D1714595

The Reception of Kant's Critical Philosophy

Fichte, Schelling, and Hegel

The essays in this volume consider both the development of Kant's system of transcendental idealism in his three *Critiques, Metaphysical Foundations of Natural Science,* and *Opus Postumum,* as well as the reception and transformation of his idealism in the work of Fichte, Schelling, and Hegel.

The contributors include many of today's preeminent philosophers of German idealism. The volume will be of critical importance to philosophers concerned with this period and to intellectual historians.

List of contributors: Sally Sedgwick, Paul Guyer, Jeffrey Edwards, Henry E. Allison, Allen W. Wood, Karl Ameriks, Günter Zöller, Robert Pippin, Daniel Breazeale, Manfred Baum, Dieter Sturma, Stephen Houlgate, Béatrice Longuenesse, and Kenneth R. Westphal.

The Reception of Kant's Critical Philosophy

Fichte, Schelling, and Hegel

Edited by

SALLY SEDGWICK
Dartmouth College

CAMBRIDGE
UNIVERSITY PRESS

B
2799
.I42
R43
2000

PUBLISHED BY THE PRESS SYNDICATE OF THE UNIVERSITY OF CAMBRIDGE
The Pitt Building, Trumpington Street, Cambridge, United Kingdom

CAMBRIDGE UNIVERSITY PRESS
The Edinburgh Building, Cambridge CB2 2RU, UK   http://www.cup.cam.ac.uk
40 West 20th Street, New York, NY 10011-4211, USA http://www.cup.org
10 Stamford Road, Oakleigh, Melbourne 3166, Australia
Ruiz de Alarcón 13, 28014 Madrid, Spain

First published 2000
Printed in the United States of America

Typeface Times Roman 10/12 pt.   *System* MagnaType™ [AG]

A catalog record for this book is available from the British Library.

Library of Congress Cataloging in Publication Data
The reception of Kant's critical philosophy : Fichte, Schelling, and Hegel / edited by
Sally Sedgwick.
    p.   cm.
Includes bibliographical references and index.
ISBN 0-521-77237-0 (hardcover)
    1. Kant, Immanuel, 1724–1804. 2. Idealism, German – History – 18th century. 3. Kant,
Immanuel, 1724–1804 – Influence. 4. Fichte, Johann Gottlieb, 1762–1814. 5. Schelling,
Friedrich Wilhelm Joseph von, 1775–1854. 6. Hegel, Georg Wilhelm Friedrich,
1770–1831. I. Sedgwick, Sally S., 1956–
B2799.I42 R43 2000
193 – dc21   99-053159

ISBN 0 521 77237 0 hardback

Contents

Notes on the Contributors

HENRY E. ALLISON is Professor of Philosophy at Boston University, Professor Emeritus at the University of California, San Diego, and Adjunct Professor at the University of Oslo. He is also former president (1996–7) of the Pacific Division of the American Philosophical Association. He is the author of several books on Kant and other figures in the history of modern philosophy as well as more than fifty articles. His books include: *Kant's Transcendental Idealism* (1983), *Benedict de Spinoza: An Introduction* (1987), *Kant's Theory of Freedom* (1990), and *Idealism and Freedom: Essays on Kant's Theoretical and Practical Philosophy* (1996). Currently, he is working on a book on Kant's *Critique of Judgment.*

KARL AMERIKS is Hank-McMahon Professor of Philosophy at the University of Notre Dame. He has cotranslated Edmund Husserl, *Experience and Judgment* (1973), and Immanuel Kant, *Lectures on Metaphysics* (1997). He has coedited *The Modern Subject: Conceptions of the Self in Classical German Philosophy* (1995), and is editing the *Cambridge Companion to German Idealism.* He has written *Kant's Theory of Mind* (1982, second edition forthcoming), and *Kant and the Fate of Autonomy* (forthcoming 2000).

MANFRED BAUM is Professor of Philosophy at the Bergische Universität Gesamthochschule Wuppertal as well as coeditor of *Kant-Studien.* He is the author of many articles on German idealism, including "Zur Methode der Logik und Metaphysik beim Jenaer Hegel" (1980), "Anmerkungen zum Verhältnis von Systematik und Dialektik bei Hegel" (1986), and "Kants Prinzip der Zweckmäßigkeit und Hegels Realisierung des Begriffs" (1990). His books include *Deduktion und Beweis in Kants Transzendentalphilosophie* (1986) and *Die Entstehung der Hegelschen Dialektik* (1986, second edition 1989).

DANIEL BREAZEALE is Chair and Professor of Philosophy at the University of Kentucky. He is the cofounder of the North American Fichte Society and has published numerous articles on German philosophy from Kant to Nietzsche, with a focus on Fichte and other early post-Kantians. He is also the editor and translator of three volumes of Fichte's writings, including *Fichte: Early Philosophical Writings* (1988), *Foundations of Transcendental Philosophy*

(Wissenschaftslehre) nova methodo (1992), and *Introductions to the Wissenschaftslehre and Other Writings* (1994).

JEFFREY EDWARDS is Assistant Professor of Philosophy at the State
University of New York at Stony Brook. He earned his Ph.D. at Philipps-
Universität Marburg, Germany. His articles include "Egoism and Formalism in
the Development of Kant's Moral Theory" (1999), "Self-Love, Anthropology,
and Universal Benevolence in Kant's Metaphysics of Morals" (1999), and
"Der Ätherbeweis des *Opus postumum* und Kants dritte Analogie der Er-
fahrung" (1991). His book, *Substance, Force, and the Possibility of Knowledge
in Kant's Philosophy of Material Nature*, is forthcoming with University of
California Press. He is also one of the translators of Kant's complete works for
Cambridge University Press.

PAUL GUYER is the Florence R. C. Murray Professor in the Humanities at the
University of Pennsylvania. His books include *Kant and the Claims of Taste*
(1979, second edition 1997), *Kant and the Claims of Knowledge* (1987), *Kant
and the Experience of Freedom* (1993), and *Kant on Freedom, Law, and
Happiness* (2000). He edited the *Cambridge Companion to Kant* (1992), and
with Allen W. Wood edited and translated the *Critique of Pure Reason* (1998)
in the *Cambridge Edition of the Works of Immanuel Kant*, of which he is
General Coeditor. He and Eric Matthews have recently completed a new edition and translation of the *Critique of the Power of Judgment* for the same
series (forthcoming 2000).

STEPHEN HOULGATE is Professor of Philosophy at the University of War-
wick and editor of the *Bulletin of the Hegel Society of Great Britain*. He was
President of the Hegel Society of America from 1994 to 1996. He has published numerous articles on Kant, Hegel, and post-Hegelian philosophy, including "Hegel, Kant and the Formal Distinctions of Reflective Understanding" (1995), "Necessity and Contingency in Hegel's *Science of Logic*" (1995),
and "Hegel, Derrida and Restricted Economy: The Case of Mechanical Memory" (1996). His books include *Hegel, Nietzsche and the Criticism of Metaphysics* (1986), *Freedom, Truth and History: An Introduction to Hegel's Philosophy* (1991), and *The Hegel Reader* (1998).

BÉATRICE LONGUENESSE is Professor of Philosophy at Princeton University. She is the author of many articles on Kant and Hegel, including "L'Effec-
tivité dans la Logique de Hegel" (1982), "Hegel, Lecteur de Kant sur le
Jugement" (1991), and "Logique et Métaphysique dans le Système Critique:
l'Exemple de la Causalité" (1994). She collaborated on the volume: *Hegel:
Notes et Fragments, Iena 1803–1806: Texte, Traduction et Commentaire*
(1991). Her books include *Hegel et la Critique de la Métaphysique*, (1981),

Kant et le Pouvoir de Juger (1993), and the revised English version of *Kant and the Capacity to Judge* (1998).

ROBERT PIPPIN is the Raymond W. and Martha Hilpert Gruner Distinguished Service Professor in the Committee on Social Thought, the Department of Philosophy, and the College and the Chair of the Committee on Social Thought at the University of Chicago. He has published more than one hundred articles and reviews on Kant, German Idealism, the nature of European modernity, and theories of self-consciousness. His books include *Kant's Theory of Form* (1982), *Hegel's Idealism: The Satisfaction of Self-Consciousness* (1989), *Modernism as a Philosophical Problem: On the Dissatisfaction of European High Culture* (1991), *Idealism as Modernism: Hegelian Variations* (1997), and *Henry James and Modern Moral Life* (1999).

SALLY SEDGWICK is Associate Professor of Philosophy at Dartmouth College. Her articles include: "On Lying and the Role of Content in Kant's Ethics" (1991), "Can Kant's Ethics Survive the Feminist Critique?" (1990 and 1997), "Hegel on Kant's Antinomies and Distinction Between General and Transcendental Logic" (1991), "McDowell's Hegelianism" (1997), and "McDowell, Hegel, and Recent Defenses of Kant" (2000). She is writing a book on Hegel's critique of Kant.

DIETER STURMA is Professor of Philosophy at the University of Essen. He is author of *Kant über Selbstbewußtsein* (1985) and *Philosophie der Person: Die Selbstverhältnisse von Subjektivität und Moralität* (1997), coeditor (with Karl Ameriks) of *The Modern Subject: Conceptions of the Self in Classical German Philosophy* (1995), and has written numerous articles on classical German philosophy, contemporary philosophy, philosophy of mind, and ethics. He is now completing a book on Jean-Jacques Rousseau.

KENNETH R. WESTPHAL is Associate Professor of Philosophy at the University of New Hampshire. He is author of *Hegel's Epistemological Realism* (1989) and *Hegel, Hume und die Identität wahrnehmbarer Dinge* (1998). He edited *Pragmatism, Reason, and Norms* (1998) and Frederick L. Will's essays, *Pragmatism and Realism* (1997). He is completing a book entitled *Kant, Hegel, and the Objective Validity of Categorial Concepts*.

ALLEN W. WOOD is Professor of Philosophy at Stanford University. He is general coeditor of the Cambridge Edition of the Writings of Immanuel Kant. His publications include: *Kant's Moral Religion* (1970), *Kant's Rational Theology* (1978), *Karl Marx* (1981), *Hegel's Ethical Thought* (1990), "Fichte's Philosophical Revolution" (1991), and *Kant's Ethical Thought* (1999).

GÜNTER ZÖLLER is Professor of Philosophy at the University of Munich. He is the author of numerous articles on Kant and German idealism. His books include: *Theoretische Gegenstandsbeziehung bei Kant* (1984); (coeditor) *Minds, Ideas, and Objects: Essays on the Theory of Representation in Modern Philosophy* (1993); (coeditor) *Figuring the Self: Subject, Individual, and Others in Classical German Philosophy* (1997); *Fichte's Transcendental Philosophy: The Original Duplicity of Intelligence and Will* (1998); and (editor) *The Cambridge Companion to Fichte* (in preparation).

Acknowledgments

Drafts of most of the papers in this volume were presented at a conference at Dartmouth College, "The Idea of a System of Transcendental Idealism in Kant, Fichte, Schelling, and Hegel," in August of 1995. My first debt of gratitude is to Burkhard Tuschling, whose work on German idealism has inspired that of several of the contributors to this volume including my own. He both proposed the idea of the conference and was of much help in the planning and organization of it. I also wish to thank the National Endowment for the Humanities, Dartmouth College, The John Sloan Dickey Center, and the North American Kant Society for the financial support without which the conference would not have become "objectively real." Finally, I am grateful to Keith Zorn and especially Ulrich Meyer for technical and editorial assistance with the preparation of this volume for publication.

Introduction:
Idealism from Kant to Hegel

SALLY SEDGWICK

The development of German idealism after Kant is in large part a story of the various ways in which features of Kant's Critical philosophy get either pre-served or transformed in the systems of Fichte, Schelling, and Hegel. While Fichte and Schelling represent their forms of idealism as basically consistent with the main principles of the Critical philosophy, Hegel tells us that an adequate form of idealism can be achieved only by parting ways with Kant in fundamental respects. An adequate form of idealism, Fichte, Schelling, and Hegel agree, is an idealism that provides a genuine alternative to subject-object dualism. It is in fact in order to challenge dualism, according to these thinkers, that philosophy comes into existence at all.[1] The central task of philosophy or of idealism in particular is to achieve harmony or reconciliation, to replace dichotomy with "identity."[2] To varying degrees, each of these later idealists believes that, although Kant's philosophy invites the charge of dualism, it also contains resources for overcoming it.

With one exception, the authors contributing to this collection have written their papers with the intention of illuminating the reception and interpretation of Kant's Critical philosophy by Fichte, Schelling, and Hegel.[3] They represent a wide range of views in their estimation of the claim of the later idealists to have developed or completed a philosophical program already defended by Kant. They also represent a diversity of opinion with regard to the question whether the transformation of idealism from Kant to Hegel counts as an in-stance of philosophical progress.

Rather than summarize the papers of this volume, I provide in this introduc-tion background material that I hope will aid the reader in appreciating them. Beginning with the "deduction" of Fichte's *Wissenschaftslehre,* I offer a guide to key moments in the development of German idealism, highlighting topics covered in greater detail in the essays which follow. In common with the contributions to this volume, my introduction presupposes some familiarity with Kant. It is intended for the reader who, although relatively well acquainted with the transcendental philosophy of the *Kritik der reinen Vernunft,* has not yet explored in any depth the systems of Fichte, Schelling, and Hegel. The reconstruction I offer, I should also point out, reflects a certain interpretative bias. My topic is the development of idealism from Kant to Hegel, and my account of that development is guided by Hegel's portrayal of it in his Jena writings of 1801–3. To be sure, Hegel's is only one of the many ways in which this complicated story can be told.

I. Fichte's Defense of Idealism over Dogmatism in the *Wissenschaftslehre*

In his two Introductions to the *Wissenschaftslehre* of 1794, Fichte announces his intention to dedicate his life to the task of providing a correct rendering of Kant's philosophy. The "transcendental idealism" of the *Wissenschaftslehre,* he writes, is "nothing other than Kantianism properly understood."[4] "Properly understood," Fichte goes on to tell us, Kant's Critical philosophy is not the "dogmatism" it is commonly taken to be, but indeed a form of "idealism."

The dogmatist contends that the cause and explanatory ground of our ideas both of our freedom and of objects of nature derives from outside self-consciousness or intelligence, from what Fichte refers to as the realm of "things-in-themselves."[5] The dogmatist, he writes, "wants . . . to assure to [the thing-in-itself] reality, that is, the necessity of being thought as the ground of all experience, and will do it if he proves that experience can really be explained by means of it, and cannot be explained without it . . . "[6] The idealist reverses this order of explanation and asserts that objects are instead grounded in human intelligence. This does not mean that, according to the idealist, human self-consciousness has the capacity to bring mind-independent objects or things-in-themselves into being. Rather, objects are grounded in human intelligence for the idealist in the sense that self-consciousness grounds or makes possible objects as they are *experienced* or *thought* by us. Because the thing-in-itself is defined as independent of the forms of intelligence, it is for the idealist not a possible object of human experience or consciousness. This is why Fichte tells us that it is "disposed of" in the *Wissenschaftslehre.*[7]

Below I will have more to say about this idealist assumption that objects are determined by or grounded in self-consciousness. But, first, how does Fichte defend his preference for idealism over dogmatism? One problem with dogmatism, he says, is that it cannot account for the "fact of presentation." Dogmatism, that is, has no means of demonstrating how something so utterly unlike our ideas could be their cause and explanatory ground.[8] On the assumption that intellect and object are distinct kinds of thing, intellect and object in Fichte's words, "inhabit two worlds between which there is no bridge."[9]

Fichte goes on to admit, however, that the *consistent* dogmatist has no reason to assume that intellect and object are distinct kinds of thing. For the consistent dogmatist, the soul or intellect is simply the product of interactions among things-in-themselves. But even if what this implies is that the consistent dogmatist need not be concerned about the problem of bridging the gap between object and idea referred to above, Fichte draws our attention to a further reason for choosing idealism over dogmatism. Since the consistent dogmatist claims that the soul or intellect is nothing other than a product of interactions among things-in-themselves, the soul or intellect cannot according to this form of dogmatism be free. It is this implication that is decisive for Fichte. Neither idealism nor dogmatism can successfully refute the other on theoretical grounds, he says; our choice between the two systems must therefore in the end be practical. Since a consistent dogmatism implies fatalism, in his view, it is not a position that can be affirmed by those fully conscious of their freedom.[10]

II. Fichte's Interpretation of Kant as an Idealist

As noted above, Fichte claims that idealism is implied by a proper understanding of Kant's first *Kritik*. This interpretation of Kant as an idealist accords, if not with the "letter" of Kant's philosophy, he says, surely with its "spirit."[11] It is true that there are passages in the *Kritik* that appear to support the dogmatic reading – for example B 1, where Kant asks: "[H]ow should our faculty of knowledge be awakened into action did not objects affecting our senses partly of themselves produce representations . . . ?"[12] Fichte notes that passages such as this are typically taken to support the view that, according to Kant, our consciousness of objects of experience is "founded upon something outside self-consciousness . . . "[13] But although Kant writes of our being "affected by objects," he cannot mean by "object" a content independent of the synthesizing activity of the intellect, in Fichte's view. He cannot mean this, Fichte insists, because the argument of the transcendental deduction of the first *Kritik* demonstrates that "object" can refer only to the product of an act of combination or synthesis performed by the understanding on some manifold of either pure or empirical intuition. What Kant, in other words, establishes in the transcendental deduction is that in the absence of that synthesizing activity, nothing can be thought or known by us as an object at all.

So Kant's philosophy is idealistic rather than dogmatic, according to Fichte, because the transcendental deduction implies that the thing-in-itself is not a possible object of human consciousness, and therefore not an object we can ever know to cause or explain our ideas. The *Wissenschaftslehre* is a system of idealism because it consistently carries out the implications of Kant's transcendental deduction.[14] In common with Kant's philosophy, it sets out from the "absolutely basic principle" that: "*[A]ll consciousness* . . . stands under conditions of the original unity of apperception."[15]

III. Intellectual Intuition and the Deduction of Fichte's *Wissenschaftslehre*

Given Fichte's intention to reformulate Kant's transcendental deduction in a way that discourages the dogmatic reading, it is puzzling that in his

4 SALLY SEDGWICK

Introductions to the *Wissenschaftslehre* he chooses the name "intellectual intuition" [*intellectuelle Anschauung*] for the faculty of self-consciousness that
Kant in the first *Kritik* refers to as "pure apperception."[16] This is puzzling for
two reasons: First, an intuition that is intellectual, in Kant's definition, does not
depend upon being affected by a given sensible content; it produces its content
or objects out of its own intuiting activity. Second, it is precisely because
intellectual intuition produces its objects that it can know them, according to
Kant, as they are in themselves. As we have seen, however, Fichte rejects the
dogmatist's assumption that we can know things-in-themselves. Furthermore,
he is committed to the view that we must in experience rely upon sensible
affection. Why, then, is "intellectual intuition" his name for that act of self-
consciousness upon which all our acts of consciousness depend? Given his
insistence upon the inaccessibility, for our form of knowing, of things-in-
themselves, why does he claim that intellectual intuition is a faculty of human
cognition at all?

Clearly what intrigues Fichte about Kant's conception of intellectual intuition is the fact that this form of cognition, in producing objects out of its own
activity, is in *immediate* cognitive contact with them.[17] For this form of cognition, that is, there simply is no worry about whether its ideas or representations
of things are capable of revealing the nature of the things themselves. Fichte
wants to claim that human understanding has this capacity of intellectual
intuition and thus this kind of immediate cognitive contact with its objects. But
how can a form of understanding that does not create but must be affected by a
given sensible content be in immediate cognitive contact with its objects?

The answer to this question requires us to consider once again Fichte's
understanding of the implications of Kant's transcendental deduction. In §6 of
his Second Introduction, Fichte writes that, "certainly our knowledge all proceeds from *an affection;* but not an affection *by an object.* This is *Kant's* view
and also that of the *Wissenschaftslehre.*" We must indeed be sensibly affected
in experience, in Fichte's view; nonetheless, we cannot claim that what affects
us are objects. Why not? Because of the conception of object that follows from
the argument of Kant's transcendental deduction: Something can be an object
for consciousness only if synthesized by the faculty of pure apperception.
When Fichte suggests that human understanding is in immediate cognitive contact with its object, he therefore means by "object" an *already conceptualized content.* For the idealist in contrast to the dogmatist, the pre-
synthesized matter of sensation (the "thing-in-itself"), *qua* unsynthesized,
lacks the credentials of objecthood.[18]

So, in Fichte's view, if we have understood the argument of Kant's transcendental deduction correctly, there will be for us nothing contradictory about
asserting both that we must, in experience, be sensibly affected, and that we are
nonetheless in immediate cognitive contact with objects. Our form of intellec-

tual intuition is in immediate cognitive contact with its objects simply because, as Fichte points out, it is that act of "spontaneity" responsible for combining the given content of sensible intuition into a thinkable content. Intellectual intuition is "by its nature objective," he says, since by means of its activity objects of consciousness first come to be.[19]

To summarize the points covered so far: Fichte's project of promoting the "spirit" if not the "letter" of Kant's idealism is driven by his conviction that idealism must be chosen over dogmatism on practical grounds: Idealism is the only system compatible with our experience of ourselves as free. His strategy for defending idealism relies on what he understands is the idealist implication of Kant's transcendental deduction: that the object of human consciousness is "posited and determined" by the cognitive faculty, not "the cognitive faculty by the object."[20] Without denying that our form of intelligence must in experience be sensibly affected, Fichte claims that objectivity is nonetheless the contribution of self-consciousness or intellectual intuition. For our form of understanding, the object of experience is an already conceptualized content, a "conceptualized sensory intuition . . ."[21] As an already conceptualized content, it is a unity of form and content – a unity, Fichte writes in one passage, of the a priori and the a posteriori.[22] The "thing-in-itself" is "disposed of" in the *Wissenschaftslehre* because, as an unconceptualized content, it is unthinkable and therefore of neither explanatory nor justificatory significance.

IV. The Incompleteness of the Deduction of the *Wissenschaftslehre*

We can now turn to that feature of Fichte's idealism that is the most important for our discussion of Hegel below, since it is the feature that Hegel believes is responsible for the inadequacy of Fichte's idealism. The feature in question is the incompleteness of Fichte's deduction. On the one hand, Fichte introduces intellectual intuition as the act that demonstrates the absolute self-sufficiency of reason – that in other words demonstrates, in opposition to the dogmatist, that there is nothing (of epistemic import) outside or independent of the "I's" self-positing. But then he tells us, on the other hand, that the deduction cannot be completed if we rely on this original act of intuition alone. Not only can it not be completed, it cannot even get started, in his view.[23] Intellectual intuition seems not to be self-sufficient after all.

By examining Fichte's reasoning step-by-step, we can see how he arrives at these conclusions. As noted above, the deduction is supposed to demonstrate that objects are "posited and determined" by the cognitive faculty. Its First Principle, "I am I," expresses what Fichte refers to as the most "primordial" act of the subject: the intellectual intuition or preconceptual awareness of its own free activity.[24] Anyone can become aware of this activity, he claims, by performing the Cartesian exercise of withdrawing attention from external objects

6 SALLY SEDGWICK

of cognition and focusing on the act that must accompany all cognition as a pre-condition: the act of thinking itself. What intellectual intuition reveals, Fichte writes, is that everything that the self is, is "founded in itself, and explained solely from itself, and not from anything outside it . . ."[25] This intuition in other words is supposed to reveal a subjectivity at the foundation of all acts of consciousness that is itself "absolutely self-sufficient" or "self-posited," as he famously puts it.[26] As self-posited or self-constructed, this form of subjectivity is nothing other than what it posits itself to be. It is at once the "activity [of positing] and the product of that activity" – "a necessary identity," in Fichte's words, "of subject and object: a subject-object . . ."[27]

But the intellectual intuition or awareness of our own free subjectivity, Fichte claims, is not yet knowledge or even consciousness of any object. What is more, intellectual intuition can provide no evidence in support of the idealist's central hypothesis: that out of the "I's" self-positing activity, we deduce "*specific* presentations: of a world, of a material, spatially located world existing without our aid . . ."[28] We can expect to derive evidence for this hypothesis, he says, only from the deduction itself. The deduction is supposed to demonstrate, then, that the self-posited "I am I" not merely accompanies but completely determines all objects of consciousness in what Fichte sometimes characterizes as its own capacity for self-limitation or self-legislation.[29]

But no sooner does Fichte assert the "absolute" self-sufficiency of the "I am I" than he seems to need to take it back. Although the first act is necessary for the possibility of all consciousness, it is not in his judgment sufficient. Taken in isolation, he says, the "I am I" is indeterminate or empty. As mentioned above, it is not yet even an act of consciousness. This is because consciousness according to Fichte is necessarily consciousness *of something,* of some *object.* Consciousness therefore requires some means of distinguishing the self-consciousness that thinks from the thing that is thought. In Fichte's words, "If I am to present anything at all, I must oppose it to the presenting self."[30] As we have just seen, however, what the preconscious awareness or act of intellectual intuition discloses is not opposition but identity: the identity of the subject that posits and the product of its positing. In order to proceed from the self-positing activity of the "I" to a deduction of objects of consciousness, Fichte tells us that a second and equally absolute or self-sufficient act or principle must be introduced: the principle that "not-I is not equal to I." The first act or "I am I" only gains determination (is only able to make the transition from the preconscious awareness of itself as a free subjectivity to a consciousness of objects) when brought into relation to something other than itself: an equally absolute "not-I."[31]

As it turns out, then, we cannot simply proceed from the "I am I" to specific presentations or objects, in Fichte's view. In absence of the "not-I," "I am I" is indeterminate: it is neither already a consciousness of objects, nor capable of

providing for their deduction. What was first set up as the fundamental principle of the deduction, "I am I," for this reason ends up depending for its
determination on something else. And this second principle, Fichte goes on to
argue, in turn requires a third. In the absence of a third principle, the second
principle, too, is insufficiently determinate. What the third principle states is
that neither the first nor the second principle is the nullification of the other.
The "not-I" is required if the first principle is to have determination and if we
are to be able to deduce objects, but it does not cancel out or replace the first
principle. It cannot do this, because there of course can *be* no "not-I" without
an "I." According to the third principle, then, the "I" is only *in part* "not-I," and
vice versa. So, just as the second principle is necessary for the determination of
the first, the third principle is necessary for the determination of the second.
With each additional positing we achieve further determination or limitation.
In Fichte's words, what is *"first set up as a fundamental principle and directly
demonstrated in consciousness is impossible unless something else occurs
along with it, and . . . this something else is impossible unless a third something also takes place, and so on until the conditions of what was first exhibited
are completely exhausted, and this latter is, with respect to its possibility, fully
intelligible.* Its course is an unbroken progression from condition to condition;
each condition becomes, in turn, a conditioned whose condition must be sought
out."[32]

We can perhaps now understand why Fichte comes to admit that the deduction of the *Wissenschaftslehre* must remain incomplete. The claim that each
condition "becomes . . . a conditioned whose condition must be sought out,"
suggests that on his account the deduction not only does not begin with a
condition that is itself unconditioned, but also never concludes with one. The
"I" of the intellectual intuition which was initially presented as "absolutely
self-sufficient" and so responsible for completely determining or grounding
the existence of all "specific presentations," turns out on Fichte's own estimation to at best determine only what presentations *ought* to be produced or
posited. The "I," he writes, "is posited as what *ought* to contain within itself the
ground of the existence of the 'not-I'."[33] The deduction is thus most accurately
described as a striving or task, because, as Fichte puts it, the "absolutely
posited is impossible."[34]

V. Hegel on the Deduction of Fichte's *Wissenschaftslehre*

As noted above, the incompleteness of Fichte's deduction is in Hegel's judgment responsible for the inadequacy of the idealism of the *Wissenschaftslehre*.[35] By reviewing Hegel's reasons for this assessment, we can derive clues
for understanding what motivates his own alternative.

Hegel correctly represents Fichte's idealism as an attempt to dispense with things-in-themselves, that is, as an attempt to argue against the dogmatist that objects are posited and produced by the "I" and that there is nothing outside the "I's" self-positing.[36] In opposition to the dualism assumed by "ordinary" consciousness between what Hegel calls "pure consciousness" (the "I" of intellectual intuition) and (objects of) "empirical consciousness," Fichte sets out to demonstrate that objects of empirical consciousness are, in Hegel's words, "completely grounded in, and not just conditioned by, pure consciousness . . . "[37] This is, in Hegel's estimation, a worthwhile undertaking; moreover, he believes that Fichte starts off on the right track by grounding his system in intellectual intuition, the faculty Hegel describes as "pure thinking of itself, pure self-consciousness, I = I, I am."[38] Indeed, Fichte's First Principle, "I = I," Hegel writes, is "the authentic principle of speculation boldly expressed."[39]

But Fichte is not successful in demonstrating what he sets out to demonstrate: that objects of empirical consciousness are posited by self-consciousness and as such "completely grounded in" self-consciousness. As we have just seen, this seems to be Fichte's assessment of the deduction of the *Wissenschaftslehre,* and it is Hegel's as well. Far from self-sufficient, the act of self-positing with which the deduction begins turns out to be an expression of deficiency and dependency.

The cause of this failure, according to Hegel, is neither Fichte's goal of dispensing with the thing-in-itself, nor his insight that intellectual intuition is the act with which the deduction must begin. Responsible for the failure, rather, is Fichte's particular conception of that act. On the one hand, he correctly discovers in the intellectual intuition of the activity of self-consciousness grounds for asserting an "identity" between subject and object: The self-positing "I" is not dependent upon any object outside itself; what it is, is completely determined by its act of positing. In addition, Fichte correctly envisions the project of his deduction as demonstrating, against the dogmatist, that objects of empirical consciousness are grounded in the positing activity of the "I" and that therefore the dualism of pure self-consciousness and objects of empirical consciousness is derivative (a product of abstraction) rather than original. Where Fichte goes wrong, in Hegel's judgment, is in characterizing the first act or principle of the deduction as empty and in need of completion by further independent acts of positing. The problem is not Fichte's recognition that all consciousness presupposes some way of distinguishing the "I" that presents and the thing presented (presupposes, that is to say, an opposition between the "I" and the "not-I"). The problem is rather his insistence that we can only achieve such opposition by appealing *outside* the first act to a second, and then a third, and so forth. The problem, in other words, is Fichte's conviction that opposition and therefore determination is *not already given in or a moment of the original act of the "I" itself.*

One of the ways in which Hegel expresses this objection is to say that Fichte's understanding of the act of intellectual intuition is limited by his adherence to the "logic of reflection." According to the logic of reflection, "A = A" is an expression of a "pure unity" (unity without opposition). Hegel contrasts this with the interpretation of "speculative logic," which takes "A = A" to express both identity and opposition. For speculative logic, in his words, "A = A contains the difference of A as subject and A as object together with their identity . . . " Presumably the "difference" Hegel has in mind here refers to the distinction presupposed in this judgment between the "A" that is the subject-concept and the "A" that is the predicate-concept.[40] Fichte's "I = I" is properly characterized as a "pure unity" or a "unity in abstraction from opposition," then, just because it does not recognize this difference, or just because it is determined by the logic of reflection.

This is why Fichte's idealism is unsuccessful in sustaining its thesis, against the dogmatist, of the self-sufficiency of self-consciousness or of the "identity" of subject and object. Because of his adherence to the logic of reflection, Fichte must assume that the "I" and the "not-I" are absolutely opposed. Did he not rely on this assumption, Hegel points out, he would not need to portray the self-positing act of the "I" with which his deduction begins as deficient or empty, as dependent for its determination upon further acts not derivable from the first. It is in other words because Fichte adheres to the logic of reflection that the emptiness or deficiency of the "I," its absolute opposition to the "not-I," must become, in Hegel's words, "the principle of [the deduction's] advance . . . "[41]

Far from successful in providing an alternative to dogmatism, therefore, Fichte is in a certain respect unable to escape its hold. This is because, far from demonstrating that objects are "completely determined" by self-consciousness, the *Wissenschaftslehre* is committed to the thesis that, as Hegel puts it, "[T]he object of the theoretical faculty necessarily contains something not determined by the Ego."[42] Again, Fichte's deduction is unable to achieve its aim because it is carried out within the narrow confines of the logic of reflection. Fichte has no option but to interpret the "I" as a pure identity or unity, as containing within itself no difference or opposition. He therefore cannot understand the "I" of intellectual intuition to express an original identity of subject and object. As Hegel says, the "I" for Fichte remains something "subjective": a "subjective Subject-Object."[43]

VI. Hegel on the Inadequacy of Fichte's Practical Philosophy

Hegel's assessment of Fichte's idealism is no more positive when its object is the deduction of Fichte's practical philosophy. Once again deriving inspiration from Kant, Fichte insists that, in its practical employment, reason has a special kind of causal power, the power to bring "moral objects" (moral intentions and behaviors) into being.[44] His hope is that, armed with this special productive power, practical reason will succeed where theoretical reason failed: in establishing the identity of the "I" and the "not-I" or in demonstrating that in the realm of the practical the object is absolutely determined by the subject. But Fichte ends up conceding failure in this domain as well. In effect, he gets caught between contradictory aims: On the one hand, he seeks to establish, against the dogmatist or dualist, the self-sufficiency of practical reason. To this end, he portrays practical reason as the bearer of objectivity, as responsible for positing its objects. On the other hand, he insists that in order to gain determination practical reason requires relation to something absolutely opposed to itself — something that *cannot* merely be the product of its own positing. As we have seen, these contradictory demands are what undermine his effort to deduce the "not-I" from the "I" in the theoretical domain, and they are equally destructive of his effort in the domain of the practical.[45] Fichte thus finds himself in the position of having to admit that practical reason is no more self-sufficient than its theoretical counterpart. Practical reason *ought* to have the power to realize morality, it *ought* to be able to bring our empirical nature into conformity with its demands as well as insure that our good intentions are rewarded with happiness. But, in Hegel's words, "this supreme demand remains, in Fichte's system, a demand."[46]

We might sum up Hegel's critique of the idealism of the *Wissenschaftslehre* in the following way: Fichte is unable to demonstrate the identity of self-consciousness and objects of empirical consciousness, according to Hegel, because of a feature his conception of self-consciousness shares with Kant's. The "I" of Fichte's intellectual intuition and the "I think" of Kant's discursive understanding, rather than self-sufficient, are in fact essentially *dependent* forms of consciousness. For both philosophers, Hegel tells us, the unity or harmony of the "I" and the "not-I" is at best an idea, postulated as a task, and as a task that can never be completed. It cannot be completed because this would violate a principle apparently dearer to both philosophers than the goal of identity: namely, the principle required by the logic of reflection of the "absolute opposition" of the "I" and the "not-I." The demand for harmony in both idealisms thus not only cannot be realized, it is a "self-destructive" demand, according to Hegel. It is "self-destructive," he says, because it is a demand that can only be met at the expense of the logic of reflection. Its fulfillment, for Fichte as well as Kant, therefore "must not happen."[47]

VII. The Influence of Schelling on the Young Hegel

We have seen that since the "I" of intellectual intuition is for Fichte a dependent form of consciousness, absolutely opposed to the "not-I" upon which it must rely for determination, it remains ultimately "subjective" on Hegel's characterization. But what about the "not-I" of Fichte's idealism? It is as much "*in itself,* as the Ego," Hegel says.[48] The "not-I" is as much "in itself" because on Fichte's account it must represent what is absolutely other to self-consciousness: something "essentially determined and lifeless,"[49] "a sense-world lacking [internal] organization."[50] Containing within itself no form or rationality, nature in Fichte's idealism, Hegel tells us, thus assumes features of Kant's thing-in-itself and of the sense content of "ordinary empiricism."[51]

Fichte's conception of nature is, of course, no more acceptable in Hegel's estimation than his conception of self-consciousness. While the "I" of Fichtean intellectual intuition is too subjective (a "subjective Subject-Object"), the "not-I" to which the "I" is supposed to be absolutely opposed is too objective. This is why in the Preface to the *Differenzschrift,* Hegel writes of the need to "recompense nature for the mishandling that it suffered in Kant and Fichte's systems." In the name of achieving a more adequate form of idealism, an idealism that does not rest on the assumption of absolute opposition, we need to dispense not merely with Fichte's conception of the "I" as "pure subject" but also with his conception of the "not-I" as pure or "lifeless" matter. A truly adequate form of idealism, Hegel tells us there, sets "Reason itself in harmony with nature, not by having Reason renounce itself or become an insipid imitator of nature, but by Reason recasting itself into nature out of its own inner strength."[52]

The goal, then, is to "recompense nature" by providing an alternative to the "empiricist" representation of it as "something essentially determined and lifeless."[53] Otherwise put, the goal is to defend the thesis that nature is not merely object but somehow a unity or identity of subject and object. For Hegel, a nature that is not merely object but also subject is a nature that is self-positing or self-determining. It is a nature that contains features of free self-consciousness.

In the *Differenzschrift,* Hegel praises his friend Schelling for defending this alternative conception of nature. Schelling, Hegel writes in his Preface, "sets the objective Subject-Object beside the subjective Subject-Object and presents both as united in something higher than the subject." For Schelling, what is subject or Spirit is not something external to or "higher" than nature but rather a part of nature, something that dwells in nature. We should think of nature, he tells us, as an organism. It does not rely for its form or organization on anything outside itself; it is a whole or totality and as such responsible for or productive of its parts. As he explains in his 1797/1803 essay "Ideas on a Philosophy of Nature as an Introduction to the Study of this Science,"

Every organic product bears the ground of its existence within *itself,* for it is its own cause and effect. No single part could *arise* except *in* this whole, and this whole exists only in the *interaction* of the parts . . . Thus every organization is based on a *concept;* for wherever there is a necessary relationship of the whole to the parts, and of the parts to the whole, there is a *concept.* But this concept dwells within *the organization itself* and cannot be separated from it. It *organizes itself* . . . [54]

12 SALLY SEDGWICK

Again, what Hegel finds attractive about this conception is that it articulates the way in which nature is self-positing or self-determining and, as such, contains subjectivity or is, in his words, an "immanent ideality."[55] This is in contrast to the "empiricist" conception, according to which nature derives whatever form or organization it has from some *external* cause or purpose.[56] As we have seen, Kant and Fichte must think of nature in this latter way, because each is committed to the thesis that objects of the sense world are absolutely opposed to self-consciousness. The most each can admit is that the idea of nature as an organism satisfies interests or ends of human reason. In the sections on "Teleological Judgment" in his third *Kritik,* Kant argues that the stronger claim that nature is *itself* an organism can only be successfully defended by an understanding that, unlike ours, is intuitive and therefore capable of actually producing or determining the manifold of its experience out of its intuiting activity.[57] It follows from the fact that our form of understanding is discursive or dependent, however, that we cannot produce or create the content of experience but must rely on being sensibly affected. For this reason, we can have no warrant for claiming that the content of experience itself necessarily conforms to our idea of it as organized or purposive. As Kant puts it at §75, "because we do not really observe the ends [*Zwecke*] of nature as purposive [*absichtliche*] but rather add this concept . . . in our thinking, such ends are not given to us by the object." Kant admits the possibility of a form of cognition that knows nature as an organism; he must however deny to human subjectivity this form of cognition because, again, he (as well as Fichte) adheres to the view that our understanding is "absolutely opposed" to the given content of experience in the sense that, because dependent, it cannot completely determine that content.[58]

According to a more adequate form of idealism, a form of idealism that takes as its point of departure not absolute opposition but absolute identity, "every speck of dust," Hegel writes, "is an organization."[59] Nature on this conception, he says,

. . . is not a stillness of being, it is a being that becomes; or in other words, it is not split and synthesized from the outside, it sunders itself and unites itself by itself; and in all of its shapes it posits itself freely . . . Its non-conscious development is a reflection of the living force which . . . posits itself in every limited shape . . . [60]

For a form of idealism that "sets the objective Subject-Object beside the subjective Subject-Object and presents both as united in something higher," nature and self-consciousness are not absolutely opposed. As Schelling puts it, nature is "visible Spirit" and self-consciousness or subjectivity is "invisible nature."[61] Each is the manifestation of an original identity or unity that is "higher."

Although it is true that as early as 1807 Hegel parted ways with Schelling philosophically, we should not understand this break to suggest that he lost faith in Schelling's conception of nature. Far from that, the idea of nature as "visible spirit," as object that is also subject, as a domain in which what is rational is actual, assumes a permanent place in Hegel's idealism. Hegel does, however, come to reject Schelling's understanding of how we are supposed to *know* the absolute or original identity of subject and object. Our knowledge of identity, Schelling claims, is an intellectual intuition, an immediate grasping or experiencing that has more in common with faith than with either observation or thinking, and that in addition involves an abstraction from difference or particularity. Hegel is too much of an Enlightenment rationalist not to be suspicious of claims to immediate knowledge in any form. In his view, Reason knows the Absolute not by means of an intuitive grasping, but only as the consequence of a laborious process of self-discovery and self-criticism in which it subjects its various claims and counterclaims to careful scrutiny. Moreover, since for Hegel a truly adequate idealism must conform to the rules not merely of a "logic of reflection" but also of "speculative" logic, it can discover identity only where there is also opposition or difference.[62] For a truly adequate form of idealism, absolute identity is therefore not, as Schelling seems to suggest, what remains once we have abstracted away difference or particularity. (It is not, as Hegel famously puts it in the Preface to his 1807 *Phänomenologie*, a night in which "all cows are black.") Absolute identity for Hegel, then, is an identity, but not a "pure" identity; it is an identity that contains difference. Thus his highly obscure definition of the "Absolute" (already in the *Differenzschrift*) as "the identity of identity and non-identity . . . "[63]

VIII. Concluding Summary

From the above discussion we can extract three critical steps in the development of idealism from Kant to Hegel.

The first is Fichte's reliance upon the "spirit" of Kant's transcendental deduction in the name of defending idealism over dogmatism. Idealism must be defended, Fichte insists, because it is the only philosophical system true to the thinking subject's experience of itself as free. In the service of this end, the *Wissenschaftslehre* assumes as its point of departure the "self-posited" and "absolutely self-sufficient" "I" of intellectual intuition. The "I" is free because it is not caused or determined by anything outside itself; it is at once the activity of positing and the thing posited, and as such an "identity" of subject and object. Moreover, it is the absolute ground of all other objects, of the "not-I." As we have seen, Fichte does not mean by this that self-consciousness brings "things-in-themselves" into being. Deriving his inspiration from Kant's account of the role of transcendental apperception, his view is rather that objects are grounded in self-consciousness in the sense that without the free activity of the "I" nothing could be thought by us as an object at all. Fichte's vision of the deduction of the *Wissenschaftslehre* is in this way faithful to the "principle of idealism" according to which, as Hegel puts it, the "world is a product of freedom and intelligence."[64]

But Fichte's system fails to achieve a satisfactory alternative to dogmatism. This brings us to the second key moment: Hegel's diagnosis of the inadequacy of Fichte's deduction. In opposition to the dogmatist, Fichte's system is supposed to set out from the intellectual intuition of the identity of the "I" and the "not-I," and so to establish at its foundation the absolute freedom or self-sufficiency of self-consciousness. But because, like Kant, his thinking is governed by the "logic of reflection," he, like Kant, must assume at the foundation of his system not identity but opposition. Fichte claims, on the one hand, that the "I" of intellectual intuition is identical to the "not-I," and that this identity is exhibited in the *Wissenschaftlehre*'s deduction of all objects of empirical consciousness from the "I." On the other hand, however, he is forced to conclude that the "I" is deficient and unable to provide for the deduction's completion. Because he relies exclusively on the logic of reflection, Fichte cannot understand how opposition or difference is already given in or a moment of the self-positing of the "I" itself.[65] Both the "I" and the "not-I" of Fichte's idealism therefore remain pure identities (identities without difference), on Hegel's analysis: The "I" of intellectual intuition remains a pure subjectivity, and the "not-I," although posited by the "I," is nonetheless conceived of as retaining the character of the not posited, a "lifeless matter" upon which the "I" must depend. According to the *Wissenschaftslehre,* Hegel writes, objects of empirical consciousness turn out not to be "product[s] of absolute freedom" at all.[66]

It is in order to "recompense nature" for this result that, in the third and final step in our story of the development of idealism, Hegel turns to Schelling for inspiration. If we are to provide a successful alternative to dogmatism, we need to dislodge the thesis of absolute opposition; this in turn requires that we establish at the basis of our system of idealism a new way of understanding not merely the "I" but also the "not-I." Standing in our way, according to Hegel, is the logic of reflection that defines each as a "pure identity," an identity without difference. In the name of achieving a successful alternative to dogmatism, however, we need to avail ourselves of the resources of a "speculative logic," according to which both subject and object contain difference or opposition as essential moments. For speculative logic, the "I" is neither "merely subject," nor (as Schelling argued) is the "not-I" "merely object," absolutely opposed to the "I" and thus incapable of any form of self-determination or freedom. "For absolute identity to be the principle of an entire system," Hegel writes, "it is necessary that both subject and object be posited as Subject-Object."[67]

Notes

1. Dualism, Hegel writes, "is the source of *the need of philosophy.*" "Differenz des Fichteschen und Schellingschen Systems der Philosophie," in *G. W. F. Hegel,*

Werke in zwanzig Bänden, Theorie Werkausgabe vol. II, *Jenaer Schriften 1801–1807.* (Frankfurt am Main: Suhrkamp Verlag, 1970), p. 20. Except where otherwise noted, I rely on the translation by H. S. Harris and Walter Cerf, *The Difference Between Fichte's and Schelling's Systems of Philosophy* (Albany: State University of New York Press, 1977), p. 89. Hereafter I refer to this work as the *"Differenzschrift,"* and first cite page references of the Suhrkamp and then of the Harris and Cerf editions. (In this case, e.g., the citation is *"Differenzschrift* 20/89.")

In his 1797/1803 essay, "Ideen zu einer Philosophie der Natur als Einleitung in das Studium dieser Wissenschaft," Schelling writes that philosophy presupposes dichotomy, "because without it there would be no need to philosophize." "As soon as man sets himself in opposition to the external world . . . , he takes his first step towards philosophy." In *Friedrich Wilhelm Joseph von Schelling: Schriften,* vol. I. (Frankfurt am Main: Suhrkamp Verlag, 1985), p. 251. I rely on the translation of "Ideas on a Philosophy of Nature as an Introduction to the Study of this Science," by Priscilla Hayden-Roy in *Philosophy of German Idealism,* ed. Ernst Behler (New York: Continuum Publishing Company, 1987), pp. 168–9.

2. As Hegel writes in *Differenzschrift* 21/90: "The sole interest of Reason is to suspend . . . rigid antithesis."

3. The exception is the paper by Jeffrey Edwards, which does not explore the reception of Kant's idealism. Edwards's paper does, however, explore Kant's reflections on his own idealism in the *Opus postumum.* And according to some commentators (most notably Edwards as well as Burkhard Tuschling), these reflections suggest that, in his later years, Kant was concerned to revise his idealism in a way that idealists such as Fichte, Schelling, and Hegel would have found most welcome.

4. *Zweite Einleitung in die Wissenschaftslehre* (1797), §6. Except where otherwise indicated, I rely on the translation of both Introductions and of the 1794 *Grundlage der gesammten Wissenschaftslehre* by Peter Heath and John Lachs in *J. G. Fichte: Science of Knowledge* (Cambridge, U.K.: Cambridge University Press, 1984).

5. For Fichte as well as Hegel (and in contrast to Kant), "thing-in-itself" refers not just to the object understood as independent of the forms of intuition space and time, but to the object understood as independent of the forms of human self-consciousness (the categories). See, for example, *Zweite Einleitung,* §6 where Fichte writes of the dogmatist's confusion: "Their thing is [supposed to be] produced by thinking; yet at the same time it is a thing-in-itself, that is, something not produced by thinking" (my translation).

6. *Erste Einleitung in die Wissenschaftslehre* (1797), §4.

7. *Zweite Einleitung,* §6.

8. *Erste Einleitung,* §§4–6.

9. Ibid., §6. Schelling raises similar points in "Ideen zu einer Philosophie der Natur" (cited above). See the section entitled "Über die Probleme, welche eine Philosophie der Natur zu lösen hat."

10. See *Erste Einleitung,* §5.

11. *Zweite Einleitung,* §6 note.

12. Unless otherwise indicated, I rely on the Norman Kemp Smith translation of Kant's *Critique of Pure Reason* (New York: St. Martin's Press, 1929), and cite page numbers of the "A" and "B" Akademie editions.

13. *Zweite Einleitung,* §6.

14. Fichte furthermore tells us that the task of his deduction is also to "complete" the deduction of the first *Kritik.* Kant claimed but did not demonstrate that the categories as well as the forms of space and time are "conditions of self-consciousness."

While he surely "envisaged" such a deduction, Fichte writes, he never in fact provided it. (See *Zweite Einleitung,* §6.)

15. See in the 1794 *Wissenschaftslehre* Part I, §1, and in the *Zweite Einleitung,* §6.

16. In his *Zweite Einleitung,* §6, Fichte identifies his notion of intellectual intuition with the faculty of pure apperception of the first *Kritik.*

17. See ibid.

18. Fichte explains his conception of the object at *Erste Einleitung,* §7: "the thing is nothing other than *all these relationships* [spatial, temporal, causal, etc.] *combined by the imagination* . . . ; the object is in fact the original synthesis of all these concepts. Form and matter are not separate items . . . " (my translation).

19. *Zweite Einleitung,* §4. There is an ambiguity in Fichte's treatment of intellectual intuition in this Introduction to the 1794 *Wissenschaftslehre* that I have passed over. Sometimes he characterizes intellectual intuition as the self's nonconceptual awareness of its faculty of self-consciousness. The self "reverts into itself" [*geht zurück in sich selbst*] and via this act of self-observation comes to recognize that the spontaneity of self-consciousness is the condition of all consciousness. (See §§4, 5.) On other occasions, however, Fichte identifies intellectual intuition as the faculty of self-consciousness or spontaneity itself, the faculty that confers objectivity on all our representations and that is referred to by Kant as "pure apperception" (§§5, 6).

20. *Erste Einleitung,* Vorerinnerung.

21. *Zweite Einleitung,* §5.

22. *Erste Einleitung,* §7.

23. With this formulation, I paraphrase Frederick C. Beiser in his fine Introduction to *The Cambridge Companion to Hegel,* ed. Frederick C. Beiser (Cambridge, U.K.: Cambridge University Press, 1993), p. 14.

24. In the order of discussion, the proposition "I am I" precedes the proposition "I am" in Part I, §1 of the 1794 *Wissenschaftslehre.* Fichte does, however, go on to tell us that the "I am I" turns out to be based or founded on an activity of the mind: the self's positing of itself, represented in the proposition "I am."

25. *Zweite Einleitung,* §6.

26. *Erste Einleitung,* §7; *Zweite Einleitung,* §§4, 6.

27. *Wissenschaftslehre,* Part I, §1 note (my translation). Fichte refers to the "sich selbst construirende Ich" in his *Zweite Einleitung,* §4.

28. *Erste Einleitung,* §7.

29. See, for example, *Erste Einleitung,* §7.

30. *Wissenschaftslehre,* Part I, §2.

31. I write "not-I" here because this is the literal translation of what Fichte writes, "nicht-Ich." "Nicht-Ich" is, however, often translated as "non-I" because "non-I" better captures what Fichte actually seems to intend.

32. *Erste Einleitung,* §7.

33. *Wissenschaftslehre,* Part II, §4 E (my translation).

34. *Erste Einleitung,* §7.

35. Fichteans will no doubt be tempted to respond here by saying that Hegel's reading suffers from the fact that it does not take into account the developments of Fichte's system that occur after 1794.

36. See, for example, *Differenzschrift* 53f/120f.

37. Ibid., 52/119.

38. Ibid.

39. Ibid., 11/81.

40. See, for example, Hegel's discussion of this topic in *Differenzschrift* 37ff./106ff.
41. "Glauben und Wissen oder Reflexionsphilosophie der Subjektivität in der Vollstän-digkeit ihrer Formen als Kantische, Jacobische und Fichtesche Philosophie," in *G. W. F. Hegel, Theorie Werkausgabe*, vol. 2, *Jenaer Schriften 1801–1807*, p. 399. Except where otherwise noted, I rely on the translation by Walter Cerf and H. S. Harris, *Faith and Knowledge* (Albany: State University of New York Press, 1977), p. 158. Hereafter I refer to this work as "*Glauben und Wissen*," and first cite page references of the Suhrkamp and then of the Cerf and Harris editions. (In this case, for example, the citation is "*Glauben und Wissen* 399/158.")
42. *Differenzschrift* 67/132; see also 63/128. And in *Glauben und Wissen* 397/156: "Fichte's Ego is an identity upon which determination supervenes subsequently as something alien [*fremde*], something which is incomprehensible since it does not originate in the Ego."
43. *Differenzschrift* 69/133. "Because the Ego is subjective Subject-Object, there is a side from which it continues to have an object that is absolutely opposed to it and from which it continues to be conditioned by the object" (ibid., 72/136). The "identity" (of the starting point) is in fact not "absolute," but merely conditioned or "formal" (ibid., 97f./159).
44. Practical reason, Kant writes, is an "efficient [*selbst wirkende*] cause through its ideas." *Kritik der praktischen Vernunft* [Ak 48]. All translations of this text are mine.
45. As Hegel puts it, "The Ego *ought* to nullify the objective world, it ought to have absolute causality with respect to the not-Ego [*nicht-Ich*]. But this is found [by Fichte] to be contradictory, for it would imply suspending the not-Ego . . . " (*Differenzschrift* 68/132; my translation).
46. Ibid., 67f./132. For Fichte, "absolute identity exists only for faith [*Glauben*] and not for cognition and knowledge" (*Glauben und Wissen* 396f./156). Cf. in Kant's *Kritik der praktischen Vernunft* [Ak 124f.]: "the acting rational being in the world is . . . not at the same time the cause of the world and of nature itself . . . Since it is not through its will the cause of nature, it cannot out of its own strength bring nature into thoroughgoing harmony with its practical principles."
47. *Differenzschrift* 70/134.
48. *Glauben und Wissen* 417/175.
49. *Differenzschrift* 76/139.
50. *Glauben und Wissen* 421/179.
51. See ibid., 403/162 where Hegel writes, "nature [for Fichte] is nothing but the world of the senses. Ordinary empiricism suffers this [one] change: it gets deduced."
52. *Differenzschrift* 13/83.
53. "empiricism gives up hope of creating spirit and an inwardness itself, and bringing its dead [stuff] to life as Nature" (ibid., 137/193f.).
54. In the Suhrkamp edition (cited above, note 2), pp. 278f; in the Behler edition, p. 190.
55. *Differenzschrift* 107/166.
56. Ibid., 105/165.
57. An intuitive understanding, Kant writes at §77, "proceeds from the *synthetic-universal* (from the intuition of a whole, as a whole) to the particular, that is, from the whole to the parts . . . " (all translations of this text are mine). Unlike our discursive form of understanding, it therefore does not rely on the particular's being given; in intuiting the whole it intuits or determines the parts.
58. "The synthesis of nature as determined and yet also not determined by

understanding, is supposed to remain a mere Idea in a sensuous understanding; and *for us men* it is quite impossible that explanation in the mechanical mode should ever converge with purposiveness" (*Differenzschrift* 103/163).

59. *Differenzschrift* 97/157.
60. Ibid., 108f./168.
61. In the Suhrkamp edition, p. 294; in the Behler edition, p. 202.
62. See, for example, *Hegels Enzyklopädie der philosophischen Wissenschaften im Grundrisse (1830), Erster Teil: Die Wissenschaft der Logik*, §82 Zusatz, where he says in opposition to those (such as Schelling and Spinoza) whose theory of identity pays the price of difference: "If we say . . . that the Absolute is the unity of the subjective and the objective, this is indeed correct but nonetheless one-sided, in so far as what is here emphasized is the *unity*, although in fact the subjective and the objective are not merely identical, but also different" (my translation).
63. *Differenzschrift* 96/156.
64. Ibid. 65f./130.
65. Or, as Hegel puts it in *Glauben und Wissen*, Fichte does not begin with "genuine [*wahrhaft*] intellectual intuition," which is the identity of opposites. 401/159, 394/154.
66. *Differenzschrift* 65/130.
67. Ibid., 94/155. I owe thanks to the students of my seminar on Hegel's critique of Kant at Harvard University in the spring term of 1997. Their patience and intelligence were of much help to me in working through this material. I also wish to express my gratitude to both Rolf-Peter Horstmann and the Alexander von Humboldt-Stiftung for the generous support that made the completion of this paper possible.

1

The Unity of Nature and Freedom: *Kant's Conception of the System of Philosophy*

PAUL GUYER

I

In the last stage of his last attempt at philosophical work, the "First Fascicle" of the *Opus postumum,* Kant was apparently trying to unify his theoretical and practical philosophy into a single system of the ideas of nature and freedom. In this work, Kant seems to have wanted to show that the constitution of nature through our forms of intuition and understanding must be compatible with the content of the moral law and our capacity to act in accordance with it, as represented by our idea of God as supreme lawgiver, because both the concept of nature and the idea of God have their common ground in human thought itself. One of the many drafts of a title page that Kant wrote for this never-completed work suggests his intent:

> THE HIGHEST STANDPOINT OF
> TRANSCENDENTAL PHILOSOPHY
> IN THE SYSTEM OF THE TWO IDEAS
> BY
> GOD, THE WORLD, AND THE SUBJECT WHICH
> CONNECTS BOTH OBJECTS,
> THE THINKING BEING IN THE WORLD.
> GOD, THE WORLD, AND WHAT UNITES BOTH
> INTO A SYSTEM:
> THE THINKING, INNATE PRINCIPLE OF MAN IN
> THE WORLD (*MENS*).
> MAN AS A BEING IN THE WORLD,
> SELF-LIMITED THROUGH NATURE AND DUTY.
> (*OP,* I.III.4, 21:34; Förster, p. 237)[1]

Some commentators[2] have interpreted texts like this to mean that in his final years Kant undertook a radical revision of his previous critical philosophy. On this view, Kant's earlier "critical idealism,"[3] which argued that human beings could and must impose on a single experience grounded on an unknowable external reality two different but compatible frameworks, the theoretical and practical points of view defined by the forms of intuition and understanding on the one hand and the formal principle of practical reason on the other, would be replaced by a more dogmatic metaphysical doctrine in which the natural and moral worlds would be seen as two products of a single common substratum, human thought itself. This new metaphysical doctrine would be akin to Spinoza's conception of the orders of nature and thought as two modes of the single substance God, a conception that was enjoying a revival in the 1790s among the emerging German idealists such as Schelling and his followers. I will argue, however, that Kant's final attempt to unify the *ideas* of nature and God in the common substratum of human thought was a project continuous with his earlier view that the laws of theoretical and practical reason, or of nature and of morality, must be unifiable within a theory of *reflective* judgment, or a theory of the necessities of *human* thought that claims no validity beyond the human point of view. Kant's numerous references to Spinoza in his final writings are only meant to emphasize the *difference* between his own theory of the systematicity of human thought as a product of reflective judgment and what he took to be the dogmatic monistic metaphysics of Spinoza as revived by Schelling and his followers. The philosophers of Schelling and his generation may have acquired their taste for a single all-embracing philosophical system of reality from Kant, but rebelled against his restriction of such a system to the realm of reflective judgment or mere "ideas."

Some well-known statements from Kant's three *Critiques* might suggest that he had originally considered the concepts and laws of theoretical and practical reason to constitute two compatible but independent systems of thought rather than the single system of ideas contemplated in the *Opus postumum,* and thus that Kant's late work represents a radical change in his views. This remark from the published Introduction to the *Critique of Judgment* is often invoked in defense of the interpretation of Kant's Critical philosophy as an insuperable dichotomy of theoretical and practical viewpoints: There is "an incalculable abyss fixed between the domain of the concept of nature, as the sensible, and the domain of the concept of freedom, as the supersensible, so that no transition is possible from the first to the second (thus by means of the theoretical use of reason)" (*CJ,* Introduction II, 5:175–6). Although the paragraph from which this remark is taken immediately proceeds to argue that there must be some way to bridge this gulf, the subject matter of the ensuing body of the work, the realm of the aesthetic on the one hand and of a methodological conception of teleological judgment on the other, seems to imply that any unification of the two realms of theoretical and practical thought can only take place in the highly subjective realms of analogy, symbolism, methodological principles, and so on, and that the theoretical and practical must remain two essentially distinct forms of thought.

I will argue, however, that there is much less difference between the conception of the systematic unity of nature and freedom in Kant's three *Critiques* and the conception to which he was apparently working in his final days as a functioning philosopher than may initially meet the eye. In fact, Kant had always insisted that the systems of nature and freedom, of theoretical and practical reason, must themselves be able to be conceived as comprising a single system of nature and freedom, although this conception would itself be valid only "from a practical point of view" – precisely as the citation from the *Critique of Judgment* suggests, which after all denies only that the gulf between the domains of nature and freedom can be bridged *by means of the theoretical use of reason.* Although Kant worked at refining his characterization of the practical point of view to the end, there are no arguments in his last writings to suggest that he had fundamentally revised the fundamental content of this conception. Specifically, I will defend the following theses:

(1) In all three *Critiques,* Kant argues that we must be able to conceive of *nature,* and not any other realm, as receptive to the realization of the intended outcome of morality, in the form of the *highest good,* and thus be able to conceive of the realms of nature and freedom as constituting a single system, although such a conception of the single system of nature and freedom is held to be valid only from a practical point of view.

(2) In the *Opus postumum,* Kant suggests that it is the possibility of the recognition and performance of *duty* that must be reconciled with the universality and necessity of natural law by seeing both as having a common ground in human thought; but in my view this represents more of a change of emphasis than a fundamental change in doctrine, not only because the compatibility between nature and duty is already insisted upon in the second *Critique,* but also because there is an essential and intrinsic connection between the concepts of duty and of the highest good. The latter is not a hybrid concept of the merely natural end of happiness as constrained by the moral condition of duty, but is rather a conception of the *object* or intended *outcome* of duty, although not an appropriate characterization of the morally praiseworthy *motivation* for the performance of duty.

(3) Throughout the three *Critiques,* Kant suggests that the concept of the highest good is a necessary and sufficient ground, from a moral point of view, for the postulation of the existence of God as an author of nature distinct from ourselves. In the *Opus postumum,* he states that the idea of God is nothing but a representation of our own capacity to give ourselves the moral law and act in accordance with it, an "idea, the product of our own reason" (e.g. *OP,* VII.X.1, 22:117, Förster 201). Yet this does not constitute a fundamental change in dogma, only a clarification of the subjective significance of the idea of God that had always been part of the meaning of Kant's claim that the postulation of the existence of God was valid only from a practical point of view.

(4) Finally, even if the conception of nature and God as constituting a single system because grounded in the single substratum of human thought did represent a fundamental departure from the earlier conception of the realms of nature and human freedom as constituting a single system because grounded in a single author of nature, this would hardly count as a move *toward* Spinozism, on which nature and human thought are merely two modes of a real God. Rather, it would be an even more radical statement of the theoretical and practical anthropocentrism to which Kant had been working throughout his mature philosophy.

In what follows, I will argue for these theses by a commentary upon key arguments of the three *Critiques,* followed by a commentary upon some representative notes from the final stages of the *Opus postumum,* the Seventh and First Fascicles.

II

Kant's first introduction of the concept of the highest good as well as his first statement of the argument that this concept can serve as the ground for the conception of God is found in the "Canon of Pure Reason" of the "Doctrine of Method" of the *Critique of Pure Reason.*[4] By a "canon," Kant means the "sumtotal of the a priori principles of the correct use of certain cognitive faculties in general" (*CPuR,* A 796/B 824),[5] or a set of positive rules that can serve as grounds for further thought or action rather than a mere critique of unfounded thoughts or actions. The point of the section is to argue that while sensibility and understanding supply a canon for theoretical inquiry and judgment, theoretical reason does not, furnishing instead only metaphysical illusions; it is only reason in its practical use that can supply a canon, in the form of the pure principles of reason that are the foundation of morality and the further assumptions necessary for us to act on these principles. This thesis is stated in the first section of the "Canon," which announces that "the ultimate end of our pure use of reason" is grounded "uniquely and solely in its practical interest" (A 797/B 825). After providing an initial statement of his theory of freedom in this first section, Kant goes on in the second to give his first account of "the ideal of highest good, as a determining ground of the ultimate end of pure reason" (A 804/B 832): Suggesting that he will abjure detailed discussion of the question "What should I do?" as purely practical (although he does not entirely do so), he proposes to discuss the highest good in answer to the question "If I do what I should, what may I then hope?" as "simultaneously practical and theoretical" (A 805/B 833). The key points about the highest good that Kant makes in the "Canon" are themes that will remain constant throughout the rest of his career: First, that the maximal happiness that it includes should be conceived of as the appropriate outcome of virtuous action; second, although there is some ambivalence about this, that this happiness must be conceived of as realizable in nature, thus as requiring a unity of the systems of nature and freedom and their ground in a common author; but, third, that this postulation of the realizability of the highest good and thus of the reality of the single system of nature and freedom and of their author can only be conceived to be valid from a practical point of view.

(1) Kant begins the discussion by drawing a firm distinction between the practical law that has *happiness* as its *motive,* which would be merely "pragmatic," and the practical law that has *worthiness to be happy* as its sole motive, which would be "moral" (*CPuR,* A 806/B 834). But he proceeds to suggest that happiness in accord with moral laws must be conceived to be possible because such happiness would be the intended although not motivating *outcome* of virtuous action, and it would be incoherent to undertake such action if its intended outcome were impossible. Kant defines "the world as it would be if it were in conformity with all moral laws" as a "moral world," and says that in the first instance the conception of the moral world is also the conception of an "intelligible world, since abstraction is made therein from all conditions (ends) and even from all hindrances to morality in it." Yet he also states that this idea of a moral world should be conceived to have "objective reality, not as pertaining to an object of an intelligible intuition . . . but as pertaining to the world of the senses" (A 808/B 836). In other words, the idea of a moral world does not give us theoretical knowledge of a world existing independently of or beyond the sensible world; rather, it gives us a practical ideal for the guidance of our conduct in the same sensible world that we know by means of the senses and the understanding.

Next, Kant claims that "in an intelligible world," "a system of happiness proportionately combined with morality also can be thought as necessary, since freedom, partly moved and partly restricted by moral laws, would itself be the cause of the general happiness, and rational beings, under the guidance of such principles, would themselves be the authors of their own enduring welfare and at the same time that of others" (*CPuR,* A 809/B 837). Kant's subsequent works will suggest that this claim is grounded on the following argument: (i) since what the law of pure practical reason to which we should be motivated to conform by the virtuous desire to be worthy of happiness rather than by the merely natural desire for happiness itself requires us to do is to respect rational agency in ourselves and others, and (ii) since what making rational agency in both ourselves and others our ultimate end in this way requires is that we do what we can to preserve and promote the necessary conditions for ourselves and others realizing our other ends, whatever they may be, and even strive for the realization of those ends, to the extent that so doing is compatible with the general respect for rational agency itself,[6] yet (iii) since happiness is just the term for the maximal collective satisfaction of the ends of agents, which can in fact be brought about only under the condition of this general respect for agency itself, therefore (iv) the respect for rational agency itself would in fact bring about maximal collective happiness under the ideal circumstances in which each agent acted in conformity with this ideal and no natural conditions external to these agents intervened between their actions and their intended outcomes that would disrupt those outcomes. Under these conditions, a group of agents all motivated by respect for rational agency and the desire to be worthy of being happy would produce their own maximal collective happiness, even though that outcome of their actions would not be the motive of their actions.[7] Kant is quick to observe that no individual is relieved from his obligation under the moral law by anyone else's failure to live up to it, but at the same time he continues to maintain that the connection between "the hope of being happy [and] the unremitting effort to make oneself worthy of happiness" is "necessary" (*CPuR*, A 810/B 838). Subsequent works will suggest that what this means is that it would be irrational for us to act to bring about an end or object that we did not believe to be possible – or knew to be impossible – even if bringing about that end is not the *motivation* of our action. Thus it will be rational for us to act as morality requires only if the sphere within which we have to act can be conceived as one where it is possible to realize the outcomes of our action; it is in this way that nature and freedom must constitute a single system.

(2) Such a necessary connection, Kant next claims, "can be hoped for only if it is at the same time grounded on a **highest reason,** which commands in accordance with moral laws, as at the same time a cause of nature" (*CPuR*, A 810/B 838).[8] If we have to think of the laws of nature as compatible with the realization of an end that is in fact commanded by the moral law, then we have to think of nature as being caused in a way that makes this true, and the most natural way for us to do this, given our own understanding of causation, is to think of nature as being caused by an intelligent author who in designing it takes the demands of morality into account as well, "a wise author and regent" (A 811/B 839). Kant then introduces an argument, prominent in both of the two subsequent critiques as well, that only morality can lead to a *determinate* conception of God as "single, most perfect and rational," a specification of His predicates to which "speculative theology" could never lead even if it could legitimately lead to the idea of a first cause at all (A 814/B 842).

At this point, Kant takes a next step that will not be repeated in his subsequent expositions of the doctrine of the highest good. He argues that although "we must assume the moral world to be a consequence of our conduct in the sensible world," the senses "do not offer such a connection to us," and the realization of the highest good that we must be able to suppose to be a consequence of our conduct must therefore be supposed to lie in "a world which is future for us" (*CPuR,* A 811/B 839), a "world which is not now visible to us but is hoped for" (A 813/B 841). Here Kant treats the postulates of both God and immortality as conditions necessary for the realization of the maximal happiness contained in the concept of the highest good. He postulates God as the cause of the connection between virtuous action and its appropriate outcome, but defers the realization of this happiness to a life beyond the sensible world, thereby having to postulate immortality as well. This partially undermines the unity of nature and freedom that has just been established, for now it seems as if nature must be conceived as necessarily compatible with the *intention* to do what morality requires of us, but not as necessarily compatible with the *realization* of the appropriate outcome of virtuous action, which apparently can be deferred beyond the realm of nature.

What would have to be a key premise for any such argument for an afterlife – namely, the assumption that happiness proportionate to virtue is not just *not evident* in the sensible world but actually *impossible* in the sensible world – goes undefended here, although without such a premise one could argue that the laws of nature merely need to make such happiness *possible* for action that would have it as its intended outcome to be rational.[9] Furthermore, Kant retreats from this position almost as soon as he states it, for he next argues that "this systematic unity of ends in this world of intelligences" must be conceivable as both a sensible and an intelligible world, and thus "leads inexorably to the purposive unity of all things that constitute this great whole, in accordance with laws of nature"; he goes on to say that "the world" – without qualification – "must be represented as having arisen out of an idea if it is to be in agreement with that use of reason without which we would hold ourselves unworthy of reason," and that for this reason "[A]ll research into nature is thereby directed toward the form of a system of ends, and becomes in its fullest development physico-theology" (*CPuR,* A 815–16/B 843–4). Here Kant again suggests that we can only make the actions required by the moral use of reason fully rational if we conceive of a single world – that in which we act – as being described by the laws of both nature and freedom, and of those laws as constituting a single system describing one and the same world.

(3) No sooner has Kant argued that the postulation of a determinately conceived author of nature is the necessary condition of the highest good
than he also insists that we must hold this concept of God to be correct
"not because speculative reason has convinced us of its correctness but
because it is in perfect agreement with the moral principles of reason":

> Thus, in the end, only pure reason, although only in its practical use, always has
> the merit of connecting with our highest interest a cognition which mere spec-
> ulation can only imagine but never make valid, and of thereby making it into not
> a demonstrated dogma but yet an absolutely necessary presupposition in rea-
> son's most essential ends. (*CPuR*, A 818/B 846)

Kant argues that we cannot infer a theoretical *is* from a moral *ought:* we
can treat God and the unity of the natural and moral that he grounds as a
presupposition of our conduct but not as an object of our knowledge.

Just what this means is a difficult issue, about which Kant will have
something but perhaps not enough more to say. At this juncture, however, I only want to suggest that in the few pages of the "Canon of Pure
Reason" Kant has already staked out three claims from which he will not
depart in more than style and emphasis even in his last writings: (i) the
appropriate outcome of virtuous action is the highest good, (ii) we must
conceive of the world in which we act as described by a single set of
both natural and moral laws with a single author for it to be rational for
us to act as duty requires, but (iii) the postulation of this systematic unity
of nature and freedom and its ground must always remain a presupposition of conduct and not a claim of speculative theology or dogmatic
metaphysics.

III

I now turn to Kant's treatment of the highest good in the *Critique of Practical
Reason.*[10] The treatment of the highest good and of its implications for the
systematic union of nature and freedom in the second *Critique* is largely
continuous with that in the first. Thus, as before, the main points are first, that
the collective maximization of happiness contained in the concept of the highest good is in fact an appropriate object of virtuous conduct, not its motive, but
also not a merely natural end that is externally constrained by the requirement
of virtue; second, although there is still some wavering on this issue, on the
whole Kant treats the happiness-component of the highest good – indeed, ever
more than the virtue-component – as something that must be capable of being
realized in nature or the sensible world, which requires that the laws of nature
be compatible with the laws of morality and that nature have a moral author
but third, again Kant insists that the postulation of such a common author of the
enabling legislation of both the natural and the moral world is valid only from a

practical point of view, and now he spells out a little more clearly what that restriction means.

(1) The *Critique of Practical Reason* initially appears to be the most formalistic of Kant's ethical writings: Its opening exposition of the fundamental principle of morality equates the categorical imperative with the requirement of the universalizability of maxims[11] and omits any mention of the requirement of respect for rational agency as the end in itself that even in the *Groundwork* is adduced as the ground of the possibility of the categorical imperative.[12] This makes Kant's introduction of the highest good opaque, and has led some[13] to suppose that the concept of the highest good is a hybrid concept, which combines the moral but purely formal requirement of virtue as a concern for universalizability without regard to ends with a merely natural concern for happiness that may be subjected to a requirement of maximization by reason as a general striving for the unconditioned but not by practical reason in any specifically moral sense. On this account, the requirement that virtue be perfected or maximized *constrains* the pursuit of happiness, or subjects it to a moral condition, but does not entail any properly moral interest in the realization of happiness, let alone in the maximization or systematization of happiness. But it is clear that this is not Kant's position, although he does not make his grounds for rejecting it very clear. On the contrary, although he is again at pains, as he was in the "Canon," to stress that an interest in happiness cannot be any part of the *motive* for the pursuit of the highest good (*CPracR,* 5:109, 113), Kant is again also at pains to stress that the happiness-component of the highest good is a genuine *object* of morality. This is clear in the following *locus classicus:*

> That virtue (as the worthiness to be happy) is the **supreme condition** of all that which may seem desirable to us, thus of all our striving for happiness, thus that it is the **supreme good,** has been proven in the Analytic. But it is not on that account the whole and complete good, as the object of the faculty of desire of rational finite beings; for in order to be that, **happiness** is also required, and not merely in the partial eyes of the person who makes himself into an end, but even in the judgment of an impartial reason, who considers the former in general as an end in himself in the world. (*CPracR,* 5:110)

Although highly compacted, this passage is significant both in what it says and what it does not say. It does not say that the desire for happiness is a merely natural desire, or a desire of a merely natural being; on the contrary, it suggests that the desire for happiness is a *rational* desire of a finite being, and one that is recognized by reason as such in regarding a being who is both rational but also placed in a world as an end in himself. Thus, although talk of an end in itself has heretofore been excluded from the *Critique of Practical Reason,* at this crucial point it appears, suggesting that what underlies the concept of the highest good even here is the view that what morality requires, out of respect for reason rather than a mere desire for happiness, is respect for rational agency as such. But rational agents or ends in themselves are finite creatures who *have* ends, so that what respect for them *as* ends requires is respect for, or the preservation and promotion of, their capacity to *have* and *pursue* ends; and since what happiness consists in is the attainment of ends, virtue therefore actually requires and does not just constrain the impartial pursuit of happiness. It is in this way that the happiness-component of the highest good is part of the object of morality – the other part, of course, being the cultivation of the virtuous *motivation* of duty itself – and not just a merely natural end externally constrained by morality.

(2) Second, although there is still one point of obscurity on this issue, for the most part the second *Critique* stresses more clearly than the first that the happiness that comprises part of the highest good is to be conceived of as realizable *in nature* and therefore requires the postulation of a morally motivated author *of nature.* Early in his discussion, Kant argues that the proposition that striving after happiness itself produces a virtuous disposition is "**absolutely false,**" but that the proposition that striving after virtue produces happiness is not absolutely but only "**conditionally** false," for it is false if considered as a claim about a "form of causality in the sensible world" but might be true if "my existence is thought of as a noumenon in an intellectual world" (*CPracR,* 5:114). This might be taken to imply that the happiness that is to be connected with virtue in the highest good need not and perhaps cannot be thought of as a happiness that is to be realized within the sensible realm of nature, but somewhere else. Kant does not, however, draw this conclusion. Rather, he only denies that the connection between virtue and happiness in nature is *immediate:* He states that "it is not impossible that the morality of disposition have if not an immediate than a mediate and indeed necessary connection as cause (by means of an intelligible author of nature) with happiness as an effect in the sensible world" (5:115). Such a connection would be merely contingent in the case of a nature that contains merely our own powers as revealed by our own senses, but, Kant implies, if nature is regarded *both* as object of the senses and as the product of an intelligent author, then the connection would be necessary rather than contingent.

By bringing God into the argument from the highest good in the form of the intelligent author of nature, in other words, Kant implies that the happiness required by the highest good must be realizable within nature and not elsewhere. He continues to imply as much when he dramatically separates the postulation of immortality from the postulation of God in the ensuing discussion. Conceiving of the highest good as requiring the maximization of both virtue and happiness (not, as he is sometimes taken to suggest, mere proportionality between the two),[14] Kant argues that the maximization of virtue, or development of a holy will, cannot be expected to occur in a finite phenomenal lifetime, and that we must think of that as something that takes place in immortality (*CPracR,* 5:122–3). But he does not go on to say the same thing about happiness and God as its ground. Instead, he argues that the existence of God must be postulated as the "cause of the whole of nature" in order to explain "the possibility of the second element of the highest good." This only makes sense if the happiness that is required by the concept of the highest good is envisioned as occurring within nature.

Kant's argument for this point is tricky. He begins by stating that the "acting rational being in the world is not at the same time the cause of the world and of nature itself," and thus that there cannot be a ground of a "necessary connection between morality and the happiness proportionate to it" in the constitution of an ordinary agent considered by itself (*CPracR,* 5:124). The next claim Kant makes, however, is not what we might expect, namely that God must be postulated as the ground of such a necessary connection; rather, he argues that a supreme cause of nature must be postulated as "the ground of the agreement of nature not merely with a law of the will of rational beings but of the representation of this *law,* in so far as they make it into the **supreme determining ground of their will,** thus of agreement not merely with the form of morals, but with their morality as the determining ground of that, i.e., with their moral disposition"; thus the highest good is only possible "insofar as a supreme cause of nature is assumed which has a causality in accord with the moral disposition" (5:125). In other words, a moral cause of nature is postulated here in order to insure that human beings as natural creatures are capable of forming moral intentions, or being virtuous. Nevertheless, Kant goes on to claim that the God so introduced, as the "**highest original good,**" is the ground of "a **highest derived good** (of the best world)," and then to argue that it is our duty "to endeavor to produce and advance the highest good in the world" (5:126). Since it is the complete highest good and not just virtue as one of its two components that is to be produced in the world, the implication is clear that not only virtuous intention but happiness as its intended outcome must be conceived by us as possible within the world, not somewhere else, and that God as a moral author is being postulated as the ground of the possibility of both virtue and happiness in the world, the same sensible world where we ourselves could connect these two components only contingently but where God can make their connection, or the systematic union of nature and freedom, necessary.

(3) As in the first *Critique,* however, Kant also immediately restricts the force of this argument with the claim that it is valid "only from a practical point of view" (*CPracR,* 5:133). This is now presented as a complex restriction: the coherence of moral conduct requires (i) that we postulate the *possibility* of the realization of the happiness called for in the concept of the highest good in the sensible or natural world, which in turn requires (ii) that we postulate the *actual existence* of God, where, however, (iii) that postulation is not entailed by any theoretical considerations whatsoever but is only a practical presupposition of our conduct in accord with the demands of morality and where, moreover, (iv) the *predicates* for the *determination* of this concept of God cannot be furnished by any theoretical speculation but only by the demands of morality. In order to understand Kant's notion of a postulate of practical reason and thus the epistemic status of his conception of the systematic unity of nature and freedom, we need to touch on each of these points, even if only briefly.

(i) What we must postulate in order to make action rational is the *possibility* of realizing the end foreseen and intended by that action, not a guarantee of the actual realization of that end. Thus at the outset of the section from which we have been quoting Kant says that the moral law must "lead to the possibility of the second element of the highest good" (*CPracR,* 5:124), and at the end of its first long paragraph he writes that "the postulate of the possibility of the **highest derived good** (of the best world) is at the same time the postulate of the actuality of a **highest original good,** namely the existence of God" (5:125). This point is important, for it sometimes seems as if Kant thinks an endeavor is rational only if its success is in some sense guaranteed,[15] but here he clearly suggests that as long as an enterprise is *motivated* by sufficiently weighty grounds, as morality above all is, then its pursuit is rational as long as its successful outcome is *not impossible.*[16]

(ii) To explain how we can conceive of nature as a sphere in which the realization of the highest good is even guaranteed to be *possible,* however, we must think that the *actual* ground of its existence is the existence of God, not merely that God is a possible cause of it. Presumably the thought here is that if God is merely a possible cause of nature, but there are other possible causes of it as well, then if one of those other causes is the actual cause of nature, the realization of the highest good in nature may not even be possible; but if God is the actual cause of nature, then the realization of the highest good is assuredly possible. Thus the content of the postulation of God is an existence-statement, not a merely possibility-statement: "the possibility of this highest good . . . occurs only under the presupposition of the existence of God" (*CPracR*, 5:125).

(iii) At the same time, however, Kant hedges the semantically existential *content* of the practical postulate of God with restrictions on its epistemic *force*. Thus he immediately follows the last remark cited with the statement that "this moral necessity is **subjective,** i.e., a need, and not **objective,** i.e., itself a duty; for there cannot be any duty to assume the existence of a thing (since this pertains merely to the theoretical use of reason" (*CPracR*, 5:125). Alternatively, he goes on to say that from a theoretical point of view the assumption of the existence of God would be, as a ground of explanation, a mere "hypothesis," although with regard to "an object set for us by the moral law" it can be a "**belief** and even a pure **belief of reason**" (5:126). Kant clarifies this distinction by suggesting that there are two conditions for a practical postulate. First, the concept to be postulated must itself be *not impossible* or free from contradiction, even from a purely theoretical point of view. Second, the affirmation of the reality of the concept, even if itself unwarranted by any theoretical ground, must still not be arbitrary, for then it would be mere theoretical hypothesis; instead, it must be something that we must believe if it is to be rational and coherent for us to act in a certain way, where acting in that way is itself morally requisite. Kant suggests these two conditions when he writes, first, that the postulates of practical reason are "(transcendent) thoughts in which there is nothing impossible," which implies that they must have noncontradictory theoretical content, and then that what would otherwise be "**transcendent** and merely **regulative** principles of speculative reason" become "**immanent** and **constitutive** insofar as they are grounds for **making actual** the **necessary object** of pure practical reason (the highest good)" (5:135). This, perhaps especially the use of the phrase "making actual," suggests that a rational belief is something that must be believed in order to make a form of conduct coherent, but that it has no force outside of that context.

Thus far, then, we have the claims that the highest good must be considered to be *possible* in nature, and that its ground, a moral Author of nature, must be considered to be *actual* from a practical point of view, where that in turn means that it must be *theoretically* possible and a necessary presupposition of a mode of *conduct,* but not otherwise grounded. Finally, Kant adds the last element of his position, the claim that (iv) the concept of God can be given *determinate content* only from a practical point of view, that is, the only predicates that can be ascribed to him in order to amplify the vague conception of him as the author of nature are those that are necessary to conceive of him as the ground of the realizability of the highest good. This argument is expanded beyond the hint at it offered in the "Canon," but still not developed at the length it will be in the *Critique of Judgment*. The argument is essentially a tacit response to Hume's critique of the argument from design in his *Dialogues concerning Natural Religion:* Kant agrees with the Philo of Dialogue XII[17] that the most that we could infer from the amount of "order, design and magnitude" we observe in nature is that it has an author who is to *some* degree "wise, beneficent and powerful," but responds that we can only infer that this author is "all-knowing, all-good and all-powerful" (*CPracR,* 5:139) on the ground that these are the qualities necessary for him to ground the possible realization of the highest good. Thus, God must be conceived of as "**all-knowing** in order [for him] to know my conduct in its innermost disposition in all possible cases and throughout the future," or in order to judge my virtue, and he must be "**all-powerful**" and "**all-present**" in order "to apportion to it the appropriate consequences" (5:140). Thus, Kant's moral theology consists not merely in the claim that only morality gives us a ground for *believing* in the *existence* of God; it also includes the claim that only morality gives us a *determinate conception* of God.

On the basis of this conception, however, we can then conceive of the systematic union of nature and freedom through their common author; the concept of this single system is thus reached through the concept of the highest good, which is itself a morally necessary concept, and is therefore valid though only from a practical point of view, as itself a postulate for which God is the ground. Let us now see whether Kant modifies that thought at all at the next stage of his thought.

IV

The *Critique of Judgment* is a work of great complexity as well as obscurity. One measure of the complexity of the work is that although its division into the two main parts of a *Critique of Aesthetic Judgment* and a *Critique of Teleological Judgment* might be taken to suggest that there are two main objects for the single power of reflective judgment that is supposed to be under analysis in the work as a whole, namely objects of beauty on the one hand and natural organisms on the other, in fact at least *five* distinguishable objects of reflective judgment are actually discussed: two in the aesthetic sphere, namely (i) particular objects of *beauty,* the internal quasisystematicity of whose parts is recognized by aesthetic judgment rather than by conceptual judgment, but which may be either naturally occurring objects or products of human intentional artistic activity, and then (ii) boundless regions of nature, which are the causes[18] of the experience of the *sublime;* and three connected with the idea of teleology, namely: (iii) individual natural objects, the internal organization of whose parts can be judged under a concept of reciprocal causation rather than by merely aesthetic judgment, or *organisms;* (iv) the system of empirical scientific *concepts* standing under the purely formal laws of nature furnished by the categories and manifesting further internal organization in the form of homogeneity, specificity and affinity; and, finally, (v) the whole of *nature* itself as a system, including but by no means limited to those internally systematic parts of nature that are themselves systems, that is, organisms. Kant explores many relations and analogies among these various objects, making his argumentation in this work particularly dense.

But in fact the work begins and ends with a claim with which we are already familiar. This is the claim that even though – or precisely because – the great abyss between nature and freedom cannot be bridged by the *theoretical* use of reason, it can and must be bridged by the *practical* use of freedom, from whose point of view nature must be able to be seen as a realm within which morality's demands on both our actions and their outcomes can be satisfied. In Kant's words, the concept of freedom "**should** have influence" on the concept of nature, "namely the concept of freedom should make the end which is set forth through its laws actual in the sensible world; and nature must therefore be able to be so conceived that the lawfulness of its form is at least in agreement with the possibility of the end which is to be effected within it in accordance with the laws of freedom" (*CJ,* Introduction II, 5:176). That is to say, in this work Kant reiterates two theses already made clear in the previous *Critiques,* that the fundamental principle of morality does not just constrain our natural ends but itself sets an overarching end for us, the highest good, and that this end must be capable of being realized in nature in order for our actions that have it as their end to be rational and coherent; and the reiteration of this theme within a general theory of reflective judgment and its regulative principles only clarifies the position, already suggested as "the practical point of view," that this conception of the unity of nature and freedom is to be treated, like a maxim for the conduct of inquiry, as a principle that may have the form of a proposition about objects but that is not asserted to have an ordinary objective truth-value.

The argument underlying Kant's *Critique of Teleological Judgment* can be outlined like this. Starting from the side of theoretical judgment,[19] we see that the peculiar complexity of individual organisms makes it necessary for us to conceive of them as if they were products of intelligent design, that the necessity of so conceiving of individual organisms also makes it inevitable for us to conceive of nature as a whole as a systematic product of intelligent design, but that although there is thus a purely theoretical impetus for us so to conceive of nature as a whole, it is not in fact possible for us to form any *determinate* and *unique* conception of nature as a whole as a system except by treating some part of that system, namely humankind, as *its* end because it is an end *in itself,* a characterization that is possible only from a moral point of view. At the same time, morality itself requires that we conceive of humankind as an end in itself and also conceive of the moral perfection of humankind, in the form of the highest good, as something possible within nature and indeed as the end of nature as a whole. So the ultimate argument of Kant's teleology is that the scientific point of view contains an idea of systematicity that can only be satisfied by the moral point of view, and conversely that the moral point of view requires us to conceive of nature as a sphere within which humankind can successfully work out its moral vocation. Yet whether we start from the scientific or the moral end of this argument, in either case what we get is a regulative principle of conduct rather than a theoretical principle of cognition.

Kant's commitment to such an argument is confirmed by several striking outlines of it among his notes. The first such outline, which neatly shows the steps from individual organisms to a view of nature as a purposive system as a whole and then the need to bring in moral considerations in order to make that system determinate, apparently dates from the 1780s:

> **Moral proof.** We find **ends** in the world; these give our insight an indication of a being which would be in accordance with **the analogy** of an **intelligent cause** of the world. But its **concept is not determined** through this [analogy] either for the theoretical or practical principles of our use of reason: Because it **explains nothing** in regard to the former and **determines nothing** in regard to the latter.
>
> Only reason, through the **moral law,** gives us a **final end.** This cannot be attained through our powers, and yet we are to have it as our aim. It can be brought about **only in the world,** consequently so far as **nature agrees with it.** A nature, however, which agrees with a moral final end, would be a **morally effective** cause. Thus we must assume a being **outside** of nature as its author, which would be a **moral being,** a cause of the world equipped with understanding and will. (R 6173, 18:477–8)

The first paragraph shows that the idea of particular systems within nature introduces at best an indeterminate idea of nature as a whole as a system; the second paragraph shows that the final end of morality, the highest good, necessarily introduces a certain view of nature as compatible with that end and of its author as determined above all by the moral predicates necessary to explain that compatibility.

A second note from the next decade outlines the second stage of this argument particularly clearly:

> First the representation of the world as a system of the *nexus finalis physici* (*causarum finalium physicarum* among which mankind must also be). Thus an intelligent primordial being, but not yet God, because the concept of the perfection of the world from experience is not adequate for that. Now the representation of the world as of a *systematis causarum finalium moralium* for the highest good. For humankind, which is a member of the *nexus finalis physici* but also touches on a principle of a higher *nexus*

finalis in itself, also relates its existence in regard to the same intelligent author; but the concept of that is that of a being as the author of the highest good, because this alone is appropriate to the end-relation of the moral human. (R 6451, 18:723).

Here Kant skips the first step of the argument, but again spells out clearly that only a moral conception of God that is in fact based on the moral end of human beings can provide a determinate conception of the world as a whole as a system of causes.

Let us now look at the details of this argument in its fullest exposition in the *Critique of Judgment.*

(1) First, the Introduction to the third *Critique* lays out the framework of Kant's argument: the critique of teleological judgment is to bridge the gap between the realms of nature and freedom precisely by showing us that it is *possible* to realize within nature the final end the pursuit of which is made *necessary* by practical reason. As Kant puts it,

> The effect in accordance with the concept of freedom is the final end [*Endzweck*] which (or the appearance of which in the sensible world) should exist, for which the condition of its possibility in nature (in the nature of the subject as sensible being, namely as human being) is presupposed. What the power of judgment presupposes *a priori* and without regard to the practical yields the mediating concept between the concepts of nature and the concept of freedom, which makes possible the transition from the purely theoretical to the purely practical, from the lawfulness in accordance with the former to the final end in accordance with the latter, in the concept of a **purposiveness** of nature: for thereby is the possibility of the final end known, which can become actual only in nature and in harmony with its laws. (*CJ*, Introduction IX, 5:195–6).

That is, a teleological view of nature that is not itself dictated by morality will nevertheless show nature, above all our own nature as creatures in the sensible world, to be suitable for the realization of the final end that is dictated by morality.

(2) Next, the opening move of the *Critique of Teleological Judgment* in particular is to argue that the teleological viewpoint that is forced upon us by the attempt to comprehend individual organisms in nature also makes it natural for us to conceive of nature as a whole as a system that is designed by an intelligent author and must therefore have or be compatible with a final end. In my view, Kant's interest in making this point is what motivates him to discuss the problem of understanding organisms at all.[20] For present purposes, we will have to take for granted Kant's argument that organic processes such as growth, self-mainte-nance, and reproduction (*CJ*, §64, 5:371–2) involve a kind of reciprocal causation that cannot be understood through our mechanical model of temporally unidirectional causal influence, but instead require, precisely

in order to accommodate them to our ordinary conception of the temporal direction of causation, the postulation of an antecedent design of the organism and therefore an antecedent designer (§65, especially 5:373) – an argument that has, to say the least, been put into question by the modern synthesis of genetics and natural selection. The point to be emphasized here is Kant's next move, the argument that once we have conceived of particular organisms or "physical ends" as systematically organized products of design, it then becomes irresistible for us to conceive of nature as a whole as a systematic organization with an end. This is in fact the final move of the "Analytic of Teleological Judgment":

It is only matter, insofar as it is organized, which necessarily carries with it the idea of it as a natural end, since its specific form is at the same time a product of nature. But now this concept necessarily leads to the idea of the whole of nature as a system in accordance with the rule of ends, to which idea now all mechanism of nature in accordance with principles of reason must be subordinated (at least for the investigation of natural appearance thereby). The principle of reason is permissible only subjectively, i.e., as a maxim: Everything in the world is good for something, nothing in it is in vain; and through the example which nature gives in its organic products one is justified, indeed invoked to expect nothing in it and its laws except what is purposive in the whole. (CJ, §67, 5:378–9)

. . . if we have once discovered in nature a capacity for bringing forth products which can only be conceived by us in accordance with the concept of final causes, then we go further and may also estimate those which do not (either in themselves or even in their purposive relation) make it necessary to seek out another principle for their possibility beyond the mechanism of blindly efficient causes as nevertheless belonging to a system of ends. (5:380–1)

Two points must be noted here. First, as Kant stresses in the first of these paragraphs, in the following §68, and then in the whole of the following "Dialectic of Teleological Judgment," from a purely theoretical point of view we are not justified in conceiving of a teleological view either of natural organisms or of the whole of nature as anything more than a heuristic, methodological or regulative principle intended to encourage and guide us in investigations ultimately aimed at discovering mechanical explanations of natural phenomena (of precisely the type that modern evolutionists have discovered): The term "purposiveness" "signifies only a principle of the reflective, not the determinant power of judgment and therefore should not introduce a special ground of causality, but only add to the use of reason another sort of research than that in accordance with mechanical laws in order to supplement the inadequacy of the latter itself for the empirical investigation of all the particular laws of nature" (*CJ*, §68, 5:383). Even from the theoretical point of view then, let alone the practical point of view, the conception of systems within nature, and presumably the idea of nature as a whole as a system that is suggested by the first, remain subjective ideas rather than objective dogmas. Second, as Kant stresses at the outset of §67, the idea of nature as a system as a whole, room for which is created by the special condition necessary for us to conceive of organisms, does not itself yield any *unique* and *determinate* way of seeing nature as a whole as a system: we might think that grass is necessary to nourish cattle and cattle in turn to nourish humans, but from a purely scientific point of view we cannot see any reason why we should not instead think that the purpose of both cattle and humans is just to facilitate the growth of grass (5:378; §82, 5:427).

(3) Kant's next move, then, will be to argue that in order to form a unique conception of nature as a determinate system aimed at the promotion of any particular end, we must introduce the idea of something that is intrinsically final or an end in itself, something that is not just chosen arbitrarily as the endpoint of a system of final causes but that must be conceived as an end and that imposes on us a view of the other elements of nature as organized in its service. Such a conception can only be provided by morality, which dictates that we conceive of mankind and its highest good as an end in itself; and morality in turn requires that we be able to conceive of nature as an arena within which the end it imposes can be achieved. Thus the teleological perspective that is necessitated by the intellectual puzzle of organisms opens up for us a possibility of seeing nature as a whole as a system, but this cannot be made determinate without appeal to morality, and in any case morality requires us to take a view of nature as well as reason as purposive, so the possibilities of the scientific view of nature and the necessities of the moral view of nature ultimately coincide. This is the complex point for which Kant argues in the "Methodology of Teleological Judgment," precisely because this is nothing less than the investigation of the ultimate conditions for the *application* of teleological judgment.

Kant begins the "Methodology" by reiterating that teleology furnishes no constitutive principles for either natural science or theology, but only reflective principles, principles for the critique of the use of judgment that will show us how natural science and theology must ultimately, although only subjectively, be combined (*CJ*, §79, 5:417). Next, going beyond his earlier suggestion that teleological principles have a purely heuristic function in encouraging and guiding us in the search for mechanical explanations, he argues that mechanical explanations of the development of natural forms, even a completely worked out

theory of evolution[21] (§80, 5:418–19), "only push the explanation further back" (420) and still require some explanation of why it is purposive for nature to be constituted with such mechanisms, which can only
be provided by an appeal to an end and its intelligent author (421). We
must thus conceive of the mechanisms of nature as "the instrument of an
intentionally acting cause, to whose end nature in its mechanical laws as
subordinated" (§81, 5:422). Kant then asserts that "the possibility of the
union of two such different types of causality" must lie in the "supersensible substrate of nature," for there our ignorance prevents us from
explaining but at the same time prevents us from precluding such a
combination; but he then also insists that we can conceive of an intelligent and purposive creation of nature through mechanical means only
if we can find something *in* nature that is itself intrinsically final and
gives the rest of nature a point. Reiterating his claim that the means-end
relation we introduce into the system of nature as a whole must not be
arbitrary, Kant in effect lays down two conditions on the nonarbitrary
end of nature.

First, he states that "the ultimate end of creation here on earth" must
be one "which can form a concept of ends for itself and can through its
reason make a system of ends out of an aggregate of purposively formed
things" (*CJ*, §82, 5:426–7). Kant does not state explicitly why the final
end *in* nature must be capable of forming a conception of ends when that
final end is also conceived of as the final end *of* a supersensible cause;
but we can take this claim to be a reminder that we are after all within the
realm of reflective judgment, and that this whole story of ends is an
artifact of our own judgment that will be inconceivable unless we ourselves can conceive of ends and of nature as a system of and for this end.
In any case, however, the requirement that the ultimate end of nature
itself be able to form the conception of ends is only a necessary, not a
sufficient condition for the view of nature as a system of ends. For Kant
next argues that the end that this ultimate end of nature conceives must
not itself be a merely natural end, such as mere happiness, but an
unconditional end the value and the setting – if not the realization – of
which is independent of nature. Kant stresses the most obvious reason
why a merely natural condition such as happiness per se cannot be the
ultimate end of nature, namely that nature does not seem particularly
well adapted to produce this condition (§83, 5:430–1); but he leaves
tacit the more important point that even if nature did produce happiness,
then there would still be nothing to distinguish this natural condition as
the putative end of nature from any other natural condition and thus give
a unique end to the system of nature as a whole. So what is necessary is
an end that makes its agent an end in itself from a rational and not

merely natural point of view. This, like the first condition of being able to conceive of ends at all, is only satisfied in the case of a human being, and is satisfied in particular only by "the formal, subjective condition of setting ends for himself in general and (independent of nature in his determination of ends) of using nature as an appropriate means for the maxims of his free ends in general" (431). In other words, what makes man an end in himself in the moral point of view, namely the intrinsic value of free and rational agency, is the only unconditional end that can be conceived to be the end of the system of nature as a whole as well, and the final end that is sought by scientific judgment in its attempt to conceive of nature as a system can only be the one furnished by moral reason, which would in any case impose this idea upon nature.

The contrast that Kant draws in the present argument between "happiness on earth" (431) on the one hand and "the culture of discipline" on the other, that which consists in "the liberation of the will from the despotism of desires, through which, by our attachment to certain natural things, we are made incapable of choosing for ourselves" (432), might appear to undercut the claim I have been making that throughout the three *Critiques* Kant sees the unity of nature and freedom as the possibility of the realization of the highest good, which of course includes happiness, and indeed happiness that is to be possible "on earth." This appearance is misleading, however, for what Kant is excluding as the ultimate end of nature is only mere happiness, or happiness conceived of as being produced by merely natural means rather than by human choice governed by reason; if the highest good is conceived of as containing not merely happiness proportionate to virtue but happiness produced *through* the virtuous exercise of human freedom, then this remains the intended end of virtuous human action and thus the ultimate end of nature. This should already be clear from the characterization of that capacity that makes human beings the ultimate end of nature as the capacity to be rational *in setting ends,* for rational agents set ends in order to realize them, and in the realization of ends lies happiness. But the point is also clear in the language Kant uses in his own summaries of the argument we have just rehearsed. Thus, drawing its exposition to a close, he writes:

Now we have only a single sort of being in the world whose causality is teleological, i.e., directed to ends, and yet at the same time so constituted that the law in accordance with which it has to determine its ends is represented by it as unconditional and independent of natural conditions but necessary in itself. The being of this sort is mankind, but considered as noumenon; the only natural being in which we can yet cognize a supersensible capacity (**freedom**) and even the law of its causality together with its object, which it can set before itself as the highest end (the highest good in the world) on the part of its own constitution. (*CJ*, §84, 5:435)

Even though man must be regarded as noumenal in order to be regarded as free, the sphere of his activity and thus where he has to realize his own highest good, which is as it were transitively the ultimate end of the whole of nature, the end to which so far as man can "he must subject the whole of nature," is "in the world." Likewise, summing up his whole critique of the eighteenth-century natural theology or argument from design and his alternative of a moral theology several sections later, Kant lays even more stress on the earthly arena within which the end of morality must be realizable. Using something very much like the dual formula I have used, that the highest good unifies nature and freedom because it must be seen as the ultimate end of both, Kant writes:

> The moral law as formal rational condition of the use of our freedom obligates us for itself alone, without depending on any end as material condition, but it nevertheless also determines for us, indeed *a priori*, a final end, to strive after which it makes obligatory for us: and this is the **highest good in the world** possible through freedom. (*CJ*, §87, 5:450; Kant's emphasis)

Thus, the third *Critique* maintains the position that even though the highest good is nonnatural in the sense of being made an end by freedom rather than nature, it must be realizable in nature, and nature and freedom must be able to be conceived of as a single system with a common ground in order to satisfy that condition.

(4) In the *Critique of Teleological Judgment,* Kant states the argument that it is only the necessity of postulating a condition for the realizability of the highest good that justifies us in postulating the existence of an intelligent Author of nature and only these same conditions that allow us to ascribe determinate predicates to this God at even greater length than he did in the *Critique of Practical Judgment* (*CJ*, §§85–87). Befitting his new presentation of his moral theology as part of a general theory of reflective and regulative judgment, he is also more explicit than before about the "Limitation of the validity of the moral proof" (§88, 5:453). His new discussion of this limitation is worth our attention because the light it sheds on Kant's conception of a practical postulate will be crucial in determining whether the *Opus postumum* represents any radical change in Kant's view of the unity of nature and freedom. The two key points that Kant here suggests are implied by the restriction that "the idea of a final end in the use of freedom" has "a subjectively-**practical** reality" (453) are, first, that from a theoretical point of view all that can be established is that the object of the postulate, the highest good or its ground, the existence of God, is not contradictory or impossible, and

second, that the representation of this object from a practical point of view as not just possible but actual serves not to ground any cognitive claim but to direct our energies in moral conduct. Kant makes the first of these points when he writes:

> The actuality of a highest morally-legislative Founder is therefore sufficiently demonstrated merely **for the practical use** of our reason, without determining anything theoretically in regard to its existence. For [reason] requires for the possibility of its end, which is set for us by its own legislation, an idea, through which the incapacity of prosecuting it in accordance with the merely natural concept of the world would be removed (adequately for the reflective judgment). (456)

Here, the point is that in order for our pursuit of the end of reason to be noncontradictory, we must be able to conceive of that object and its ground as free of contradiction. Second, Kant stresses that the point of the postulation of these ideas is not cognition but conduct:

> The final end is merely a concept of our practical reason and cannot be deduced from any data of experience for theoretical judgment, nor be related to their cognition. No use of this concept is possible except solely for practical reason in accordance with moral laws; and the final end of creation is that constitution of the world which agrees with that which we can determinately produce only in accordance with laws, namely the final end of our pure practical reason . . . – Now through the practical reason which sets this end for us we have, in a practical regard, a ground, namely the application of our powers for effecting it, for assuming its realizability . . . (§88, 5:455)

The role of the idea of the realizability of the highest good is simply to encourage us to use our own powers to bring it about, and Kant's claim is that it has no validity outside of this use. Postulates of practical reason, then, are "subjectively-practical" in the sense that they must be theoretically noncontradictory and practically necessary and efficacious in directing our conduct toward purely moral goals, and have no other force.

(5) Before leaving the *Critique of Judgment,* I want to spend a moment on the issue of Spinozism, which is a recurring although by no means dominant theme in the work. Two key objections that he makes to this doctrine, as he understands it, are, first, that Spinozism eliminates any conception of intentionality, design and choice both within the world and within the substance that is its ground; and, second, that Spinozism eliminates any recognition of contingency in our objects of either knowledge or action. These are both grave objections from Kant's point of view, and it would take strong evidence to prove that he ever gave up these objections.

Both of these points are made in the "Dialectic of Teleological

Judgment." Kant first objects that Spinozism is a system of *fatality,* and that the "fatalism of purposiveness" is also an *idealism* thereof, that is, a view on which there is the mere appearance but no reality of design and choice both on the part of God and of any of his modes, such as ourselves. Kant's reason for saying this is his view that, while according to Spinoza the "conception of the original being is not to be understood," it is clear that the connection of ends in the world "is derived from a primordial being, but not from its understanding, hence not from any intention, but from the necessity of its nature and the unity of the world that stems from that" (*CJ,* §72, 5:391–2). Now, it might not seem fair for Kant to charge Spinoza with advocating a mere "idealism" with regard to ends, whether in God or in his modes, since Kant himself, after all, insists that the purposiveness of the world and its author and perhaps even ourselves is demonstrable only from the practical point of view and not from a theoretical point of view. But that is precisely Kant's point: In his view, Spinoza's argument for a necessitarian God who has no freedom and intention in himself and therefore eliminates all freedom and intentionality from the world is based on an illegitimate elevation of the theoretical and mechanical worldview of empirical science into a metaphysical dogma and an elimination of any practical conception of God. This seems to be what Kant means when he asserts that Spinozism is based on "a mere misinterpretation of a universal ontological concept of a thing in general": Spinoza's theory is a version of "physicotheology," which excludes a teleological conception of nature simply by carrying "mere theoretical principles of the use of reason" beyond their legitimate empirical application into a theological application, with no appeal to the moral point of view (§85, 5:440). Indeed, this could even explain what Kant means by his otherwise remarkable assertion that Spinoza is convinced "that there is no God and (since it follows in the same way in regard to the object of morality) no future life" (§87, 5:452): Since on Kant's account there can be neither a determination of the predicates of God nor a proof of his existence except as presuppositions of the realizability of the highest good, Spinoza's purely theoretical metaphysics has eliminated any basis for a rational conception of and belief in God.

Second, Kant also objects that Spinoza's system eliminates all *contingency.* He states that "on account of the unconditional necessity of the [substrate of natural things] together with those natural things as accidents inhering in it," Spinoza leaves to natural forms "the unity of ground which is requisite for all purposiveness, but at the same time rips from them the contingency, without which no **unity of end** can be conceived, and with that takes away everything **intentional,** just as he takes all understanding away from the primordial ground of natural things" (*CJ,* §73, 5:393). Here, the point seems to be that intentionality and choice must be conceived as being exercised on material that is to some extent independent of that choice, or contingent with respect to what the intention and choice try to make necessary. Whether this leads to a theology any more orthodox than Spinoza's may be questionable – it would seem to lead to the pagan conception of a demiurge rather than to the Judaeo-Christian conception of a creator *ab nihilo* – but it may well be argued that it leads to a more coherent conception of *human* action than Spinoza has to offer, one on which human action must take place in an arena that it does not literally create, in which therefore success in the pursuit of any end, a fortiori in the pursuit of the ultimate end, must be able to be seen as *possible* but not as *guaranteed.* This would certainly fit with the doctrine that we have now seen Kant advocate in both the second and third *Critiques,* namely that we must conceive of God as the ground of the laws of nature as well as of morality so that we may conceive of success in our moral action as *possible.* If we were to see such success as impossible, it would be patently incoherent for us to attempt to act as morality demands; but at the same time, if we were to see success in our actions as *guaranteed,* that, too, would undermine the seriousness of our efforts to concentrate our moral powers in our ac-tions. The only coherent conception of nature for Kant the moralist to adopt is one in which success in our morally obligatory enterprises is possible in accordance with the laws of nature but guaranteed, if at all, only by the rigor and vigor of our own efforts in accordance with the laws of freedom. This is precisely the conception of nature as grounded in a morally intelligent author who yet has a healthy respect for con-tingency that Kant opposes to Spinozism.

As deeply seated as this conception of nature is in Kant's conception of morality, it would be striking indeed if he were to have given it up in his final years. Let us now conclude with a look at the *Opus postumum* to see if that text warrants the conclusion that Kant did radically revise the conception of the system of nature and freedom that he had evolved without fundamental change throughout his three *Critiques.*

V

In his final years, Kant worked on a project he called the "Transition from the Metaphysical First Principles of Natural Science to Physics," in which he attempted to argue for the existence of an all-pervasive ether,[22] a detailed yet a priori system of forces, and so on, and also worked on a more general restate-ment of the principles of transcendental philosophy. Whether these efforts represent a refinement and extension or a radical revision of his earlier views continues to be debated. Here, I will join this debate only on a narrow front, and suggest that a view for which Kant argued prominently in the final stages of his work, the Seventh and then the First Fascicles, namely that both God and the world-whole are not ontological realities existing outside of human thought but are rather ideas imposed on and realized in human experience by human thought, does not represent a radical revision of Kant's earlier thought but only a restatement of it, and that Kant makes this continuity clear by a *contrast* between his own transcendental idealism and Spinozism, a contrast continuous with what he had already offered in the *Critique of Judgment.*

Kant defines the conception of transcendental idealism that he held at the end of his life in passages like these:

There is a God, not as a world-soul in nature but as a personal principle of human reason (*ens summum, summa intelligentia, summum bonum*), which, as the idea of a holy being, combines complete freedom with the law of duty in the categorical imperative of duty; both *technical-practical* and *moral-practical* reason *coincide* in the idea of God and the world, as the *synthetic unity of transcendental philosophy.* (*OP,* I.II.1, 21:19; Förster, 225)[23]

and:

God and the world are ideas of moral-practical and technical-practical reason, founded on sensible representation; the former contains the predicate of personality, the latter that of [*gap*]. Both together in one system, however, and related to each other under one principle, not as substances outside my thought, but rather, the thought through which we ourselves make these objects (through synthetic *a priori* cognitions from concepts) and, subjectively, are self-creators of the objects thought. (*OP,* I.II.3, 21:21; Förster, 228)

Kant makes the following claims in such passages. Both God and the world are ideas originating in our own thought, but imposed upon sensible representation, as an irreducibly external element in experience, and producing objects, as combinations of both intuition and concept, through this imposition. The idea of God is generated in connection with our recognition of our duty, as an image of the source of unconditional legislation that actually lies within our own practical reason, and is thus the "moral-practical" idea. The idea of the world is the idea of the unitary and law-like spatiotemporal realm imposed on our sensible representation by sensibility and understanding, but also the idea of the natural sphere within which we can perform our duty and realize our ends, and is thus a "technical-practical" idea. As much the product of our own reason as the idea of God, the laws of nature must be compatible with the moral legislation summed up in our idea of God and indeed subordinated to it, in the sense that we must always conceive of nature as a sphere in which the performance of duty and the achievement of its intended ends are possible.[24] But in both cases God and the world cannot be thought of as substances existing independently of our thought, and are instead constructions generated from our thought, the idea of God from our consciousness of our duty and our freedom to perform it and the idea of the world both from our theoretical forms of intuition and understanding but also from our idea of nature as a sphere within which we can successfully perform our duty. Thus Spinozism is right in its general form of seeing both nature or the order of causes and thought or the order of reasons as modes of an underlying substance, but wrong in identifying God as that substratum of which nature and ourselves are modes. We ourselves are the substratum from which both God and nature are projected unities. Kant may indeed mention Spinoza more often in the *Opus postumum* than ever before, but only to make even more pointedly the kind of contrast he had already suggested in the *Critique of Judgment.*

To sustain my view that these claims are continuous with Kant's previous conception of the unity of nature and freedom, there are three points we need to look at in some more detail: first, Kant's introduction of the idea of God as the image of our unconditional duty rather than the condition of the possibility of the highest good; second, Kant's claim that a moral-practical God and a technical-practical nature are mere ideas rather than propositions about external existences that are valid only from a practical point of view; and third, Kant's comments about Spinoza. On each of these issues I suggest that there is less change than may initially meet the eye.

(1) There can be no doubt that in these last stages of the *Opus postumum* Kant links the idea of God to the idea of duty in a way that he had not previously emphasized. He repeatedly states that the idea of God is an image of our own capacity as legislators of unconditionally binding moral law; for example,

> The categorical imperative is the expression of a *principle of reason* over oneself as a *dictamen rationis practicae* and thinks itself as law-giver and judge over one, according to the categorical imperative of duty (for thoughts accuse and exonerate one another), hence, in the quality of a person. Now *a being which has only rights and no duties is **God.*** Consequently, the moral being thinks all duties, formally, as divine commands; not as if he thereby wished to certify the existence of such a being: For the supersensible is not an object of possible experience (*non dabile sed cogitabile*) but merely a judgment by analogy – namely, to think all human duties *as if* divine commands and in relation to a person. (*OP,* VII.X.2, 22:120; Förster, 202–3)

By conceiving of the commands of duty that in fact originate in our own reason *as if* they were commands of a divine person, we can make clear to ourselves several key points about duty, above all its unconditionally obligatory character and also the fact that it may be in conflict with our merely sensual inclinations, and thus can seem to us like the command of another person if we identify – as of course we should not – our own personality solely with our merely sensual side. The first of these points in particular might seem to be confused by Kant's suggestion that God is a being who has rights but no duties at all; he could hardly be an image of our own obligation under duties if he has none. Perhaps Kant puts the point he is driving at here better in other passages when he writes that "The concept of God is . . . the concept of a being that can *obligate all moral beings* without itself being obligated" (*OP,* VII.X.2, 22:121; Förster, 203; see also VII.X.3, 22:124, 127; Förster, 205, 207); this can be taken to express the primacy of obligation over duty in Kantian ethics, or the fact that our duties arise from obligations we place ourselves under because of the demands of our own practical reason rather than from rights as claims made upon us by others independently of our own legislation.[25]

A first point to note here is that Kant does not introduce the idea of God just as an image of our power to *legislate* moral laws, but also as an image of our power to *judge* ourselves morally, and, even more importantly, as an image of our power to *execute,* that is, act in accordance with, moral laws. Thus he writes: "The concept of God is the idea of a moral being, which, as such, is judging [and] universally commanding. The latter is not a hypothetical thing but pure practical reason itself in its personality, with reason's moving forces in respect to world-beings and their forces" (*OP,* VII.X.1, 22:118; Förster, 201–2); and he defines the idea of God as "the idea of an omnipotent moral being, whose willing is a categorical imperative for all rational beings, and is both all-powerful with regard to nature as well as unconditionally, universally commanding for freedom" (*OP,* VII.X.4, 22:127; Förster, 207). Likewise, in this context Kant explicitly asserts the principle that "If I *ought* to do something, then I must also be *able* to do it" (*OP,* I.II.1, 21:16; Förster, 223), thereby suggesting that if our own capacity to command is reflected in our image of God then so is our capacity to perform. Throughout this discussion, then, Kant states that God, that is, our own reason, is efficacious not just in giving commands but in imposing its "moving forces" on nature, that is, "world-beings and their forces." So just as he here immediately interprets the categorical imperative as "the expression of a moral and holy, unconditionally commanding will" (*OP,* VII.X.3, 22:123; Förster, 205), which we imagine as in God but that is actually in ourselves, so he also equally immediately infers from the categorical imperative a capacity to act in nature but in accordance with that law, which we imagine as being in God but that is actually in ourselves. Through the image of God we therefore represent both the laws of freedom themselves and also the unity of nature and freedom that we must postulate in order to think of ourselves as capable of actually acting in accordance with these laws.

Now it might seem as if we have here come upon several fundamental differences between Kant's position in the *Opus postumum* and in his earlier works. First, while earlier Kant had postulated God in order to ground our conception of the realizability of the *ends* of duty in the form of the highest good, here he seems to bring God into the picture much earlier as an image of our capacity to recognize and act in accordance with duty regardless of any consideration of its ends. There are reasons, however, why we should not take this fact to indicate any fundamental change of view. (i) First, at least once in the *Critique of Practical Reason* Kant had already argued that the postulation of God was neces- sary for our recognition the possibility of the virtue- as well as of the happiness-component of the highest good, that is, to explain our capacity to perform our duty as well as the likelihood of that perfor- mance having its intended outcome (*CPracR*, 5:125). (ii) Second, since there is a direct connection between the concept of duty and the concept of happiness in the highest good, namely that our duty is in fact to preserve and promote rational agency as the capacity to set and pursue ends and happiness just is the successful pursuit of ends, Kant does not need to make any special mention of happiness and the highest good; a genuine capacity to act in accordance with moral law will also bring happiness in its train, at least so far as the contribution of human agents is concerned. (iii) Finally, it should be noted that at least once in these late fascicles Kant does explicitly mention the highest good; thus he suggests that "[T]he intelligent subject which grounds the combination of God with the world under a principle" is the source of:

The highest nature
The highest freedom
The highest good   (blessedness
                     happiness)
(*OP*, I.II.3, 21:23; Förster, 229)

So in Kant's argument that the idea of God is the image of our capacity to recognize and perform our duty rather than the conception of our ground for expecting happiness seems to be a change more in emphasis than in doctrine.

(2) One could well ask, however, if there is not an important change in Kant's conception of God from the object of a postulate of pure practical reason to a mere idea. Here, too, I would suggest that the change in Kant's form of expression is striking but not radical. It is true that in Kant's earlier work he tended to conceive of a practical postulate as something that had the logical *form* of an existential proposition, assert- ing that an entity or condition, in this case God, actually exists, but with

only the *force* of a presupposition of action rather than any genuine cognition, whereas here Kant speaks of a mere idea of God without any logically propositional assertion of his existence at all. But in fact the sort of thing Kant says about the force of this idea is very similar to what he earlier said about the force of a practical postulate. On the one hand, Kant repeatedly insists that God cannot be proven to exist "as substance outside the subject," but is, rather, "thought" (*OP,* I.II.3, 21:23; Förster), and this seems an even more subjectivist claim than in the earlier writings, where God seems to be conceived of as existing outside us but cannot be theoretically proven so to exist. Indeed, often Kant even goes so far as to suggest that because God is so clearly an idea, the proposition that He exists outside of us, the thinkers, does not even make any sense:

The concept of such a being is not that of substance – that is, of a being which exists independent of my thought – but the idea (one's own creation, thought-object, *ens rationis*) of a reason which constitutes itself into a thought-object, and establishes synthetic *a priori* propositions, according to principles of transcendental philosophy. It is an ideal: There is not and cannot be a question as to whether such an object exists, since the concept is transcendent. (*OP,* I.III.1, 23:27; Förster, 231)[26]

And even when Kant continues to use the language of postulation, he qualifies the existence-claim in a way that he did not before:

The existence of such a being, however, can only be *postulated* in a practical respect: Namely the necessity of acting in such a way as if I stood under such a fearsome – but yet, at the same time, salutary – guidance and also guarantee, in the knowledge of all my duties as divine commands . . . ; hence the *existence* of such a being is not postulated in this formula, which would be self-contradictory. (*OP,* VII.X.1, 22:116; Förster, 200)

On the other hand, even as Kant modifies his language, he makes it perfectly clear that the force of entertaining the idea of God is precisely the same as the force that he previously assigned to the postulation of his existence, namely it is a representation without theoretical force but one which plays an essential role in making our conduct coherent. In the passage just cited, for example, Kant referred to a necessity of *acting* rather than *asserting,* and in this striking comment further down the same sheet he appropriates the Pauline language of the traditional theologian into his own framework of the presuppositions of conduct rather than cognition: "In . . . the idea of God as a moral being, we live, move and have our being; motivated through the knowledge of our duties as divine commands" (22;118; Förster, 201). Here we have knowledge of the divinity of our own moral commands but not of the actual existence of any source for them but ourselves. The purely practical necessity of the idea of God is likewise stressed here:

> It is not a *substance* outside myself, whose existence I postulate as a hypothetical being for the explanation of certain phenomena in the world; but the concept of duty (of a universal practical principle) is contained identically in the concept of a divine being as an ideal of human reason for the sake of the latter's law-giving. (*OP,* VII.X.2, 22:123; Förster, 204)

As in his earlier works, Kant's real concern is not with the issue of whether or not we assert an existential proposition about God with a theoretical truth-value, but rather with the point that whatever our representation of God, mere idea or more complex proposition, it plays no theoretical role in "the explanation of certain phenomena," but rather functions as an ideal in our self-legislation and its execution.

Above all, what Kant is concerned to stress is that the idea of God is an ideal for our own conduct and not a piece of theory; this passage, I suggest, reveals the role that the concept of a rational being in general should be recognized to have had through Kant's exposition of his ethics, an ideal to which we aspire rather than a theoretical concept for the explanation of anything:

> There are two ways in which men postulate the existence of God: they say sometimes: There exists a divine *judge* and *avenger,* for wickedness and *crime* require the extinction of this loathsome race. On the other hand, reason thinks of an *achievement* of which man is capable – to be able to place himself in a higher *class,* namely that of autonomous (through moral-practical reason) beings, and to raise himself above all merely sensuous beings . . . ; he is such a being, not merely *hypothetically,* but has a destination to enter into that state, to be the originator of his own rank – that is, obligated and yet thereby self-obligating. (*OP,* VII.X.1, 22;117–18; Förster, 201)

This passage clearly expresses the view that what practical reason requires and provides is a coherent set of ideals within which to pursue our conduct, not a theoretically demonstrable set of cognitions; this was Kant's view during the critical period, and here we have evidence that it remained such until the end of his life. And the unity of nature and freedom under a God who is a projection of our own capacity to construct both moral and natural law remains firmly within this framework.

(3) I will conclude with a comment on Kant's final attitude toward Spinoza. Kant mentions Spinoza far more frequently in the last two fascicles of the *Opus postumum* than in any earlier writing, but that fact itself only raises the question of whether he does this because his views have moved closer to some form of Spinozism or because he is more concerned than ever to clarify his difference with Spinoza (perhaps due to

the increasing approval of Spinoza among his younger contemporaries). My view is that the latter is the case. We have just seen that throughout his final stage Kant remains committed to the view that metaphysics can only have a moral-practical rather than theoretical foundation, which was already the basis for his critique of Spinoza's theology in the *Critique of Judgment*. But we are not limited to indirect arguments like that; Kant also tells us quite explicitly what he thinks is wrong with Spinoza's whole approach. "Spinoza's concept of God and man, according to which the philosopher intuits all things in God, is enthusiastic," Kant tells us (*OP*, I.II.1, 21:19; Förster, 225), and "A concept is enthusiastic if that which is in man is represented as something which is outside him, and the product of his thought represented as thing in itself (substance). *Principia sunt dictamina rationis propriae*" (*OP*, I.II.4, 21:26; Förster, 231). Spinoza is right to conceive that there is a common ground of the orders of nature and freedom, in other words, but wrong to think that this can be anything other than the principles of our own proper reason, above all our own practical reason. Thus, nearly as many times as Kant mentions Spinoza, he insists that Spinoza has "reversed" or "transformed" genuine idealism: "Not that we intuit in the deity, as Spinoza imagines, but the reverse: that we carry our concept of God into the objects of pure intuition in our concept of transcendental philosophy" (*OP*, VII.V.4, 22:59; Förster, 216).[27] And even when Kant seems to indicate acceptance rather than rejection of Spinoza, it is only a Spinoza whose view has already been transformed into Kant's own moral-practical transcendental idealism: "According to Spinoza, I see myself in God who is legislative within *me*" (*OP*, VII.V.3, 21:54; Förster, 213). Throughout these pages, Kant contrasts to anything resembling the views of the historical Spinoza a conception of our images of both God and the world as founded in the ideals of our own practical reason. It was precisely his failure to adopt such a viewpoint, Kant had already argued in the *Critique of Judgment,* that prevented Spinoza from producing a valid argument for God.

There seems to me ample evidence, then, to conclude that the conception of the unity of nature and freedom that Kant was striving to formulate for his final statement of transcendental philosophy is not merely compatible with but in all essentials identical with that which he had advocated throughout his critical years, and that for all the changes in detail in argumentation and application which he made during the two decades after 1781, Kant's grand vision of the foundation of the unity of nature and freedom in the power of human reason remained largely unchanged.

Notes

1. *OP* stands for *Opus postumum;* the following numbers signify, first, fascicle, sheet, and page numbers, and then volume and page number of the text in the *Akademie* edition (*Kants gesammelte Schriften,* edited by the Royal Prussian (later German) Academy of Sciences, Berlin: Walter de Gruyter [and predecessors], 1900–); these are then followed by the page number from the translation by Eckart Förster and Michael Rosen, *Immanuel Kant: Opus postumum* (Cambridge, U.K.: Cambridge University Press, 1993), referred to as "Förster." Other Kantian works will be cited by the following abbreviations and by references to the volume and page numbers in the *Akademie* edition, except in the case of the *Critique of Pure Reason,* where, as is customary, the pagination of its first and second editions is used:
   CPuR: Critique of Pure Reason
   CPracR: Critique of Practical Reason
   CJ: Critique of Judgment
   Rel: Religion within the Limits of Reason Alone
   R: Reflexionen from the *Handschriftliche Nachlaß*
   Unless otherwise indicated, translations from these works are my own. I use boldface type rather than italics to indicate emphasis in Kant's texts, since the original printed versions of Kant's main books indicated emphasis by the use of *Fettdruck* (larger, fatter type) rather than the *Sperrdruck* (spaced type) of later German publications or the italics of English publications.
2. See Burkard Tuschling, in a series of papers including "The Concept of Transcendental Idealism in Kant's *Opus postumum,*" in *Kant and Critique: New Essays in Honor of W. H. Werkmeister,* ed. R. M. Dancy (Dordrecht: Kluwer, 1993), pp. 151–67; "Die Idee des transzendentalen Idealismus im späten Opus postumum," in *Übergang: Untersuchungen zum Spätwerk Immanuel Kants,* ed. Forum für Philosophie Bad Homburg (Frankfurt: Vittorio Klostermann, 1991), pp. 105–45; and "System des transzendentalen Idealismus bei Kant? Offene Fragen der – und an die – *Kritik der Urteilskraft,*" *Kant-Studien* 86 (1995): 196–210; and Jeffrey Edwards, "Spinozism, Freedom and Transcendental Dynamics in Kant's Final System of Transcendental Idealism," this volume.
3. See *Prolegomena to any Future Metaphysics,* 4:294.
4. All our evidence is that at the time of the composition and publication of the first edition of the *Critique of Pure Reason,* Kant intended to proceed immediately to the composition of his long-intended metaphysics of nature and metaphysics of morals, and thus that he conceived of the preliminary statement of the foundations of his moral philosophy provided in the "Canon" as all that would be necessary before he proceeded to the substantive exposition of his normative moral philosophy. The publication of the *Groundwork of the Metaphysics of Morals* in 1785, the *Critique of Practical Reason* in 1788, and even the extensive "Doctrine of Method" in the *Critique of Teleological Judgment* of 1790 before he finally published the *Metaphysics of Morals* in 1797 clearly show that he changed his mind about the adequacy of the "Canon" as the foundation for his moral philosophy; but none of these works, I suggest, radically revised the concept of the highest good and its use in the "Canon"; the major changes in the subsequent works have to do with the exposition of the fundamental principle of morality and the theory of freedom, not the highest good or the system of nature and freedom.
5. For extensive although inconclusive discussion of what Kant meant by "canon," see

Giorgio Tonelli, *Kant's Critique of Pure Reason within the Tradition of Modern Logic,* ed. David H. Chandler (Hildesheim: Georg Olms, 1994), esp. pp. 92–98 and pp. 110–18.

6. For a defense of this interpretation, see Paul Guyer, "Kant's Morality of Law and Morality of Freedom," in *Kant and Critique,* pp. 43–89, and "The Possibility of the Categorical Imperative," *Philosophical Review* 104 (1995): 353–85, reprinted in Guyer, ed., *Kant's Groundwork of the Metaphysics of Morals: Critical Essays* (Lanham: Rowman & Littlefield, 1998), pp. 215–46, as well as Barbara Herman, *The Practice of Moral Judgment* (Cambridge, Mass.: Harvard University Press, 1993), esp. Chap. 10.

7. For an especially clear statement of this view, with its emphasis on collective rather than individual happiness and a clear distinction between happiness as the impermissible motive of virtue and happiness as the ideal object of virtue, see the essay *On the Old Saying: That may be right in Theory but does not work in Practice,* Section I, esp. 8:279–84 of vol. VIII of the *Akademie* edition of *Kants gesammelte Schriften.*

8. In fact, Kant actually calls the "idea of such an intelligence" that would be "cause of all happiness in the world, insofar as it stands in exact relation with morality . . . [,] **the ideal of the highest good**," instead of reserving that title for the condition which such an intelligence would cause. See also *CPrR,* 5:125, where he describes the condition of maximal virtue conjoined with maximal happiness the "highest derived good" and God as the putative source of this condition the "highest original good."

9. And in the *Critique of Practical Reason,* Kant will argue that the assumption that virtue cannot be followed with happiness in the sensible world is itself a merely subjective assumption (5:145).

10. For further exposition of my views on several of the issues taken up in this section, see my "In praktischer Absicht: Kants Begriff der Postulate der reinen Vernunft," *Philosophisches Jahrbuch* 104 (1997): 1–18.

11. See particularly §4, Theorem III, 5:26–7.

12. See *Groundwork,* 4:428; for discussion, see my article "The Possibility of the Categorical Imperative" (see note 6).

13. Notably Lewis White Beck; see *A Commentary on Kant's Critique of Practical Reason* (Chicago: University of Chicago Press, 1960), esp. pp. 242–5.

14. In other words, the highest good is not any part of a doctrine of punishment or retribution: It does not imply that the virtuous should be rewarded with happiness and the vicious punished with unhappiness, but simply that the object of morality is to strive for the maximum of virtue and the maximum of happiness. In making this claim, I reject the supposition frequently made that Kant's doctrine of the highest good rests on a principle of proportionality that itself has no clear basis in his conception of principles of pure practical reason. For another critique of this supposition, see Andrews Reath, "Two Conceptions of the Highest Good in Kant," *Journal of the History of Philosophy* 26 (1988): 593–619.

15. For instance, in the Introduction to the *Critique of Judgment,* he writes as if we must adopt the principle that nature *is* systematic if it is to be rational for us to strive to find systematic concepts of it (*CJ,* Introduction IV, 5:183–4).

16. The same point is also made in a striking comment in a note from the 1790s, which was incorporated into Jäsche's edition of Kant's *Logic.* Here Kant writes that belief in the practical postulate of the highest good " . . . is the necessity of assuming the objective reality of the highest good, i.e., the possibility of its object as *a priori*

necessary object of choice. If we look merely to actions, we do not need this belief. However, if we would go beyond actions to the possession of the end that is possible through them, then this must be thoroughly possible" (R 2793, 16:515; see *Logic,* 9:69n.).

17. See David Hume, *The Natural History of Religion and the Dialogues concerning Natural Religion,* ed. A. Wayne Colver and John V. Price (Oxford: Clarendon Press, 1976), pp. 244–5.

18. It might seem natural to say that regions of nature (mountain ranges, seas, etc.) are the *objects* of our experience of the sublime, but Kant actually denies this because he wants to emphasize that what we ultimately admire and enjoy in the experience of the sublime is not nature as such but rather our own capacities of theoretical and practical reason to both form the idea of the magnitude of nature and also to resist its threats; see *CJ,* §23, 5:245–6.

19. I have explored this argument further in "From Nature to Morality: Kant's New Argument in the *Critique of Teleological Judgment,*" forthcoming in the proceedings of a conference on "System and Architectonic in Kant's Philosophy" held in Vienna in 1997, edited by Jürgen Stoltzenberg and published by Felix Meiner Verlag.

20. For further discussion of this point, see my "Organisms and the Unity of Science," in *Kant and the Sciences,* ed. Eric Watkins (New York: Oxford University Press, 2000).

21. I use this word here in its contemporary sense, not in Kant's own sense in which it refers to a theory of "individual preformation" according to which all natural forms in nature as originally created (*CJ,* §81, 5:423), a sense diametrically opposed to the contemporary sense of "evolution."

22. See my "Kant's Ether Deduction and the Possibility of Experience," in *Akten des Siebenten Internationalen Kant-Kongresses,* vol. II/1, ed. G. Funke (Bonn: Bouvier, 1991), pp. 119–32.

23. The use of italics to indicate both emphasis and Latin in quotations from the *Opus postumum* follows Förster's edition (see note 1).

24. For example, "God and the world are not coordinated beings, but the latter is subordinated to the former" (*OP,* VII.X.1, 22:127; Förster, 201), and "The complex of all beings as substances is God and the world. The one is not coordinated as an aggregate with the other, but subordinated to it in its existence, and combined with it in one system; not merely technically but morally-practically" (*OP,* I.I.1, 21:12; Förster, 220, translation modified).

25. For an account of the primacy of the concept of obligation over that of right in Kantian ethics, see Onora O'Neill, *Constructions of Reason: Explorations of Kant's Practical Philosophy* (Cambridge, U.D.: Cambridge University Press, 1989), for example, pp. 187–93.

26. Another relevant citation: "It is not a *substance* outside myself, whose existence I postulate as a hypothetical being for the explanation of certain phenomena in the world; but the concept of duty (of a universal practical principle) is contained identically in the concept of a divine being as an ideal of human reason for the sake of the latter's law-giving [*breaks off*]" (*OP,* VII.X.2, 22:123; Förster, 204). For further instances of the claim that God is not "outside" but "inside" the human thinker, see *OP* VII.V.2, 22:51 and 53 (Förster, 211, 212); VII.V.3, 22:56 (Förster, 214); VII.V.4, 22:60 (Förster, 217); and I.VII.2, 21:92 (Förster, 252).

27. See also *OP,* VII.V.3, 22:56 (Förster, 214); I.II.3, 21:22 (Förster, 228); and I.IV.4, 21:50 (Förster, 241).

2

Spinozism, Freedom, and Transcendental Dynamics in Kant's Final System of Transcendental Idealism[1]

JEFFREY EDWARDS

I

In the final fascicles of the *Opus postumum*, Kant intends to work out a plan for a comprehensive system of transcendental idealism. It is a system that includes the cardinal principles of both our experience of sensible nature and our experience of freedom. One of the most intriguing aspects of Kant's thinking regarding this system is his increasingly affirmative view of Spinoza and Spinozism. Kant repeatedly attributes to Spinoza the idea that we "intuit everything in God." He treats this idea as something that either itself furnishes, or else is necessarily connected with, a formal principle of unity.[2] This Spinozistic principle is what governs the investigation of the formal determinacy of cognition (*das Formale der Erkenntnis*), and Kant clearly weighs the option of making it a, if not the, founding principle of his transcendental theory. Moreover, he explores the possibility of making Spinoza a representative of transcendental idealism and even goes so far as to identify this idealism as a form of Spinozism. These passages from Fascicle VII and Fascicle I give a fair sense of this line of reflection:

Spinoza: that we intuit everything in God and, indeed, according to the formal principle of unity. (22:61.2–3)

Transcendental idealism is the Spinozism of positing the object in the total complex [*in dem Inbegriff*] of its own representations.

Of Spinoza's idea of intuiting all objects in God. That means as much as comprehending all concepts constituting the formal determinacy of cognition, i.e., the elementary concepts, under *one* principle. (22:64.6–11)

The transcendental idealism of that of which our understanding is itself the author. Spinoza. – To intuit everything in God. (21:15.6–7)

Reason leads the way with the projection of its forms (*forma dat esse rei*) because it alone conveys necessity. *Spinoza.* The elements of cognition and the moments of the determination of the subject through them. (To intuit everything in God.) (21:15.19–22)

[Transcendental philosophy] is the *intussusception* of a system of Ideas (inventions [*Dichtungen*] of pure reason) through which the subject makes itself into the object of thought according to a principle and [thus] grounds synthetic unity *a priori* by means of concepts. It is a principle of the forms (1) of personality in me, (2) of the portrayal of the world, *cosmotheoros,* outside of me, (3) (according to Spinoza) of the system of entities which (in opposition to the principle of experience) [must] be conceived as in me and thereby as outside of me. (21:101.5–12)

We must keep one basic point firmly in mind when attempting to fathom the significance of conceptual sketchings like these. It is that Kant's appropriation of Spinoza and Spinozism takes place entirely within the framework of his Critical philosophy. We thus should not regard his affirmative view of certain features of Spinozism as a surrender or retreat to a form of philosophic enthusiasm or metaphysical dogmatism. Acknowledging this point is essential for interpreting in a coherent manner the range of judgments on Spinoza delivered in the late fascicles. It puts us in a position to consider what appears to be the outright rejection of all elements of Spinozistic doctrine in a number of passages as part of Kant's effort to divest that doctrine of its enthusiastic (*schwärmerische*) and dogmatic elements, thus making it receptive to combination with the fundamental tenets of Critical philosophy.[3] We are currently a long way from having clarified adequately the historical presuppositions of Kant's appeals to Spinoza.[4] Accounting for all these factors requires intensive research of a sort that is now only at its inception. Yet, however that research turns out, the most basic question that guides it will still have to be the following: Why is Kant at all willing to entertain the proposition that *Spinoza* qualifies as a representative of transcendental *idealism?* After all, even a critical appropriation of Spinoza remains an appropriation of – Spinoza. We must therefore ask why Kant is willing to engage in such an exercise when his published writings and the pertinent metaphysical reflections prior to the *Opus postumum* show that he had decisive reason for rejecting any attempt to place his concept of transcendental idealism in proximity with any kind of Spinozistic standpoint.

These questions become pressing in view of the persistently negative judgment passed on Spinozism in writings from the central period of the Critical philosophy (i.e., the 1780s and earlier 1790s).[5] The treatment of Spinozism in the second *Critique*'s "Critical Elucidation of the Analytic of Pure Practical Reason" (5:100.15–102.36) reveals especially well the deep-seated motives for Kant's standard evaluation of Spinoza. In the Critical Elucidation, the reality of transcendental freedom is seen to require the distinction between the finite acting subject as thing-in-itself and that same subject as appearance. Transcendental freedom thus presupposes the transcendental ideality of time and space, since Kant holds that the attribution of spatial and temporal properties to things-in-themselves must result in the "fatalism [*Fatalität*] of actions" (5:101.19). This consequence holds true as well when the notion of the causality of God as the universal primordial or highest being is entertained. For if we assume the transcendental reality of time, then we must also accept that the causality of an infinite being is the complete determining ground of the finite subject's actions. Moreover, when existence in time is regarded as an attribute necessary to all finite things-in-themselves, then (so Kant argues) the creative causal activity of the infinite highest being would itself have to be temporally conditioned.[6] But this implication is inconsistent with the assumption of that being's infinitude and with the postulation of its ontological independence with respect to all finite things. Hence, when the causality of a primordial being is contemplated, and when the distinction between this causality and the finite subject's causality through freedom is demanded by practical reason, only the transcendental idealism of time and space allows us to escape the clutches of Spinozism and its deterministic ramifications:

[I]f one does not assume that ideality of time and space, *Spinozism* alone remains, in which space and time are essential determinations of the primordial being itself, but in which the things dependent upon it (including ourselves) are not substances, but rather merely inhering accidents: for if these things exist merely as that being's effects *in time,* which would be the condition of their existence in itself, even the actions of these entities would have to be its actions, which it carries out anywhere and at any time. (5:101.37–102.7)

Given considerations like these, it is reasonable to suppose that any movement on Kant's part toward making his conception of transcendental idealism compatible with any type of Spinozistic standpoint would call into question the pivotal concept of the critical metaphysics of morals, namely, the transcendental concept of freedom. We would expect Kant to avoid doing that at practically all costs. This concept of freedom provides not merely the basis for the critically grounded moral theology whose possibility he is implicitly addressing in the passages just bespoken.[7] It is also, as he asserts in the Preface to the *Critique of Practical Reason,* the "*keystone* [*Schlußstein*] of the entire architectonic edifice of a system of pure reason, even of speculative reason" (5:3.25–4.1). Thus, it seems that the attempt to accommodate elements of Spinozism must threaten the systematic integrity of the Kantian critical project in both its theoretical and its practical dimensions. Yet the move toward some form of critically adapted Spinozism is precisely what does occur in those passages from the final fascicles of the *Opus postumum* where Spinoza is treated as a representative of transcendental idealism.

I will maintain that this move is necessitated by the dynamistic conception of material nature that Kant elaborates in the *Opus postumum.* More particularly, I will contend that the problem of Spinozism (as Kant understood it) is inherent in the most striking feature of the epistemological reflections associated with that dynamistic conception, namely, Kant's concern to work out a theory of objective experience based on the idea that there is a necessary connection between the faculty of representation of the sensuously embodied self-conscious subject and the material world-whole of dynamical interactions. To understand this concern, let us begin by discussing the theory of self-positing (*Selbstsetzung*) at issue in the late fascicles of the *Opus postumum*. This will allow us to have a better grasp of the account of transcendental philosophy and transcendental idealism that supplies the immediate context of Kant's late considerations on the problem of Spinozism.

II

Between August 1799 and April 1800, Kant presents in Fascicle X/XI the rudiments of a theory of objective experience by describing how a universal system of dynamical interactions is constituted for the subject as the object of perceptual knowledge. This constitution takes place when the knowing subject affects itself by means of given moving forces of matter in accordance with its a priori specifiable subjective cognitive functions and its characteristic forms of intuition. In this way, the subject establishes its relation to the unified material system of dynamical interactions that composes the general object of physics.[8] Evidently as a result of his critical encounter with certain arguments from contemporaneous debates about the concept of idealism, Kant comes to regard the cognitive activity of the self-affecting subject as a form of self-positing.[9] Between April and December 1800, he undertakes to explore the implications that the theory of self-positing holds for his general critical account of theoretical and practical cognition. Primarily in Fascicle VII of the *Opus postumum,* he seeks to demonstrate how the knowing subject establishes its a priori necessary relation to the unified whole of physical existence in space. He attempts to clarify how the subject is able to conceive of itself as something related cognitively to the all-encompassing field of appearances, and is therefore able to regard itself as both observer and author (*Zuschauer und zugleich Urheber,* 22:421.9–10) of the whole of the manifold of intuition in space and time.[10] He thus shows that the subject is conscious of itself as theoretically self-posited through its relation to the entire objective field of appearances that is to be investigated by physics as a transcendentally and metaphysically grounded empirical science.[11]

The theory of self-positing adumbrated in the later fascicles has a practical as well as a theoretical dimension. The subject constitutes itself not merely as determined by its relation to the unified whole of physical or material existence. It also constitutes itself as *person.* The subject posits itself as a being that knows itself to be free by virtue of its consciousness of the categorical imperative.[12] It thereby knows itself through practical reason to be a being that has rights and duties.[13] As a rights-bearer and moral agent, the subject is necessarily motivated to act out of respect for the moral law. Thus motivated, it is called upon to posit the existence of God as the supreme moral author with reference to which the particular duties made discernible by means of the categorical imperative can be regarded as duties enjoined by divine commands.[14] Insofar as the reference to the morally purposive creative activity of the divine lawgiver allows the subject to think the inviolability and systematic integrity of the complex of moral and juridical duties, Kant's proof of the existence of God as *ens rationis* (or *ens rationabile*) serves as the apex of practical self-positing.[15] The moral proof does not establish the existence of God as a transcendent substance. Nevertheless, the proposition that the divine lawgiver exists as the object of human thought furnishes a constitutive principle of morally practical reason.[16] This principle is therefore central to the human experience of freedom.

It is in view of the theory of theoretical and practical self-positing that Kant ultimately redefines his concept of transcendental philosophy. He attempts this mainly in the final fascicle of the *Opus postumum* that, conveniently enough, has been handed down to us under the title of Fascicle I. It is certainly no easy task to determine exactly what Kant's new definition of transcendental philosophy is, for there are some 150 different versions of it in Fascicle I alone.[17] But in any event, it is fully evident that Kant envisages a comprehensive system of theoretical and practical philosophy based on a concept of transcendental idealism. It is also clear that the point of entry for comprehending this transcendental idealist system is what Kant calls the "Highest Standpoint of Transcendental Philosophy."[18] This standpoint represents the conjunction of three concepts of reason: God, World, and the Human Being.[19] In this conceptual triad, the idea of the human being allows for the transition between, on the one hand, the rational concept of God (and consequently the fundamental principles of ethics and the doctrine of right) and, on the other hand, the concept of world. That idea supplies the ground, or basis, for this transition by virtue of the fact that the human being is not only a sensuously determined being (*Weltwesen*), but is also a moral agent. The human being, then, is not merely a subject that posits itself theoretically in relation to the world of the senses. For it also knows itself as a being capable of exercising its causality through freedom in this subjectively constituted phenomenal world in conformity with laws that it can regard as commands of a morally purposive creator.[20] Hence, the idea of the theoretically *and* practically self-positing human being is what unifies the domains of freedom and sensible nature.

Such is the immediate context of Kant's concern with Spinozism in the late fascicles of the *Opus postumum*. It is not easy to detect in the presentation just given anything that would *constrain* Kant to revise the negative judgment passed on Spinozism in the classical writings of his Critical philosophy. There is, after all, no strikingly obvious reason to assume that Kant's view of transcendental cognition has changed fundamentally with respect to those writings.[21] Accordingly, we could argue that the foundations of Kant's original theory of transcendental idealism are never subjected to serious doubt in the final fascicles, even if the doctrine of self-positing may call for some fairly substantial alterations in the architectonic configuration of the critical system. We could thus contend that the approach to the problems of theoretical and practical cognition discernible in the *Opus postumum* is basically the same purely formalistic approach found in the earlier critical texts. We could, it seems, maintain that the description of theoretical self-positing does nothing more than refine the presentation of the a priori anticipation of the form of possible experience already offered in the first *Critique*.[22] It does not, therefore, crucially alter the standardly accepted foundational account of the relation between the subjective, *a priori* determinable formal conditions of theoretical cognition and the empirically given.[23] We could also maintain that Kant's employment of the transcendental concept of freedom and his applications of the moral-theological proof in the doctrine of practical self-positing do not entail anything really novel with regard to the *Critique of Practical Reason,* the *Critique of Judgment* or, say, the *Religion* of 1793.[24]

Historically, the view that I have just summarized has been widely represented in the constructive exegesis of Kant's late manuscripts,[25] and it is clearly the most attractive option for the conservatively predisposed interpreter of Kant's critical thought. But close inspection of the final fascicles shows that view to be greatly compromised by Kant's considerations on existence in space and the moving forces of matter.[26] In keeping with his conception of synthetic a priori knowledge from concepts, which in this context is explicitly linked to the name of Spinoza (21:89.23–25), Kant proposes that, in order to posit itself theoretically in relation to the all-encompassing field of outer appearances, the subject must generate (*Dichten,* 89.21) the idea of the *existence* of a universal continuum of material forces as the general object of outer intuition. He contends that this idea furnishes a condition of experience as an *absolute* unity (22:107.7), and that it is necessary for the cognition of space as something outside the subject, as distinguished from a subjective form of intuition. By means of such an idea of existence, the subject posits itself as something determined by its relation to the real objective referent of its thought, that is, the universal continuum of moving forces that constitutes the objective field of appearances or physical existence in space. The subject's thinking itself as a being determined by its relation to this general object of the outer sense thus involves thinking the reality of the object as a necessary condition of the real unity of experience. The actual existence of the object must therefore be thought to furnish an a priori condition of cognition. For the very requisiteness of the idea of the object's existence as an epistemic condition is established by the principle of possible experience. And according to this principle, which Kant understands in terms of a principle of complete determination (*omnimoda determinatio,* 22:89.1–2), the self-positing subject's act of generating the idea of the unified whole of material existence amounts to the absolute position of the object constituting that whole as a condition of the absolute unity of the subject's experience.

Clearly, positing any condition like this is inconsistent with the most elemental stated tenets of the classical critical theory of our a priori knowledge of objects. According to this theory, the attribution of material necessity in existence with respect to any object of the senses is expressly prohibited;[27] and the principle that all existence is completely determined is not supposed to entail its converse, as is in fact assumed in the passages concerned with the material or dynamical determination of space.[28] In short, the account of synthetic a priori knowledge from concepts underlying Kant's description of self-positing in the *Opus postumum* presupposes a theory of the formal determinacy of cognition that is far broader in scope than the classical critical theory of a priori knowledge could possibly allow for. There is thus good reason to think that Kant's theory of self-positing is not compatible with the theory of our *a priori* knowledge of objects presented in the first *Critique*.

How does Kant arrive at this position? And what exactly follows from it? To respond to these queries, let us turn to the so-called aether deduction of the *Opus postumum*.

III

The basic issue that any expository treatment of Kant's late manuscripts must contend with is the notion of a transitional science, which Kant refers to as "Transition" (*Übergang*). This science is intended to mediate between, on the one hand, the principles of a special metaphysical science – notably, those principles formulated in the *Metaphysical Foundations of Natural Science* of 1786 – and, on the other hand, the particular concepts and methods of empirical physics.[29] In accomplishing its purpose, the transitional science is supposed to fill in a gap in the structure of the Kantian metaphysics of nature, and thus fill out the architectural plan of Kant's transcendental philosophy.[30] The actual passage from metaphysical principles to the empirical part of physics is supposed to take place by means of the systematic formulation of a dynamical theory of matter. This theory of matter is founded on the concept of a cosmic aether. Kant treats this physical aether as a continuum of moving forces that furnishes the material ground of interaction between all empirically knowable corporeal entities in space.[31] And he comes to consider an a priori proof of the aether's existence as something necessary for philosophically grounding his transitional science.[32]

The aether proof, or aether deduction, is found mainly in the collection of manuscripts bearing the title Transition 1–14 (*Übergang* 1–14). It is a procedure of transcendental argumentation through which Kant professes to reveal and to submit to a priori determination the causal setting within which the perceptual relation of an embodied knowing subject to an objective world is at all possible. The deduction represents in particular the endeavor to demonstrate, by means of a series of strictly a priori arguments, the reality of the aether as a continuum of material forces present throughout empirically knowable cosmophysical space. In Transition 1–14, Kant intends to ground his transitional science by showing that the existence of such a material entity is a transcendental condition for our experience of objects in general.[33] This condition, or setting, is defined in terms of the action of attractive and repulsive forces. Kant repeatedly attempts to determine the possible forms of interaction between these forces; for it is their activity that constitutes the universal field entity, an entity designated as aether (*Äther*), caloric (*Wärmestoff*) and light-matter (*Lichtstoff*).[34] The aether[35] is internally self-motive and perpetually in motion, its uniform and uninterrupted wave action being rooted in the efficacy of attractive and repulsive force.[36] By virtue of its spatial omnipresence and the uniformly lawful quality of its activity – a quality that receives its most general expression in the Newtonian law of universal gravitation – the aether furnishes the subject-independent causal basis for the perception of any and all external objects.[37] It is thus *a* condition of our possible experience of the accessible totality of objects; and it is *the* condition necessary for our experience of this totality to demonstrate what Kant calls a collective unity, as distinguished from a merely distributive unity.[38] The aether is, at the same time, the "*one* object" (*das Eine Objekt*) of this experience, although its existence is not ascertainable by empirical means in the way that the existence of individually identifiable objects of empirical intuition is ascertainable.[39]

The basic aim of the aether deduction is to establish, in conformity with a subjective principle of "*one* all-encompassing [*allbefassende*] experience,"[40] that our experience of nature is necessarily rooted in an overarching union between subjective and formal conditions and material conditions. Accordingly, the deduction is meant to establish that the "*one* object" of that experience must itself be understood to have a transcendental function within the cognitive process. How exactly are we to conceive of the transcendental function of the universal continuum of forces? More particularly, how do we understand this function in relation to the knowing subject's constitutive a priori cognitive accomplishments? Our main problem here is to understand how the active function of the universal force continuum relates to the specifically subjective transcendental functions. In other words, we need to understand how the transcendental function of cosmic matter relates to the particular functions of unity among our representations through which the knowing subject, *qua* individual human subject, establishes synthetic unity in its representations of objects.

In undertaking to justify his idea of the necessary union between subjective and material conditions in accordance with the subjective principle of the *one* all-encompassing experience, Kant intends to show how the human faculty of representation can be related to the whole of materially filled space. How, then, does he understand this relation? To answer this, let me bring to light the main thesis supported by arguments in a number of representative texts from Transition 1–14. (I refer in particular to these passages from Sheets 11 and 12: 21:578.3–579.4, 601.23–603.2, 603.24–605.4.) Kant contends that the object of the one all-encompassing experience, i.e., the aether regarded as the total complex of the moving forces of matter, is the "basis for the representation of the whole of *one* experience." It is also, *at the same time,* the "principle of the unification of all moving forces" (21:578.20–579.2). As the *one* object of external perception, the aether exerts an all-embracing causal influence that includes the subject's faculty of representation. It thereby constitutes, objectively speaking, the subject-independent basis for the generation of particular perceptions in the subject. But since it is precisely by virtue of this function that the aether constitutes the *one* object represented by the subject, the aether must be conceived in subjective terms as well as objectively. In other words, the single, unified, lawfully operating entity that constitutes the enveloping objective causal basis for the generation of all particular perceptions (or all particular empirical representations) is what makes possible the representation of one and the same entity as the *one* object that is known through the subjective synthesis of perceptions. As Kant puts it, the subjective aspect of the dynamical world matter is identical to the objective aspect of the same:

Now *regarded subjectively,* those perceptions are effects of the moving forces of matter (namely, as empirical representations) and belong as such to the collective unity [*Gesamteinheit*] of *possible* experience. But the collective unity of the moving forces is objectively the effect of the absolute whole of the elementary material [*Elementarstoff*] . . . Hence, the subjective moment [*das Subjektive*] of the effects of the . . . agitating forces, i.e., the whole of perceptions, is at the same time the *presentation* of the aforementioned matter and is thus: identical with the objective moment [*das Objektive*]; that is, this elementary material, as a given whole, is the *Basis* of the unification of all forces of matter into the unity of experience. (21:601.23–602.11)

Kant here wants to account for the origin of our cognitive relation to an objective world by showing that the entire unified complex of matter itself provides a condition of formal unity in the connection of empirical representations. The aether thus furnishes an objective *material* condition of formal and subjective unity. That is to say, it furnishes a material condition of cognition without which there could be no combination of any given empirical manifold *into* a necessary synthetic unity, namely, the synthetic unity required by our experience of objects in space could not take place.

In the passages I am summarizing, Kant makes it clear that the *particular* formal determinations of the moving forces that affect the senses are, as he puts it, "to be developed out of" (21:578.5–8) the synthetic and nonempirical consciousness of the affected subject. In this way, he seeks to show that various operations of the material forces constituting the aether necessarily correlate with certain subjective synthetic functions that can be specified by means of *a priori* concepts. Kant's analytic of the subjective side of the subject-object relation thus supports the central thesis that the aether deduction is intended to establish, that is, the thesis that the unity of our experience of objects depends on the aether's capacity to *sustain* the affective relation of the percipient subject's faculty of representation to the represented collective whole of material forces. This thesis implies that our perceptual experience of the external world depends on the a priori determinable sustentative function of the nonsubjective and material universal condition of that unified experience.

The thesis from Kant's late philosophy implies that the unity of perceptual consciousness depends not only on the synthetic functions of pure understanding with respect to what is given in space and time. For this unity depends, too, on the a priori determinable function of dynamical cosmic matter. Thus, the thesis concerning the transcendental function of this dynamical plenum undermines the notion that the constitutive principles of our a priori knowledge of objects could be grounded sufficiently by means of the exposition of space and time as a priori forms of intuition, and through the analysis and deduction of pure understanding's synthetic functions in relation to these formal conditions of sensibility.

Whatever else it does, Kant's thesis concerning dynamical aether's transcendental function seems to make highly problematic the description of transcendental idealism generated by the adherence to this purely formalistic conception of the a priori necessary conditions of objective experience, which is characteristic of Kant's expressly stated epistemological position in the *Critique of Pure Reason* and other writings of his Critical philosophy prior to the *Opus postumum*.[41] That is, the thesis renders problematic the description of transcendental idealism as a merely formal idealism or, in other words, as the doctrine according to which "everything intuited in space or time, and therefore all objects of any experience possible to us, are nothing but . . . mere representations, which, in the manner in which they are represented, have no independent existence outside our thoughts" (CPR B 518–519). And perhaps even more significantly, Kant's thesis raises issues about the status of the principle of the transcendental unity of apperception, a principle that during the classical critical period forms the centerpiece of the theory of transcendental idealism as well as the system of transcendental philosophy planned in conjunction with that theory. The thesis of Kant's late philosophy implies that the synthetic unity of nonempirical consciousness itself depends on the a priori determinable epistemic function of the object of experience. Accordingly, the unity of apperception with respect to particular objects involves the necessary correlation between the unitary self-consciousness of the knowing subject and the *one* object whose concept refers to the universal material condition of the synthetic unity of empirical representations, that is, the cosmic continuum of moving forces. This, however, raises a basic question about the concept of original synthetic unity at issue in Kant's principle of the transcendental unity of apperception. Kant asserts in the *Critique of Pure Reason* (B 133) that the synthetic unity of apperception is the "highest point" of *all* use of the understanding. But what exactly does this mean if unified self-conscious experience of spatial objects is not possible apart from the overarching material transcendental condition furnished by the *one* object experienced?[42] To put it mildly, the aether deduction gives rise to significant problems for interpreting Kant's philosophic enterprise from the first *Critique* on.[43] The late fascicles of the *Opus postumum* are devoted to supplying responses to these problems from the standpoint of a theory of the self-positing subject's theoretically and practically constitutive cognitive activity.

One way of disposing of the set of questions raised by the aether deduction would be to maintain that it represents merely an episode in Kant's thinking within the corpus of system fragments that make up the *Opus postumum*.[44] There is something to be said for this claim. In the system sketches written prior to the spring of 1799 the aether deduction is either absent from, or else is not obviously a central ingredient of, Kant's reflections on his transitional science.[45] In the sketches dating from late summer of the same year, it *appears* to be a rather marginal theme wherever it does plainly emerge.[46] But two decisive objections can be directed against the claim in question. First, it is simply not true that the aether deduction is ever conclusively eliminated from the a priori groundwork of physics and the corresponding theory of the constitutive cognitive accomplishments of the knowing subject. Its role in the doctrine of self-affection and self-positing is never definitively fixed. But in all the later manuscripts it is at important junctures still fully in evidence as a significant factor in Kant's reflections.[47] Second, and far more important; in whatever way we view the fate of the aether deduction in the *Opus postumum*, we must recognize that the most basic insight supported by this transcendental procedure is never abandoned. That insight is that our experience of objects and physical events *in* space is possible only on the condition that the whole of space is completely determined *as* a dynamical continuum or plenum of material forces – and that this space is thus determined as the *one* object of outer experience.[48] Throughout the later manuscripts, including Transition 1–14, the condition embraced by Kant's insight is treated in a variety of ways and under different terminological headings.[49] But the problem of dynamically determined cosmic space does not disappear from the horizon of Kant's continuing reflection on the conditions of possible experience. It makes its appearance at crucial junctures in the theory of self-affection and self-positing. And there is reason to maintain that it is a primary problem that determines the advancement of Kant's thinking toward a new conception of transcendental idealism and transcendental philosophy in the final fascicles.[50]

Whether or not he uses the actual vocabulary of his aether theory, Kant does not cease to treat the universal continuum of moving forces in terms similar to those employed in Transition 1–14. He thus continues to conceive of the dynamical continuum as the condition for the "realization of space as a single object of the senses" (21:564.2–3). He understands it as "hypostatically conceived space" or as "hypostatized space itself, so to speak [*gleichsam*], in which everything is in motion" (21:221.13–14, 224:11–12), and that constitutes a "principle of the possibility of perceptions" (22.524.6). He thereby supplies the elements for an exposition of a concept of space. According to this exposition, "hypostatized" space must, despite its material quality, pertain to an a priori and necessary representation that undergirds all outer intuition. In effect, Kant works out the rudiments of a *metaphysical* exposition of a concept of space. In doing this, however, he does not maintain that space, regarded as an a priori condition, is but a mere *form* of intuition or pure intuition.

This challenges the fundamental tenet of the doctrine of space formulated in the Transcendental Aesthetic of the *Critique of Pure Reason,* that is, the thesis that the quality of space as a condition of the existence of things "lies in our mode of intuition" (CPR B 69) – that space, transcendentally speaking, is merely something ideal. Kant tries, and he tries at great length, to mediate between the earlier and later expositions of the concept of space. In the major late manuscripts of the *Opus postumum,* he stresses repeatedly that space in its *primary* signification is but the form of outer intuition, and so cannot be an object of perception. In keeping with this position, he maintains that the concept of space denotes merely the formal determinacy of our receptivity for objects of the senses. Accordingly, space is not something objective. It is merely subjective; it is "in me" and is not something "outside of me."[51] Kant thus gives the impression of taking it for granted that there is no fundamental inconsistency between the assumptions underlying his account of hypostatically conceived material space, as formulated in the *Opus postumum,* and the conclusions that are drawn from the doctrine of space presented in the Transcendental Aesthetic of the first *Critique.* He is quite often content simply to treat side-by-side the two different accounts of space in question, and to maintain that each of them makes an a priori condition of experience recognizable. Yet precisely these juxtapositions must lead us to question the sense in which the underlying theory of space in the later manuscripts can be deemed internally coherent. I quote here from a passage in Transition 1–14 that exemplifies the difficulties implicitly confronting Kant:

Just as every object of the sensibility, we represent to ourselves space in two distinct ways: *first* as something *conceivable* (*spatium cogitabile*), since as a magnitude of the manifold whose parts are outside one another,[52] it lies as a mere form of the object of pure intuition solely in our faculty of representation; but *second,* we represent it also as something perceptible (*spatium perceptibile*), as something existent apart from our representation, which we perceive and can draw to our experience and which as an empirical representation constitutes an object of the senses, i.e., the material that fills space.

An empty space is conceivable, but not perceptible; i.e., is no object of possible experience . . .

Matter, therefore, merely with the quality [of being] a sensible space, and thus dynamically present in all that is corporeal, must be a self-subsistent, all-penetrating, and uninterruptedly and uniformly diffused whole, and a material that serves as the basis of the moving forces with their motion for the possibility of *one* experience (of all possible coexistents).[53] (21:235.19–27–236.15–20)

On first reading, it looks as though all this might easily fit inside the doctrinal framework of the Transcendental Aesthetic and the theory of objective experience that it supports. There is, of course, the requirement that space must be regarded as something that exists *apart* from our representation. But with that, it seems that Kant is just referring to the objective perception that springs from the unification of the manifold of a given intuition or, more precisely, to the empirical representation of the object of outer intuition as an object out there *in* space.[54] To use a formulation that Kant employs elsewhere in Transition 1–14, that requirement would constrain us to consider space as "something given outside us in the representation" (*ein außer uns in der Vorstellung gegebenes* - 21:542.5–6), whereby the expression "in the representation" could be interpreted as indicating that space is not something outside us in any transcendental sense.[55]

If this were an adequate explication of the concept of material space at issue, the passage quoted would indeed contain nothing novel vis-à-vis the first *Critique.* But the account is not exhaustive. Consider the phrase "something existent apart from our representation" (paragraph 1) in conjunction with Kant's conclusion that the dynamical cosmic matter serves as the basis for the possibility of *one* experience (paragraph 3). In other words, consider that phrase in conjunction with the implication that this matter supplies an a priori condition for all outer experience as a synthetic unity. Now since it is precisely this objective a priori condition that exhibits the property of being a "sensible (i.e., a material) space" (paragraph 3), it is evident that the concept of material space in question cannot be referred to a *merely* empirical representation. Furthermore, since material space (as an a priori condition) is constituted as a "self-subsistent whole" of matter (paragraph 3), and since this whole of matter provides the subject-independent causal basis of all outer perception, then the demand for us to consider space as something apart from our representation cannot, it seems, conduce us to consider it as something given outside us *solely* in our *representation* of objects. In short, matter or sensible/material space cannot be something that is merely *called* external or that is represented merely in thought as being outside us, as the classical critical theory of space would have us maintain.[56] And it certainly pertains directly to the a priori knowable features of outer experience. This interpretation is confirmed by a good number of further passages in Transition 1–14 and also in the manuscripts composed after it.[57]

It is here unnecessary for us to take up the question of whether a substantival or else a relationist view of space is implicated by the concept of material space in the *Opus postumum*. The crucial point to underscore is merely this: Despite the strictures against any objectivistic account of space that are entailed by the proposition that space is a mere sensible form or form of intuition, space must nonetheless be conceived as something given in reality apart from our representation *independently* of our sensibility.[58] Space must be thought of in this way to the extent that it is known as something completely determined by the *existence* of the universal dynamical continuum as the *one* object of outer experience.[59] Thus, unless Kant is prepared to concede that the sum-total of the matter of outer experience is literally created *ex nihilo* by the individual finite mind in each particular act of perceptual cognition, then the reality attributable to what he calls hypostatically conceived space must be, in some sense, an *absolute* reality. But, naturally, it follows from this that the quality of space relevant to transcendental cognition can no longer consist in its ideality (or at least not in its ideality alone). Space is, in some sense, transcendentally real.

It would, of course, remain Kant's prerogative in the *Opus postumum* to argue that our cognition of the structural properties of materially determined perceptual (i.e., physical) space must conform to the formal constitution of the type of sensibility that underlies all human cognition of an outer world. Specifically, he could (and in fact does) maintain that the space of our actual outer experience is three-dimensional and Euclidean in nature.[60] There thus remains at least this aspect of compatibility between the treatment of space in the *Opus postumum* and the expositions of the concept of space in the Transcendental Aesthetic.[61] Nevertheless, the general doctrine of space at work in the *Opus postumum* seems unavoidably to conflict with the earlier treatment: If we suppose that the aether, grasped as the *self-subsistent* material whole or as hypostatically conceived space, provides a principle of the possibility of perceptions, then we must regard such space as something not only empirically real; for it is essential to the meaning of that supposition that space must remain *something* even when considered in complete abstraction from the strictly subjective condition of all outer appearances.[62] After all, it is the stated purpose of Kant's reflections on the "hypostatization" of space to show that space must be considered in exactly this way, given that the existence of the universal continuum of material forces (i.e., cosmic aether) serves as an a priori specifiable necessary condition of all outer experience. But that means that space is not only something empirically real. It is transcendentally real as well. And that is to say, on Kant's own terms, that its reality is absolute.[63]

IV

I have confined my analysis to Kant's treatment of space in the *Opus postumum*. A more thorough discussion of the underlying issues would have to take into account the closely connected treatment of time, which pertains to the aether's role as the material principle of the conservation of motion in the ongoing process of cosmogenesis that shapes our natural history.[64] But at any rate, the considerations on space in the *Opus postumum* confirm the assertion made earlier that Kant's conception of the transcendental function of cosmic matter undermines any pure formalism of intuition and understanding as the basis for a critical theory of our a priori knowledge of objects. They allow us to recognize at least one substantive reason intrinsic to the developmental context of the *Opus postumum* itself that would lead Kant to treat seriously a Spinozistic standpoint. As we have seen, questioning the transcendental ideality of space (and time) is, on Kant's own terms, tantamount to raising the specter of Spinozism. Objectively, then, the systematic problem that results from the aether deduction and the corresponding treatment of dynamically determined space is to find a way to integrate elements of what Kant himself had previously deemed to be a position of Spinozistic realism with the (or a) theory of transcendental idealism. That Kant in fact recognized and reflected on this problem is evidenced in the final fascicles of the *Opus postumum*, particularly in the following remarkable passage from Fascicle I:[65]

The first act of thought contains a principle of the ideality of the object in me and outside of me as appearance, i.e., of me as a subject affecting itself [*des mich selbst affizierenden Subjekts*] in a system of ideas containing merely the formal determinacy of the advancement towards experience in general; i.e., transcendental philosophy is an idealism; for experience is not merely an arbitrary aggregate of perceptions . . .

We can know objects, either in us or as found outside us, only insofar as we inject into ourselves the *actus* of cognition according to certain laws. The mind of the human being is Spinoza's God (as far as the formal determinacy of all objects of the senses is concerned) and transcendental idealism is realism in the absolute sense. (21:99.5–22)

We witness here the kind of conceptual tension that parallels what we have just encountered in discussing dynamically determined space in relation to space as the form of outer intuition. On the one hand, the conception of the ideality of appearances touched upon in the first paragraph lends itself to explication in terms consistent with expressly stated classical critical doctrine – in this case, in terms of the essential connection that prior to the *Opus postumum* Kant establishes between transcendental idealism and empirical realism on the basis of his supposition that space and time are transcendentally ideal.[66] In view of that connection, the existence of *appearances* is granted only relative to the conditions of human sensibility. Consequently, outer appearances (and of course space itself) cannot be treated as anything self-subsistent.[67] On the other hand, it is exceedingly difficult to see how the realism in the *absolute* sense mentioned in the second paragraph could incorporate the assumption of such relativity.

One way around the difficulty at hand might be to regard the mention of this sort of realism as nothing more than an oblique reference to the Kantian refutations of material idealism, which are meant to establish that the empirically determined consciousness of one's own existence (in time) involves the immediate consciousness of the spatial existence of external things.[68] But the argument that the existence of outer objects of the senses does not need to be mediately inferred obviously does not require, or indeed permit, us to renounce the assumption that the existence of objects, as appearances, is relative to the formal conditions of human sensibility. That is, it does not permit us to reject the tenet that is essential to Kant's original account of empirical realism and that in effect makes this a realism in the merely relative sense, insofar as it concerns the existence of objects as appearances. Now, it is unclear what a realism in the absolute sense could mean in this context if it does not involve the renunciation of just the kind of relativity regarding the existence of these objects that is demanded by Kant's earlier conception of empirical realism. The difficulty becomes decisive when we consider that the phrase "realism in the/an absolute sense" is employed in an interpretation of self-positing that identifies the self-legislative cognitive activity of the human subject with Spinoza's God. For we must recall that the Spinozistic standpoint goes together with the denial of the transcendental ideality of space and time, and that this ideality is the foundation of the classical Critical conception of the correlation between empirical realism and transcendental idealism understood as a merely formal idealism.

In view of the background discussed thus far, it makes sense to think that Kant simply means what he appears to be saying, namely that the account of the ideality of objective appearances must somehow be made compatible with elements of an absolute (or transcendental) realism, if the self-positing human subject is to constitute for itself a unified perceptual world. Now, that *may* permit the construction of a system of transcendental philosophy based on a concept of transcendental idealism. But this concept of idealism would have to be radically different from the terminologically corresponding notion from the central critical period. To satisfy its requirements, one would have to see one's way beyond the familiar dualities of the forms of realism and idealism that define the terminological, conceptual, and historical terrain upon which the three *Critiques* were built.

Recognizing the theoretical need to move beyond this terrain is a very significant part of what motivates Kant to redefine transcendental idealism by means of a doctrine of self-positing that he characterizes with reference to the figure of Spinoza. According to this doctrine, the Highest Standpoint of Transcendental Philosophy is generated by an idea of the origin of the subject-object relation that cannot be made consistent with the view of transcendental idealism as a merely formal idealism. For the attempt to integrate that inherently Spinozistic standpoint with a critical theory of transcendental cognition requires an account of the sustentative material basis of the object-relation of self-consciousness that militates against the particular doctrine of space presupposed by any merely formal idealism.

We thus see that Kant was led toward the characterization of his final system of transcendental idealism as a form of Spinozism by way of reflection on the implications of his dynamistic conception of material reality. But that kind of reflection, of course, cannot fail to have serious repercussions for the doctrine of the practical self-activity of the subject as well, given that any move to accommodate elements of Spinozistic realism must unavoidably call into question the conception of the *causa noumenon* that is inseparably linked to the classical doctrine of causality through freedom. In short, the philosophical standpoint that Kant was impelled to occupy as the result of his explorations on the transcendental dynamics of material nature inevitably challenges the particular concept of transcendental freedom that during the 1780s and 1790s was supposed to provide the keystone in the architectonic edifice of the system of pure reason.

Kant was no longer able to come to grips directly with this last implication of his Critical doctrine of self-positing. Nevertheless, the textual inventory of the *Opus postumum* does make it fully clear that the problem of transcendental freedom was indeed the crucial factor in Kant's decision to expand the doctrine of self-positing to include a practical as well as a theoretical dimension.[69] If we bear in mind that this practical dimension is the least developed aspect of the *Opus postumum* as a whole, then we will have every reason to suppose that Kant ultimately would have faced squarely the ramifications of the fact that by 1800 he had rendered problematic the entire basis of his previous critical account of transcendental freedom. That is to say, he would have done so had old age not put an end to the *forward* movement of his late thought.[70]

Notes

1. I treat the issues discussed in this paper more extensively in Chapters 8 and 9 of my *Substance, Force, and the Possibility of Knowledge in Kant's Philosophy of Material Nature* (Los Angeles: University of California Press, 2000).

Apart from the *Critique of Pure Reason*, all references to Kant are to the volume, page, and line numbers of *Kants gesammelte Schriften*, Königlich Preußische (now Deutsche) Akademie der Wissenschaften (Berlin: G. Reimer [now de Gruyter]), 1902-). References to the *Critique of Pure Reason* (abbreviated as CPR) are to the standard A and B pagination of the 1781 and 1787 editions. All translations from Kant's German are my own.

2. See 22:55.1–2, 56.13–14, 59.21–24, 61.1–2, 64.9–11; 21:15.6–7, 19.14–25, 43.22–24, 48.26–27, 51.12–17. In the Inaugural Dissertation (1770), the view that we intuit all things in God is ascribed to Malebranche and implicitly linked to the Cambridge Platonist and Newtonian metaphysics of space and time (2:409.28– 410.16). But there is some evidence showing that Kant attributes the view to Spinoza very early on and, moreover, that he does so explicitly by the 1780s at the latest (see Reflections 4749–450 and 6051). I discuss these issues in Chapter 9 of my *Substance, Force, and the Possibility of Knowledge.*

3. See, for example, 22:59.21–24; 21:19.14–15, 48.26–27, 50.13–15.

4. It is important to recognize fully the historically convoluted character of Kant's appropriation of Spinoza and Spinozism in the *Opus postumum*. The assessment of this appropriation will eventually have to take into account not only the entire record of Kant's own criticisms of Spinoza from the 1760s through the 1790s. It also will have to do justice to the fact that Kant's appropriation presupposes his reading of Lichtenberg's epistemological reflections and, at least indirectly, his acquaintance with Schelling's *System des transzendentalen Idealismus* of 1800. A proper understanding of Kant's concern with the name of Spinoza therefore demands a detailed investigation of the role of Spinozism in German philosophy during the second half of the eighteenth century, above all during the 1790s. Perhaps most importantly in this connection, it will be necessary to interpret the treatment of Spinoza given in Volume II of Lichtenberg's *Vermischte Schriften* which Kant studied closely during the period in which he composed *I. Konvolut*. We also will need to determine how Schelling (see, e.g., 21:87.29–31) fits into the linkage between Lichtenberg's and Kant's appeals to Spinoza.

5. For analysis, see Giuseppe De Flaviis, *Kant e Spinoza* (Florence: Sansoni, 1986), pp. 91–242; Henry Allison, "Kant's Critique of Spinoza," in *The Philosophy of Baruch Spinoza,* ed. Richard Kennington (Washington: Catholic University of America Press, 1980), pp. 199–222.

6. Paul Guyer, *Kant and the Claims of Knowledge* (Cambridge, U.K.: Cambridge University Press, 1987), pp. 352–4, demonstrates the unsoundness of the corresponding argument in the first *Critique* (see CPR B 71–2).

7. See 5:124.4–146.12, 436.3–461.10; 6:3.3–6.11.

8. See, for example, 22:300.10–31, 324.5–327.20, 346.1–350.26, 359.15–361.8, 388.1–390.30, 402.15–404.9, 457.1–30, 463.1–467.18, 467.10–469.3, 483.7– 484.10.

9. See the references to Aenesidemus-Schluze, Beck, Fichte, Reinhold, Schelling, and Theatetus-Tiedemann in the Factual Notes to Immanuel Kant, *Opus postumum,* ed. and trans. Eckart Förster, trans. Michael Rosen (Cambridge, U.K.: Cambridge University Press, 1993).

10. See, for example, 22:333.21–334.16, 364.12–365.6, 384.9–18, 465.14–28, 484.3– 10, 535.16–17, 411.26–412.2, 418.16–25, 421.7–10; 21:122.14–18, 128.3–9.

11. See, for example, 22:325.8–326.10, 363.14–365.13, 385.3–14, 388.1–389.20, 32.5–18, 73.8–74.5, 77.11–78.14, 81.25–82.21, 82.23–89.12, 418.16–25; 21:26– 13–14, 34.3–4.

12. See, for example, 22:51.16–17, 53.11–15, 60.3–4, 125.8–16; 21:14.14–16, 16.16–28, 21.11–14, 37.11–18, 41.6–7, 43.27–33 48.30–49.2, 55.25–26, 62.15–19, 74.18–21.
13. See, for example, 22:50.11–19, 51.16–17, 52.9–12, 65.6–14, 108.19–27, 119.16–18; 21:13.21–28, 14.8–16.
14. See, for example, 22:53.3–6, 54.9–19, 57.22–25, 58.30–32, 61.16–20, 64.21–29, 105.6–10, 117.7–15, 120.1–15; 21:15.6–9, 22.28–29, 25.15–21, 28.11–17, 50.20–22.
15. See, for example, 22:52.25–53.6, 53.26–56.2, 57.26–58.32, 104.7–18, 108.11–27, 108.28–110.8, 112.8–17, 115.19–117.15, 119.6–1234.19; 21:11.1–3, 13.1–20, 19.25–20.4, 35.24–28, 37.11–21, 49.3–8, 55.16–19, 144.3–7, 147.4–9.
16. See, for example, 22:52.25–53.2, 54.14–55.11, 108.11–18, 109.12–25, 119.16–18, 120.16–122.9, 123.1–5, 125.23–126.3; 21:14.3–7, 20.16–19, 21.11–32, 27.14–28.7, 32.10–33.16, 51.2–4, 56.3–6, 74.7–9, 94.15–23, 144.19–28, 147.4–9.
17. Cf. De Flaviis, *Kant e Spinoza,* p. 247 (n. 4).
18. Cf. 20:300.3–37. The term *"höchster Standpunkt der Transzendentalphilosophie"* is used by J. S. Beck with reference to his *Erläuternder Auszug aus den critischen Schriften des herrn Prof. Kant* (1793–6). (See Beck's letters to Kant of June 17 and September 16, 1794, as well as Kant's letter to Beck of July 1, 1794 and Reflections 6353, 6358. Cf. 12:222.25–223.29; 13:468.18–471.28.) For Beck, however, the Highest Standpoint is furnished by the concept of the transcendental unity of apperception, not by the conjunction of the ideas of God, World and the Human Being.
19. See 21:22.1–17, 23.1–19, 27.1–12, 31.1–5, 34.10–18, 39.8–23, 42.18–43.7, 46.1–23, 48.4–9, 79.25–80.4.
20. See, for example, 22:52.3–11, 54.14–22, 57.4–5, 63.9–18, 114.12–19, 116.4–117.6; 21:11.1–11, 33.7–14, 48.11–19, 91.16–27, 145.3–5, 149.18–24, 149.29–150.5.
21. On Kant's concept of transcendental cognition, see Tillman Pinder, "Kants Begriff der transzendentalen Erkenntnis," *Kant-Studien* 77 (1987): 1–40. For an investigation of the changes that this concept undergoes between the first *Critique* and the *Opus postumum,* see Eckart Förster, "Kant's Notion of Philosophy," *The Monist* 72 (1989): 285–304.
22. On Kant's conception of the form of possible experience and its a priori anticipation, see CPR A 118 and B 303. See also CPR A 110, 127; B 195–196, 218–219, 267, 273.
23. See, for example, CPR B 34, B 124–125, B 208–209, B 217–218, B 223, B 265, B 269, B 220–222, B 272–273, B 279–280, B 748, B 751.
24. See 6:168.18–169.3 and the passages cited in note 10 above.
25. See, most recently, Vittorio Mathieu, *Kants Opus postumum,* (Frankfurt am Main: Klostermann, 1989), pp. 268–273. For summary treatments of the secondary literature, see Mathieu, *La filosofia trascendentale e l' "Opus postumum" di Kant* (Turin: Biblioteca di Filosofi 12, 1958), pp. 107–132; Burkhard Tuschling, *Metaphysische und transzendentale Dynamik in Kants Opus postumum* (Berlin: de Gruyter, 1971), pp. 8–13.
26. The summary of Kant's position contained in the rest of this paragraph is based especially on the following passages, which are cited in chronological order: 22:88.27–89.12, 106.20–22, 107.1–21; 21:23.27–31, 59.28–60.13, 89.7–26, 122.14–18.

27. See CPR B 279–280.
28. See CPR B 601–608 and 20:301–302 (note the reference here to the idea of the *omnitudo realitatis* as an intrinsically Spinozistic concept). The most striking formulations concerning the equivalence of the two principles are in Transition 1–14 of the *Opus postumum* (see especially 21:603.4–19; cf. CPR B 609–611). For a treatment of the metaphysical issues involved in these formulations, see Peter Rohs, "Kants Prinzip der durchgängigen Bestimmung alles Seienden," *Kant-Studien* 67 (1978): 170–180.
29. See, for example, 21:162.14–21, 168.15–20, 359.11–17, 368.27–387.14, 402.20–403.9, 407.29–408.5, 477.15–20, 478.23–26, 524.28–525.12, 582.6–16; 22:254.4–7, 263.1–6. (These passages are not cited in keeping with the chronological order of the manuscripts. For the sake of the reader not already well acquainted with the textual composition of the *Opus postumum,* I have simplified standard procedure of citation in the notes pertaining mainly to the earlier fascicles.)
30. For a different interpretation of the "gap" in Kant's system, see Eckart Förster, "Is There 'A Gap' in Kant's Critical System," *Journal of the History of Philosophy* 25 (1987): 536–555.
31. This conception is already evidenced in the *Oktaventwurf* (see, e.g., 21:378.7–379.6, 383.15–34), but it is articulated most carefully in Transition 1–14 (see 21:219.1–10, 223.10–224.2, 226.25–227.8, 229.23–30, 233.5–8, 235.4–16, 247.2–12, 535.17–537.12, 539.27–540.12, 547.20–548.4, 564.6–12, 565.2–15, 588.17–589.3, 592.7–10). See also the following passages from Fascicle XI: 22:425.23–426.6, 431.4–9, 440.3–15, 457.20–27.
32. For discussions of these reasons, see B. Jeffrey Edwards, "Der Ätherbeweis des Opus postumum und Kants 3. Analogie der Erfahrung," in *Übergang: Untersuchungen zum Spätwerk Immanuel Kants,* ed. Siegfried Blasche (Frankfurt am Main: Klostermann, 1991), pp. 77–104; Eckart Förster, "Die Idee des Übergangs," in *Übergang,* ed. Blasche, pp. 28–48.
33. Regarding the concept of transcendental condition at issue, see Edwards, "Der Ätherbeweis," p. 90.
34. See, for example, 21:560.10–11, 562.2/9, 563.11, 565.8, 572.6–7, 574.21.
35. I will use only this term in referring to Kant's universal force-continuum. Kant uses "caloric" (*Wärmestoff*) more often than "aether." But by *A. Elementarsystem* in the Opus postumum at the latest, nothing essential hinges on the different names given to the material entity.
36. See, for example, 21:561.7–12, 563.3–4, 565.10–15, 573.6–8, 575.12–15/24.
37. See, for example, 21:560.1–5, 561.28–30, 562.3–10, 562.21–563.15, 564.25–27, 565,3–15, 572.3–10/20–24, 573.1–8/20–22, 573.25–574.12, 575.20–24.
38. See, for example, 21:561.24–27, 563.11–15/21–27, 564.6–12/22–24, 571.21–24, 572.16–573.13, 574.5–12/25–26, 574.29–575.8.
39. See, for example, 21:559.5–8/10–19, 561.22–23/28–30, 562.14–19, 563.17–564.12, 571.1–5, 571.14–572.2, 572.16–573.13, 573.25–575.8. It is difficult to see how Kant's conception of the aether as both an epistemic condition and the object of experience can be reconciled with the following claim from the first version of the Paralogisms of Pure Reason: "Now it is indeed very evident that what I must presuppose in order to know an object at all is not something that I could know as an object" (A 402). For a criticism of Henry Allison's interpretation of the issues involved in this claim in *Kant's Transcendental Idealism: An Interpretation and Defense* (New Haven: Yale University Press, 1983), p. 110, see Edwards, "Der Ätherbeweis," p. 93 n. 58.

74   JEFFREY EDWARDS

40. See, for example, 21:563.14–15; 564.4–6.
41. On this, see the Introduction to my *Substance, Force, and the Possibility of Knowledge.*
42. The correlativity of the unity of consciousness and the unity of the object in question here is not the same as the correlativity thematized by Henry Allison's well known "reciprocity thesis" (see *Kant's Transcendental Idealism,* pp. 144–148, 294; and *Idealism and Freedom: Essays on Kant's Theoretical and Practical Philosophy* [Cambridge, U.K.: Cambridge University Press, 1996], p. 51). The thesis discussed by Allison concerns the necessary correlation that Kant establishes in the *Critique of Pure Reason* between the transcendental unity of apperception, as a purely formal unity, and an object in its "judgmental or logical sense" (*Kant's Transcendental Idealism,* p. 146). The thesis therefore relies on the broad conception of object at issue in §17 of the 1787 Transcendental Deduction, where Kant defines "object" as "that in the concept of which the manifold of a given intuition is *united*" (CPR B 137). Moreover, the thesis asserts the reciprocity between the synthetic unity of apperception and the representation of an object exclusively on grounds of Kant's general argument that the pure concepts of the understanding are conditions of both the unity of apperception and the representation of objects (on this, see Allison's *Idealism and Freedom,* p. 51). Now Kant's physical aether can be characterized formally in terms of his broad conception of object, since it furnishes what Kant calls the "*one* object" of outer intuition. Also, nothing that Kant says in the aether deduction denies that pure intellectual concepts are conditions of the unity of apperception *and* the representation of objects. Nevertheless, the reciprocity thesis that emerges from the 1787 Transcendental Deduction is not a sufficient basis for determining the aether's role in Kant's late transcendental theory. The correlativity conception of the *Opus postumum* implies that if the *one* object of all outer sensible intuition did not itself provide a condition of synthetic unity for our empirical representations, then there could be no experience of particular objects in space. Consequently, apart from the unifying function of the aether's (i.e., dynamical cosmic matter's) activity, no pure concept of the understanding could serve as a condition of unity in the representation of such objects *as* objects of experience. And if this is so, then the synthetic unity of apperception that correlates with *that* representation is not achievable apart from the unifying function of dynamical cosmic matter. In the context of the aether deduction, there is indeed complete reciprocity between the synthetic unity of apperception and the unity of an object as far as our a priori knowledge of the objects of outer intuition is concerned. But this kind of reciprocity cannot be understood in abstraction from the transcendental function of the universal continuum of moving forces. Thus, if the principle of the synthetic unity of apperception is to be based on a concept of the unity of consciousness that denotes the "highest point to which one must attach all employment of the understanding" (CPR B 133), *including* the understanding's employment in relation to the objects of sensible intuition, then it must be linked to a principle that specifies an objective material condition of a priori synthetic unity. But the 1787 Transcendental Deduction does not provide any basis for establishing this link, since it does not recognize the possibility of such a material transcendental condition.
43. It also gives rise to new ways of approaching old problems. It is worth noting that the correlativity conception of the *Opus postumum* allows us to focus on the reasons Kant may have had for attempting the aether deduction in view of the difficulties inherent in the proof structure of the 1787 Transcendental Deduction. These well-known difficulties stem from Kant's procedure of establishing a necessary connec-

tion between the categories and the data of human sensibility (i.e., appearances) on the basis of an *analytic* principle of the synthetic unity of apperception (see CPR B 135, B 138; cf. Allison, *Idealism and Freedom,* pp. 47–52 and Guyer, *Kant and the Claims of Knowledge,* pp. 132–133, 142–143). But as long as it is true that the pure concepts of the understanding are conditions of both the unity of apperception and the representation of objects (see note 42 above), there would be no problem in establishing that connection in the context of the aether deduction. The necessary correlativity of the unity of apperception and the unity of the object at issue in the aether deduction is meant to guarantee that outer appearances will be so constituted that they can be subjected to the conditions of the understanding's unity (contrast CPR B 123). Interestingly, Kant insists on the analyticity of the principle that asserts the aether's existence (see, e.g., 21:559.5–14, 591.1–593.5, 600.1–601.3).

44. Regarding the fragmentary character of the manuscripts and the resulting difficulties for the systematic interpretation of the *Opus postumum,* see Erich Adickes, *Kants Opus postumum dargestellt und beurteilt, Kant-Studien* Ergänzungsheft 50 (1920): 36–154; Gerhard Lehmann, *Kants Nachlaßwerk und die Kritik der Urteilskraft,* Habilitationsschrift Greifswald (Berlin: Neue deutsche Forschungen, no. 247, 1939), pp. 30–40; and "Zur Frage der Spätentwicklung Kants," *Kant-Studien* 54 (1963): 491–495, 507; Tuschling, *Metaphysische und transzendentale Dynamik,* pp. 4–14.

45. On this point, particularly with reference to the merely hypothetical status of the aether's existence in the earlier sketches, see Adickes, *Kants Opus postumum,* pp. 422–450; Mathieu, *La filosofia trascendentale,* pp. 231–234; Tuschling, *Metaphysische und transzendentale Dynamik,* pp. 23–30, 73–75, 83–84, 131, 141, 172–175.

46. See, for example (in chronological order), 22:324.5–327.8, 330.6–331.31, 337.5–339.12, 346.3–350.26, 377.5–378.24, 388.2–390.30, 402.16–405.12, 459.31–462.28, 463.1–465.28, 470.15–472.8 (cf. 474.25–476.6).

47. Besides the passages cited in note 26 above, see 22:425.23–426.6, 431.4–9, 440.3–15, 457.20–27, 84.5–28, 88.30–89.12, 93.11–15 (cf. 21:603.4–19), 106.23–107.21, 110.9–11, 115.3–4, 117.16–19; 21:55.1–6, 55.27–56.2, 59.28–60.15, 89.2–30, 124.21–24.

48. See, for example, 21:550.11–16, 577.16–578.2. 583.20–32, 586.7–24, 603.4–19; 22:306.5–12, 364.24–27, 494.28–32, 497.20–498.11, 449.2–20, 88.30–89.12, 93.11–15.

49. The most notable of which are *"spatium sensibile/perceptibile"* (see, e.g., 21:219.5–10, 228.24–27, 550.28–551.6, 561.28–562.19; 22:508.11–14, 517.25–518.14, 538.7–23, 431.4–24, 434.11–28, 436.14–22, 440.4–15) and "indirect appearance" or "appearance of the appearance" (see, e.g., 21:561.22–23, 562.14–19, 573.6–9, 574.21–24. 22:325.8–327.3, 327.20–26, 338.7–339.28). See also 21:59.27–60.15, 71.21–23, 124.21–24; 22:10.15–30, 107.16–21, 109.16–19, 110.9–11, 115.4–5, 117.16–19, 118.9–12.

50. See, for example, 22:325.8–326.14, 330.20–331.4, 332.2–14, 339.17–28, 351.1–6, 474.25–476.6, 507.12–18, 513.27–514.5, 515.19–24, 517.25–519.8, 521.11–523.29, 524.1–539.4, 18.17–19.2, 106.23–107.21, 110.9–14, 113.25–114.11, 115.3–4, 124.2–12, 420.2–421.3; 21:47.1–26, 51.23–52.3, 54.2–28, 59.28–60.15, 66.22–67.10, 124.21–25, 150.20–22. Note that when Kant refers to empty space in a number of these passages, he is referring either to mechanically empty space (i.e., to a space that offers no resistance to the motion of bodies) or else to space as dynamically determined by the force of attraction but not filled by the force of

repulsion (on this see 4:496, 511–513, 517, 562–564). Although he does ordinarily maintain that space is determined by both of the constitutive forces of matter, Kant can entertain the notion that space could be dynamically determined without thereby being materially filled. Michael Friedman recognizes this point. But since he does not acknowledge the dynamist presuppositions of Kant's late aether theory, he overlooks the problem of space generated by the aether deduction. See *Kant and the Exact Sciences* (Cambridge, Mass.: Harvard University Press, 1992), pp. 317, 320–341.

51. Cf. CPR B 59; A 370–376.
52. Regarding this translation of "eine Größe des Mannigfaltigen außer einander," see CPR B38, B 40 (3:52.23–24, 53.20).
53. The final clause ("welcher den bewegenden Kräften mit ihrer Bewegung zur Basis dient zur Möglichkeit Einer Erfahrung [aller zugleich möglichen] zusammen zu stimmen") defies translation. The continuation of the line of argument (see 21:236.21–237.16) shows that Kant has in mind the unified material basis that makes possible the combination of the moving forces into the collective unity of experience. But my translation gives the weakest feasible interpretation of the connection between cosmic matter and the principle of possible experience.
54. Cf. CPR B 137, B 202–203, B 207–208, B 277–278; 4:481.2–22.
55. Cf. CPR A 375.
56. Cf. CPR A 370–373.
57. See 21:221,10–13, 223.15–24, 228.6–27, 231.8–13, 235.4–8, 236.15–20, 539.27–540.12, 547.7–12, 553.6–17, 563.24–564.4, 589.27–590.9, 593.24–28/594.16–23; 22:331.23–31, 332.21–233.14, 475.3–476.1, 486.12–16, 524.1–16, 531.13–19, 538.7–25, 430.27–431.24, 440.4–15, 20.14–23, 88.30 - 89.12, 92.26–29, 117.16 19, 420.17–421.3; 21:59.28–60.15.
58. Cf. CPR A 369, A 375–376, A 385.
59. See note 48 above.
60. See, for example, 22:475.1–11, 22.21–23, 22.29–23.5, 23.11–14, 25.12–21, 27.16–20, 29.16–29, 74.10–18, 80.17–81.2, 81.27–29; 21:59.28–60.4, 66.22.24.
61. See CPR B 37–45.
62. Cf. CPR B 42, B 49, B 52, B 59; A 375. According to Kant's definitional criteria (see CPR B 69–71, 274–279), any attempt to absorb this feature of transcendental reality into a doctrine of the transcendental ideality of space must ultimately result in a full-blown material idealism.
63. Cf. 2:403.23–404.2; CPR B 44, 56–57; A 369–373.
64. See, for example, 21:423.29–424.6, 378.7–379.6, 310.3–13, 256.1–19, 22:194.17–195.26; 21:216.16–218.7, 579.20–580.10; 22:10.15–30; 21:38.9–11.
65. See also, e.g., 22:18.16–19.31; 21:52.18–53.14, 54.18–55.15, 66.5, 70.23–31, 100.23–101.15, 149.29–150.5, 151.3–6. Note that the concept of transcendental egoism (as distinguished from moral egoism – see 22:128.29–129.2) at issue in these passages is consistently linked to the notion of Spinozism throughout Kant's philosophical development. On this, see 2:389.22–390.4; 28:206.12–207.20; Reflections 3803, 5390 (cf. Reflection 6051; Wolff, *Psychologia rationalis* §38; Baumgarten, *Metaphysica* §§392–393, 395, 348); see also De Flaviis, *Kant e Spinoza*, pp. 46–50.
66. See CPR B 42–44, B49–53, B 69–71, B 274–275; A 369–370, A 378–379.
67. Cf. CPR B 49; A 369–378.
68. See CPR B xl–xli, B 69–71, B 275–279; A 366–380; Reflection 6312 (18:612.23–613.8), 6313–6316, 6323.

69. See 22:48.10–65.16 (Fascicle VII, Insertion [*Beilage*] V) in conjunction with 22:304.13–15 (cf. 12:290.32–291.15) and the corresponding editorial note by Lehmann (22:821.). Note well that Kant's initial concern with the problem of transcendental freedom in the autumn of 1799 is explicitly linked to the problem of Spinozism.

70. Orthodox Kant interpretation has often enough regarded most everything novel that Kant has to say in the *Opus postumum* as nothing more than evidence of his increasing mental debilitation. Eckart Förster's introduction to the 1993 Cambridge translation of selections from the work contains everything necessary to factually debunk the debilitation thesis as applied to textual materials composed before the second half of 1801 (see Kant, *Opus postumum*, pp. xxiv–xxix).

3
Is the *Critique of Judgment* "Post-Critical"?

HENRY E. ALLISON

Dualism, formalism, subjectivism: These for Hegel constitute the unholy trinity of the Kantian philosophy, the grounds for characterizing it in *Glauben und Wissen* as a "philosophy of reflection," as opposed to a speculative philosophy, which is alone capable of doing justice to the nature of reason.[1] In this same work, however, Hegel also claims to find in the third *Critique,* particularly in the conceptions of reflective judgment and the intuitive understanding, an anticipation of the speculative principle of the identity of subject and object, thought and being. Moreover, this privileging of the third *Critique* is not merely a passing phase of the young Hegel; for in his later writings he continued to regard the intuitive intellect as a genuine anticipation of the concrete universal and he attributed to it the functions of grounding the purposiveness of nature, the beautiful in art, and the ultimate unity of nature and freedom.[2] To be sure, in spite of his positive appraisal of certain aspects of the *Critique of Judgment,* Hegel remained highly critical of Kant's procedure in that work as a whole, suggesting that he failed to grasp the implications of his own insights and thus lapsed back into a disastrous subjectivism. Nevertheless, the fact remains that for both the young and the mature Hegel the third *Critique* was seen as postcritical in essential respects, as pointing the way to a new, more adequate mode of philosophizing.

Recently this Hegelian or "speculative" reading of the third *Critique* has been reaffirmed by Burkhard Tuschling. What is particularly interesting about Tuschling's approach, however, is that he does not impose the Hegelian critical apparatus on Kant in an external way. Instead, he argues that even from "the classical or authentic Kantian starting point of the understanding," it can be shown that "Kantian Transcendental Idealism involves elements of the Hegelian or speculative understanding."[3] He also claims that Kant himself came to recognize this, not only in the *Opus postumum,* but already in the *Critique of Judgment.* On his view, by 1790 Kant was well aware of "substantial, if not fatal shortcomings of his Transcendental Idealism" and intentionally made this known to his contemporaries.[4]

According to Tuschling, Kant's innovations in the third *Critique* are to be seen within the context of his ongoing and never satisfactorily resolved struggle with the problem of integrating the empirical, contingent features of particular experience into a system of knowledge grounded in the a priori principles of the understanding.[5] This struggle, which culminates in the final reformulation of transcendental idealism in the *Opus postumum,* is a direct result of Kant's break with the theocentric paradigm of the rationalists and their ideal of a *mathesis universalis* grounded in the intuitive intellect of God. That is to say, it is a consequence of what is usually referred to as Kant's "Copernican revolution" in philosophy, which consists essentially in the replacement of this divine understanding with the discursive human understanding as the "lawgiver to nature." This revolution is the source of all of the dichotomies (e.g. form-matter, sensibility-understanding, a priori-a posteriori, analytic-synthetic, appearance-thing in itself), which characterize the Kantian philosophy and, therefore, of its deepest and most intractable problems. Paramount among these is the incompatibility of the contingency of the brute, given features of experience with the universal lawfulness supposedly imposed by the understanding.

The claim, then, is that Kant attempted to deal with this and related problems in the Introduction to the third *Critique* through the appeal to a "new transcendental principle," the purposiveness of nature, which is itself founded on the concept of an intuitive understanding. Moreover, this new principle is not introduced merely to ground the possibility of an additional mode of experience (aesthetic experience), but rather to secure the very results that were supposedly established in the first *Critique.* In fact, Tuschling claims that without this principle, *"the whole system of transcendental concepts and principles,* centered around the concept of the transcendental, original synthetic unity of apperception, would cease to be applicable."[6] Tuschling further contends that Kant's appeal to this new principle entails the abandonment of the most basic assumption of the initial critical position: "that the discursive human understanding is the final, legislative and supreme ground of the unity of nature."[7] Accordingly, this new principle is "superordinate to apperception, categories and the principles of pure understanding;"[8] and this gives to the "new transcendental deduction" (presumably of the principle of purposiveness) a "'speculative' character" in the sense indicated by the young Hegel.[9]

It is this claim of radical revision that I propose to examine here. The question is not whether there are any significant innovations or developments in the third *Critique.* I think it obvious that there are. Nor is it whether one can profitably read the third *Critique* through Hegelian spectacles in order to understand the central themes and claims of German idealism.[10] This, too, is readily conceded. At issue is only whether the *Critique of Judgment* contains something like an abandonment of the basic commitments and principles of the first *Critique.* I shall argue that it does not and that in the third *Critique* Kant is best seen as building upon rather than attempting to reconstruct his original "critical" edifice.

I

In claiming that the purposiveness of nature is a new transcendental principle, first introduced in the third *Critique,* Tuschling is obviously assuming its absence from the first; and in this respect at least he would seem to be in agreement with Rolf-Peter Horstmann and others. Although he emphasizes the extreme ambiguity of the argument of the Appendix to the Transcendental Dialectic in which Kant takes up the topics of systematicity and purposiveness, Horstmann insists that both the idea of the systematic unity of knowledge and the purposiveness of nature (understood as a specific form of systematic unity) are there regarded as logical rather than transcendental principles.[11] Similarly, Paul Guyer has argued that for the Kant of the first *Critique* all of the genuinely transcendental work is accomplished in the Analytic, where it is shown that the categories and the principles based upon them are themselves sufficient to ground the unity of experience, even at the empirical level, that is, to ensure the applicability of empirical concepts and laws to whatever may be given in sensible intuition.[12] Guyer admits that there are indications of a different view in the Appendix, since Kant there seems to grant an essential regulative role to reason's idea of systematicity. But he also insists that Kant is there not really serious about such a position and that he therefore retreats to the view that systematicity is a desideratum pursued by reason, which does not stand in any essential connection with the operations of the understanding.[13]

By contrast, my own view is that the Analytic attempts to accomplish much less than Guyer suggests and leaves ample room for the assignment of genuine transcendental status to reason's principle of systematicity.[14] Consider Kant's significant, yet generally ignored remark in the Second Analogy that he is concerned with determining merely the "formal conditions of empirical truth" (A 191/B 236). I take this to mean that the Transcendental Analytic is concerned mainly with the determination of a set of a priori rules (or epistemic conditions), which determine what can count as an object of possible experience. As "formal," these rules serve to preclude certain (logically) possible scenarios, such as changes that are not alterations of enduring substances or alterations without causes. Consequently, they may be said to provide the "norm" to which all empirical laws must conform in order to count as laws (A128); for, as Kant himself notes, no cognition can contradict them without "at once losing all content, that is, all relation to any object, and therefore all truth" (A 62–3/B 87). Indeed, that is why they can be used as a "canon for passing judgment upon the empirical employment of the understanding" (A 63/B 88). It does not follow from this, however, that they suffice to ground any particular causal law or even to guarantee that such laws are there to be found.[15] In Kantian terms, that would give them the status of an organon rather than merely that of a canon.[16]

Armed with this view of the Analytic, the claim of the Appendix to the Dialectic that reason has its own transcendental principle of systematicity seems somewhat less mysterious. But before considering that matter it must be emphasized that we are dealing with what is purported to be a genuinely *transcendental* principle. To be sure, Kant introduces the "systematic unity of the manifold of [empirical] knowledge" as a *"logical* principle," the function of which is to assist the understanding by means of ideas" in order to secure such unity or coherence (A 648/B 676). And, considered as such, it is only subjectively necessary, as method. In order to avoid a complete misunderstanding of Kant's position, however, it is crucial to keep in mind that this initial characterization is presented as a provisional conclusion from the initial account of the hypothetical employment of reason, which is quite different from proclaiming *tout court* that it is in fact merely a logical principle.[17] Thus, there is no contradiction involved when, after a brief analysis of the regulative function of the idea of a fundamental mental power, Kant goes on to argue that this logical principle, as articulated in the complementary demands for homogeneity, specificity, and affinity, presupposes a transcendental principle (A 654/B 682).

But if there is no contradiction, there is certainly a major shift in emphasis, indeed, one that has seemed opaque to many commentators. For Kant proceeds to claim that, as transcendental, this principle must be assumed to be necessary and objectively valid (A 651/B 679), or at least to possess "objective but indeterminate validity" (A 663/B 691).[18] In short, the claim is that this principle is more than a mere methodological recommendation to look for homogeneity, specificity, and affinity; that in spite of its regulative function, it involves some (albeit indeterminate) presupposition about what is to be encountered in experience. And this raises the puzzle about how a principle could have both transcendental status and a merely regulative function.

The transcendental status assigned to this principle is clearly based on its alleged necessity with respect to empirical inquiry. In support of this necessity, Kant claims that without the law requiring us to seek systematic unity, "we should have no reason at all, and without this no coherent employment of the understanding, and in the absence of this no sufficient criterion [*Merkmal*] of empirical truth" (A 651/B 679). And, in a similar vein, he remarks:

If among the appearances which present themselves to us, there were so great a variety . . . that even the acutest human understanding could never by comparison of them detect the slightest similarity (a possibility which is quite conceivable), the logical law of genera would have no sort of standing; we should have not even the concept of a genus, or indeed any other universal concept; and the understanding itself, which has to do solely with such concepts, would be non-existent (A 654/B 682).

In considering these texts, it is instructive to contrast the characterization of the transcendental principles of the Analytic as "formal conditions of empirical truth" with the Appendix's view of systematicity as that without which we would have "no sufficient criterion of empirical truth."[19] Clearly, Kant is not claiming that systematicity is, *of itself,* a sufficient criterion of empirical truth, as if the systematic embeddedness of an empirical generalization or "law" in an overarching theory or set of laws were sufficient to account for its truth. The claim is rather that systematicity is necessary in order to have a sufficient criterion of empirical truth and, therefore, a coherent employment of the understanding or, as the second passage suggests, virtually any valid employment of the understanding at all.

Unfortunately, as is frequently noted, Kant offers precious little in the way of argument in support of these bold claims. But setting that large issue aside for the moment, I would like simply to note several points that have emerged from our brief consideration of the Appendix to the Dialectic. First, as is clear from the passage cited above, already in the first *Critique* Kant links systematicity with the possibility of forming empirical concepts; indeed, that is why it is necessary for understanding. Thus, we cannot accept Horstmann's claim that this is an insight unique to the third *Critique.*[20]

Second, given Kant's equation of experience with empirical knowledge, it follows from this that systematicity must in some sense be regarded as a necessary condition of the possibility of experience. This does not conflict with the Analytic, however, since this principle conditions experience in a different way and at a different level than the categories and principles of the understanding.[21] As formal conditions of empirical truth, the latter or, more specifically, the Analogies, serve as rules for the unification of appearances in a single time. As such, these rules collectively condition experience in the sense of determining the forms of the thought of an objective temporal order (hence their "formal" status). For the same reason, they are also conditions of objects of experience, which accounts for their constitutive status. By contrast, systematicity is concerned with the connectability, and hence the coherence, of the first-order empirical claims regarding objects falling under these formal conditions.[22] Consequently, systematicity is not itself a direct condition of objects of experience, which is why it has a regulative rather than a constitutive function.

Third, and most important, this regulative function is not incompatible with its transcendental status. The common view that it is stems from the erroneous assumption that "regulative" means something like "merely heuristic" or optional. This is erroneous, because the whole purpose of the Appendix is to argue for the indispensability of reason and its ideas with respect to the empirical use of the understanding. To claim such indispensability is to claim a transcendental status, if not a constitutive function. And that is why the analysis culminates in the transcendental deduction of the ideas, which supposedly "will complete the critical work of pure reason" (A 670/B 698).[23]

II

Turning from the Appendix to the Dialectic of the first *Critique* to the two versions of the Introduction to the third, we find both some common ground and some significant differences. The basic difference is, of course, the shift in focus from the hypothetical use of reason to the reflective capacity of judgment. In the first *Critique,* Kant does not seem to have recognized that judgment might have such a capacity or function, while in the third it is the main topic, providing the very raison d'être for a *Critique of Judgment.*[24] Also, reflective judgment's peculiar principle, the purposiveness of nature, is obviously far broader than reason's concept of systematicity. And, perhaps most significantly, the first *Critique*'s vague appeal to an "indeterminate objective validity," which is claimed first for systematicity and later for the ideas, is replaced by the explicit acknowledgement of the subjective, reflexive character of judgment's principle of purposiveness. As Kant puts it in both versions of the Introduction, it is a matter of the "heautonomy" rather than the autonomy of judgment, of judgment legislating merely to itself rather than to nature (see 20:225; 5:185).[25]

Nevertheless, "logical purposiveness," the form of purposiveness with which Kant is initially concerned in the Introductions, does correspond to reason's principle of systematicity. In fact, he explicitly links it with what in the first *Critique* were described as the principles of homogeneity, specificity, and affinity (5:185). Moreover, Kant is emphatic regarding the transcendental status of this principle. Thus, in an important footnote in the first Introduction, Kant affirms that, in spite of its apparently logical and tautological character, this principle is both synthetic and transcendental, since it specifies the "condition under which we can apply logic to nature" (20:211–12 note). And in the second Introduction, he insists that it requires a transcendental deduction (5:182).

Unfortunately, Kant is not so clear in his accounts of the epistemic function of this principle. In particular, it is not clear whether it concerns the possibility of unifying empirical laws into a system (theory construction), of formulating empirical laws in the first place, of forming empirical concepts, of classifying "natural forms" into genera and species, or of attributing necessity to empirical laws. Kant makes all of these claims at one point or another, without ever explaining the connection between them.[26]

This unclarity concerning the function of the principle of logical purposiveness or systematicity carries over to its transcendental deduction, which is provided in both versions of the Introduction, even though it is only characterized as such in the second. Underlying this deduction are two key premises: (i) that because of their formal character, the transcendental laws underdetermine the particulars falling under them, that is to say, these laws are compatible with any number of possible empirical laws and arrangements; and (ii) that it is necessary to distinguish between a system of nature according to empirical laws and such a system that is graspable by the human mind. Kant's position seems to be that, even though the necessary lawfulness of nature at the transcendental level somehow guarantees that nature will also constitute a system of laws at the empirical level, it does not guarantee that it will be one that the human intellect can grasp.[27] As he puts it in the first Introduction:

For the empirical laws might be so diverse and heterogeneous that, though we might on occasion discover particular laws in terms of which we could connect some perceptions to [form] an experience, we could never bring these empirical laws themselves under a common principle [and so] to the unity characteristic of kinship. We would be unable to do this if – as is surely possible intrinsically (at least as far as the understanding can tell *a priori*) – these laws as well as the natural forms conforming to them, were infinitely diverse and heterogeneous and manifested themselves to us in a crude and chaotic aggregate without the slightest trace of a system (20:209).

The deduction turns on the claim that judgment, in its reflective capacity, cannot accept the possibility of such a state of affairs, but must instead presuppose that nature is systematically organized in a way that is accessible to our cognitive requirements. Since this is a subjective requirement of judgment, the claim is not that nature must *be* purposive – as if judgment could impose the conditions of its successful operation on nature – it is rather that judgment must necessarily regard nature as purposive as a condition of engaging in empirical inquiry.

The crucial question, however, remains why it is necessary to presuppose such a principle at all. Is Kant perhaps here inflating a desideratum into an absolute requirement? Or, even worse, is he claiming that success must somehow be guaranteed as a precondition of engaging in inquiry? Presumably, the most that Kant is entitled to claim is the necessity of presupposing that the possibility not be ruled out in advance; for that would render the project of inquiry absurd. Accordingly, if the deduction is to succeed, it must be shown that logical purposiveness or systematicity is a condition of the very *possibility* of acquiring empirical knowledge, and in this sense a condition of the possibility of experience. When this issue first arose in connection with the Appendix to the Dialectic I postponed a discussion of it. But if we are to understand Kant's claim in both *Critiques* regarding extracategoreal, yet transcendental conditions of empirical knowledge, the issue must be addressed.

Like Hannah Ginsborg, I think it best to begin with a consideration of the question of the conditions of the formation of empirical concepts.[28] Since such concepts are obviously essential for empirical knowledge, if logical purposiveness or systematicity can be shown to be necessary in this regard, its transcendental status would be sufficiently established for the purposes of the deduction. And Kant, indeed, does make such a claim when, in the first Introduction, he characterizes the principle as stating "that for all natural things *concepts* can be found that are determined empirically" (20:211). The question therefore becomes why nature's systematic ordering, the classifiability of its constituents into something like genera and species corresponding to natural kinds, should be a *necessary* condition of the possibility of forming empirical concepts rather than merely a desideratum, which would greatly facilitate the process. Clearly, *some* similarity is necessary if the mind is to form general concepts, but it might seem that Kant is requiring too much.

The key to the answer lies in Kant's expression "determined empirically," which I take it means being determined by underlying, empirically real features of things rather than merely by superficial features, which reflect the contingencies of the way in which we happen to encounter these things in experience. In other words, Kant's claim is not that systematicity is a condition of the possibility of forming *any* empirical concepts, since any common features would provide reflective judgment with something to compare; it is rather a condition of forming empirical concepts that are cognitively significant, that "carve nature at its joints" if you will. Consider Kant's oft cited remark regarding Linnaeus:

One may wonder whether Linnaeus could have hoped to design a system of nature if he had had to worry that a stone which he found and which he called granite, might differ in its inner character from any other stone even if it looked the same, so that all he could ever hope to find would be single things – isolated, as it were, for the understanding – but never a class of them that could be brought under concepts of genera and species (20:215–16 note).

Kant is here claiming that a classificatory system such as that of Linnaeus presupposes that the observable similarities and differences on which conceptualization and classification are based correspond to real similarities and differences in the inner nature of things. Expressed in Lockean terms, the point would be that systematicity is required if we are to have knowledge of "real" as opposed to "nominal" essences. Or, adopting Kant's distinction between judgments of perception and judgments of experience to the case of concepts, one might say that unless we presuppose a systematic arrangement in nature, we would have to regard all our concepts as mere "concepts of perception" rather than "concepts of experience."[29]

Moreover, as Ginsborg has shown, this analysis can easily be extended to empirical laws and their necessity. For one thing, without assuming something like natural kinds we could not even begin to look for empirical laws or hope to distinguish such laws from contingent regularities. For another, determinate empirical concepts presuppose known causal laws, since the inner properties in terms of which we conceptualize and classify things must include causal properties. Finally, the necessity and, therefore, the nomological character of relatively specific laws, such as that of the solubility of gold in aqua regia, are a function of their derivability from higher level laws, such as those that hold at the molecular and atomic levels.[30] For all these reasons, then, it is necessary to presuppose that "[N]ature, for the sake of the power of judgment, makes its universal laws specific into empirical ones, according to the form of a logical system" (20:216).

Admittedly, much more would have to be said in order to make this fully convincing. But even this superficial sketch should suffice to show that there is no abandonment of "critical" principles in this account of the purposiveness of nature as a transcendental principle of reflective judgment. In particular, there is no basis for Tuschling's claim that Kant viewed this principle as in some sense "superordinate to apperception, categories and the principles of pure understanding." Nor, may I add, should he have done so. To argue to the contrary is to conflate the *insufficiency* of the transcendental principles of the understanding to account for the possibility of empirical knowledge with the *inadequacy* of the grounding of these principles themselves. Nothing in the third *Critique* indicates that Kant had any second thoughts about the latter and, as we have already seen, he had readily acknowledged the former in 1781. Otherwise expressed, it is not that Kant belatedly came to the conclusion that he could not account for the applicability of the transcendental laws apart from the presupposition of the purposiveness of nature; it is rather that he continued to recognize that these laws, as "formal conditions of empirical truth," do not of themselves yield a "sufficient criterion of empirical truth."[31]

III

In light of these considerations, we are in a position to consider Tuschling's thesis that in the third *Critique* Kant abandoned his essential principle that the discursive human understanding is the ultimate source of the unity of nature and that he granted ultimacy instead to the intuitive intellect. Central to this reading is the assumption of an essential connection between purposiveness in its various forms and the idea of an intuitive intellect, which is introduced in §77 as a contrast to the discursive variety. Whereas the latter is defined by its dependence on given sensible data, which it subsequently subsumes under "analytic universals," the former is characterized by its independence of any such data. Thus, rather than having to subsume sensibly given particulars under abstract, analytic universals, a putative intuitive intellect would generate its own content through its "synthetic universals." Moreover, as a direct result of this, the contingency of fit between universal and particular, which is endemic to a discursive intellect and the ground of the dualities characteristic of the Kantian philosophy, would be overcome.

As textual support for this thesis, we are given Kant's remark in the published Introduction that since the universal laws of nature (the formal, transcendental principles) have their ground in the human understanding, "the particular empirical laws must, as regards what the universal laws left undetermined in them, be viewed in terms of such a unity as they would have if they likewise had been given by an understanding (even though not ours) so as to assist our cognitive faculties by making possible a system of experience according to particular laws" (5:180). Assuming that this other and more than human understanding is to be identified with the intuitive intellect of §77, it might then seem that the latter is being assigned the function of grounding the lawfulness of nature. And from this it is but a short step to the conclusion that this same intellect also grounds the beautiful in art and organic unity in nature.

Even setting aside the question of the identification of the two more than human intellects, however, such a reading is hardly compatible with the merely regulative function Kant assigns to the idea of purposiveness. As a principle of reflective judgment, it prescribes how we (as finite, discursive cognizers) are rationally constrained to regard nature, not how it "really is" *an sich.* Moreover, although this identification seems natural and was certainly made by Hegel, it is actually quite problematic. This has been clearly shown by Manfred Baum, who notes that Kant links the idea of purposiveness specifically to our discursive form of understanding, while an intuitive intellect is by definition one for which this idea and the associated contingency of fit has no place.[32] Thus, it is difficult to see how the latter could function as the ground of purposiveness on the Kantian account. Similarly, we cannot, as Hegel attempted to do, explain the regulative function assigned to the idea of purposiveness in terms of the merely ideal status of the intuitive intellect. On the contrary, if we could assume the reality of such an intellect, there would be no room for purposiveness in any form.[33]

What then is the function of this intuitive intellect and why does Kant appeal to two distinct, perhaps even incompatible, conceptions of a more than human understanding? These are not simple questions and I can here do no more than to sketch the outline of an answer. To begin with, the idea of an intuitive intellect has two distinct tasks in the resolution of the Antinomy of Teleological Judgment. The first is a straightforward limiting function: to underscore the claim that the need to represent organic beings in accordance with the idea of purpose is a function of the discursive nature of our intellect. From this, Kant concludes that it is a merely subjective necessity, not applicable to every conceivable intellect, for example, an intuitive one, and, therefore, without any ontological import.[34] The second function is to account for the possibility that mechanism and teleology are not merely logically compatible *qua* maxims, but also that they are unifiable in a single overarching account. For unless this were the case, "they could not both enter consistently into the same survey of nature"

(5:412). In other words, without such unifiability, the requirement that empirical laws cohere in a system would have to abandoned in the biological domain, since mechanistic and teleological explanations could not be combined in a single research program. The ground for this unifiability is provided by the idea of an intuitive intellect precisely because what for our discursive intellect requires the idea of purpose would be grasped by such an intellect as necessary independently of any appeal to purposes.

By contrast, the idea of the nonhuman understanding of the Introduction serves to regulate judgment in its reflective capacity rather than to limit reason in its transcendent pretensions. Within the context of the Introduction's concern with logical purposiveness, this idea is necessary in order to conceive of the possibility of the multiplicity of empirical laws constituting an order graspable by a human (discursive) intellect. Similarly, in the Dialectic of Teleological Judgment, the idea of a creative intelligence is supposedly needed for the representation by a discursive intellect of the unique whole-part relationship, which is claimed in the Analytic to be criterial for organic beings. In both cases, then, this intelligent cause is conceived according to the model of a discursive understanding, since it is viewed as operating according to the idea of a purpose or design (something which is explicitly denied of the intuitive intellect.)

This suggests that the idea of a divine or more than human intellect is characterized as nondiscursive (and therefore as proceeding nonpurposively) when it functions as a limiting concept and as discursive and purposive when it functions regulatively.[35] But no matter how one stands on that question, it should at least be clear that Kant consistently links purposiveness with the discursive rather than the intuitive intellect.

Finally, it should also be noted that because of the way in which the intuitive intellect is characterized, what Tuschling views as a breakthrough to a new speculative standpoint would have been regarded by Kant as a regression to a precritical position. Tuschling is well aware of this problem with respect to the young Hegel's own appeal to the intuitive intellect. Thus he insists that for Hegel this does not mark a regression because (i) it leads to a new logic of absolute thought, which denies the principles of non-contradiction and identity, and (ii) that Hegel's metaphysics is not an analytic "concept-metaphysic" in the manner of Wolffian rationalism, but rather demonstrates the concept as the "immanent structure of empirical existence."[36] But however accurate this may be as a characterization of Hegel's view, the fact remains that such an appeal to the intuitive intellect would have been regarded as a regression by Kant. And let us not forget that Tuschling's basic claim was that even the authentic Kantian would have to acknowledge these results.[37] It is only this claim that I have challenged here. This leaves untouched the larger question of the cogency of Hegel's Kant-critique; but I would hope that by clarifying the

Kantian position in the third *Critique,* this chapter might contribute at least indirectly to the discussion of that overriding issue.

Notes

1. Hegel, *Glauben und Wissen,* vol. IV, ed., *Gesammelte Werke,* Hartmut Buchner and Otto Pöggler (Hamburg: Felix Meiner Verlag, 1968), pp. 325–46.
2. See especially, *Enzyklopädie der philosophischen Wissenschaften* 1830, §55 and *Vorlesungen über die Geschichte der Philosophie* III (Frankfurt am Main: Suhrkamp Verlag, 1971), pp. 372–82. For a helpful discussion of these texts and the whole issue of Hegel's understanding of Kant's conceptions of purposiveness of nature and the intuitive intellect, see Klaus Düsing, "Naturteleologie und Metaphysik bei Kant und Hegel," in *Hegel und die Kritik der Urteilskraft,* ed. Hans-Friedrich Fulda and Rolf-Peter Horstmann (Stuttgart: Klett-Cotta, 1990), pp. 141–57, and Manfred Baum, "Kants Prinzip der Zweckmässigkeit und Hegels Realisierung des Begriffs," in the same volume, pp. 158–73.
3. Burkhard Tuschling, "The System of Transcendental Idealism: Questions Raised and Left Open in the *Kritik der Urteilskraft," System and Teleology in Kant's Critique of Judgment* (Spindel Conference 1991) Volume xxx, Supplement *The Southern Journal of Philosophy,* ed. Hoke Robinson, 1992, p. 111. I shall here be focusing primarily on Tuschling's views in this article and in his "Intuitiver Verstand, absolute Identität, Idee. Thesen zu Hegels früher Rezeption der *Kritik der Urteilskraft," Hegel und die Kritik der Urteilskraft,* pp. 174–88.
4. Tuschling, "The System of Transcendental Idealism," p. 112.
5. See Tuschling, "Intuitiver Verstand, absolute Identität, Idee," pp. 174–80.
6. Tuschling, "The System of Transcendental Idealism," p. 115.
7. Ibid., p. 121.
8. Ibid., p. 119.
9. Ibid., pp. 118–19.
10. This approach is taken, for example by Robert Pippin in "Avoiding German Idealism: Kant and the Reflective Judgment Problem," *Proceedings of the Eighth International Kant Congress, Memphis 1995,* ed. Hoke Robinson (Milwaukee: Marquette University Press, 1995), pp. 977–97.
11. Rolf-Peter Horstmann, "Why Must there be a Transcendental Deduction in Kant's *Critique of Judgment?"* in *Kant's Transcendental Deductions, The Three "Critiques" and the "Opus postumum,"* ed. Eckart Förster (Stanford: Stanford University Press, 1989), pp. 157–76, esp. pp. 165–8.
12. See Guyer, "Reason and Reflective Judgment: Kant on the Significance of Systematicity," *Nous* 24 (1990): 29–30; and "Kant's Conception of Empirical Law," *Proceedings of the Aristotelian Society,* supp. vol. (1990): 224.
13. Guyer, "Reason and Reflective Judgment," pp. 33–4; and "Kant's Conception of Empirical Law," pp. 227–8.
14. See Allison, *Kant's Transcendental Idealism: An Interpretation and Defense* (New Haven: Yale University Press, 1983), pp. 229–32; and "Causality and Causal Law in Kant: A Critique of Michael Friedman," *Kant and Contemporary Epistemology,* ed. Paolo Parrini (Dordrecht: Kluwer, 1994), pp. 291–307.
15. Admittedly, there is a sense in which the existence of causal laws is guaranteed by the causal principle itself or the mere concept of causality. Thus, Michael Friedman has argued that, since the causal relation for Kant involves strict universality and necessity, to say that A is the cause of B is to affirm a universal law to the effect that

"all events of type A are necessarily followed by events of type B." See his "Causal Laws and the Foundations of Natural Science," *The Cambridge Companion to Kant,* ed. Paul Guyer (Cambridge, U.K.: Cambridge University Press, 1992), pp. 161–97. But it hardly follows from this that in experience we shall ever encounter more than a single event of each type and therefore be in a position to discover empirical causal laws. In short, for all that can be inferred from the concept of causality, the possibility remains open that there might be nothing more than what could be termed "instantaneous laws," that is, laws with merely a single instance. And such "laws" could never become empirically known as such. This latter point has been put clearly by J. D. McFarland, *Kant's Concept of Teleology* (Edinburgh: University of Edinburgh Press, 1970), esp. pp. 8–11.

16. On the distinction between a canon and an organon, see the *Critique of Pure Reason,* A 21/B 26, A 61/B 85, and especially A 63/B 88, where Kant states that the "transcendental analytic should be used only as a canon for passing judgment upon the empirical employment of the understanding . . . "

17. In German, the sentence reads: "Man sieht aber hieraus nur, dass die systematische oder Vernunfteinheit der mannigfaltigen Verstandeserkenntnis ein *logisches* Prinzip sei, um, da wo der Verstand allein nicht zu Regeln hinlangt, ihm durch Ideen fortzuhelfen, und zugleich der Verschiedenheit seiner Regeln Einhelligkeit unter einem Prinzip (systematische) und dadurch Zusammenhang zu verschaffen, soweit als es sich tun lässt" (A 648/B 676).

18. See also A 656/B 684; A 660/B 688; A 664/B 692; and A 680/B 708. Kant's position is that each of the three maxims or logical principles presupposes a corresponding transcendental law.

19. The contrast is also noted by Helga Mertens, *Kommentar zur ersten Einleitung in Kants Kritik der Urteilskraft* (Munich: Johannes Berchman Verlag, 1975), p. 38.

20. See Horstmann, "Why Must there be a Deduction?" pp. 169–70. Although Horstmann connects empirical concept formation with purposiveness rather than systematicity and notes that purposiveness has a rather restricted meaning in the first *Critique,* I do not think that this affects the main point at issue.

21. The importance of paying attention to the different levels of Kant's analyses, particularly with respect to the contributions of understanding and reason, has been emphasized by Gerd Buchdahl. See particularly, *Metaphysics and the Philosophy of Science* (Cambridge, Mass.: MIT Press, 1969), esp. pp. 651–65; "The Kantian 'Dynamic of Reason' with Special Reference to the Place of Causality in Kant's System," in *Kant Studies Today,* ed. L. W. Beck (La Salle, Ill.: Open Court, 1969), pp. 187–208; "The Conception of Lawlikeness in Kant's Philosophy of Science," in *Kant's Theory of Knowledge,* ed. L. W. Beck (Dordrecht: Reidel, 1974), pp. 128–50.

22. This reflects Kant's view that the proper object of reason is the understanding, which is a central tenet of the Dialectic. See, for example, A 306–7/B 363; A 321/B 378; A 326/B 383; A 327/B 384.

23. Very roughly, I take it that the goal of this "deduction," which Kant admits is quite distinct from the deduction of the categories, is to establish a necessary connection between the three official transcendental ideas and reason's governing idea of systematicity. Each of these ideas posits the "object in idea," which must be necessarily presupposed in the quest for homogeneity, specificity, and affinity. This also explains the connection between the two parts of the Appendix, a topic which is seldom even discussed.

24. In the first Introduction Kant explicitly states that the concept of purposiveness

must be assigned to reflective judgment rather than reason on the grounds that the purpose is not posited in the object but rather in the subject and its capacity to reflect (20:216). In short, the subjectivity of the principle is the reason offered for not attributing it to reason.

25. The introduction of the notion of heautonomy is emphasized by Mertens (*Kommentar zur ersten Einleitung,* p. 36) as the major difference between the Appendix to the Dialectic and the third *Critique.*

26. The point is emphasized by Guyer, who claims that Kant affirms both a "taxonomic" and "explanatory" versions of systematicity and that they are unrelated. See Guyer, *Kant and the Claims of Taste,* pp. 44–5.

27. Admittedly, there is a tension in Kant's thought at this point, since, as Guyer notes, he appears to waver between the view that there might be no laws at all and that there might be laws that are not discoverable by the human mind. See Guyer, "Reason and Reflective Judgment," pp. 36–8, "Kant's Conception of Empirical Law," pp. 233–4. I am assuming, however, that the latter reflects Kant's considered opinion (or at least what he ought to have maintained), since the Second Analogy of itself entails that there must be causal laws of some sort (albeit not necessarily ones that can be recognized as such).

28. See Hannah Ginsborg, *The Role of Taste in Kant's Theory of Cognition* (New York and London: Garland Publishing, 1990), pp. 171–91. What follows owes a great deal to her account, which I regard as by far the most insightful discussion in the recent literature of the issues regarding the epistemic role of the principle of purposiveness.

29. Important support for this thesis, at least as a reading of Kant, is provided by Kant's anthropological-biological writings, such as *Von den verschiedenen Racen der Menschen,* in which he sides with Buffon, against Linnaeus, insisting on the necessity of finding and appealing to real rather than merely nominal types or species. Thus, he accepts Buffon's definition of species in terms of real consanguinity (a causal property) rather than superficial similarities. For a useful recent discussion of this issue, see John H. Zammito, *The Genesis of Kant's Critique of Judgment* (Chicago and London: The University of Chicago Press, 1992), pp. 199–213.

30. On this point, see Ginsborg op. cit. p. 190.

31. Similar considerations apply, *mutatis mutandis,* to Guyer's much more guarded claim of conceptual innovation. As already noted, Guyer takes the reassignment of systematicity from reason to judgment and the unambiguous attribution to it of transcendental status as at least pointing in the direction of making it into a virtual condition of apperception and of demoting the unity of experience to a regulative idea. In so doing, he is apparently presupposing that if something is a condition of experience, it must also be a condition of apperception; and further, that if such a condition is a regulative idea, then the unity of experience must likewise be merely regulative. But this is simply to ignore the different levels at which Kant analyzes the conditions of experience, which, in turn, leads to the failure to recognize that for the Kant of 1781 as well as of 1790 something could be a condition of possible experience without being a condition of objects of experience.

32. See Manfred Baum, "Kants Prinzip der Zweckmässigkeit und Hegels Realisierung des Begriffs," esp. pp. 167–73.

33. Also relevant to this point is the similarity between the idea of an intuitive intellect and Spinoza's God/substance, which acts by virtue of the necessity of its nature rather than in light of an idea. After criticizing Spinoza on the grounds that one cannot account for the purposiveness in nature by deriving it from a first cause that

92   HENRY E. ALLISON

acts by virtue of the necessity of its nature (5:393–4), Kant could hardly endorse the derivation of such purposiveness from an intuitive intellect that proceeds in an analogous fashion. The similarity is noted by Kevin Thompson, "The Antinomy of Teleological Judgment and the Concept of an Intuitive Intellect: Transformation and Conflict," *Proceedings of the Eight International Kant Congress,* volume II, part 1 (Milwaukee: Marquette University Press, 1995), pp. 445–52, esp. p. 448. Tuschling traces the distinction between the discursive, finite intellect and the nondiscursive, divine intellect to Descartes, especially *Principles* I, 23, but this does not affect the issue. See Tuschling, "Intuitiver Verstand," p. 175 n. 5.

34. I analyze this issue in more detail in "Kant's Antinomy of Teleological Judgment," in *System and Teleology in Kant's Critique of Judgment,* pp. 25–42.

35. The two distinct senses in which Kant construes the divine intellect in the context of the Antinomy of Teleological Judgment has also been noted and emphasized by Kevin Thompson, op. cit. But whereas Thompson regards this as an ambiguity that renders the resolution of the Antinomy problematic, I see it as a distinction between the limitive and the regulative functions of the idea of such an intellect.

36. Tuschling, "Intuitiver Verstand," p. 187.

37. I am grateful to Robert Pippin for calling attention to this regression problem with respect to Tuschling's analysis, particularly insofar as it concerns the Kantian position. See his "Avoiding German Idealism: Kant and the Reflective Judgment Problem," note 10.

4

The "I" as Principle of Practical Philosophy

ALLEN W. WOOD

Fichte founded a revolutionary philosophical movement and invented an entirely new kind of philosophy; and he did so knowingly and intentionally. Yet, paradoxically, he did all this merely in the course of attempting to complete the philosophical project of Kant and protect the Critical philosophy against the possibility of skeptical objections. Kant had distinguished the activity of *critique* from that of *science,* and advertised the *Critique of Pure Reason* as a propaedeutic or methodological inquiry, examining our powers of cognition so as to clear the ground for philosophy as a systematic science and to indicate how such a science might be made actual (KrV A xxi/B xxxv–xxxvii).[1] Fichte saw his task as that of bringing Kant's work to completion by turning the new Kantian philosophical standpoint into a science by constructing the system to which Kant's *Critiques* were merely preparatory.

In order to accomplish this task, Fichte thought he had to overcome several obstacles remaining in the standpoint of Kantian critique itself. Kant had seen that skepticism must be answered by starting from the condition for the possibility of cognition and providing a transcendental justification of knowledge by grounding it in those conditions. But he had undertaken this project using an account of cognition that was not sufficiently fundamental, because it already assumed some things that were likely objects of skeptical doubt. Or as Fichte puts it, Kant had incorporated into the standpoint of transcendental critique a good deal that belongs to "metaphysics," which operates within the "ordinary point of view" and tries to explain it (SW 1:33). The task of a genuinely scientific system of transcendental philosophy, however, must be to purify itself both of metaphysics and the ordinary standpoint, so as to derive both from a wholly transcendental standpoint.

To begin with, Kant took for granted the division of our cognitive capacities into passive sensibility and active understanding. Regarding the former, he left unanalyzed the presupposition that we are affected by objects external to us, thereby assuming a realism about those objects that was not only open to question but even inconsistent with his own basic insight that a transcendental theory of cognition must show how our own representation of its objects makes those objects possible. Regarding the latter, he arrived at the categories of understanding by taking the traditional formal logic and its theory of judgment as his guiding thread, without exploring the transcendental grounds of this received theory, as was again required, in Fichte's view, by a consistent application of Kant's own transcendental standpoint. The scientific system of transcendental philosophy could not be content merely to reorganize the contents of Kant's *Critiques* and work out the applications of the a priori principles they had uncovered.

I. From Transcendental Critique to Critical System of Transcendental Philosophy

In order to turn the Critical philosophy into a scientific system, we must provide this system with a more fundamental grounding. Kant's methodological inquiries had won a new standpoint for philosophy: the transcendental standpoint. Those who would build on this must start from this standpoint, but display the transcendental ground even of what Kant had, for critical or methodological purposes, taken for granted. Fichte coins a new name for a systematic philosophical science that grounds all human cognition transcendentally in this way: He calls it a "doctrine of science" (*Wissenschaftslehre*).

A doctrine of science must begin with a single "first principle," which is wholly certain, and it must proceed to other propositions in the system through rigorous transcendental argument that communicates this certainty to them (SW 1:40–42). Thus, Fichte thinks that Reinhold had been on the right track in seeking for the fundamental elements of transcendental philosophy, and in grounding the system on a single, self-evident first principle from which the entire system might be derived. But the skeptical attacks of G. E. Schulze convinced Fichte that Reinhold's "principle of consciousness" – which takes as its starting point the representation that relates subject to object while distinguishing itself from both – is inadequate as the starting point for a transcendental system.

The first principle of Fichte's doctrine of science is the "I." Fichte states this principle in a variety of ways, as "I am" (SW 1:20, 1:95, 1:425, 6:295), or "I am I" (SW 1:69, 1:93–5), or "the I posits itself (absolutely)" (SW 1:22, 1:69, 1:96, 2:441). From these different formulations, as well as the different uses Fichte makes of his first principle, it is anything but self-evident what precisely this first principle is supposed to assert. But the "I" evidently recommends itself to Fichte as a first principle for the doctrine of science on several compelling grounds. Since Descartes, the assertion of one's own existence appeared to even the most skeptical as possessing both the greatest and the most immediate certainty, even if there is considerable room for dispute about what the assertion means. The "I" also seems eminently qualified to serve as a principle grounding human knowledge as a systematic whole, since there is no cognition except for an "I," and the "I" seems to be equally present in all modes of consciousness, whether sensitive or intellectual, active or passive, and whether they are concerned with knowing the world or with agency in it. This ubiquity of the "I," which Kant had seen as the ground of the synthetic unity of all possible experience, also seems closely tied to the "I"'s function of providing whatever unity, coherence, and systematicity our knowledge may acquire. Fichte attributes the certainty of his first principle to the absolute unity of content and form, the total coincidence of what is cognized in the principle and what is known about it (SW 1:49). For in the act of self-awareness, when it is considered purely for itself and unmixed with any other awareness that may accompany it, the self of which we are aware is nothing different from the awareness we have of it. In this way, self-awareness is also unique in that it is a kind of knowledge whose object is immediately identical with the subject of that same knowledge. The "I" is, in Fichte's famous phrase, the "subject-object" and the content of self-awareness is nothing but the knowledge of the identity of subject and object (SW 2:442). It therefore seems to contain in itself the ground of every relation of a subject to an object, and thereby also the form of every possible subject-object relation, hence the sole sufficient condition for the possibility of all cognition.

The "I" also possesses a unique kind of certainty, in that it is a certainty always available to us however much or little knowledge we may have about anything else. Both the "I" itself and our certainty about it are, moreover, entirely at our disposal, and depend at every moment solely on our choice. For we are always free to become aware of ourselves; and even in cases where something outside us occasions our becoming self-aware, we never become aware of ourselves without performing a free act through which the self-awareness comes about. This is due to another noteworthy fact about the "I" – that not only the certainty but even that of which we are certain – the "I" itself – is something generated entirely through our own free act. Fichte's formula: "the I posits itself absolutely" refers to the remarkable fact that the subject-object of self-awareness is something whose very existence depends on its own free agency. Consequently, in self-awareness the subject stands in an active cognitive relation to its object, or is an *intellectual intuition*.

This feature of the "I" was, for Fichte, the key to solving a second problem presented by Kant's way of carrying out his critical project: Kant's fundamental division of philosophy into theory and practice.

In the *Critique of Judgment,* Kant himself had recognized a problem here, and had attempted to bridge the "great gulf" between theoretical understanding and practical reason through reflective judgment. But once it is accepted that transcendental philosophy as a doctrine of science must begin with a single fundamental principle, it becomes unacceptable to bridge the gulf between theory and practice through the use of any mediating faculty. Instead, the only way to deal with the problem is to discover a first principle that can serve simultaneously as the ground of both theoretical and practical philosophy. No doubt even for Kant the "I" be recognized as the ground of both our theoretical cognition of nature and our practical awareness of moral duty. For in his account the unity of experience rests on apperception, just as the possibility of obligation rests on autonomy. But in the Kantian system it remains enigmatic how the theoretical "I" whose understanding synthesizes the contents of experience relates to the practical "I" whose reason gives itself the moral law. The "I" that is to serve as the first principle of a doctrine of science must in some way be simultaneously theoretical and practical. Further, the entire possibility of a doctrine of science will have to depend on the way this identity is understood in the first principle and then worked out in the structure of the system.

II. What Is the "I"?

Before we can deal with the unity of the theoretical and the practical in Fichte's first principle, we must get clearer about the meaning of the principle itself. Fichte holds that every consciousness involves an awareness of the "I" (SW 1:435, 1:526–527). At the same time, Fichte denies that the "I," in the sense in which it is a first principle, is ever anything actual as an appearance or object of experience (GA 4/2:26). Rather, it is the first and most original of a series of necessary acts that make experience possible (SW 1:91). We reach the first principle by becoming self-aware and noticing how we do it. This involves an act of abstraction, in which we must be careful to think only what is required, and not mix this thought with other aspects of experience that are generated only by other acts whose necessity for experience is to be established only subsequently (SW 1:91, 1:338, 1:501, 1:521).

When he claims that the "I" is present in every consciousness, Fichte seems to have in mind here what Sartre was later to call the "pre-reflective" or "non-positional" self-consciousness we have even when our attention is focused on objects entirely distinct from the self.[2] If I am reading a novel, for example, my attention is not on myself (or my reading activity) but on the characters in the story, and what they are doing. But if my reading is interrupted by someone asking me what I am doing, I reply immediately that I am (and have for some time been) reading; and the self-awareness on the basis of which I answer the question is not something acquired at just that moment but a consciousness of myself that has been present to me all along.

For Fichte, what is crucial about this awareness is not only its ubiquity and certainty, but equally the fact that it is an awareness of *activity*, which is present even in our most passive states of perception. In every thought, "you directly note activity and freedom in this thinking, in this transition from thinking the I to thinking the table, the walls, etc. Your thinking is for you an *acting*" (SW

1:522). What Fichte means by "I," regarded as the absolute principle of all philosophy, is nothing but this awareness of our own activity, which is an inevitable ingredient in any awareness and provides us with an ineluctable consciousness of our freedom.

If Fichte derives the ubiquitous certainty of the "I" from prereflective self-awareness, that does not mean that he intends to exclude *reflective* self-awareness from the first principle. For the free activity in which prereflective awareness consists is precisely the source of the constant possibility I have of reflecting on myself, and making myself an object of a concept. Fichte often describes the awareness through which we grasp the first principle as the one I achieve when I construct a concept of myself and notice how I do this (SW 1:491, 1:521, 2:441, 4:16). In prereflective activity the "I" "posits itself absolutely"; but in reflection it "reiterates this positing" or "posits itself as self-posited" (SW 1:274, 276).

In forming a concept of itself, the "I" necessarily distinguishes itself from something else, since every act of conceptualization involves distinguishing the item brought under a given concept from those excluded from it. This means that the primary act of the "I," through which it posits itself, necessitates a second act in which it "counterposits" that which is distinct from it, the "not-I" (SW 1:101–5). This means that the activity of the "I" must be twofold: that of the "I," directed toward a not-"I" and that of a "not-I," directed back against the "I" as a "collision" or "check" (*Anstoss*) of the "I"'s activity (SW 1:208–19). Since both are conditions of the "I"'s existence, Fichte regards both as activities of the "I": the former is "ideal" activity, the latter "real" activity (SW 1:267–70).

By exhibiting the necessity of positing a "not-I" as a condition of the "I"'s own self-awareness, Fichte transcendentally deduces the distinction between passivity and activity, sensibility and understanding, which Kant had merely taken for granted, and has done so without the need to assume dogmatically a thing in itself that acts on our faculties. At the same time, he has provided a ground for the distinction between the theoretical and practical functions of the "I." In reflecting on itself, the "I" is aware of the opposition of ideal and real activities, whose boundary point separates the "I" from the "not-I." This awareness, Fichte says, is what Reinhold meant by "representation" – that which relates subject and object to each other by distinguishing them (SW 1:227–8). Reinhold's principle too, therefore, has been transcendentally deduced from the first principle of the doctrine of science. And the "I" that represents is the "I" as "intelligence," or the theoretical "I" (SW 1:248).

But the condition of this awareness of the "I"'s real activity is that the ideal activity of the "I" should meet with a check or resistance. From a transcendental standpoint, therefore, this makes ideal activity the ground of real activity, and exhibits the "absolute I" as the ground of the "not-I" (SW 1:250). It also enables us to determine the ideal activity itself more precisely. It must be an activity that opposes the real activity posited in the "not-I," yet without ever abolishing this activity, since to do so would at the same time abolish a necessary condition of the "I"'s own existence. The ideal activity of the "I" must therefore take the form of a "willing" or "striving," which is directed against the "not-I" (SW 1:261–2, 4:18–21). This reveals the "I" as practical, and also shows that the theoretical "I," or intelligence, is grounded on the practical "I," or the will (SW 1:263–5). In this way, Fichte claims to have demonstrated what Kant had only postulated, that reason can be practical (SW 1:264).

III. Theoretical and Practical Science

The sketch of Fichte's argument, which I have just presented, unfortunately still does not tell us very much about how he conceived the difference between theory and practice as parts of philosophy. Thus, it does not tell us about the distinct manner in which he conceived of the "I" as a first principle in relation to each. This question is complicated by what Frederick Neuhouser has shown, that Fichte adopted one view of the matter in the 1794 *Foundation of the Doctrine of Science,* but then changed his views significantly by the time he wrote the two Introductions of 1797 and the *System of Ethics* of 1798.[3]

According to the earlier view, presented in the *Concept of a Doctrine of Science* and the *Foundation* of 1794, the doctrine of science is supposed to ground all other particular sciences, including both theoretical and practical sciences (SW 1:63–6). Fichte intends this not in the sense that other sciences are each grounded on some particular principle or principles belonging to the *Wissenschaftslehre,* but rather in the sense that they are each grounded on the fundamental principle itself. The boundary between the doctrine of science and particular sciences is marked by the way the first principle is taken. "As soon as an action which is in itself entirely free has been given a specific direction, we have moved from the domain of the general doctrine of science into that of some particular science" (SW 1:63–4). The division of theoretical from practical science is therefore based on considering the two ways in which the "I" can relate to the "not-I." If the "I" adopts a dependent relation to the "not-I," then it is determined as "intelligence" and the science is theoretical. If we consider the "I" as independent in relation to the "not-I," then its relation is one of *striving,* and we are dealing with the practical part of the doctrine of science.

This is the way Fichte presents things in the practical part of the *Foundation* of 1794 (especially §5, SW 1: 246–85). Neuhouser argues that Fichte's deduction of practical reason is supposed to consist in grounding the theoretical use of reason and then showing that reason can be theoretical only if it is also practical.[4] That he is correct is clearly indicated in the following remark: "Up to now a practical faculty of reason has been postulated, but not proved. Such a proof. . . can be achieved in no other way than by showing that reason cannot even be theoretical unless it is practical; that there can be no intelligence in the human being unless he possesses a practical faculty" (SW 1:264).

Fichte's subsequent argument in the *Foundation* is that this practical faculty, in order to be able to limit its distinct practical drives by one another and to bring them into harmony through "interdetermination," must include a drive to absolute activity for its own sake, or a "drive for drive's sake," that is, a capacity to give itself "an absolute law or categorical imperative" (SW 1:327). The "I" as practical principle is transcendentally deduced from the theoretical "I."

By 1797, however, Fichte had changed his mind both about the strategy for justifying practical reason and about the relation between the doctrine of science and its theoretical and practical parts. In the *First Introduction to the Doctrine of Science* of 1797, he famously maintains that there are only two consistent philosophies, dogmatism (or materialism) and idealism (or criticism). Philosophy before Kant was based entirely on the principle of dogmatism, that of the thing in itself, which leads necessarily (Fichte insists) to determinism, fatalism, authoritarianism, the denial of human dignity, and resignation to the unfreedom and injustice that has reigned in human society up to now; the new or Critical philosophy is grounded on the principle of idealism, the "I," which leads necessarily to the affirmation of freedom, morality, and the unlimited possibility of progress in human history. The principle one follows, the philosophy one chooses, depends on the kind of person one is. Neither philosophy can refute the other, because each begins with a different principle, and each of the two principles from the outset excludes the other (SW 1:425–35). Idealism and dogmatism, therefore, each begin with a faith in which their respective systems resolve to persevere (SW 4:25–6).

Such remarks may lead us to think that Fichte has simply abandoned the whole idea of establishing a doctrine of science on the basis of an absolutely certain first principle, and is resorting instead to a blind leap of faith as the ground of his system of idealism. But a closer look at what he says will remove this impression. For the apparent strength of dogmatism, its ability to withstand the challenge of criticism and maintain itself as a faith in the minds of its adherents, is due not to any evidence in its behalf or to any weakness in the evidence for criticism. Instead, it is due entirely to the freedom-fearing closed-mindedness of the dogmatic mindset, and in the end to either the weakness or viciousness of character on the part of the dogmatists themselves.

Fichte regularly ascribes to idealism two advantages, each decisive from the standpoint of reason, which it has over dogmatism. In the first place, whereas the dogmatist's principle – the thing in itself – is a mere presupposition, a thought that can never be given in intuition, the principle of idealism – the "I" 's freedom – is at every moment directly exhibited in consciousness, given to us as an intuition in our most inward feeling (SW 1: 428, 445–6, 4:44, 54, GA 4/2:20–21). We can take the practical standpoint only insofar as we ascribe freedom to ourselves, and this standpoint is unavoidable – even as a theorist I must take it insofar as I deliberate about what hypotheses to test, how to test them, and what conclusions to draw from the evidence. To be sure, dogmatism consistently rejects its own self-generated awareness of freedom – on the authority of dogmatism's principle – as a delusion. But dogmatism can neither deny the experience of freedom that is inseparable from the practical stand-point, nor offer any comparably self-evident experience in evidence of its principle. Dogmatism's faith is therefore adopted willfully and contrary to experience, where idealism's faith is nothing but a confidence in what it directly experiences (SW 4:26). This is a faith born of the fear to use one's own reason, a fear reinforced by social traditions and hierarchies that depend on the denial of the fundamental freedom and equal dignity of every rational being.

Idealism's second advantage, according to Fichte, is that it can be completed as a philosophical system, whereas dogmatism cannot. Thus idealism's starting point can be demonstratively guaranteed, whereas dogmatism's cannot (SW 1:466). Idealism can even explain how we come to ascribe the representations of consciousness to a thing in itself. But dogmatism is unable to explain our consciousness of freedom on its principles, and it therefore can only reject this consciousness as an illusion (SW 1:435–40). The dogmatist, moreover, is "unable to offer a clear account of how representations could be produced within any creature by the influence of things" (GA 4/2:20). For, once again, the standpoint from which we have representations is the practical standpoint of a free agent, and to regard oneself as free is incompatible with regarding oneself as a thing.

The contest between idealism and dogmatism is not, therefore, an epistemic stalemate, to be settled merely by an arbitrary decision or act of faith. Fichte's claim is rather that a consistent dogmatist is someone who has on principle cut himself off both from immediate evidence and scientific demonstration through a stubborn denial of both immediate experience and scientific reason. Dogmatism, in Fichte's view, is a philosophical attitude that expresses a mor-ally corrupt character and corresponds to an unfree social order that rests on mental servitude, vanity, dishonesty, self-deception, and complacent despair over the power of reason (SW 1:434). People are drawn to dogmatism either because they benefit from the system of unfreedom or because they are victims deluded and intimidated by it who are afraid to throw off their chains. It is in this sense only that Fichte holds that dogmatists cannot be "refuted," but can only be "cultivated," "educated," or "cured" (SW 1:136, GA 4/2:21).

The fundamental change in Fichte's method between 1794 and 1797, how-ever, is that, whereas the earlier system made the practical power of reason into an object of demonstration, the later system grounds itself directly on the original Act (*Tathandlung*) through which the free "I" posits itself. This is why Fichte repeatedly asserts that no one can be compelled to adopt idealism. Fichte cannot demonstrate his starting point but can only invite his readers to initiate it for themselves (SW 1:429, 1:458, 4:8, GA 4/2:32). It is in this sense that Fichte, reversing what he said in the *Foundation* of 1794, now claims that his first principle is a "postulate": "The reader or student of philosophy must begin by doing something" (GA 4/2:29). According to Fichte, in 1794 he began with self-awareness as a fact (*Tatsache*), something found in experience, and attempted to demonstrate from this the practical freedom, the original Act (*Tathandlung*), which made it possible. But after 1797 he begins directly with the Act and the doctrine of science is to show how it generates the fact: "Here we began with the Act and arrived at the fact; but the method of the book [of 1794] was just the reverse" (GA 4/2:33). This means that now the first principle of the doctrine of science is directly a practical principle; practice is not only the ground of theory but even the starting point of philosophy as a whole.

This change reflects itself in the way Fichte conceives of the relation of the doctrine of science to the theoretical and practical sciences. In 1794, Fichte began with a general grounding of the entire doctrine of science (Part I: §§1–3, SW 1:91–122), then proceeded to the theoretical part of the doctrine of science (Part II: §4, SW 1:123–246) and finally to the practical part (Part III: §§5–11, SW 1:246–328). In the *System of Ethics* of 1798, however, theoretical and practical sciences are presented as simply two equal parts of a single unified doctrine of science, neither taking systematic precedence over the other (SW 4:15). That this is an intentional change is documented in a transcript of Fichte's lectures of 1797:

[These lectures will] follow a method of presentation that is just the opposite of that followed by the author in his compendium of 1794, where he proceeded from the theoretical portion of philosophy (i.e. from what had to be explained) to the practical part (i.e. to what was meant to serve *as the basis* for explaining the former). In the present lectures, however, the hitherto familiar division between theoretical and practical philosophy is not to be found. Instead, these lectures present philosophy *as a whole*, in the exposition of which theoretical and practical philosophy are united. This presentation follows a much more natural path, beginning with the practical sphere, or whenever it would contribute to the clarity of the exposition to do so, inserting the practical into the theoretical, in order to explain the latter in terms of the former: a liberty for which the author was not yet sufficiently self-confident at the time he published his *Doctrine of Science*. (GA 4/2:17)

Fichte apparently *always* regarded the practical as the foundation of the theoretical, so that his earlier procedure is not to be understood as founding the practical on the theoretical but, on the contrary, as a regressive method, moving from what is grounded back toward the ground. The "I," therefore, was always regarded as fundamentally a practical rather than a theoretical principle. The new presentation of the system merely makes this explicit.

IV. The "I" as Practical Standpoint and Practical Principle

But what does it mean to say that the "I" is fundamentally a practical principle? A practical principle is one according to which we guide or direct our action, in other words, an "ought"-principle. To say that the "I" is fundamentally a practical principle is to say that "I" refers fundamentally not to something a person is, but something a person ought to be, or more precisely, to a way a person ought to act. What could this mean?

The "first person standpoint," as philosophers usually call it, is typically interpreted by them as a *cognitive* standpoint, a standpoint from which things are *known* — typically, a standpoint from which people know things about their own mental states. It is the existence of this standpoint, for instance, that makes knowing "I have an itch behind my left ear" a different piece of knowledge from knowing that Allen Wood, or the only native of Seattle in this room, has an itch behind his left ear. For I would be equally certain that I have an itch behind my ear even if I forgot my birthplace or even my name. Philosophers such as Gareth Evans and Sydney Shoemaker point out that first person knowledge of mental states has a distinctive dimension of certainty or infallibility, in that it is immune in principle to errors of misidentification of the subject of those states.[5]

These philosophers are not wrong to think of the first person standpoint in this way as a cognitive standpoint with certain distinctive features. But their account is importantly incomplete if they do not realize that the first person standpoint is distinctive, and perhaps even has these special cognitive features, only because it is not originally and fundamentally a cognitive standpoint at all, but instead the standpoint of an agent, so that what is most distinctive about it is not the way it enables us to know certain things, but rather the fact that it is that unique viewpoint on the world from which things can be done.

There is no space here to develop this point as fully as it deserves,[6] but we may get the idea if we begin by reflecting on why it is that I cannot misidentify the subject of my explicitly avowed conscious intentions or purposes in the very act of avowing them. For the ascription of such intentions to myself is not fundamentally a matter of theoretical observation but an act of self-definition, which I take to be normative for my own conduct. In the avowal I am defining myself as a person with this intention or aim, and as long as I continue to do so, when my behavior fails to correspond to my aim I should criticize the behavior rather than disavow the aim. To be a person with an intention or aim is in this way to be an agent acting under self-given norms. And if, as Fichte maintains, this is what it fundamentally is to be an "I," then the "I"'s identity is more fundamentally tied to those norms than to anything else. This is the reason why I cannot, from such a standpoint, misidentify the subject of my aims or intentions: for, from a practical point of view, I am directly constituted by them. We may see how this account might be extended to more passive first person states (such as sensations or feelings) if we follow Fichte in understanding these as constituting not the properties of a thing, but merely the passive aspect of our practical field, regarded from the standpoint of a free agent (see *Foundation*, §§7–10, SW 1:287–322). Feeling, in other words, is only the passive side of a willing or striving in which I am engaged. Hence, from the practical standpoint, its subject is self-defined through the self-givenness of the norms through which I define my own willing or striving.

Christine Korsgaard has emphasized that it is essential, when we are considering the standpoint of agency, "not to confuse *being engaged in a conscious activity* with *being conscious of an activity.*"[7] The latter provides us only with a theoretical or cognitive viewpoint *on* our own agency, whereas only the former is a truly practical viewpoint, and it alone is actually the standpoint of agency itself. Korsgaard argues that the unity of the person and its identity through time is grounded not, as Derek Parfit and others would have it, on a "deep metaphysical fact" (whether genuine or bogus), but rather on practical requirements of agency. Thus, my identity with the self who will inhabit my body in the future is not based on the persistence through time of my self as a metaphysical substance, but instead on the fact that my body is the fundamental vehicle of my agency and meaningful action through this body requires a relation to a future which I actively define as mine. Korsgaard notes that "to the extent that you regulate your choices by identifying yourself as the one who is implementing something like a particular plan of life, you need to identify with your future in order to be *what you are even now.* When the person is viewed as an agent, no clear content can be given to the idea of a merely present self."[8]

The even more fundamental point here is that no clear content can be given to the idea of a self understood only theoretically, that is, as a set of events or psychological processes cognitively available (whether by empirical observation or theoretical inference). If the identity of an "I" is determined by the practical requirements of its agency, then what constitutes the "I," from the standpoint of its own agency, is less the set of processes known to have gone on in it than the project it is engaged in implementing, regarded (again from the practical point of view) as a practical or "ought"-principle that it regards itself as engaged in following (whether or not it turns out actually to obey this "ought"-principle).

Fichte calls attention to this fundamentally practical character of the "I" in many ways, but one of the most interesting of them concerns his use of it in the *System of Ethics* to derive the *intersubjectivity* of the "I." Fichte argues that reflective or conceptual awareness of the "I" must represent the "I" as "determinate" or "limited"; this implies that the "I" must not only posit its own activity, but "counterposit" the activity of a "not-I." Insofar as the "I" is a practical principle, however, its determinacy has to be understood normatively as well. Fichte puts this by saying that "true determinacy" cannot be merely "found" in me, but "I must give it to myself" through "ideal activity" (SW 4:220). Some activity, that is, must be thought of as determinately mine not merely in the sense that I observe myself engaged in it, but in the more fundamental sense that I demand or require it of myself, so that activity excluded by the requirement is not properly mine, even if (by failing to comply with this self-demand) I actually do it. Fichte then argues that the "I" can acquire the concept of such a requirement only by internalizing a requirement addressed to it from outside, which presupposes an external being capable of making such a demand on me, in other words, another "I" (SW 4:218–21). For our present purposes, the conclusion of this argument is of less interest than its premise: namely, that being a determinate "I" means subjecting oneself to a requirement, an "ought"-principle.

V. The "I" as Principle in Fichtean Ethics

Of course, Fichte insists on the fundamentally practical character of the "I" from quite early in the *System of Ethics*. But the point we have been trying to explicate, that as practical the "I" is a normative or "ought"-principle, is harder to grasp owing to the extremely abstract and formalistic character of this principle as Fichte expounds it. Fichte, like Hegel after him, regards Kant's formula of universal law not as "constitutive" but "merely heuristic," since it requires other grounds of moral judgment to determine its content (SW 4:233–4). The "I" as practical principle is formulated variously as a "tendency to absolute self-activity" (SW 4:39), "self-activity for the sake of self-activity" (SW 4:29) or "freedom for the sake of freedom" (SW 4:153–4), or as a "drive toward the whole I" (SW 4:40) or, finally as a drive to "self-determination (*Selbstbestimmung*)": "Always fulfill your vocation (*Bestimmung*)" (SW 4:150–1, 184–5).

Recent accounts of Fichte's normative ethics have been less than lavish in their praise of its accomplishments. In his treatment of Fichte's "I" as a substantive practical principle, Neuhouser distinguishes a "universalist" from an "individualist" account, judging the former to be fundamentally unsuccessful, and the latter, though more promising, to be insufficiently developed. Günter Zöller has more recently concluded that Fichte's system of ethics does not aim so much at presenting a prescriptive or normative ethics as at providing "a sustained reflection on the conditions of moral knowledge and action."[9]

Such assessments seem to me vastly to underestimate the normative content of Fichte's *System of Ethics*. It is true that Fichte approaches normative ethics through extensive and detailed reflection on the formal features of free agency and moral epistemology, but his account of moral duties is much more far-reaching and specific, for example, than the contemporaneous account given in Kant's doctrine of virtue.

In considering the application of the practical principle, Fichte distinguishes between the standpoint of a science of ethical duties and that of the actual agent, the "I" itself as it lives and enacts the struggle for its own freedom. Regarding the former, he develops a complex taxonomy of duties, he distinguishes "conditioned" (or self-regarding) duties from "unconditioned" (or other-regarding) ones, and "universal" duties (which apply equally to everyone) from "particular" duties that apply to people in virtue of social relationships – either within the family or in regard to one's estate, profession, or vocation. Here, his account involves a moral theory of society (a topic on which Kant's *Metaphysics of Morals* officially demurred), and anticipates a great deal for which Hegel's conception of ethical life has usually been given the credit.

Fichte progresses from the "I" as practical principle to this scientific theory of duties through consideration of the standpoint of the "I" as agent. This discussion certainly does deal, as Zöller says, largely with matters that could be considered under the heading of "moral epistemology." But Fichte's approach itself involves some quite distinctive and views about how we should consider moral questions in our lives. These views are substantive enough, I think, to be counted as genuinely normative and not merely "epistemological."

Fichte insists that what it is our duty to do in a given situation is not given through the practical principle itself but is a matter for theoretical inquiry (SW 4:166). The correctness of a conviction about our duty is something that must be given through a feeling of necessity conjoined with the conviction (SW 4:167). Fichte likens this theoretical inquiry to the activity of reflective judgment (in the sense of Kant's third *Critique*); it seeks a harmony, analogous to aesthetic feeling, between the pure and the empirical "I," which, when found, results in the cessation of doubt and a state of peace and satisfaction (SW 4:166–8). Fichte's moral epistemology here is formally coherentist in that it regards the search for a state of certainty as the quest for a systematic agreement among moral conceptions (SW 4:172).

This feeling of immediate certainty about our duty is called "conscience" (SW 4:173). Because in this as in every other theoretical inquiry there is no objective criterion that can be given externally (SW 4:170), duty is never known by deriving it from an objective rule or set of rules, but is to be found only through conscientious inquiry directed to one's situation and resulting in a felt conviction. The most Fichte thinks we can specify in general is the *form* of every moral conviction: that it involves ascribing to a thing a "final end" (*Endzweck*), and gives the moral law for each thing as the injunction to use it according to its final end (SW 4:171–2).

106 ALLEN W. WOOD

Fichte insists that moral convictions are worthless unless they result from one's own free thinking, and that the reliance on any form of moral authority compromises the morality of one's convictions (SW 4:173–4). Here, Fichte's theory strongly anticipates twentieth-century existentialist conceptions of a "situation ethics," except that it utterly rejects the metaethical noncognitivism and normative agent-relativism with which such views have typically been conjoined. The substantive point here is that nothing can be morally authoritative for an "I" except its own free thinking about what it ought to do, measured by the feeling of certainty as a principle of reflective judgment. This amounts to a rejection of any system of casuistry that proposes to derive what I ought to do from a "universal principle of morality," such as the principle of utility or Kant's formula of universal law, together with a set of facts to which such a principle is applied. Actions are to be directed at final ends, but these are not to be conceived according to some general conception (such as "pleasure" or "happiness") or derived (as Kant would have it) from a formal categorical imperative, but determined as good by the "I"'s reflective judgment on its situation in its full and concrete complexity and particularity. But for Fichte, as we shall see in a moment, this point in no way puts in question the objectivity of ethical values or the universal validity of ethical norms.

What is normatively distinctive in Fichte's position here is its rejection of general moral principles and its insistence on the subject's own reflective judgment as the only authoritative criterion. In this respect, the very features of Fichte's theory that make it look merely "formal" and "epistemological" may be seen as grounded in a rejection of certain assumptions about the sort of thing that a practical principle would have to be in order to have "content" or "substance." And this rejection itself involves substantive issues of value, since it asserts the "I"'s autonomy as the sole possible source of practical authority, and draws possibly controversial conclusions from this about what counts as an acceptable manner of forming our practical convictions.

What has just been said, however, may still give the impression that Fichte's moral epistemology is excessively subjectivistic or individualistic. This impression needs to be corrected by supplementing our sketch of Fichte's account of the "formal" conditions for moral action with a look at his account of its "material" conditions. Here Fichte's discussion focuses on the way in which practical inquiry must take account of the thinking of others. In other words, the subjective certainty of the "I"'s convictions must be arrived at through a social or dialectical process, and if the formal criterion of a conviction's certainty is a feeling of reflective judgment, its material criterion is rational agreement with others through a free and rational communication aiming at objective truth.

Fichte approaches this point by arguing that action that is materially free must simultaneously meet two conditions: first, that whatever limits me must be subjected to my final ends; second, that certain things in the world should limit my final ends, namely the freedom of others (SW 4:230). Then he argues that these two apparently contradictory requirements can be reconciled only if all free beings necessarily have the *same* final end, so that the free action of each simultaneously liberates all (SW 4:230–1). This can happen only on the basis of a reason that is identical with each individual "I" and simultaneously one single reason for all "I" 's. Hence, if there is moral disagreement between different "I" 's, it is the strict obligation of each to enter into a process of communication aimed at a common rational conviction concerning their moral principles and ends (SW 4:232–3). This involves both the duty to influence others through rational argument and the duty to be open to a like influence from them (SW 4:245, 6:308–11). The certainty of my own conviction about the content of the "I" as a practical principle is therefore something that can be attained only through communication with others establishing it as universally rational and valid (SW 4:246–7). What is substantively normative here is not only the idea that we cannot form rational convictions apart from a communicative interaction with others, but also Fichte's insistence on certain conditions which such communications must meet, such as their freedom from constraint, as by any authority or creed, and the continuous openness of the participants to being convinced by the rational arguments of others (SW 4:175–7, 235–8). In this respect, what is substantive in Fichte's view could be seen as anticipating Habermas's ethics of domination-free communication.[10]

This means that for Fichte, the "I" as a principle of philosophy has a content that is open-ended in two senses. First, the "I" is not some sort of fixed truth whose content is there to be theoretically apprehended; instead it is a practical principle, whose content is not what the "I" is observed to be but what it determines that it ought to be. But second, even as a practical principle, the "I" is something whose content is the projected result of an active process of self-determination, relating the "I" to itself through reflective judgment and feelings of doubt or certainty and to others through the reciprocal activity of rational communication. In both respects, what or who the "I" is is determined by what it ought to be; and what it ought to be is what it projects from the practical standpoint as the ideal result of a process of self-reflection and communicative interaction. The system of philosophy grounded on the "I" can therefore be nothing but the experience of a world as it must be constituted for a being that seeks simultaneously to actualize itself and to discover, through such relations to itself and others, the final ends it ought to actualize. Even the "I" itself, regarded as an object of cognition, has only those properties or contents determined for it by the contours of the entire practical project through which it constitutes its identity.

108 ALLEN W. WOOD

Notes

1. Kant's *Critique of Pure Reason* will be abbreviated as KrV and cited according to A/B pagination. Other writings by Kant will be cited in the Berlin Academy Edition (abbreviated "AK") by volume:page number.
   Fichte's writings will be cited according to the following system of abbreviations:
   GA *J. G. Fichte – Gesamtausgabe,* ed. Reinhard Lauth and Hans Gliwitzky (Stuttgart: Frommann-Holzboog, 1962–). Cited by part/volume:page number.
   SW *Fichtes Sämmtliche Werke,* ed. I. H. Fichte (Berlin: W. de Gruyter, 1970). Cited by volume:page number.
2. Sartre, *Being and Nothingness,* trans. by Hazel Barnes (New York: Simon and Schuster, 1978), pp. 11–15.
3. Frederick Neuhouser, *Fichte's Theory of Subjectivity* (New York: Cambridge University Press, 1990), Chap. 2.
4. Ibid., pp. 41–53.
5. See, for example, Gareth Evans, "Self-Identification," in *The Varieties of Reference,* ed. J. McDowell (Oxford: Oxford University Press, 1982), pp. 205–35, and Sydney Shoemaker, "The First Person Perspective," Presidential Address to the American Philosophical Association, *Proceedings and Addresses of the American Philosophical Association* 68 (1994): 7–22.
6. I am grateful to Henry Allison for pressing me to clarify this point as much as I can in the present context.
7. Christine Korsgaard, "Personal Identity and the Unity of Agency," *Philosophy and Public Affairs* 18 (1989): 118.
8. Ibid., pp. 113–114.
9. G. Zöller, "Changing the Appearances: Fichte's Transcendental Theory of Practical Self-Determination," *Proceedings of the Eighth International Kant-Congress* (Milwaukee: Marquette University Press, 1995) vol. I, part 3, pp. 929–42.
10. See, for example, J. Habermas, *Moralbewußtsein und kommunikatives Handeln* (Frankfurt am Main: Suhrkamp Verlag, 1983).

5

The Practical Foundation of Philosophy in Kant, Fichte, and After

KARL AMERIKS

Fichte's work, and especially his emphasis on the self's activity, has been receiving considerable attention recently, and even in America important philosophers have made claims that it points to significant improvements on Kant's philosophy.[1] Elsewhere I have challenged some of these claims, in particular as they bear on a precise understanding of the central notion of the activity of apperception,[2] and on the detailed interpretation of some key passages in Fichte regarding the "primacy of the practical."[3] On this occasion, I will present a somewhat broader view of the transition from Kant to Fichte, while expanding on my reading of this period as marked by a premature move toward a radical kind of "practical" foundationalism.

After stepping back briefly to sketch a very general picture of the peculiar context and impact of the early reception of Kant (sec. I.1), I will review the Critical texts most relevant for explaining the basic features of Fichte's reaction and the popularity of positions like Fichte's in our own time (sec. I.2). From this interpretive perspective I will then draw some critical implications for evaluating an important account of this period developed recently by Allen Wood (sec. II). Whereas Wood presents Fichte as improving in places on Kant's program, I will offer reasons for regarding Fichte's reaction as an understandable but questionable departure from the Critical philosophy.

I.1

The immediate reaction to the *Critique of Pure Reason* (1781, second edition 1787) was highly unusual. On the one hand, it was admired right away as a revolutionary masterpiece because of how it proposed a rigorous deduction of the structures of human experience in the place of heavily disputed transcendent claims of traditional metaphysics. Very soon, however, there arose a perplexing variety of interpretations and a widespread feeling that Kant's system itself was opaque, riddled with traditional weaknesses, and entangled even in outright contradictions. Within a very few years, it was thought by many that Kant's work was surpassed and obviously inferior to systems such as those advanced in the next decades by Fichte, Schelling, Hegel, and others.[4]

This feeling was growing already in the 1790s when Kant was still alive and active – a fact that constitutes one of the great mysteries in the history of philosophy and reflects a perspective rarely found in later generations. Even philosophers who are quite critical of Kant today, and more sympathetic to the later Idealists, would not go so far as to assume, as the vanguard of thinkers in turn of the century Germany did, that it is *evident* that Kant's own philosophy was outdated and at a whole level lower in eminence than its successors.

Many attempts have been made to begin to explain this development (among the best are studies by Beiser, Horstmann, and Pippin).[5] Here I will outline and elaborate on only a few basic strands of my own interpretation, which is built on a set of contrasts between four main subperiods in the Idealist era. In order not only to clarify specific historical issues but also to point to a proper approach to some systematic options of contemporary significance, I propose a sharp distinction between (i) Kant's own views, and three main phases in the immediate reaction to the *Critique:* (ii) the initial pre-Fichtean or "Reinholdian-Cartesian" phase (1788–94), (iii) the central "Fichtean-practical" phase (1794–1801), and (iv) the alternative "speculative Hegelian" phase that dominated the post-Fichtean era (1801–).[6]

The pre-Fichtean phase is most crucial and is still often overlooked. In this period Kant's own relatively modest system was transformed and replaced in the public mind by Reinhold's lucid but highly idealized vision of philosophy, an ambitious foundationalism. Reinhold made his fame in Jena originally by becoming the anointed and most influential earlier expositor of Kant, but he quickly shifted from providing a readable and lively survey of themes concerning primarily the end of the *Critique* and its popular antidogmatic results (stressing their significance for an enlightened ethics and religion), to offering what he got people to believe was a clear improvement on Kant's method and controversial premises.[7]

Because Kant appeared to – and on my reading actually did[8] – work from premises already assuming experience of objects, it was objected (by G. E. Schulze and F. H. Jacobi[9]) that the Kantian system could not defeat skepticism, and that it even had skeptical implications of its own because of its explicit attachment to a kind of idealism. Reinhold tried to meet this concern by picking up on programmatic strands in Kant's own work and on some of its more extravagant phrases. Kant had spoken of "one" principle at the base of his philosophy, he had stressed the "unity" of reason, he had proclaimed that genuine philosophy must "come forth as a science" and needed to be not a mere conjunction of theses but a full "system," a priori and certain.[10] All these claims might be given a relatively innocent reading when they are taken in the precise and full context of what Kant actually did. Reinhold, however, moved in the opposite direction and demanded an "Elementarphilosophie" that would take these claims in a bold sense. True philosophy, he insisted, needs an *absolutely certain* foundation, one that rests on *a single and self-evident* principle and allows us to move *immediately with deductive* rigor toward a *thoroughly unified* and *clearly exhaustive system.* In other words, Kantianism needs to be reformulated so that it manifestly fits a radical Cartesian ideal. Reinhold was also a close student of Leibniz, and this may help explain why he proposed as his base not Kant's judgments of experience but a bare principle of representation,[11] from which he attempted to deduce features such as space and time that had appeared in Kant's system as fundamental givens, ultimate "facts of consciousness." Here I must pass over the details and full motivation of Reinhold's philosophy of representation;[12] the crucial point is the ensemble of methodological characteristics – strict certainty, deducibility, unity, exhaustiveness, systematicity – that Reinhold managed to convince his generation to focus on and to take as the implicit ideal and most irreplaceable feature of the Kantian movement.

In the second phase of the reception of Kant, one can see Fichte as taking over the very ideal that Reinhold had used, and as replacing Kant's own more modest and complicated system with what was meant to be simply a more effective means for achieving this ideal. The specific principle at the base of Reinhold's system, and the deductions that he had offered from that base, turned out to encounter immediate objections just as severe as those made against Kant himself. In particular, no one was convinced that Reinhold had come close to solving the problem of skepticism, for it was all too easy to object that the notion of representation alone could not establish a meaningful reality, a thing beyond whatever is merely within one's own representation.[13]

There are many ambiguities, complications, and modifications in Fichte's work, but on my reading his basic strategy is to be understood as a matter of trying to solve Reinhold's problems by relying – again with some stimulus from formulations found within Kant's work – on a radical principle of the "primacy of the practical." Against those who would object that *theoretically* we cannot know, or establish with logical certainty, that there are objects beyond our representations, the Fichtean responds that it is enough if "we can't but believe" in our free action, since from this belief alone there immediately arises a commitment to external objects as needed in order to make sense of our "practical," that is, moral intentions. Theoretical skepticism is dismissed as irrelevant, and the methodological characteristics of certainty, deducibility from a privileged base, unity, exhaustiveness, and systematicity are all said to be saved from the perspective of a philosophy that claims to reflect the immediate certainty of an active "I" (a "Tathandlung" rather than a "Tatsache") and of a "primacy of practice" that is already present in our everyday lives.

This Fichtean emphasis on the practical has ramifications that are crucial at a number of levels. It is helpful to distinguish at least three different dimensions of the effect of turning to a radical "primacy of the practical":

(1) Fichte's specific use of the strategy and its immediate consequences in furthering the eclipse of Kant's own program in Jena and the cultural world determined by it;[14]

(2) the way that this strategy provoked the reaction of Hegel (and then the counterreaction of left-wing Hegelianism), who understandably criticized the "subjective" one-sidedness of a "merely practical" foundation, and then claimed in effect that the desiderata of the ambitious type of idealist system that Reinhold introduced could be met after all, albeit through an elaborate speculative substitute for the details of Reinhold's own approach and especially for his simple notion of representation; in this way, the third and final major phase in the early reception of Kant – and hence the tone of most later assumptions about Critical philosophy – remained, on my interpretation, determined not so much by the key structures of Kant's own work as rather by the dialectic of developments in the often forgotten Reinhold-Fichte period;[15]

(3) the general philosophical idea of a "primacy of the practical," which is defended today not only by well-known radical pragmatists (e.g., Richard Rorty) but also by leading Kant interpreters (Henry E. Allison, Christine Korsgaard, and, to a lesser degree, Allen Wood[16]), who advocate a version of the Critical philosophy that often understands Kant's own claims not as grounded in pure theoretical doctrines but rather as simply expressing ideas in terms of which "we can't help but" think or act.

These topics each deserve much more space than is available here. I will focus on one recent interpretation of Fichte by Allen Wood ("The 'I' as Principle of Practical Philosophy," hereafter "Wood") that bears directly on issues in areas (1) and (3), and provides a notable paradigm of precisely the kind of very influential perspective, common to interpreters in the late eighteenth century as well as the late twentieth century, for which I am proposing an alternative. But before assessing Wood's analysis, it is necessary to fill out some of the essential Kantian background of the issues at stake here.

I.2

All discussions of the primacy of the practical in this era stand, implicitly if not explicitly, under the momentous influence of Kant's introduction in the *Critique of Practical Reason* (Chap. I, part 7) of the peculiar notion of a "fact of reason" as central to morality and to the idea of freedom that he says (on the first page of the second *Critique*'s Preface) constitutes the "keystone" of his system. This "fact of reason" is said to be a "fact" because it is not derived from something prior to it, that is, something meant as acceptable to a completely neutral audience, such as the bare notion of judgment; and yet it is "of reason" because it is understood to be given to us not through contingencies of feeling but from part of our general and essential, albeit not merely theoretical, character as a rational agent.

In the first *Critique,* Kant had constructed an entire theoretical system, a global transcendental idealism (expanding the doctrine of the ideality of space and time in his Dissertation to a doctrine of the ideality of all our determinate theoretical knowledge), to make room for at least the *possibility* of asserting human freedom in an absolute rather than relative or compatibilistic sense. At that time, however, he did not work out a positive argument for human freedom, and he even skipped over discussion of the issue at the natural place for it in the Paralogisms. The dense final part (III) of his *Groundwork of the Metaphysics of Morals* (1784) finally addresses the issue of freedom's *actuality* by directly confronting the worry that our belief in such freedom, which Kant took to be essential to our very notion of morality, might be a mere "figment of the brain" (*Hirngespinst*). The argument of part III of the *Groundwork,* for all its ambiguities and obscurities, clearly presents itself as a deduction of freedom, as an argument that defends the assertion of human freedom from the starting point of general considerations such as the mere (supposedly "spontaneous") nature of judgment, considerations that do not themselves already contain practical and especially controversial moral presumptions in any "thick" Kantian sense. It is therefore a very striking shift when, in returning to the issue just a few years later in the second *Critique* (1788; the main point was anticipated in the second edition preface of the first *Critique,* 1787), Kant eschews reference to his earlier *Groundwork* argument, chooses to speak of a mere "confirmation" of freedom, and insists (Preface, note 1) that morality and the freedom which it requires rather has its sole *ratio cognoscendi* in the "fact of reason," that is, the authority of our pure *practical* reason.[17]

There are many different interpretations of these difficult texts, but one obvious approach is to take the texts at face value and to see Kant as retreating from an initial "strong" or foundational argument for freedom, one that would supposedly address even skeptics about morality, and as falling back on a moderate or "coherentist" argument that relies on the "fact" of what is already found in what is supposed to be our common moral reason. (One might compare this shift with an analogous – but only analogous – move in John Rawls' work from the arguments in the *Theory of Justice,* that are meant as relevant for nearly all practical agents, to the considerations in later works such as *Political Liberalism,* that appear to be aimed primarily at members of a certain kind of modern liberal society.) Rather than engaging in another full-scale discussion of these very controversial texts, here I will only make one observation regarding a scruple that might be raised against the present interpretation. Against the worry that Kant could not have made such a momentous reversal so quickly without marking it out even more clearly, it is worth knowing that considerable evidence has now been assembled that shows Kant went through several significant shifts in his treatment of major metaphysical issues, and especially freedom, from his early precritical period, through his lectures in the 1770s, to the time of the first *Critique* itself.[18] It is striking, for example, that he starts as a compatibilist, shifts without explanation to a vigorous anticompatibilism, and then presents strong dogmatic arguments for freedom (in his lectures) which he later chooses totally to ignore rather than repeat, let alone criticize or modify, in the first *Critique*. Somewhat similar key shifts can be found also in later aspects of Kant's thought, such as the very idea of a separate second or third *Critique*. At one point such studies seemed to be excluded or unnecessary for transcendental philosophy; and then in work very soon thereafter they were presented as essential to the Critical program.

   Many important contemporary philosophers would nonetheless dispute the sharp contrast drawn here in Kant between an early deduction that moves from broadly theoretical considerations *to* morality and a categorical assertion of freedom, and a later mere "confirmation" that moves *from* a moral fact of reason to simply an unpacking of freedom and other ideas supposedly implicit in the practical perspective that comes with that fact. One way to minimize this contrast would be to contend that the second *Critique* itself offers something that is still tantamount to a deduction of freedom,[19] but a more widespread strategy is to take the opposite approach and to contend that Kant in fact does not and need not ever claim to be giving a strict deduction of the actuality of freedom. On this strategy, it is enough if Kant can be taken always to be reminding us simply that "from a practical point of view" we "must regard" ourselves as spontaneous and thus as ultimately subject to strict moral standards. Henry Allison, for example, has suggested that we should read Kant's ethics as not making any metaphysical claims about transcendent powers but as making only a "conceptual" point about how we regard ourselves as agents.[20] This is an especially appealing strategy for his popular type of Kant interpretation because (unlike Wood and some more traditional interpreters here) Allison also takes even many components of Kant's theoretical philosophy to express what is merely a "conceptual distinction" between points of view. Thus, "phenomena" and "noumena" do not stand for two possibly distinct realms of objects but rather indicate what are simply different ways, roughly epistemic and nonepistemic, of considering a realm of empirical objects that implies nothing about anything transcendent. Christine Korsgaard and other Rawlsian neo-Kantians appear to endorse a similar strategy, for example, when Korsgaard argues that questions of personal identity for a Kantian are not a matter of absolute metaphysical status but depend rather on one's practical perspective.[21] For many readers, it understandably seems much easier, for both internal and external reasons, to defend Kant's philosophy when it is taken to back away from any traditional metaphysical and transcendent claims.[22]

Nonetheless, without claiming that Kant's own position can be easily defended, I would argue that in this area metaphysical considerations are inescapable, and for reasons both external and internal to Kant's work. Externally, it is hard to see how any philosopher today can flatly assert that "we must regard ourselves as free," even if only from "a practical perspective." If the "must" is meant to record a mere psychological fact, it goes against the deep attachment to spontaneity that Kantians usually insist on, and in any case it is directly contradicted by the army of nonlibertarian philosophers (growing ever larger since Hume's day, and certainly well known to Kant) who not only argue that their philosophy denies we are free (in Kant's noncompatibilist sense) but who also observe, accurately enough, that in daily life people in general seem to get along quite well without a belief in absolute freedom. People do use and need a belief in their own agency, but the thought that they can and do act does not entail that there is, or even that they must believe there is, nothing acting on them. Of course, this does not settle the metaphysical issue of freedom, but it does show how in the end Kant's arguments become extraordinary weak if they are taken in this way to rest on dubious psychological presumptions. On the other hand, if it is said that we "must" believe in absolute freedom simply because this is a *normative* (rather than psychological) implication of a "genuine" moral perspective, then this simply begs the issue with Kant's opponents in moral theory, and at most points to where the real discussion has to begin.

There are not only external difficulties for the position that we must merely "regard ourselves as free"; it is hard to square this reading with central concerns internal to Kant's system. One can ask: What is the *point* of this belief that we supposedly must have in freedom, what exactly is it that can't be captured by compatibilism, especially for philosophers who (unlike Kant himself on my reading) refuse to assert that there literally are any "metaphysical powers," that is, sources of agency not governed by the rules we take to cover the empirical domain? Here the talk of freedom seems like a wheel turning idly – whereas if one thinks that the idea of freedom is *not merely* part of our "conceptual standpoint" but designates an actual and separate power, then it at least involves an ineliminable existential claim. And not only is a literal notion of nonempirical agency something that would give talk of freedom a real reference and point, it appears to be clearly what Kant himself had in view. In the first *Critique* he talks explicitly of absolutely spontaneous and nontemporal sources of action, and the natural way to understand his argument in the third Antinomy is precisely as making room for some real causation that would transcend whatever action we can know empirically.[23] Confusions may arise here for readers who do not see that when Kant relies in the second *Critique* on a "fact of reason" as the ground for freedom, he is not denying a commitment to the *truth* that we have nontemporal agency, nor is he saying "we merely believe" we have such freedom. Rather, he holds explicitly that there *is a fact* here and we can be certain about it; it is just that we should not any longer suggest that we might be in the epistemic position of being able to *derive* this fact from neutral theoretical considerations, for example, the general features of judgment cited in the *Groundwork*.

All this does leave Kant in a position that makes him not only unable to defeat a moral skeptic but also weighted down by a literal belief in nonempirical agency that can embarrass many contemporaries who share an attachment to much of the content of his strict morality. There is a problem here, but I believe it is a problem that is not *much* worse than those that other philosophical systems have when faced with fundamental questions. There is a special difficulty for Kant, however, which arises from the fact that in some places he appeared to concede that a stronger reply to skepticism was *needed here,* and to suggest that he could provide such a reply. His own abandoned adventure of an argument, a categorical deduction of morality and freedom in the *Groundwork,* naturally generates the suspicion that on its own grounds Kant's final moral philosophy is insufficient. To start by calling for a deduction to defeat skepticism, and to end by relying on a "fact" is to raise and frustrate expectations that others would naturally want to see satisfied. I believe that these expectations, and the keen interest in Kant's moral philosophy from the period of its first reception, go a long way in helping to explain the incredibly intense search, after Kant, for a philosophy with an absolute foundation – that is, the remarkable Reinholdian phase noted earlier, and its strong influence on all later phases of reaction to Kant. Note, however, that while Kant's own philosophy, on my reading, naturally engenders this search for such a foundation, the *content* of his moral theory alone does not clearly require it. Kantians concerned merely with this content could have rested with moral experience as simply a fact of commonsense-like theoretical experience; in this way the projects of the first and second *Critiques* could have been accepted as having a parallel and relatively modest structure. But a peculiar combination of circumstances in the Idealist era stood in the way of such a common sense approach. Three factors were especially important:

(1) Kant's own belief in metaphysical powers as not only actual but essential to our picture of ourselves as agents (i.e., as free agents in a system that excludes compatibilism and takes nature to be governed by Newtonian laws) was responsible for keeping alive a drive for some kind of metaphysical system.

(2) The association of Kant's work with Hume, and a natural misunderstanding of its theoretical ambitions, reinvigorated the disastrous thought that Kant's philosophy, like earlier modern philosophy, has to be evaluated primarily from the perspective of how well it can answer radical skepticism.

(3) The tumultuous cultural circumstances of late eighteenth-century Germany, combined with Kant's own talk about instituting a new era of scientific philosophy and rational society, generated the thought that to lead and preserve such an era philosophy required an immediate certainty and exhaustive scope, a form that alone could give it the irreversible attachment not only of specialists but of the whole public of the Enlightenment.

II

All these background considerations provide a framework for challenging Wood's highly sympathetic interpretation of Fichte. Wood begins by presenting Fichte's system as set up to overcome two now familiar "problems" in Kant's allegedly incomplete transcendental philosophy (Wood, sec. I): the problem of meeting *skepticism* (discussed below in sec. II.1), and the problem of providing a *unity* of theoretical and practical philosophy (see sec. II.2 below). The Fichtean notion of the "I" as a fundamental "practical principle" is explicitly introduced as the key to resolving both of these problems. In discussing the *transition* in Fichte's presentation of his system between 1794 and 1798, Wood argues that, contrary to what can seem to be the case, these changes do not point to any major shift in Fichte's orientation (Wood, sec. III; see sec. II.3 below). Wood also argues, against other interpreters, that Fichte's reliance on the "I" as a practical principle is not simply formal but is closely connected with a substantive and attractive approach to *morality* (Wood, sec. IV; see sec. II.4 below).

My interpretation implies an alternative view on each of these issues. Briefly, on the first two issues – of skepticism and unity – my contention is that Fichte does not – and should not be trying to – improve on Kant. On the issue of a transition in Fichte's approach, I argue, contra Wood, that after 1794 Fichte's work does involve a significant and not adequately appreciated move to a more radical position, a position that gives a clearer but still problematic expression to the doctrine of the primacy of the practical. Finally, I argue that an excessive stress on the practical also causes problems for some of Wood's claims on behalf of the content of Fichte's moral theory.

II.1

Wood properly reminds us that Fichte's philosophy is designed as an attempt to provide a transcendental philosophy that, unlike Kant's, would be fully "scientific," because it would be absolutely certain, systematic, and complete. As I just have argued, hints of a such an approach come from Kant himself, but it is Reinhold who deserves the main credit – and blame – for issuing the call for such a philosophy. Fichte, as he himself admitted, was simply – and extremely effectively – responding to this call. It is also striking that, like Fichte, Reinhold was motivated to insist on such a special scientific philosophy because he thought it was the only way to achieve essential practical ends. Without an *unshakable* Critical philosophy in place, he feared nothing could prevent a reversal of the Enlightenment; the very "fate of reason" supposedly rested in the capacity of philosophy to resolve its disputes in a decisive and anti-metaphysical fashion.[24] That is, Reinhold saw that in attempting to replace the dogmatic schools of pre-Kantian philosophy with a Critical system, he had to meet the objection, pressed very strongly at the time, that philosophy was a scene of constant vacillation and that its claims to have achieved radical reform deserved a cynical response. Reinhold's strategy was to stress that Kant had finally established limits for our knowledge that in principle block any reversion to the old schools, and that he had done this in a way that could be reformulated in terms of principles that were not only universally valid (*allgemeingeltend*) but also universally evident (*allgemeingültig*).

In retrospect, this wild inflation of the accomplishments, goals, and value of philosophy is all too understandable in an era when, in addition to all the other crises of the time, relatively large groups of people first seriously aimed to make a living from the suspicious enterprise of secular reflection – and hence were especially motivated to show that it is indispensable to others.[25] But the initiator of the Critical philosophy had a more modest view of the role of his own work. Kant would often appeal to common claims that he (naively, we would now say) assumed no sane person of his time would put in real doubt. Such claims included the fundamentals of mathematics and logic, the general fact that there is "experience," that is, a warranted determination of empirical objects, and also the fact that we acknowledge categorical demands of morality. Kant understood transcendental philosophy to be an a priori account of these assumptions, an account that would appreciate the metaphysical complexities of alternative views, and that would offer its own framework as the best way "to save the phenomena" and to keep people from abandoning common sense in the face of modern philosophical perplexities. Often Kant's own "account" was quite limited, as when it claimed merely that transcendental idealism alone would allow us at least to accept – but not "explain" – both the absolute freedom that he insisted morality calls for, as well as the universal causality that he argued experience requires. I have called Kant's philosophy "modest" because he was willing to live with limitations. From the beginning of his career, he had maintained that sometimes it is enough if philosophy can show a way in which what we have always believed to be the case – for example, that we act imputably, or that there is genuine interaction – can at least be held to be not demonstrably impossible and to cohere well with a feasible metaphysical framework.[26] Obviously such an approach does not provide an absolutely self-evident foundation and so will not satisfy the traditional skeptic. Such a skeptic can point out that the "facts" to be accounted for are, theoretically at least, still disputable, and that the particular account offered for them surely lacks absolute certainty. Since Kant's own account ultimately was so highly metaphysical — transcendental idealism is anything but a given of common sense — it is no wonder that someone like Fichte, seeking irreversible radical change and trained by a scholar of skepticism (G. E. Schulze), would be convinced by Reinhold's ideal of philosophy, and would seek to find a foundation that, unlike Kant's own very controversial system (especially after it had been attacked as incoherent by Jacobi), would appear truly beyond dispute.

Kant was long familiar with, and opposed to, the project of attempting to derive all philosophy from one principle. He was consistent, for example, in mocking the Wolffians who thought that substantive conclusions could be derived from meager analytic premises, and that all the powers of the mind could be reduced to one basic faculty (cf. also his discussion of the general emptiness of Wolffian ontology based on the idea of "a" first principle of being[27]). Although he did not take the time to criticize Fichte's approach in detail, Kant did explicitly repudiate Fichte's system,[28] and I believe he would have pointed to similar problems with the first principle of the *Wissenschaftslehre,* that "the I posits itself absolutely."

Wood provides us with two more specific formulations of Fichte's principle, or, more precisely, of what is certain in the "I" that Fichte at first puts at the basis of philosophy. The first of these is the claim that "the self of which we are aware is nothing different from the awareness we have of it" (Wood, sec. I). The second is that this "I" has "ubiquity," such that we are and always can be aware of it in the "free act through which self-consciousness [presumably of a nonreflective sort] comes about" (Wood, sec. I). There are difficulties with each of these formulations, difficulties Kant surely would have stressed. The first formula has the problem of content; to the extent that it is allowed, to that very extent it must not be assumed to refer to anything other than itself. If the "self" that we are aware of is to be absolutely certain and really equivalent to the "awareness" of it, then as such it cannot be understood in terms of hidden or nontransparently contained aspects. Such a "self," when it exists, may be a fact not to be denied, but that does not mean that anything substantive follows from it alone, or that it has to exist. The second formula tries to provide some way out of this difficulty by claiming that this self can be brought about at any time and freely. These are new claims with strong content, but taken that way they immediately lose certainty. How do we know that this self can be brought about at *any* time? Reference to the past is no help now, and reference to our ability to reflect is also irrelevant, since this claim is about the prereflective self (cf. the example of certainty that one is reading, Wood, sec. II). Moreover, how do we *know,* when the act is brought about, that it is ever truly free, not determined by anything beyond the immediate act? It is no accident that although Kant focused on the act of thinking, he usually was very careful and backed off from any such tempting but dogmatic assertions. And it is no accident that he saw the futility of claiming to bury skepticism by trying to do without any substantive premises. To get content, one has to start with content, and the advantage Kant claimed is simply that his initial content came from what nonphilosophers already accepted. Having appreciated Hume, he saw that one cannot just immediately help oneself to certain claims of freedom at a philosophical or prephilosophical level.

II.2

Precisely to cope with these severe problems, problems which the theoretical skeptic will press eagerly, Fichteans move on quickly to saying that their disputed formulas must be taken in some "practical" sense. Wood sees that this was done initially with an eye to saving the project of a fully "scientific" first philosophy that maintains a strong unity of reason: "Once it is accepted that transcendental philosophy as a doctrine of science must begin with a single fundamental principle . . . the only way to deal with the problem is to discover a first principle which can serve simultaneously as the ground of both theoretical and practical philosophy" (Wood, sec. I). Note that one might rather have argued that the very absoluteness of the claim of freedom in (Kantian) practical philosophy is what provides a *reductio* for the notion of such "a single fundamental principle." That is, one might allow, as I have noted that Kant himself certainly did, that the claim to freedom is a special claim about a very special "fact," a "fact of reason" that theoretical philosophy, or whatever might underlie it, can never derive but rather can only assume – and if that defeats the project of a strong unity of reason, so much the worse for the tradition that is attached to such a project. Wood's Fichtean response is just the opposite, however; he asks how we can save a strong unity of reason by finding something about practical reason, or some common root with theoretical reason, that would still give us certainty and content at once. It is in this way that, in Wood's nondissenting words, "Fichte claims to have demonstrated what Kant had only postulated, that reason can be practical" (Wood, sec. II).

The claim that "reason can be practical," however, which is at issue *here,* surely must be understood in Kantian terms – for otherwise Fichte could not be demonstrating "what Kant . . . postulated" – and clearly Kant's claim is a claim about *pure* practical reason. That is, it is a claim that morality and its presumed absolute freedom is not impossible, is not a hoax, that we are not mere "turnspits" of however complex a form. Just how is it that Fichte can "demonstrate" such a strong claim?

What Wood reminds us of here is that Fichte has a story to tell about the active/passive distinction, a story to the effect that this distinction need not be simply assumed, as it is by Kant, but that it can be argued to be a condition of the self's certain self-awareness. In "forming a concept" of itself, the self supposedly must be aware of a nonself that it posits as a contrast with itself, and as not to be abolished, so that in constantly practically "striving" with it, self-consciousness can be maintained (Wood, sec. II). This is an interesting story, and it points to a central function that a kind of practical activity *can* have in the life of the self. But there are many things that this story still does *not* do. It does not show that the conditions of the process of forming a concept of a self, whatever they are, are themselves absolutely certain (for precisely on Fichte's own view, such a reflective activity is not primary). It also does not show that the "not-self" that is posited in this process is anything more than an idea within the self, that is, it is not shown that this "passivity" is "other" in ultimate reality and not simply in immediate intention. More important, it does nothing to show that the "practical striving" involved here is of a specifically moral sort at all. And, most important, it does not begin to show that the activity involved, whatever it contrasts with, and however it is oriented, is a genuinely free activity, undetermined from outside. But until it shows all these things, it has hardly "demonstrated" that "reason is practical" in the relevant sense.

Wood does provide an extra citation that bears on the claim that the self is genuinely free, and not simply active in some not clearly relevant sense. In an initial attempt to reformulate the *Wissenschaftslehre,* Fichte says that one can "directly note activity and freedom in this thinking," that is, in the transition from one thought to another (Wood, sec. II).[29] But one can't help but immediately ask, just how did this claim about "freedom" get in here, especially when one is supposed to be allowing only claims that are certain? Even if we are *not aware* that we are being determined, why should we presume – and how can we "directly note" – that we are *not* being determined?[30]

At this point it is appropriate to look at another transition of thought – this time the transition in Fichte's own presentation of his system, which on my interpretation was developed precisely as the weight of these difficulties began to be appreciated.

II.3

Following Neuhouser,[31] Wood notes that in the new "Introductions" for the *Wissenschaftslehre* in 1797 Fichte moved toward a different way of expressing the foundation of his philosophy. The original formulation of the *Wissenschaftslehre* (1794) aimed to demonstrate that "reason cannot even be theoretical unless it is practical" (cited at Wood, sec. III, n. 4).[32] This passage expresses the original ambitious idea that any mere state of awareness had by a self brings with it enough to provide a *proof* that "reason is practical." By 1797, however, "whereas the earlier system made the practical power of reason into an object of demonstration, the later system grounds itself directly on the original act (*Tathandlung*) through which the free I posits itself" (Wood, sec. III). In this way the "first principle" becomes an initial "postulate" after all, and no longer provides a supposedly absolute "demonstration" that overcomes the need for all postulates.

After drawing attention to this transition, Wood plays it down somewhat, but I would argue that its significance cannot be overemphasized. Wood holds that in both stages "the 'I' . . . was always regarded as fundamentally a practical rather than a theoretical principle" (Wood, sec. III). Methodologically, this seems to me to be a misleading way of putting things. It is true that in both stages of his thought here Fichte claims to give a major role to what he understands as a practical aspect of the "I." But in a situation where epistemic and foundational relations have been made the main focus, as they clearly have been in Fichte's concern for "science," everything hangs on the *order* of considerations. It is one thing to start, as Fichte does initially, with something not characterized as practical, and *then* to move toward the practical as its demonstrated ground; and it is something else to start, as Fichte does later, with something *already* characterized as definitely practical (a *Tathandlung*). Very loosely speaking, both procedures could be described, because of their goals, as sympathetic to a "primacy of the practical," but *in the order of reasoning* (as opposed to the order of being or value) the first procedure precisely does not give primacy to the practical. Rather, it aims to demonstrate "the practical" from something else that is given as absolutely first for us.

Although Fichte's transition to an explicitly practical starting point gives up his original version of a fully scientific philosophy, this shift is quite understandable on my interpretation. The shift responds directly to appreciating the difficulties noted earlier with his original project. For those who were asking, exactly how does one know that one really is free, the Fichtean now can say, this is not claimed to be a matter of demonstration, it is simply something that comes with one's practical orientation – an idealist just is a person who *believes* in his or her freedom and works *from* that "interest." Such a standpoint is formulated most clearly in works such as Fichte's *Vocation of Man* (1800), which focuses right on the very kind of experiences that Fichte mentioned before – the "acts" of thinking and planning – and then (in Part III) argues that while these might well seem to prove one's freedom, they do no such thing;[33] freedom is rather disclosed only as a matter of "faith." Moreover, in his later expositions, Fichte becomes much clearer that not just any "practical" premise can work as a starting point – he insists that only contexts in which one is sensitive to a categorical moral "ought" bring with them the claim of absolute freedom.

In what seems to be an attempt to tone down the implications of this shift, Wood points out various ways in which Fichte is not resorting to a blind leap of "faith" (Wood, sec. III). Wood reminds us how, in the Introductions, Fichte argues that the idealist philosophy of freedom has the advantage both of apparently fitting subjective experience and also of being able to offer some explanations from its perspective – which "dogmatism" and its mysteriously posited thing in itself cannot do. While Fichte's arguments here surely could be challenged, it must be granted that they do at least *aim* to show that there is *something* even *non*practical to be said *for* freedom, and apparently nothing to be said against it.[34] Nonetheless, on Fichte's own account the considerations do *not* defeat skepticism, and so, contra Wood, they hardly vindicate the idea of an "*absolutely certain* first principle" (Wood, sec. III). Moreover, although it is true that the considerations are hardly idiosyncratic or "blind" but rather recapitulate the familiar universal perspective of Kantian pure practical reason, they do give up on the autonomy of reason in one crucial respect. When Kant resorted to the "fact of reason" to let in the claim of freedom, he did so only after a prior theoretical investigation that aimed to show how, despite appearances, a thoroughly deterministic framework was not metaphysically required for us. Without such an investigation, he conceded that the move to "practical faith" would be illegitimate, irresponsible in the face of our apparent knowledge.[35] Fichte unfortunately does not make such an essential prior investigation. He seems to be presuming that since there are difficulties with a determinism rooted in some kind of absurd notion of a thing in itself, then all theoretical considerations can be outweighed by our practical interest. But this is to sell theory much too short, and to leap blindly after all to a radical primacy of the practical. The specific problems of the thing in itself (exaggerated in any case) still do not show that even in the domain of experience the only evidence we have is for freedom. A growing appreciation for this point, and for the strength of a kind of a Humean view, may have influenced the more explicit reliance on faith that Fichte came to acknowledge in Part III of the *Vocation of Man*.

II.4

Wood contends in the end that Fichte's principle of the "I" is to be supported because it is "not originally and fundamentally a cognitive standpoint at all . . . [and] no clear content can be given to the idea of a self understood only theoretically" (Wood, sec. IV). Here too there are highly controversial claims about the practical, claims typical of contemporary neo-Kantian pragmatism. Wood suggests, for example, that identity of the self over time is not a "deep metaphysical fact" but rather rests on the "fact that my body is the fundamental vehicle of my agency" (Wood, sec. IV).[36] But how is it that reference to a "body," of all things, no longer counts as "cognitive"? And why should even the mere "requirements of agency" have to bring in a noncognitive perspective? To act, we typically do need to plan and to think of ends, of what we believe we can do and even of what we think we should do, which is itself also a fact – but, again, as Fichte himself clearly argued in the *Vocation of Man,* all this is still possible without accepting that "reason is practical" in the relevant and deep sense that already entails absolute agency and moral freedom.

These worries do not affect the claims of Wood and others that Fichte's *System der Sittenlehre* and *Grundlage des Naturrechts*[37] have a rich normative content and improve on Kant's system in various significant ways, especially with a new proposal that we regard moral knowledge as a "quest for systematic agreement among moral conceptions" (Wood, sec. V). It is not at all clear, though, that this account follows from, rather than at best simply "fits," Fichte's general reflections on an active "I." Moreover, the account is difficult even to reconcile with his earlier and strongly foundational notion of philosophy as a science. Most important, as Wood himself suggests, and as I have documented elsewhere in an analysis of these very texts,[38] the *central* passages of these works do nothing to take back Fichte's notion of a radical primacy of the practical but rather give it a classical expression. To the extent that this notion remains highly problematic, the major methodological shift from Kant to Fichte remains anything other than a matter of clear philosophical progress, however attractive it may have seemed at first and however influential it has become again.[39]

Notes

1. My main focus will be on Allen Wood's chapter, "The 'I' as Principle of Practical Philosophy" (this volume), but see also his "Fichte's Philosophical Revolution," *Philosophical Topics* 19 (1991): 1–28, and "Autonomy in Kant and Fichte," presented at a conference at the University of Indiana, September 1997. See also Frederick Neuhouser, *Fichte's Theory of Subjectivity* (Cambridge, U.K.: Cambridge University Press, 1990); and Robert Pippin, *Hegel's Idealism: The Satisfactions of Self-Consciousness* (Cambridge, U.K.: Cambridge University Press, 1989), and *Idealism as Modernism* (Cambridge: Cambridge University Press, 1997). These discussions correspond to some important works by German scholars, for example, Dieter Henrich, *Fichtes ursprüngliche Einsicht* (Frankfurt am Main: Klostermann, 1967), and "The Identity of the Subject in the Transcendental Deduction," in *Reading Kant,* ed. E. Schaper and W. Vossenkuhl (Oxford: Blackwell, 1989), pp. 250–80; Manfred Frank, *Selbstbewusstsein und Selbsterkenntnis* (Stuttgart: Reclam, 1991), and (ed.) *Selbstbewusstseinstheorien von Fichte bis Sartre* (Frankfurt am Main: Suhrkamp Verlag, 1991).
2. See my discussion of Henrich in "Kant and Guyer on Apperception," *Archiv für Geschichte der Philosophie* 65 (1983): 174–86, and in "Kant and the Self: A Retrospective," *Figuring the Self,* ed. D. Klemm and G. Zöller (Albany: State University of New York Press, 1997), pp. 55–72; of Neuhouser in "Kant and the Self"; of Frank in "The Ineliminable Subject: From Kant to Frank," in *The Modern Subject: Concep-*

tions of the Self in Classical German Philosophy, ed. K. Ameriks and D. Sturma (Albany: State University of New York Press, 1995), pp. 217–30; and of Pippin in "Hegel and Idealism," *Monist* 74 (1991): 386–402. The broadest presentation of my interpretation of the era is in "Kant, Fichte, and Short Arguments to Idealism," *Archiv für Geschichte der Philosophie* 72 (1990): 63–85.

3. See my "Fichte's Appeal Today: The Hidden Primacy of the Practical," in *The Emergence of German Idealism,* ed. M. Baur and D. Dahlstrom (Washington: Catholic University of America Press, 1999). This article discusses passages in Fichte's *Vocation of Man* (1800), the two "introductions" to his first *Wissenschaftslehre* (1797), *System der Sittlichkeit* (1798), and *Grundlage des Naturrechts* (1796). It explains also how my reading is close to but differs slightly from interpretations by D. Breazeale and A. Perrinjaquet. For a somewhat similar recent reading, cf. also Peter Rohs, *Johann Gottlieb Fichte* (Munich: Beck, 1991), p. 128.

4. See for example, Schelling's typical and influential thoughts about Kant's philosophy as still being hostage to the age of absolutism, *Sämtliche Werke,* ed. K. F. A. Schelling (Stuttgart, 1856–), I: 157f.

5. See above, note 1, and Frederick Beiser, *The Fate of Reason* (Cambridge, Mass.: Harvard University Press, 1987); Rolf-Peter Horstmann, *Die Grenzen der Vernunft: eine Untersuchung zu Zielen und Motiven des Deutschen Idealismus* (Frankfurt am Main: Hain, 1991). See also D. Breazeale, "Fichte and Schelling: The Jena Period," in The Routledge History of Philosophy, *The Age of German Idealism,* vol. VI, ed. R. Solomon and K. Higgins (London: Routledge, 1993), pp. 138–60. It should be acknowledged that most recent writing in this area draws heavily on the research into the Jena period generated by Dieter Henrich's extensive work.

6. For a reading of Hegel in this context, see my "Recent Work on Hegel: The Rehabilitation of an Epistemologist?" *Philosophy and Phenomenological Research* 52 (1992): 177–202. Unfortunately, here I must skip over not only many details within these main phases but also very significant developments in other related movements. For example, there is much to be said about the role of Schelling in mediating the transition from Fichte to Hegel. Also, it can be argued that in the later 1790s there emerged in Jena an important "early romantic" option (Novalis, the early F. Schlegel), soon covered over by other developments, that introduced a promising alternative to the overly ambitious approach to philosophy dominating the foundationalist line of thought from Reinhold to Fichte and after. See Manfred Frank, "Philosophical Foundations of Early Romanticism," *The Modern Subject,* pp. 65–85.

7. Reinhold's most widely read works were his letters on the *Critique,* which appeared first as essays in the *Teutscher Merkur,* 1786–7, and later as *Briefe über die Kantische Philosophie,* 2 vols. (Leipzig: Göschen, 1790, 1792). Other very relevant works are: *Versuch einer neuen Theorie des Vorstellungsvermögens* (Prague and Jena: Wiedtmann und Mautke, 1789), *Über das Fundament des philosophischen Wissens* (Jena, 1791), and *Beyträge zur Berichtigung bisheriger Missverständnisse der Philosophen. Erster Band das Fundament der Elementarphilosophie betreffend* (Jena, 1790). See my "Reinhold and the Short Argument to Idealism," in *Proceedings: Sixth International Kant Congress 1985,* ed. G. Funke and T. Seebohm (Washington: The Center for Advanced Research in Phenomenology and the University Press of America: 1989), vol. II, part 2, pp. 441–53; and D. Breazeale, "Between Kant and Fichte, Karl Leonhard Reinhold's 'Elementary Philosophy'," *Review of Metaphysics* 35 (1982): 785–821. For background on Reinhold's place in the whole period, see Sabine Roehr, *A Primer on the German Enlightenment: with a Translation of Karl Leonhard Reinhold's 'The Fundamental Concepts and Principles of*

Ethics' (Columbia: University of Missouri Press, 1995); and the very helpful translations of eighteenth-century German essays in the collection edited by James Schmidt, *What is Enlightenment? Eighteenth-Century Answers and Twentieth Century Questions* (Berkeley: University of California Press, 1996).

8. See my "Kant's Transcendental Deduction as a Regressive Argument," *Kant-Studien* 69 (1978): 273–85; "Recent Work on Kant's Theoretical Philosophy," *American Philosophical Quarterly,* 19 (1982): 1–24; and my reading of Kant's "Refutation of Idealism" in *Kant's Theory of Mind,* Chap. III.

9. See materials from the period in the important collection edited and translated by George di Giovanni and H. S. Harris, *Between Kant and Hegel: Texts in the Development of Post-Kantian Idealism* (Albany: State University of New York Press, 1985); and also F. H. Jacobi, *The Main Philosophical Writings and the Novel Allwill,* ed. and trans. by George di Giovanni (Montreal: McGill-Queen's University Press, 1994).

10. See especially the Prefaces and Introduction to Kant's *Critique of Pure Reason.*

11. The classical statement of the principle is: "In consciousness representation is distinguished through the subject from both object and subject and is referred to both," as translated in Reinhold, "The Foundation of Philosophical Knowledge," *Between Kant and Hegel,* p. 70.

12. See above, notes 3 and 7.

13. This development is reviewed in Daniel Breazeale, "Fichte's "Aenesidemus Review and the Transformation of German Idealism," *Review of Metaphysics* 34 (1981): 545–68.

14. For an especially interesting account of the Fichte period in Jena and its background, see Theodore Ziolkowski, *German Romanticism and its Institutions* (Princeton: Princeton University Press, 1990), Chap. 5.

15. See again the end of my "Kant, Fichte, and Short Arguments to Idealism."

16. See the essays collected in H. Allison, *Idealism and Freedom* (Cambridge, U.K.: Cambridge University Press, 1996), and C. Korsgaard, *Creating the Kingdom of Ends* (Cambridge, U.K.: Cambridge University Press, 1996), esp. Chap. 12, "Personal Identity and the Unity of Agency: A Kantian Response to Parfit." Cf. my review of Allison in *Philosophy and Phenomenological Research* (forthcoming); my critique of earlier work by Allison and Wood in "Kant and Hegel on Freedom: Two New Interpretations," *Inquiry* 35 (1992): 219–32; and my objections to "constructivist" readings of Kant's ethics in "On Schneewind and Kant's Method in Ethics," *Ideas y Valores* 102 (1996): 28–53.

17. This development is discussed in detail in my "Kant's Deduction of Freedom and Morality," *Journal of the History of Philosophy* 19 (1981): 53–79 (*Kant's Theory of Mind,* Chap. VI).

18. See my *Kant's Theory of Mind,* which is reinforced now by the materials available in *Kant's Lectures on Metaphysics,* ed. and trans. by Karl Ameriks and Steve Naragon, (Cambridge, U.K.: Cambridge University Press, 1997).

19. Wood appears sympathetic to a position like this at one point in his "Autonomy in Kant and Freedom." This line would be closer to the view of Lewis White Beck than to opposite line of interpreters such as H. J. Paton and Dieter Henrich (see my analysis of these options in work cited above, n. 17).

20. See above, note 16.

21. Again, see above, note 16. These interpretations obviously developed under the influence of John Rawls.

22. A major source for this kind of interpretive strategy is no doubt Kant's talk about presupposing freedom "merely as an idea," at *Groundwork,* 448n (using the stan-

dard Academy pagination). This passage requires a long explanation; for a start, see above, note 17.

23. For an excellent account of the coherence of Kant's position here (which still interprets Kant in straightforward metaphysical terms), see Wood, "Kant's Compatibilism," in *Self and Nature in Kant's Philosophy* (Ithaca: Cornell University Press, 1984), pp. 57–72.

24. This theme is explored in my review of *The Fate of Reason* by Frederick Beiser, *Philosophical Review* 98 (1989): 398–401. The title and structure of Beiser's book suggests the interesting but overly dramatic notion that the fate of reason itself rested on the progress of the philosophical disputes of the age. This notion actually was assumed by one important group of thinkers, but it was not the only option present in the era, and it does not correspond to Kant's own view.

25. See A. J. LaVopa, *Grace, Talent, and Merit: Poor Scholars, Clerical Careers, and Professional Ideology in Eighteenth Century Germany* (Cambridge, U.K.: Cambridge University Press, 1988); and Laurence Dickey, *Religion, Economics, and the Politics of Spirit, 1770–1807* (Cambridge, U.K.: Cambridge University Press, 1987).

26. See, for example, Kant's early remarks as noted in the Metaphysik Herder (Ak 28:6): "Thus one should begin with the most familiar and settled concepts of a matter, and go ever higher in derivation. If there later arise propositions that contradict common sense, then one should re-examine all the preceding arguments, and not, like Wolff, treat this as silly fantasy; and thus one could proceed with an uncommon modesty."

27. See Kant's remarks as noted in Metaphysik Mrongovius, now translated in *Kant's Lectures on Metaphysics*, p. 111 (Ak, 29:749).

28. See Kant's open letter repudiating Fichte, August 7, 1799 (Ak, 12:370–71).

29. The passage is from Fichte's "Chapter One of 'Attempt at a New Presentation of the Wissenschaftslehre'," ed. and trans. Daniel Breazeale, in J. G. Fichte, *Introductions to the Wissenschaftslehre and Other Writings 1797–1800* (Indianapolis: Hackett, 1994), p. 106 (*Johann Gottlieb Fichtes Sämmtliche Werke*, ed. I. H. Fichte [Berlin: Veit, 1845–6], I: 522).

30. This point is made explicitly by Kant, as noted in Metaphysik K3 in *Kant's Lectures on Metaphysics*, p. 490 (Ak, 29:1022), and is discussed in my "Kant on Spontaneity: Some New Data," *Proceedings of the VII International Kant-Kongress 1990* (Berlin: de Gruyter, 1991), pp. 436–46.

31. See the works cited in note 1 and note 2 above.

32. Fichte, *Sämmtliche Werke* I: 264.

33. I have discussed this text in detail elsewhere; see note 3 above.

34. This point is developed in a helpful paper by Andrew Lamb, "Fichte's 'Introductions' as Introductions to Certainty," *Idealistic Studies* 27 (1997): 193–215.

35. "If we grant that morality necessarily presupposes freedom in the strictest sense . . . and if at the same time we [were to] grant that speculative reason has proved that such freedom does not allow of being thought, then . . . morality would have to yield to the mechanism of nature." Kant, *Critique of Pure Reason*, B xxix.

36. This claim is explicitly linked to Korsgaard's work. See above, note 16. For a contrasting and more metaphysical view of the problem of personal identity in Kant, see my *Kant's Theory of Mind*, Chap. IV.

37. These important works are forthcoming in English editions by Günter Zöller and Frederick Neuhouser (with Michael Baur), in the Cambridge Texts in the History of Philosophy series.

38. See above, note 3.
39. I am indebted to others in ways that go far beyond what is indicated here. I am
thankful for much (uncited) work by members of the Dartmouth conference, for
special assistance from Sally Sedgwick, Steve Scher, Dieter Sturma, and also for
much help from discussions with Eric Watkins, Andrew Lamb, Patrick Kain, John
Davenport, and Patrick Frierson.

6

From Critique to Metacritique:
Fichte's Transformation of Kant's Transcendental Idealism[1]

GÜNTER ZÖLLER

Both systematically and historically, Fichte's *Wissenschaftslehre* represents a further development of Kant's Critical philosophy, prepared and inspired by the latter's earlier reception through Karl Leonhard Reinhold, Gottlob Ernst Schulze, Friedrich Heinrich Jacobi, and Salomon Maimon.[2] Fichte's relation to his illustrious predecessor is a curious mixture of unconditional allegiance and metacritical distancing. By applying such hermeneutical devices as the distinction between the letter (*Buchstabe*) and the spirit (*Geist*)[3] of an author's philosophical system and the separation of the system itself from its various presentations (*Darstellungen*), Fichte establishes a precarious balance between loyalty and patricide in his relationship to Kant. In so doing, Fichte is supported by Kant's own claim, originally raised with respect to Plato, that it is possible for an author to be better understood by someone else than by himself or herself.[4]

The basic direction of Fichte's move with Kant beyond Kant points toward a completion of what is prepared, begun and partially executed in the latter's Critical philosophy. Fichte's project aims both at a more radical foundation and at a more extensive elaboration of the investigation of reason initiated by Kant, thereby integrating Kant's work in the three *Critiques* into a comprehensive, systematically unified account of (finite) reason. In drawing on Kant's own architectonic distinction between the "propaedeutic" and the "system of pure reason,"[5] Fichte asserts his claim of transforming the "*critique* of pure reason" into the "*system of pure reason*," which, he maintains, Kant never provided.[6]

Yet in spite of the assignment of Kant's Critical philosophy, and specifically the *Critique of Pure Reason,* to a mere preliminary stage of the *Wissenschaftslehre,* Fichte does not give up the Kantian project of preparing the ground for philosophy proper by way of introductory considerations, specifically designed to orient the reader about the task, subject matter, and method of philosophy.[7] On the contrary, the first major phase of Fichte's work on the *Wissenschaftslehre* (1793–1800), roughly coinciding with his professorship at Jena (1794–9), is characterized by a parallel process of critical or introductory writings and systematic writings. Fichte's sustained theorizing *about* the *Wissenschaftslehre* accompanies the development of the *Wissenschaftslehre* during the Jena years like a running commentary in which he articulates the nature of his philosophical project with increasing clarity as well as polemical force.

At the center of Fichte's critical thinking about the *Wissenschaftslehre* stands the conception of transcendental idealism as the doctrinal core that assures the ultimate identity of his system with that of Kant. Occasioned by the misinterpretations and misunderstandings that the *Wissenschaftslehre* encountered upon its first appearance, Fichte advances a self-interpretation of transcendental idealism that combines insight into the origin of transcendental-idealist reasoning with the recognition of the extension and specifically the limits of all such thinking. Fichte thus supplements Kant's critical investigation of the possibility of objective knowledge and its systematic completion in the *Wissenschaftslehre* through a critical investigation of philosophical knowledge itself, thereby radicalizing the project of philosophical critique from philosophy's critique of the knowledge of objects to the metacritique of philosophical knowledge.

While much work has been done on Fichte's doctrinal extensions and revisions of Kant's transcendental philosophy, the methodological and meta-philosophical issues that inform Fichte's relation to Kant have not yet received sufficient attention. The present essay, which is designed to fill that lacuna, compares and contrasts the status and function of transcendental idealism in Kant and Fichte. It is organized in three sections. The first assesses the role of transcendental idealism in Kant's Critical philosophy. The second examines Fichte's self-interpretation of the *Wissenschaftslehre* as a system of transcendental idealism. This middle section is based on Fichte's programmatic brochure *On the Concept of the Wissenschaftslehre* (1794) as well as the (so-called First) Introduction to the fragmentary *Attempt at a New Presentation of the Wissenschaftslehre* (1797). The concluding section examines Fichte's meta-critical assessment of transcendental idealism in the *Crystal-Clear Report to the General Public on the Essence of the Newest Philosophy* (1801). In articulating the methodological differences between Kant's and Fichte's transcendental idealism, the essay documents what every traveler knows: you can't get going if you don't leave your point of departure behind.

I. The Systematic Significance of Transcendental Idealism in Kant

During the 1780s Kant's conception of a critique of pure reason evolved from the originally planned single work under that title (1781), suitably characterized as a "critique of pure speculative reason," to include two further installments in the form of a critique of practical reason (1784) and a critique of reflective judgment (1790). According to Kant, the unity of the critical trilogy is assured by the unity of reason in its threefold employment as theoretical understanding, practical reason and aesthetico-teleological judgment.[8] The three-step development of the Critical philosophy is evident in the expansion of the central critical question "How are synthetic judgments a priori possible?" from theoretical judgments concerning nature to practical judgments concerning the grounds of volition and to reflective judgments concerning the grounds of pleasure and displeasure.[9] In each case, the answer to the question involves the appeal to a priori subjective conditions that first make possible one of the three principal forms of nonempirical judgmental synthesis.

The parallel grounding of specifically different claims to objective validity in universal and necessary but subjective conditions might suggest a generic idealism of epistemic, thelematic and hedonic forms.[10] Yet in Kant the extension of the transcendental question does not go hand in hand with an analogous extension of the doctrine of transcendental idealism. On the contrary, the latter remains specific to the first, theoretical *Critique* and its restriction of all (theoretical) knowledge to the realm of appearances, whereas the second and third *Critiques* supplement the phenomenal restriction of theoretical knowledge with the practical and reflective extension of knowledge beyond the limits of experience through moral and teleological thinking. Thus, Kant's theoretical transcendental idealism is balanced by a critically mitigated nonempirical realism on ethical and ethico-teleological grounds that rehabilitates metaphysics in a moral guise.[11]

But not only does Kant not extend the appellation of "transcendental idealism" to all doctrines involving a priori subjective conditions of claims for objective validity. Even within the *Critique of Pure Reason,* he restricts the phraseology of transcendental idealism and transcendental ideality to those aspects of the work that appeal to the role of sensibility in the constitution of objective knowledge. In the Transcendental Aesthetic, the predicate "transcendental ideality" is originally attributed to the a priori forms of sensible intuition and secondarily to that of which they are the forms, viz., the appearances. The introduction of the very term "transcendental idealism" in the Paralogisms of Pure Reason in the first edition (A369) and in the Antinomy of Pure Reason in the second edition (B519/A491) traces the phenomenal status of empirical objects to the fact that they are intuited in space and time.[12]

Conversely, neither the a priori concepts of the understanding (categories) nor the a priori concepts of theoretical reason (transcendental ideas) are ever characterized in terms of transcendental ideality or transcendental idealism. On the contrary, both the categories and the transcendental ideas are shown to originate independent of sensibility and its forms and to have some significance beyond the confines of the realm of appearances. It is only through their (theoretical) cognition-geared application to the manifold of space and time that the categories become restricted to appearances. The categories as such (as a priori forms of thinking) are not affected by the conditions of sensibility.[13]

The strict dissociation of the term and concept of transcendental idealism from the core of Kant's critique of understanding, reason and judgment points to a fundamental distinction between the Transcendental Aesthetic of the first *Critique* and the rest of the critical trilogy, including the Transcendental Logic of the *Critique of Pure Reason*. As a doctrine concerning the forms of sensibility and the features of objects due to those forms, transcendental idealism does not directly pertain to the concepts, principles, and object domains of the "upper," rational registers of the faculties of cognition, volition, and feeling examined in the three *Critiques*.

To be sure, the doctrine of transcendental idealism is of fundamental importance in Kant's critical project, because it allows the theoretical realization of the categories in some pure sensible manifold in the first *Critique* and negatively delineates a conceptual space for nontheoretical cognition and faith in the second and third *Critiques*. Still, the presentation of the doctrine remains outside of the critique of the *rational* capacities – as indicated by the historical origin of the Transcendental Aesthetic in the semicritical theory of the form and principles of the sensible world in the Inaugural Dissertation (1770).[14]

Moreover, the very term "transcendental ideality," as employed in the Transcendental Aesthetic of the *Critique of Pure Reason*, points back to the precritical and pre-Kantian understanding of "ideality" as "nullity" (*Nullität*) and of "transcendental" as "concerning the absolute nature of things." Predicating "transcendental ideality" of space and time *qua* forms of sensibility means denying that they have any "meaning" (*Bedeutung*) for the way things are independent of our forms of sensing, or asserting that they are "nothing" (*nichts*) with respect to things in themselves.[15]

The unique position of the Transcendental Aesthetic and its doctrine of transcendental idealism within the critical trilogy can be traced back to a crucial difference between the *sensible* a priori conditions of appearances elucidated in the Transcendental Aesthetic and the various *rational* conditions of objective validity established in the three *Critiques*. Space and time are the a priori forms of the mind's undergoing affections; they are the ways in which the mind receives determination. By contrast, the a priori forms and principles of the understanding, of reason and of judgment are the ways in which the mind actively brings about determination: by determining the object, determining the will, or determining the feeling of pleasure and displeasure, respectively.[16]

But Kant's continued insistence on the equivalence between the ideality or nullity of representations (with regard to their forms) and the mind's passivity or receptivity in having those representations, not only introduces a fundamental distinction between the theory of sensibility and the theory of spontaneous reason. It also entails a distinction between the receptive and spontaneous sides of space and time themselves. Whereas the Transcendental Aesthetic treats of space and time as passive forms of *intuiting,* the Transcendental Analytic considers space and time as *intuited* or as objects in their own right that reflect the formative influence of some activity, thereby effectuating the required mediation between sensibility and the understanding.[17] It therefore comes as no surprise that the very doctrine that pioneered the transcendental turn in Kant, viz., his theory of a priori forms of sensibility, became a chief target of the post-Kantian revisions of Kant's work.

In addition to the systematic, architectonic reasons for not subjecting the notion of transcendental idealism to a comprehensive enlargement and making its scope coextensive with that of the entire transcendental project, there may well have been strategic considerations that spoke against such a move in Kant's eyes. After all, it was the doctrine of transcendental idealism that attracted some of the most vehement attacks and misunderstandings in the early reception of the *Critique of Pure Reason,* which led Kant to advance the alternative appellations "formal" and "critical idealism" for his doctrine.[18]

The original restriction of transcendental idealism to the theory of sensibility in Kant is also evident in the fact that he does not resort to formulations such as "system of transcendental idealism" to characterize his overall project of a critique of reason.[19] Kant's extensive reflections on the architectonic of philosophy in general and that of the critical philosophy in particular[20] are not cast in any specifically idealist terminology. For Kant, transcendental idealism is a "doctrinal concept" (*Lehrbegriff*), designed to account for the peculiar status of space and time as nondiscursive yet a priori representational forms.[21]

Moreover, to Kant's ear the phrase "system of transcendental idealism" would not have designated the sum total of transcendental philosophy. When used in connection with "doctrinal concepts" such as preestablished harmony and occasionalism, to which one might add Kant's own transcendental idealism, the term "system" in Kant retains its older meaning of an account developed in order to explain a certain range of phenomena, as in talk about the Ptolemaic and Copernican "systems" in astronomy.[22] The range of phenomena to be explained by Kant's strict, narrow conception of transcendental idealism does not warrant any identification of that system with transcendental philosophy *tout court.*

II. The *Wissenschaftslehre* as System of Transcendental Idealism

The Kantian basic terms "critique," "system," and "idealism" figure prominently in Fichte's sustained reflection on the form, method and goal of the *Wissenschaftslehre.* Yet in Fichte those terms enter into a constellation that makes them differ in significant respects from their earlier usage in Kant.[23] The terms in question receive their revised meaning from their relation to the fundamental notion of the *Wissenschaftslehre* itself.

Fichte's choice of the term "*Wissenschaftslehre*" for his project of a radicalized transcendental philosophy draws on the etymological connection as well as the semantic proximity of the German words for "science" and "knowledge" (*Wissenschaft, Wissen*). For Fichte, philosophy is concerned with the nature of knowledge as such and can be described as the search for knowledge regarding knowledge. More specifically, the knowledge peculiar to philosophy is the knowledge of the most general features of knowledge, a meta-knowledge that can be termed "transcendental" in that it transcends the specifics of any particular kind of knowledge.

While the term "*Wissen*" ("knowledge") in Fichte primarily designates the epistemic modality of philosophy *qua Wissenschaftslehre*, distinguishing the latter from mere opinion (*Meinung*) as well as belief or faith (*Glaube*), the term "*Wissenschaft*" ("science") addresses the epistemic form or structure of philosophy and indeed of all knowledge. That form is "systematic form"[24] or the form of a system, in which individual instances of knowledge receive their character as knowledge (*Gewißheit*) from their relation to basic propositions or principles (*Grundsätze*) that function as the ultimate source of certainty in all knowledge. Fichte stresses that systematic form is not sufficient for knowledge in that the form of a system also can pertain to a body of beliefs built on some groundless and improvable principle such as the existence of aerial spirits.[25] Moreover, systematic form belongs to science only contingently. The form of a system is not the purpose of a science but only its means required by the contingent fact that human beings know very little with certainty and need to establish certain knowledge by tracking their beliefs to paradigmatic instances of certain knowledge.[26]

In Fichte's first conception of the *Wissenschaftslehre,* as published in 1794–5, the systematic form of philosophy involves the initial presentation of the supreme principles of all knowledge, which in turn constitute a subsystem of knowledge, and the subsequent derivation of the main features of all knowledge from those principles.[27] But soon Fichte came to replace the beginning of the *Wissenschaftslehre* by way of separately presented principles with an alternative presentation, first offered in lecture form in 1796–7, that takes its departure from the postulate of reflecting on the form and structure of one's knowledge, thus integrating the foundations of knowledge into the development of its principal structure.[28]

Fichte's use of the term "system" to designate the architectonic form of knowledge is not restricted to the system of philosophical knowledge. Fichte argues that the very possibility of developing a system of knowledge regarding knowledge in the *Wissenschaftslehre* presupposes that knowledge as such have systematic form; hence "the object of the *Wissenschaftslehre* is . . . the system of human knowledge."[29] Thus, the term "system" designates both the form of philosophical knowledge and the form of the object of philosophical knowledge. What links the two instances is the systematic nature of knowledge in general, of which philosophical knowledge regarding knowledge is just one instance.

Fichte tends to transfer the designation "system" as applied to the overall system of human knowledge to the mind as such and to characterize the object of the system of philosophical knowledge as "the system of the human mind."[30] To be sure, not everything contained in the mind is part of the mind's system. Fichte distinguishes between the representations (*Vorstellungen*) in the mind that arise freely and arbitrarily and hence without systematic connection to the rest of the mind, on the one hand, and the representations that arise with necessity, thus exhibiting systematic connection, on the other hand. The mind *qua* system is the system of the latter kind of representations, which Fichte also terms "the system of experience,"[31] stressing the compulsory nature of objective representations.[32]

The task of philosophy is to determine the ground of experience so conceived. Since the ground of experience falls necessarily outside experience, a basic distinction is introduced between knowledge regarding experience, including the sciences, and philosophical knowledge regarding the nonempirical ground of knowledge. According to Fichte, both kinds of knowledge admit of systematic form.

In determining the nonempirical ground of all empirical knowledge, the *Wissenschaftslehre* provides a representation (*Darstellung*) of the system of the human mind. Fichte captures the representational nature of the *Wissenschaftslehre* with respect to the mind *qua* system of knowledge in the following description of the philosopher's activity:

We are not lawgivers of the human mind but its historiographers; to be sure, not journalists but writers of pragmatic history.[33]

While stressing the independence of the mind's system from its theoretization in the system of philosophical knowledge, the analogy to historiography still suggests the philosopher's active and purpose-oriented role in writing the transcendental history of the mind.[34]

In addition to designating both the scientific form of human knowledge in general and that of specifically philosophical knowledge regarding all other knowledge, the term "system" in Fichte also refers to any particular philosophical system developed as an account of the ground of experience. The procedure of reconstructing the nonempirical ground of empirical knowledge originates in the philosopher's freely chosen act of separating what is united in experience, focusing on one element of experience at the expense of any other, thereby ascending from the level of actual experience to that of the latter's structural condition or ground.

Since the only principal factors that are connected in and through experience are the experienced thing (*Ding*) and the experiencing intelligence (*Intelligenz*), the procedure of philosophy results in two and only two alternative accounts of the ground of experience. If the thing experienced is raised from its status as a factor of experience to that of the ground of experience and considered in abstraction from experience, then the thing is reconfigured as a "thing in itself" (*Ding an sich*); if the intelligence undergoing experience is elevated from the status of an ingredient of experience to that of its ground and considered in isolation from experience, then the intelligence is reconfigured as an "intelligence in itself" (*Intelligenz an sich*) or "I in itself" (*Ich an sich*).[35]

Fichte terms the procedure of accounting for experience by way of a thing in itself "dogmatism" and calls the opposite procedure of explaining experience by appeal to some "intelligence in itself" "idealism." In assessing the difference between the two philosophical systems, Fichte stresses that the thing in itself of the dogmatic system is a mere "fiction" (*Erdichtung*) that has no reality in experience as such and could only be validated through the successful derivation of the system of experience from the thing in itself. By contrast, the absolute intelligence or "I" of the idealist system is not merely a hypothetical device awaiting confirmation through its explanatory potential but figures within consciousness as the "immediate self-consciousness . . . that occurs in a free action of the mind."[36] As an object of philosophical consciousness, the "I in itself" is of a unique kind: It is neither entirely made like a fictional being nor is it entirely given like an independently existing thing. Rather, it is given in its existence, while being determinable through the free intelligence with regard to its determinations.[37]

Fichte maintains that neither of the two principal philosophical systems is able to refute the other, but he still argues for the speculative as well as practical superiority of the idealist system over the dogmatic system. The materialist monism implied by dogmatism is unable to account for the structural difference between intelligent beings, which are what they are for themselves – thus exhibiting a characteristic duality of being and knowing one's being – and nonintelligent beings, which are what they are not for themselves but only for others.[38] Moreover, the delegation of all independence from experience to some thing in itself fails to do justice to the human interest in absolute independence to be realized through free self-determination.[39] Yet none of these arguments will convince the dogmatist, who – on Fichte's account – simply lacks the belief (*Glaube*) in freedom that motivates the systematic pursuit of freedom by means of idealism.[40]

For Fichte, the philosophical systems of idealism and dogmatism are not products of some detached, artificial reasoning, but are deeply rooted in an individual's overall disposition. More specifically, one's philosophical system reflects which of the two one believes to be originally absolute and independent of the other, whether the thing or the self. Fichte himself explains the matter in commenting on his well-known *dictum* that the philosophy one chooses – whether dogmatism or idealism – depends on the human being one is:

> . . . a philosophical system is not some lifeless household item one can put aside or pick up as one wishes, but is animated by the soul of the human being whose system it is.[41]

Fichte's outright existentialist grounding of the philosophical system in an individual's protophilosophical outlook, together with his own profession of a basic belief in the original independence of the self from all thingly reality, leads him to advance an idealist philosophical system centered around the notion of the self as spontaneous intelligent activity (*Tun*) that is originally independent from anything other than itself. Yet the freedom from all external influence that lies at the heart of Fichte's idealism is not tantamount to lawless irregularity or personal caprice. Rather, the intelligent activity operates according to laws that are part of its own being and that provide determination to its activity and to the products of that activity. The "fundamental law" (*Grundgesetz*) behind all particular laws of the intelligent activity is that the intelligent being "gives itself its own laws in the course of its acting."[42]

Fichte contrasts his own "critical or transcendental idealism," which presupposes the original determination of the intelligence through its own laws and thus admits of a "system of necessary modes of acting,"[43] to "transcendent idealism," whose presupposition of an absolutely lawless intelligent activity contradicts the very idea of a system of the mind.[44]

Within critical or transcendental idealism, Fichte further distinguishes between a "higher, complete criticism,"[45] which actually derives the system of mental activities from the basic laws of the intelligent being, on the one hand, and an incomplete idealism, which merely abstracts those laws from the objects of experience, on the other.[46] The latter form of transcendental idealism is incomplete in that it explains only the formal relational properties of a thing through the laws of the intelligent activity but leaves the very matter (*Stoff*) unexplained, thus inviting a dogmatic interpretation of the thing as originally independent from the intelligent activity. By contrast, in "complete transcendental idealism"[47] the thing *qua* matter as well as its formal properties are shown to originate according to the laws of the intelligent activity. Thus, the thing in its entirety is derived from the "total" legislation of the intelligent activity.

The systematically incomplete idealism is deficient in yet another regard. It is limited to the laws governing external experience, thus neglecting to address large parts of the "system of reason," notably practical reason and reflective judgment, and amounting to a "half criticism."[48] Although these criticisms could be taken to address Kant's work, Fichte takes great care not to identify incomplete transcendental idealism with Kant's own position but only with that of some of his followers – a move that allows Fichte to credit Kant with the insight that "the object is given neither entirely nor half but rather is made."[49]

The conceptual development of the terms "system" and "transcendental idealism" from their separate usage in Kant to their combined employment in Fichte's notion of a radically idealist system of the mind's dynamic structure also includes a revised understanding of the nature and place of "critique" within the overall enterprise of philosophy. Fichte contrasts the philosophical system proper with the introduction into the system, in which the philosophy presented in the system becomes the object of a philosophical inquiry into its possibility, conditions, and rules. Fichte's title for such a metaphilosophical introduction into philosophy proper is "critique." He even grants the introductory investigations undertaken in a critique the status of a system in its own right.[50]

According to Fichte, the relation between critique and philosophy proper – the latter being alternatively referred to as "metaphysics" and *"Wissenschaftslehre"* – is analogous to the relation between the *Wissenschaftslehre* and the ordinary, nonphilosophical standpoint. In both cases, philosophy – in its capacity as critique or as *Wissenschaftslehre,* respectively – critiques a form or level of thinking: In one case it is philosophical thinking itself that is being critiqued, in the other case what is critiqued is natural thinking.[51] The relation of double critique thus established between philosophical thinking and its object allows Fichte to retain the specifically critical stand of philosophy introduced by Kant, while enlarging the critical project by a metacritique of philosophy's critique of natural thinking.

In Kant, Fichte finds the two levels of philosophical critique confused and the so-called critique for the most part concerned with metaphysics. The inverse deficiency still holds, as Fichte himself concedes, for the *Wissenschaftslehre,* whose elaborations so far given include elements of an introductory or metacritical nature. Moreover, for Fichte advances in metaphilosophical understanding and advances in the presentation of the *Wissenschaftslehre* go hand in hand. A complete systematic account of the procedure of the *Wissenschaftslehre* is only to be expected once a "pure presentation of the *Wissenschaftslehre* itself" becomes possible.[52]

III. The Metacritique of Transcendental Idealism

In addition to addressing the relation between the idealist and the dogmatist system of philosophy, Fichte's sustained metaphilosophical reflections also include extensive discussions of the relation between the viewpoint of philosophy and the viewpoint of ordinary consciousness. In response to objections and misunderstandings encountered by the first presentations of the *Wissenschaftslehre,* Fichte addresses the very nature of the *Wissenschaftslehre,* stressing the limits as much as the possibilities of his radically idealist system. The central concern of his metacritical self-interpretation is to dispel the contemporary perception of the *Wissenschaftslehre* as an ontological idealism that teaches the production of the world through the mind. Fichte clarifies the scope of systematic idealism by emphasizing the role of extraphilosophical reality and by focusing on the reconstructive nature of the *Wissenschaftslehre*.

Fichte's critical reflections on the relation between philosophy and reality are part of his response to the critique of the *Wissenschaftslehre* in two open letters addressed to him in 1799, each written by a leading figure of late eighteenth-century German thought, viz., Kant and Jacobi.[53] In his "Declaration Regarding the *Wissenschaftslehre*," Kant distances himself from a self-proclaimed follower who had become a liability to the Kantian movement by getting embroiled in a series of professional scandals, culminating in atheism charges and the loss of his professorship at Jena. Kant turns against the *Wissenschaftslehre* itself Fichte's charge that Kant had only provided a philosophical propaedeutic, arguing that, far from being genuine metaphysics, the *Wissenschaftslehre* itself is merely a logic, thus devoid of content and without reference to reality.

Jacobi's open letter treats the *Wissenschaftslehre* as a case study in the spiritual dangers of the Kantian revolution in philosophy. For Jacobi, the transcendental idealism introduced by Kant and radicalized by Fichte dissolves reality into a mere figment of the mind. Rather than combating skepticism, Fichte's *Wissenschaftslehre* is seen as supporting doubt in everyday reality by replacing the realist world view of ordinary consciousness with the idealist production of a world that is nothing but appearances and hence appearances of nothing. In his earlier critique of Kant, Jacobi had already coined the term "nihilism," which he reuses in the letter to Fichte to brandish the metaphysical and moral implications of transcendental idealism.[54]

In the *Crystal-Clear Report,* Fichte responds to his prominent critics by claiming an identical "tendency" in Kant's, Jacobi's, and his own philosophy, viz., the recognition that all thinking, whether philosophical or ordinary, has its basis as well as its end in experience.[55] Following Jacobi, Fichte designates the reality provided by experience through the term "life."[56] Both in Fichte and in Jacobi, the notion of life as the sustaining core of reality goes beyond the narrowly biological and conveys the presence of subjective mental, even spiritual, factors that animate reality. Fichte explicitly excludes an absolutist reading of life as detached from possible or actual consciousness.[57]

Fichte expands Jacobi's notion of life to include even the detached ("speculative") life form of philosophy. Rather than merely contrasting life and speculation, Fichte links the two by distinguishing them as gradations of life, termed "potencies" (*Potenzen*).[58] Ordinary consciousness and its world of objects is the first potency of life, on which all further gradations are based. In ordinary consciousness the self is completely immersed in its experience, to the point of forgetting itself and its role in the constitution of experience.[59] By raising itself to the level of reflection on experience, consciousness actualizes the second potency of life, in which the consciousness present at the first level becomes an object for philosophical consciousness.

Fichte stresses that life in the first potency is fully functional and complete. The higher gradations of life, of which only the first one is philosophically interesting and all subsequent ones consist in empty iterations, do not complete the most basic, primary potency of life but supplement it through contingent mental efforts. Hence, the fundamental difference between the two potencies of life remains. The essential character of life in the first potency is its pre-givenness: objects appear to consciousness as ready-made and as imposing themselves on the mind. By contrast, life in the second potency is entirely the product of the mind's spontaneous activity.[60]

Their radical distinction notwithstanding, ordinary and philosophical consciousness are also intimately related. Life in the second potency is about life in the first potency. To be sure, philosophical life does not simply repeat ordinary life. Rather, it provides an account of the latter that seeks to understand the inner, hidden workings of ordinary consciousness. Fichte likens the business of philosophy as conducted in the *Wissenschaftslehre* to the demonstration of a watch. Explaining the workings of a watch involves the exhibition of its design, which accounts for the systematic arrangement of the parts in a functioning whole. Analogously, the idealist explanation of experience exhibits the systematic constitution of experience by relating the principal parts of experience to some overall unifying conception.[61] Philosophical life is as little capable of replacing ordinary life as the demonstration of a watch can be a substitute for an actual timekeeper.[62]

Now, given the restrictions of human knowledge, the teleological explanation of the systematic features of experience through the *Wissenschaftslehre* cannot presuppose some actual cosmic artisan that would make the world of experience, as it were, tick.[63] Moreover, on Fichte's account, the elements and laws that constitute the system of experience are not of a merely mechanical nature but have the organic qualities of self-motion and "self-generation" (*Selbsterzeugung*).[64] Unlike the demonstration of a watch, which involves the theoretical reinvention of a previously invented artifact, the philosophical reinvention of experience involves the construction of a system that as such exists only in and through contingent philosophical reflection. More precisely, philosophical reflection does not actually produce that system but functions as the occasion for the self-generation of the system of experience out of a presupposed first principle.

To be sure, the consciousness thus generated under the philosopher's observing eye is not ordinary consciousness or life in the first potency itself but the latter's "image" (*Abbildung*).[65] The systematic structure of experience does not belong to experience per se but to experience speculatively considered. Fichte thus returns to Kant's usage of the term "system" to designate primarily a philosophical account of some object domain, or that object domain insofar as it is considered by philosophical reason. Accordingly, the term "image" as applied to the philosopher's account of ordinary experience should be taken to convey the formed, artificially shaped nature of that consciousness, due to which it serves as a model – in Fichte's view, as the only acceptable model – of experience in its systematic unity.

The model-theoretical understanding of the imaging relation between ordinary consciousness and its philosophical reinvention receives further confirmation from Fichte's account of the applicability and indeed application of the former to the latter. According to Fichte, the freely initiated but lawfully generated determinations of consciousness are not merely internally consistent but predictive of the determinations of actual consciousness and thus permit a priori knowledge of the latter's principal features.[66] Fichte compares the relation between the two sets of determinations to that between pure geometry and its application to field measurements. Just as the a priori geometrical relations that hold in pure space apply to empirical space, so the a priori features of philosophically reconstructed consciousness apply to ordinary consciousness.

As in the earlier analogy between philosophical activity and the demonstration of a watch, Fichte resorts to teleological thinking in order to explain the match between imaged and actual consciousness. This time an analogy is set up between the philosophical reconstruction of ordinary consciousness and spatial measuring as the geometrical reconstruction of some empirically given space. In both cases the reconstruction is carried out under the presupposition of an original construction that is to be reconstructed through judgment and measurement, respectively. And as in the analogy with the watch, the presupposition is a methodological device with no implication as to the actual existence of some divine watchmaker or spacemaker.[67] Actual consciousness is considered "as though" (*als ob, gleichsam, gleich als ob*)[68] it were the result of some actual construction along the lines of its virtual construction in philosophical consciousness.

Fichte outright calls the philosophical account of ordinary consciousness a "fiction" (*Fiktion*) that is not to be confused with a "narrative of some true event which occurred at some particular time."[69] The original construction of ordinary consciousness, as presupposed in the latter's philosophical reconstruction, is an artificial model of ordinary consciousness that allows the prediction of the main features of experience. It should not be taken to imply a generation or construction on the part of actual ordinary consciousness. On Fichte's understanding, the life of ordinary consciousness is not a matter of generating or constructing but of finding:

Our existing world is all ready. . . . Life is not a producing but a finding.[70]

Fichte's insistence on the facticity of actual life and on the fictional nature of philosophy point toward a system of transcendental idealism that is quite akin to the teleological interpretation of mind and world in the *Critique of Judgment* with its treatment of systematic unity on the basis of an analogy to human design.[71] Fichte's metaphilosophical reflections at the close of the first period of the *Wissenschaftslehre* place the systematic idealist account of knowledge in the broader context of an account of human existence that acknowledges the presence of a dimension that sustains knowledge while resisting its grasp. The later developments of the *Wissenschaftslehre* are further stages in Fichte's realization of the ground and limits of the transcendental-idealist system. The Kantian inspiration preserved by Fichte in these endeavors is the critical animus of ascertaining the limits of knowledge by considering what lies beyond them.

Notes

1. Work on this essay was supported by a Faculty Scholarship from the University of Iowa and carried out during my association with the Center for Literary and Cultural Studies, Harvard University, in the spring of 1995. The essay also forms the first chapter of my book *Fichte's Transcendental Philosophy: The Original Duplicity of Intelligence and Will* (Cambridge, U.K.: Cambridge University Press, 1998).

2. Fichte's works are quoted and cited from *J. G. Fichte-Gesamtausgabe,* ed. R. Lauth et al. (Stuttgart: Frommann-Holzboog, 1962–), abbreviated as "GA," followed by a combination of Roman and Arabic numbers, indicating the series and volume, respectively, and the page number(s).

   The following abbreviations refer to English translations of Fichte: EPW: *Early Philosophical Writings,* ed. and trans. D. Breazeale (Ithaca: Cornell University Press, 1988); IWL: *Introductions to the Wissenschaftslehre and Other Writings. 1797–1800,* ed. and trans. D. Breazeale (Indianapolis: Hackett, 1994); and CCR: "A Crystal-Clear Report to the General Public Concerning the Actual Essence of the Newest Philosophy: An Attempt to Force the Reader to Understand," in *Philosophy of German Idealism,* ed. E. Behler (New York: Continuum, 1987), pp. 39–115.

   The *Critique of Pure Reason* is cited by the pagination of the second and first original editions, indicated by "B" and "A," respectively. All other works by Kant are cited from *Kant's gesammelte Schriften,* ed. Royal Prussian Academy and its successors (Berlin: Reimer, later de Gruyter, 1900–), referred to as "AA."

3. Cf., for example, GA I/4: 231n.; IWL, pp. 63f.n. On the difference between letter and spirit, cf. also the manuscript remains pertaining to the later, unpublished parts of Fichte's lectures on the vocation of the scholar held in Jena during the summer semester of 1794 (GA II/3: 291–342; partial translation in EPW, pp. 192–215).

4. Cf. *Critique of Pure Reason* B 370/A 314. On Fichte's interpretation of Kant, cf. Manfred Zahn, "Fichtes Kant-Bild," in *Erneuerung der Transzendentalphilosophie im Anschluß an Kant und Fichte,* ed. K. Hammacher and A. Mues (Stuttgart: Frommann-Holzboog, 1979), pp. 479–505.

5. *Critique of Pure Reason,* B 869/A 841.

6. Cf. GA I/4: 230n.; IWL, p. 63n (Fichte's emphases).

7. On Fichte's distinction between critique and system with respect to his own work, cf. GA I/2: 159f.; EPW, p. 97.

8. For an account of the overall nature and the modes of employment of reason in Kant in the context of the practical orientation of classical German philosophy in general and Kant's doctrine of the primacy of practical reason in particular, cf. my essay "Kant and the Unity of Reason" (unpublished manuscript; originally presented as an invited paper at the Central Division Meeting of the American Philosophical Association in Kansas City in May 1994). For an alternative account of the unity of reason in terms of the latter's practico-regulative function, cf., Susan Neiman, *The Unity of Reason: Rereading Kant* (New York: Oxford University Press, 1993). Cf. also my review of Neiman's book in *Journal of the History of Philosophy* 34 (1996): 306–8.

9. The formulation of the critical task through the question "How are synthetic judgments *a priori* possible?" first occurs in section 5 of the *Prolegomena to Any Future Metaphysics* (1783; AA IV, 276; Immanuel Kant, *Prolegomena to Any Future Metaphysics*, introd. L. W. Beck [Indianapolis: Bobbs-Merrill, 1982], p. 23), from where it is taken over into the second edition of the *Critique of Pure Reason* (1787; B 19ff.).

10. For a reconstruction of Kant's systematic idealism in aesthetics, cf. my essay "Kant's Aesthetic Idealism," in *The Iowa Review* 21 (1991): 52–7.

11. On Kant's project of a practico-dogmatic metaphysics of postulates of pure practical reason, cf. AA XX, 252–332, esp. 296–301 (*Preisschrift über die Fortschritte der Metaphysik*); *What Real Progress Has Metaphysics Made in Germany Since the Time of Leibniz and Wolff?* Trans. and introd. T. Humphrey (New York: Abaris, 1983), pp. 127–37.

12. Cf. *Critique of Pure Reason*, A 369 and B 519/A 491, respectively.

13. On the systematic place of transcendental idealism in the *Critique of Pure Reason*, cf. also my *Theoretische Gegenstandsbeziehung bei Kant* (Berlin and New York: de Gruyter, 1984), pp. 289–96.

14. Cf. AA II, 398–406 (*De mundi sensibilis atque intelligibilis forma et principiis*); Immanuel Kant, *Theoretical Philosophy 1755–1700*, trans. and ed. R. Meerbote and D. Walford (Cambridge, U.K.: Cambridge University Press, 1992), pp. 391–400. Although the term "ideal" (*ideale*) is applied to space in the *Inaugural Dissertation* (AA II, 403; *Theoretical Philosophy*, 397), Latin equivalents of the coinages "transcendental ideality" and "transcendental idealism" are not yet to be found in that work.

15. Cf. *Critique of Pure Reason*, B 44/A 28 and B 52/A 36.

16. For an account of the role of reason in the generation of the feeling of pleasure, cf. my essay "Toward the Pleasure Principle: Kant's Transcendental Psychology of the Feeling of Pleasure and Displeasure," in *Akten des Siebenten Internationalen Kant-Kongresses*, ed. G. Funke (Bonn: Bouvier, 1991), pp. 809–19.

17. Cf. *Critique of Pure Reason*, B 160n., B 176ff./A 137ff. For an account of Kant's controversial notion of "formal intuition" in the context of the relation between sensibility and understanding, cf. my exchange with Patricia Kitcher in *The Southern Journal of Philosophy* 25 (1986), Supplement (*The B-Deduction*): 137–55.

18. Cf. AA IV, 293f. (*Prolegomena*, Section 13, Remark III); *Prolegomena to Any Future Metaphysics*, 41.

19. The only exception to this is to be found in Kant's late, fragmentary reflections on the "highest standpoint of transcendental philosophy" in the *Opus postumum* (in the last, so-called First Fascicle; cf., e.g., AA XXI, pp. 32ff.; Immanuel Kant, *Opus postumum*, ed. E. Förster [Cambridge, U.K.: Cambridge University Press, 1993], pp. 235ff.). In those passages, Kant can be seen as a reacting to, and even

144 GÜNTER ZÖLLER

participating in, the post-Kantian undertaking of completing transcendental philosophy in the idealist spirit.

20. Cf. *Critique of Pure Reason,* B 860ff./A 832ff.; AA V, pp. 170–9 (*Critique of Judgment,* Introduction, I.-III.) and AA XX, pp. 241–7 (*First Introduction to the Critique of Judgment,* XI.); *Critique of Judgment: With the First Introduction,* trans. W. Pluhar (Indianapolis: Hackett, 1987), pp. 9–18 and pp. 431–7.

21. Cf. *Critique of Pure Reason,* A 369; B 519/A 491; B 37–40/A 22–25 and B 46–48/ A 30–32.

22. On the notion of system before and in Kant, cf. my essay " 'Die Seele des Systems': Systembegriff und Begriffssystem in Kants Transzendentalphilosophie," forthcoming in a volume on system and architectonic in Kant edited by Hans Friedrich Fulda and Jürgen Stolzenberg.

23. For an account of the role of Reinhold in Fichte's conception of philosophy as system, cf. Wolfgang Schrader, "Philosophie als System – Reinhold und Fichte," in *Erneuerung der Transzendentalphilosophie im Anschluß an Kant und Fichte,* pp. 331–44. On Fichte's and Reinhold's different assessment of the role of popular thinking in philosophy, cf. my essay "Die Unpopularität der Transzendentalphilosophie: Fichtes Auseinandersetzung mit Reinhold (1799–1801)," forthcoming in an essay collection on Reinhold edited by Wolfgang Schrader (Stuttgart: Frommann-Holzboog).

24. GA I/2: 112; EPW, p. 101.

25. Cf. ibid.

26. Cf. GA I/2: 113f.; EPW, p. 102.

27. On the architectonic of the first published presentation of the *Wissenschaftslehre,* cf. my essay "Setzen und Bestimmen in Fichtes *Grundlage der gesammten Wissenschaftslehre,*" in *Der Grundansatz der ersten Wissenschaftslehre Johann Gottlieb Fichtes – Der Stand der Fichte-Forschung,* ed. E. Fuchs and I. Radrizzani (Neuried: Ars Una, 1996), pp. 178–92.

28. Cf. GA IV/2: 16f. and Johann Gottlieb Fichte, *Wissenschaftslehre nova methodo: Kollegnachschrift K. Chr. Fr. Krause,* ed. E. Fuchs (Hamburg: Felix Meiner Verlag, 1982; second edition 1995), pp. 10f. Johann Gottlieb Fichte, *Foundations of Transcendental Philosophy (Wissenschaftslehre) nova methodo (1796/99),* ed. and trans. D. Breazeale (Ithaca and London: Cornell University Press, 1992), pp. 85f.

29. GA I/2: 140; EPW, p. 125.

30. Cf., for example, GA I/2: 146; EPW, p. 130.

31. GA I/4: 190; IWL, p. 13.

32. Cf. GA I/4: 186; IWL, pp. 7f.

33. GA I/2: 147; EPW, p. 131 (translation modified). Cf. GA I/2: 365; SK, 198f. The contrast between ephemeral and pragmatic historiography can be traced back to Kant's identification of "pragmatic" (*pragmatisch*) with "prudential" (*klug*) and his conception of pragmatic history as instruction in pursuing one's advantage in the world. Cf. AA IV, pp. 416f. (*Grundlegung zur Metaphysik der Sitten,* II.); *Foundations of the Metaphysics of Morals,* trans. L. W. Beck (Indianapolis: Bobbs-Merrill, 1983), p. 34. The transposition of the term "pragmatic history" from the political sphere to that of the philosophical account of the mind occurs in Ernst Platner's *Philosophical Aphorisms* (*Philosophische Aphorismen,* third edition of part I; Leipzig: Schwickert, 1793), on which Fichte based the lectures on logic and metaphysics, which he offered during each of the eight semesters that he taught at Jena. For Platner's use of the phrase "pragmatic history of the human faculty of cognition" (*pragmatische Geschichte des menschlichen Erkenntnißvermögens*), cf. the

reprint of his *Philosophical Aphorisms* in GA II,4 Supplement, p. 16. On Fichte's critical appropriation of Platner's term in the context of his Jena lectures on logic and metaphysics, cf. GA II,4: 46, 52; GA IV,1: 204f.

34. For an account of Fichte's alternative self-interpretation of the *Wissenschaftslehre* as a scientific experiment, cf. my essay "An Eye for an I: Fichte's Transcendental Experiment," in *Figuring the Self: Subject, Individual, and Others in Classical German Philosophy*, ed. D. Klemm and G. Zöller (Albany: State University of New York Press, 1996), pp. 73–95.

35. Cf. GA I/4: 188, 190; IWL, p. 11 (translation modified), p. 13.

36. GA I/4: 191; IWL, p. 14.

37. Cf. GA I/4: 189; IWL, p. 12.

38. For an account of the I's ideal-real double nature, cf. my essay "Original Duplicity: The Ideal and the Real in Fichte's Transcendental Theory of the Subject," in *The Modern Subject: Conceptions of the Self in Classical German Philosophy*, ed. K. Ameriks and D. Sturma (Albany: State University of New York Press, 1995), pp. 115–30, and my book *Fichte's Transcendental Philosophy*.

39. Cf. GA I/4: 194; IWL, p. 18.

40. Cf. GA I/4: 194f.; IWL, p. 18f.

41. GA I/4: 195; IWL, p. 20 (translation modified).

42. GA I/4: 201; IWL, p. 27 (translation modified).

43. GA I/4: 201; IWL, p. 27.

44. Cf. GA I/4: 200; IWL, pp. 26f.

45. GA I/4: 202; IWL, p. 29 (translation modified).

46. Cf. GA I/4: 201f.; IWL, p. 27f.

47. GA I/4: 204; IWL, p. 30.

48. GA I/4: 203; IWL, p. 29 (translation modified).

49. Cf. GA I/4: 203n.; IWL, p. 29n. (translation modified).

50. Cf. GA I/2: 159; EPW, p. 97. The text under consideration is the preface to the second edition of this work, published in 1798.

51. Ibid.

52. GA I/2: 160; EPW, p. 98 (translation modified).

53. Kant's open letter, which is dated 7 August 1799, appeared in the *Intelligenzblatt* of the *Allgemeine Litteratur-Zeitung* on 28 August 1799. Jacobi's extensive, rhapsodic letter, which is dated 3 March 1799, was first sent to Fichte and subsequently published in expanded form in the fall of 1799. For Kant's letter, cf. *Fichte im Gespräch*, 6 vols, ed. E. Fuchs, (Stuttgart: Frommann-Holzboog, 1980), 2: 217f.; for Jacobi's letter, cf. GA III/3: 224–81; for the printed version, cf. *Transzenden-talphilosophie und Spekulation. Der Steit um die Gestalt einer Ersten Philosophie (1799–1807)*, ed. W. Jaeschke (Hamburg: Felix Meiner Verlag, 1993), pp. 3–43; English translation of the printed version under the title "Open Letter to Fichte" in *Philosophy of German Idealism*, pp. 119–41. On Fichte's position between Kant and Jacobi, cf. my essay " 'Das Element aller Gewissheit': Jacobi, Kant und Fichte über den Glauben," *Fichte-Studien* 14 (1998): 21–41.

54. Cf. *Fichte im Gespräch*, 2: 245; cf. also ibid., pp. 238, 240f.

55. GA I/7: 194; CCR, p. 47. Many of the metaphilosophical points of the *Crystal-Clear Report* are already to be found in Fichte's unpublished draft of an essay, entitled *Rükerinnerungen, Antworten, Fragen*, written in 1799 as part of his defense in the atheism dispute (cf. GA II/5: 103–86).

56. On the concept of life in Fichte, cf. Wolfgang Schrader, *Empirisches und absolutes Ich* (Stuttgartt: Frommann-Holzboog, 1972); ibid., "Philosophie und Leben im

Denken Fichtes um 1800," in *Kategorien der Existenz: Festschrift für W. Janke,* ed. K. and J. Hennigfeld (Würzburg: Königshausen und Neumann, 1993), pp. 77–86.

57. Cf. GA I/7: 202, 204; CCR, pp. 54f., 56.

58. GA I/7: 203ff.; CCR, pp. 56ff.

59. GA I/7: 198f.; CCR, p. 51.

60. Cf. GA I/7: 203f.; CCR, p. 56.

61. On Fichte's account, the guiding principle of the *Wissenschaftslehre* is first formulated on the basis of a "fortunate idea," which as such falls outside of the *Wissenschaftslehre,* and that is confirmed subsequently through the *Wissenschaftlehre*'s complete derivation of the main features of experience from the first principle. Cf. GA I/7: 212, 217ff.; CCR, pp. 63, 68ff.

62. Cf. GA I/7: 210; CCR, p. 61.

63. Cf. GA I/7: 216; CCR, p. 67.

64. Cf. GA I/7: 218; CCR, p. 69 (translation modified).

65. Cf. GA I/7: 218; CCR, p. 69 (translation modified).

66. Cf. GA I/7: 232f.; CCR, pp. 82f. Fichte's extended comparison between philosophical and geometrical method turns on the analogous role of intellectual intuition in the two disciplines. Cf. GA I/7: 226ff.

67. Cf. GA I/7: 232f.; CCR, pp. 82–4.

68. GA I/7: 232, 233, 249; CCR, pp. 82, 83, 98 (translation modified).

69. GA I/7: 249; CCR, p. 99.

70. GA I/7: 249; CCR, p. 98 (*Unsere bestehende Welt ist fertig . . . Das Leben ist kein Erzeugen sondern ein Finden*) (translation modified). It should be stressed that it is only the already existing world that is ready-made, not any future world that is to be brought about by human praxis. For Fichte's account of practical change, cf. my essay "Changing the Appearances: Fichte's Transcendental Theory of Practical Self-Determination," in *Proceedings of the Eighth International Kant Congress, Memphis 1995,* vol. I, part 3, ed. H. Robinson, (Milwaukee: Marquette University Press, 1995), pp. 929–42.

71. On the role of the *Critique of Judgment* in German idealism in general and in Fichte in particular, cf. Rolf-Peter Horstmann, *Die Grenzen der Vernunft. Eine Untersuchung zu Zielen und Motiven des Deutschen Idealismus* (Frankfurt am Main: Anton Hain, 1991), pp. 191–219.

7

Fichte's Alleged Subjective, Psychological, One-Sided Idealism[1]

ROBERT PIPPIN

Nach den mündlichen Äusserungen Fichtes, denn in seinem Buch war
noch nicht davon die Rede, ist das Ich auch durch seine Vorstellungen
erschaffend, und all Realität ist nur in dem Ich. Die Welt ist ihm nur ein
Ball, den das Ich geworfen hat und den es bei der Reflexion wieder fängt!!
Sonach hatte er seine Gottheit wirklich deklariert, wie wir neulich
ewarteten.

(Schiller to Goethe, 28 October, 1794)[2]

I

Most interpretations of Fichte's early (1794–1800) philosophy are very much
influenced by a decision on two large issues. First there is the question of
origins, or Fichte's early understanding of the nature of, enthusiastic commitment to, and revisions of, Kantian idealism; the distinctive position he took and
defended throughout these years, amidst the general swirl of possibilities
opened up by Kant's three *Critiques.* He had, of course, a good deal to say
about Kant, but a major text for anyone interested in this origins question
(interested, that is, in the inauguration of the distinctively post-Kantian set of
issues that were to engage Schelling and Hegel), has become his 1794 review
of G. E. Schulze's skeptical attack on Karl Reinhold. The essay has even been
called "a genuine watershed in the history of German Idealism."[3] This does not
make understanding Fichte's original idealist inspiration easy, since it involves
coming to terms with quite an unsteady and large pile of topics, some involving
figures now long forgotten: Fichte's reaction to Schulze's criticisms of Reinhold's attempted systematization of Kant's transcendental idealism.

The second major issue involves the *reception* issue: or how one understands
what was at stake in the way Fichte was taken up and criticized by two of his
most important fellow idealists, Schelling and Hegel. These early disputes with
Fichte set so much of the later agenda, and first formulated so many of the
canonical problems, that they have understandably been the focus of much
scholarly controversy. Like many philosophers, Fichte has largely come to be
understood by understanding what he opposed, and by understanding the controversies and reactions he inspired.

An easy summary of the problems underlying both issues would be the following: Inspired by the "Aenesidemus essay" (which Schulze's attack has come to be called, after the skeptical partner in the dialogue), Fichte realized that Reinhold had not gone far enough in radicalizing Kant's idealist project, and so had not achieved a self-grounded, thoroughly systematic philosophy. Fichte, no shrinking violet, took the decisive steps with his theory of the "absolute" or unconditioned nature of the "I"'s self-positing, and so subjected himself to the criticisms that stick to standard characterizations of his idealism as surely as "Platonic" sticks to one form of "love," or "alleged" sticks to "perpetrator" in police reports. Fichte's idealism is, we all presumably know, too "subjective," only a psychological idealism; it is too "one-sided" an account of the mind-world relation, wildly underestimating the contribution and constraints of the world, and wildly overestimating the mind's capacity for self-determination. The "act" of self-consciousness all by itself is supposed both to establish the truth of idealism (that all "is" only "for the I"), and to enable us to determine a priori the forms of the subject's possible relation to the world and to other free subjects.[4]

Or so it was alleged by many of Fichte's idealist colleagues, and many historians of the period. The combination of *desiderata* – accepting Reinhold's insistence on systematic philosophy, avoiding the skeptical implications of Reinhold's and Kant's version of idealism, but "overcoming" the one-sided and subjective version of systematic idealism proposed by Fichte – is one sensible version, among several others, of the agenda set for Schelling and Hegel.[5]

My interest in the following is in the first of the questions noted above: What sort of idealist position Fichte takes himself to have formulated, and how he means to justify it. With that established, an alternative way of understanding the later idealists will be suggested.

II

According to the standard story, Fichte could only correct Reinhold's position, whose systematic aspirations he much approved of, and so save critical idealism from Schulze's skeptical attack, by means of a subjective version of quite a radical idealism. The details of this origins story, which I shall need to make the point I eventually want to make, go like this. (They all require much more comment, but to save time, I shall simply list them here.)

(1) Fichte appreciated that Reinhold was right in his attempt to revise the Kantian philosophy in order to make it more systematic. A variety of the early dissatisfactions with Kant revolved around this worry about systematicity, in one way or another. For one thing, Kant's doctrine of the dual (and completely distinct) sources of human knowledge, sensibility,

and understanding, it was charged, had not been argued for or demonstrated in any way, and so seemed to rest too much on a psychological claim. Similar sorts of objections were raised against the Metaphysical Deduction of the categories, or the claim to derive all the categories from a table of judgments. By contrast, the Critical philosophy could only be systematic and so genuinely philosophical if it relied on one supreme or unconditioned principle, a principle from which the particular forms of thought and sensibility could be derived[6] and that would have no problematic skeptical implications (problematic still, according to Fichte as well as Schulze, in Reinhold). This meant finding some sort of a "self-grounding" or self-authorizing "first principle," the analysis of which could reveal the various necessary elements of any possible experience, and ward off skeptical challenges.

Another call for revision stemmed from the fact that, for almost all of the post-Kantians, Kant had not properly clarified the nature of his claim that "we do not know things in themselves," leaving (unsystematically) too much of a skeptical remainder for Spinozists and other enemies of moral freedom.[7] This problem especially was the origin of what is sometimes called the "idealist monism" supposedly aspired to by Fichte, Schelling, and Hegel.[8]

(2) But Schulze was right that Reinhold had hoped for far too much from his *"Grundsatz des Bewusstseins,"* his "principle of consciousness," formulated by Reinhold as:

Consciousness forces everyone to agree that to every representation there pertains a representing subject and a represented object, both of which must be distinguished from the representation to which they pertain.[9]

The undeniable "fact" (undeniable for anyone making any claim at all) was consciousness itself; a fact undeniably requiring that any conscious subject can distinguish itself as subject from the representing, and the object represented from the representing. The principle formally expressing this "material fact" was the *Grundsatz,* or "principle" of consciousness.[10]

This fact alone was to establish the truth of idealism, for, with a Berkeley-like gesture, Reinhold treats references to the thing in itself as attempts to represent the unrepresentable, a consciousness of what we stipulate to be beyond the conditions of the possibility of consciousness (defined by the principle of consciousness). The air of triviality suggested by such a claim, and the potential problems looming for Kantian moral philosophy, raise issues we shall return to shortly.

(3) The air of paradox surrounding Reinhold's formulations was certainly exploited by Schulze ("Aenesidemus") in his skeptical attack on both

Kant and Reinhold.[11] Reinhold's formulations themselves immediately invite the question of how, on its own terms, the existence of anything other than representations, whether the thing in itself, or the subject in itself, could be known (unless "represented" as such, contradicting the possibility of a thing in itself).[12]

But for the most part, Schulze is out to raise a general challenge to the Kantian-Reinholdean picture of transcendental philosophy itself. Reinhold purports to know something about the mind's representational activities and Schulze basically wants to know how Reinhold knows what he claims to know. The question, Schulze charges, is: " . . . by which means has the Philosophy of Elements come to its extravagant cognition of the objective existence of this something [the faculty of representation] . . . ?"[13] The only evidence on which claims about the faculty are made, he goes on, commits the very sort of rationalist paralogism Kant inveighed against, confusing conditions of thought with those of being " . . . A conclusion is being drawn," he claims, "from the constitution of representations and thoughts in us, to the constitution of objects in themselves, outside us"[14] (objects either as the source, or "matter" of representations, and especially a conclusion about a particular object, the existence and nature of the representing subject). Later, Schulze extends the famous criticisms so associated with Jacobi, that Kant's whole theory depends on a claim about the causal influence of things in themselves which his theory itself prohibits (the principle of causality is supposed to be objectively valid only for appearances), and also argues that Kant's theory makes claims about "the mind" doing this or that, or being responsible for this or that, with no account within the theory for the status of such claims. (Schulze claims that this could only be a causal responsibility, and trots out the above criticism again.)

> Hume would therefore require its author to explain to him what right he had to apply the principle of causality in the groundwork of critical philosophy, and how he could presume, at the very outset of its construction into a system, that a circumstance such as the presence of synthetic necessary propositions in us is the effect of a cause different from them . . .[15]

"Mr. Kant," he goes on, "never indicates what this 'mind' truly is – this mind which, as he claims, we ought to think as the source of some of the components of our knowledge."[16]

(4) In his response to Schulze, Fichte makes a number of predictable, but effective points against Schulze's confusion of empirical and psychological issues with transcendental concerns, his confusing the issue of representation as a mental event, governed by its own psychological laws, with representation as a condition for the possibility of experience.

Transcendental philosophy is not supposed to be about the mind as an object, but about what is necessary for any subject to be the subject of any possible claim about any object, including the mind. But along the way, he makes three crucial points that will occupy the remainder of this discussion.

First, he flatly rejects Reinhold's Kantian skepticism about our ignorance of things in themselves, and suggests his own version of what is to remain an *idealism,* but without this *restriction.* In this respect, such an aspiration indeed signals a watershed moment in this period since it inaugurates the problem of an absolute idealism, or systematic idealism without the *Restriktionslehre.* (It also signals the problem I am interested in: that is, that understanding the nature of the idealism claim must be prior to, and is obviously crucial to, understanding the nature of the claim for absolute, or skeptically unchallengeable status, especially given the conventional ontological readings of how this is supposed to work (an idealist monism).) The "old mischief about a thing in itself" appears a Kantian dilemma, Fichte explains, because Kant's philosophy was left incompletely systematic. This meant that the forms of intuition had not been derived from a single principle, a single principle presumably comprehensive enough to ground the possibility of any possible experience of, or claim about, anything, for any being whatsoever. Because of this lack, the forms of intuition could only have the status of conditions for uniquely human experiencers, accepted as such as a sort of basic, quasifactual premise. And this meant that it would be possible to contemplate a possible form of intuition other than ours, generating the "frequently repeated distinction between things as they appear to us and things as they are in themselves."[17] But Fichte treats this distinction, somewhat remarkably, as a mere *façon de parler* in Kant himself, claiming that the distinction "was certainly intended to hold only provisionally."[18] Fichte offers an initial statement of his own idealist but nonskeptical alternative, and it is important enough for later developments to quote at length.

Should we ever discover in the future, by means of further back-tracking [*Zurückschreiten*] upon the way so gloriously opened up by Reinhold, that what is immediately certain, the *I am* [*Ich bin*], holds only *for* the I, that all non-I *is* only for the I [*daß alles nicht-Ich nur fürs Ich sey*]; that this non-I derives all the determinations of its being *a priori* only through its connection with an I; that all these determinations, however, to the extent that their knowledge is possible *a priori,* become absolutely necessary on the simple condition of the relation of a non-I to an I in general; it would then follow that a thing in itself, to the extent to which it is supposed to be a non-I not opposed to any I, contradicts itself; and that the thing is so constituted, actually and in itself, as it would have to be thought by any conceivable intelligent I, i.e., by any being who thinks according to the principle of identity and contradiction . . . [19]

The nature of this sort of idealism is not explored much in this review, but it is signalled by several striking phrases, as when Fichte, in explaining that Reinhold should not have been taken to refer to the faculty of representation as a "thing" or entity "about which" we make straightforward knowledge claims, asserts that "The faculty of representation exists *for* the faculty of representation and *through* the faculty of representation," and summarizes this by claiming, "This is the necessary circle in which any finite understanding (and this means any understanding we can think of) is locked [*eingeschlossen*]."[20] And, "All that arises in our mind is to be completely explained and comprehended on the basis of the mind itself."[21]

The next two distinctive or non-Reinholdean points are familiar to all students of Fichte. Reinhold's systematic aspirations are praised, but Reinhold erred in taking the principle or *Grundsatz* in question to "express a fact" or *Tatsache*. Instead, such a *Grundsatz* can express what Fichte calls a *Tathandlung,* a distinctive sort of activity or doing or "performance." The unconditioned condition for the possibility of any knowledge claim (not, presumably any merely human experience) is this activity, not an undeniable state or fact or event.

And the activity has a distinctive character, eventually expressed as the "I"'s absolute positing of itself, but now introduced initially as an unconditioned autonomous "positing." "The absolute subject, the I, is not given by empirical intuition; it is, instead, posited by an intellectual one; and the absolute object, the non-I, is that which is posited in opposition to the I."[22]

III

Even before raising any questions about the "*subjective* idealist" implications of the last two points, there is still question enough about the first point, Fichte's understanding of idealism generally, and especially about his entitlement to such claims. Fichte might have indeed "pushed back" his analysis "farther" than Reinhold's reliance on the "facts of consciousness," and, perhaps, shown such facts to require as a condition the assumption of some original, all determining activity. It is quite important to note and think through the fact that conscious subjects do not just come to be in intentional states; that consciousness is representational by virtue of the activity of representing, and so is in an intentional relation to an intentional or referential object by virtue of this relation having been established. But Fichte appears to think that it is simply obvious that this sort of analysis establishes idealist conclusions, differing with Reinhold only by denying that there could be any point or even intelligibility to a contrast between what is "for" or "posited" by the "I" in this sense, and what is "in-itself." (In the *Aenesidemus* review, Fichte had called the very idea of a thing conceived apart from any possible relation to representation "a piece of whimsy, a pipe dream, a nonthought" and totally "futile."[23])

This, despite Fichte's many pious references, clearly stands in marked contrast to Kant's case for idealism, since it bypasses completely the two issues that had cost Kant so much labor: the case for the ideality of space and time, or the claim that they were pure forms of intuition,[24] and the argument that the objective validity of the categories could be established only for objects of such a spatiotemporal manifold. In a way quite similar to Reinhold's analysis of the nature of representation itself (and not of any distinctive feature of human experience), Fichte appears to proceed only from the implications of the "posited" character of experience, and to claim idealist conclusions from such premises. In the words of one commentator, Fichte, like Reinhold, seems to think that there is a "short argument to idealism."[25]

If so, this raises a number of problems. For one thing, moving from the unrepresentability to the wholesale impossibility of noumena obviously greatly complicates the question of how, within even a remotely Kantian framework, we should understand the possibility of morality.[26] For another, the air of triviality in Reinhold's formulations returns, as if we were merely denying that we can represent the unrepresentable or posit or in any way take up what is stipulated to be in principle inaccessible to any positing or taking up.[27] And finally, there are all the extravagant promises which Fichte's formulations are leading him toward. Under the influence of Schulze's attack, to escape the factual and quasiempiricist claims about representation in Reinhold, Fichte has postulated (or promised to defend) an "absolutely" active, self-positing "I" as the origin of all possible experience, and apparently has promised to consider all objects, or anything "not-I," as something that could "*be*" only "for such an I."

The difficulties in interpreting the status and implications of such a first move are well known. But since Fichte links what he is doing with some claim for the priority of practical reason, and links self-positing with the experience of freedom and self-determination, and since both such links are at least intelligible, it also has become relatively common to interpret the early *Wissenschaftslehre* in such "priority of the practical" terms. But if understood straightforwardly, this would mean that such a notion simply begged the question of the *possibility* of such freedom, the great animating problem behind the whole idealist enterprise (i.e. the question of whether there *could be* beings with the relevant required capacity for freedom) and to have reformulated the problems of knowledge, concept formation, objectivity and science to the point of unrecognizability, as if, to quote one gloss on this move, "there is no other ground for any assertion of external existence other than one which the moral law implies . . . "[28]

IV

This all leaves us with either a trivial statement of idealism, or a very implausible exaggeration of the implications of some practical experience of freedom. The former gets us nowhere; the latter to just a different version of the "wild subjectivism" destination, where everything is a kind of postulate or subjective requirement of practical freedom. A more adequate (and a more interesting) interpretation would depend on a proper restatement of such founding, apparently idealist, claims by Fichte as, "all that arises in our mind is to be completely explained and comprehended by the mind itself." Or, in explaining why no one could satisfy Aenesidemus, who asks for the impossible, the "absolute existence" and "autonomy of the I . . . in itself," Fichte counters, again, apparently stating his "idealism," "the I is what it is, and because it is, for the I."

The question at issue is what Fichte means to be denying when he denies us knowledge of the "absolute" existence and autonomy of the subject in itself, and insists that the "I," and all else, can only be "for the I." This might be an idealist claim if we admit it is possible to *contrast* how things are or even must be "for the I," and how they are in themselves. But Fichte rejects this as relying on "whimsy" or the "unthought." If his only reason for doing so is that by entertaining such a contrast, we would *be* representing or positing such a thing in itself, we are back to triviality (and confusion, since it is possible to represent a possibility without thereby requiring that what is possible be itself a representation).

The obvious key to understanding what Fichte intends to say, as well as to his own understanding of his great differences with Reinhold, lies in the strict categorial difference he insists on between Reinhold's notion of representing (and by implication, Kant's notions of synthesis and judgment) and his own unique account of an original self-positing. That is the key, that is, to understanding his not treating things in themselves as unknowable because, by definition, unrepresentable.

By categorial difference I mean to stress the fact that Fichte does not regard himself as simply replacing the Reinholdean emphasis on representing with an emphasis on an original positing, but seems to believe he has reformulated the issue radically, rather than answer it in a different way, and this reformulation is not expressed directly by reference to the consciousness of the moral law, although that dimension is certainly important to him. Now Fichte himself, having complained about the misleading implications and incomplete status of Reinhold's emphasis on representation, does return frequently to the language of representation and external objects, and this can confuse things. (He frequently says that the great problem of all philosophy is "why do we assume that real things exist beyond and in addition to our representations?"[29] And he formulates an answer to this question in terms of a "feeling of necessity" that accompanies some representations and not others, contributing to the impression of some sort of "veil of positings" theory and of the even more radical claim that external objects just "are" positings accompanied by a feeling of necessity.)[30]

In the response to Schulze, however, several of Fichte's formulations suggest more a reformulation of the issue than such a standard post-Cartesian, or "New Way of Ideas" idealism. He denies several times that Schulze's various questions about the "real origin" of our representing power, either with respect to formative activity, or material ground, should be answered more adequately than Reinhold answered them (as if with a theory of "absolute self-positing" as ground in the same sense). The implication throughout is that the question is very badly posed, and must be undermined and exposed as such, not answered. The fundamental condition of experience is a kind of "absolute autonomy," which, when understood properly, cannot be grounded by reference to anything either "*in*" us or "outside" of us. And again he makes the claim, "It is plainly the business of critical philosophy to show that we are not in need of a transition [from inner to outer, or vice versa]; that all that arises in our mind is to be explained and comprehended by the mind itself."[31]

This "circle" that we cannot "overstep" is described very broadly in response to Schulze's Humeanism, which is said to "leave open the possibility that eventually one might still be able to go beyond that limitation of the human spirit," whereas "(t)he critical system demonstrates instead the absolute impossibility of such an advance . . . " *This* sort of circle is very much broader and vaguer, at the outset, than any "circle of representations."

These more comprehensive formulations are linked with Fichte's sense of the radicality of his claim that consciousness should be understood in a thoroughgoing way as an activity, that every sort of mental event or episode or imagining or perceiving or willing or even direct sensing must be understandable as something I do, and not as a special kind of happening or state or a manifestation of some underlying substance. (His sense of the real nature of the claim being made for such an idealism is signaled by the fact that his own early name for his position is more frequently "criticism" than "idealism" and by such things as, in the second edition of the essay "Concerning the Concept of the *Wissenschaftslehre*," his altering references to acts of "the human mind," a phrase that can suggest the kind of causal dependence and substantial theory he is trying to avoid, and his substituting for *Geist* the more metaphysically and epistemologically neutral term, *Intelligenz*.[32]) Appreciating this requirement means appreciating the unavailability of any "determination" of thought (meaning here such things as constraints on what can be believed, evidence deciding one view as opposed to another, etc.) *other than some other thought, some other thinking of mine.* The point he is trying to make, or the heart of what he considers idealism, involves a sweeping objection to the very possibility that there could be some such determination exogenously, that such conceivings and judgings could be determined "from without" or, in the same sense of determined (the sense he is objecting to in Reinhold) "from within." (He is, I am suggesting, shifting the question of idealism from ontological mind dependence and even from a "transcendental" or subjectively "constituting" psychology to a claim for the dependence of judgments or positings on warrants; ultimately an idealist rather than simply rationalist position because of the radicality of the claim for the self-authorizing, or self-grounding character of such warrants. "No *explanatory role* for the non-thought except as thought" is the idealist claim, not "no possible thought of a non-thought.") This is all not because of some unargued-for Fichtean theory of mental substance and the possibility of its freedom, but because of a distinctly Fichtean incompatibilism claim, an incompatibilism between such universal normativity in consciousness and any nonnormative or material grounding. Likewise, the basic objection to dogmatism is not that we cannot represent or posit the unrepresentable. The "absurdity" in question does not lie there, but in the expectation that any explanation which referred to things in themselves, to what is assumed to be a determinant of conscious mental activity, *could be* such an explanation. Whatever reasons a dogmatist offers for such a claim will not and could not be themselves explicable as reasons on the dogmatic approach. ("Dogmatism, however, is quite unable to explain what it is supposed to explain, and this alone is enough to demonstrate its inadequacy."[33]) Fichte's idealism in other words asserts the *self-sufficiency* or *autonomy* of, let us say, *the normative domain itself,* what Sellars took to calling (without actually thinking through as radically as Fichte did the implications of such an autonomy claim) "the space of reasons."

I am not claiming that Fichte would put the matter just this way, and there are numerous passages where different, and not always consistent characterizations of "the idealism thesis" abound. But there a few places where he puts his point with simple, even lapidary clarity. My favorite occurs at the end of the "The Second Introduction" to the 1796/1799 *Wissenschaftslehre (nova methodo),* translated as *Foundations of Transcendental Philosophy.* The passage I am interested in follows a general claim that "The idealist observes that experience in its entirety is nothing but an acting on the part of a rational being." There then follows a gloss on "the viewpoint of idealism."

The idealist observes how there must come to be things for the individual. Thus the situation is different for the [observed] individual than it is for the philosopher. The individual is confronted with things, men, etc., that are independent of him. But the idealist says, "There are no things outside me and present independently of me."

Though the two say opposite things, they do not contradict each other. For the idealist, from his own viewpoint, displays the necessity of the individual's view. When the idealist says, "outside of me," he means "outside of reason"; when the individual says the same thing, he means "outside of my person."[34]

Or, in an even more summary claim from Fichte's notes: "the I is reason."[35]

This is, I think, what Fichte is about in claiming that Reinhold sent Kantianism in a disastrous direction by treating the problem of knowledge in terms of "facts" of consciousness, or what we must claim about psychological activities, and their origin. To shift the question from representation to positing is not to propose a different sort of psychological ground, but to point out that the question at issue is a fundamentally normative not a psychological one. The world gets represented *by* my representing it as such and such. That means I am, in thinking any thought, thinking that *I* am thinking that thought, saying it is such and such for me and thereby "standing behind it," proposing to have reasons. To think a thought is not to entertain an idea, but to propose a claim; if a merely imagined possibility, then posited (rightly) just as an imagined possibility subject to the norms and restrictions thereof. As he says in the theoretical part of *WL,* it is to bring the wavering of the imagination to rest, or to take a stand, to posit. This means to shift the question to: the problem of reasons, warrants, and away from the issue of "what must be happening in the mind for a representation of objects to occur." That latter is a fact of consciousness question and Fichte keeps saying that is what he is trying to avoid, what Reinhold did not avoid.

The broadest way to put this would be to say that Fichte is denying that the receptivity-spontaneity distinction is *congruent* with the nonconceptual/ conceptual distinction. The "I" *is* not limited in its judgings/positings by the mere occurrence (or *Anstoß*) of some nonconceptual content, some "not-I"; the "I" always must construe itself as limited, given what it takes to be the "not-I." This puts the entire question "*within* the space of reasons," eliminates the given, and attacks the reliance on faculty language still plaguing Kantianism.

Fichte, that is, is a foundationalist but of a peculiar sort. To understand "the I as the ultimate foundation" simply means that there is no "end" to the self-critical, *self*-adjusting activity that makes up the "whole" of the self's positings. And this all means that the general strategy for the *WL* is something like: Given that any subject can warrant its claims only by "relying on itself" (= is wholly within the domain of normativity, can rely on X (say a "*nicht Ich*") as warranting P only by *having taken X* to be reliable *for reason Y* (= posited it as such), what must such an "I" be able to do to fulfil such a requirement? What norms constitute such an "absolute" self-reliance? It will turn out that such an absolute self-grounding is, finally, impossible and will provoke the famous *Streben* issue, and it will turn out that the structure of this question has a great deal to do with the structure of the question: What is the norm constitutive of free agency as such (the moral law); but it is the form of this case that, I think, Fichte began to see after his encounter with Schulze on Reinhold.

And, looked at this way, it is also possible to claim that the argument rests fundamentally on a practical experience of some sort that cannot really be "argued for," just as Fichte himself regularly asserts. In this case, such a claim does not mean to make all of experience a postulate or condition of morality. Since one cannot get someone to subject himself to the space of reasons unless he has already so subjected himself, the only possible appeal is to call his own experiences to mind in a way that will reveal he must have always already so subjected himself, and to ask him to try "not to be so subject," to act and think as if dogmatism were true. Such a subject would be in the same fix as the skeptic about practical reason, who must act under the idea of freedom if he is to act at all. To assume otherwise would still be to determine oneself to act as if determinism were true. But that would be to make it a norm for action and so to refute oneself; likewise with any attempt to exempt oneself from the space of reasons or the domain of normativity.[36]

V

There is, then, if looked at this way, no "short argument" to idealism in Fichte. But this way of posing Fichte's problem still only suggests an idealist possibility. The "long argument," the one that would establish *that there can* be such a self-authorizing by reason of its own norms, still faces two familiar Fichtean problems. The first concerns one of the systematic issues mentioned at the outset. It is still unclear in what sense such an "I" could accomplish all that Fichte is trying to establish as transcendentally necessary. The question of the nature of such a subject and the whole within which there could be such a subject still seems a legitimate and unanswered question. Even if Fichte takes himself to be formulating and answering a different sort of question, the relation between the traditionally metaphysical challenge and the normative framework must still be addressed. And, second, there is the problem of the details of some systematic deduction, some way of understanding how such an extremely abstract premise about normativity, conceived in such a radical opposition to any mythical given or ground or external or substantial foundation, could be the first move in a fuller account of the concrete normative dimensions of thinking and willing as such. The model Fichte is looking toward is obviously the model from Kant's moral philosophy, where the idea of lawfulness or rational normativity itself, it was claimed, could provide the basis for both "a theory of morality" and a "metaphysics of morals." But given the many problems faced by such an account in Kant, an even more ambitious hope for such an argument form does not look promising. Both these sorts of objections were raised by Fichte's idealist colleagues and, at least in the case of Schelling, Fichte had his turn in response.

Schelling's worries are natural ones. In many modern philosophical treatments, understanding the possibility of a strict distinction between the explanation and the justification of thinkings and actings is taken to be a metaphysical problem. Believing or acting on reasons is often treated as a distinct sort of event in the world, accomplished by necessarily distinct sorts of beings, and thereby not subsumable under the causal laws that govern the motions of particles in space and time. Since Kant, a kind of Holy Grail for modern philosophy has been finding a way to argue that "our natures" are not properly accounted for by "subsumability to causal law" without basing such an argument on any metaphysical dualism. And the problem has been: coming up with the right way to state the insufficiency of such causal explanation.[37] Functionalist accounts of the autonomy of the psychological, anomalous monism, the unique status of the subjective point of view, and so forth, are all recent successors of the basic problem first addressed in the post-Kantian German accounts of the status of human freedom.

In his early essays on idealism (and here I mean "Of the I as Principle of Philosophy, or on the Unconditional in Human Knowledge," [1795], "Philosophical Letters on Dogmatism and Criticism" [1795], and the "Treatise Explaining the Idealism in the *Wissenschaftslehre*" [1797]), Schelling is clearly concerned about the adequacy of any sort of merely categorial or wholly "practical," or any ultimately skeptically based, specification of the autonomy of the space of causes and the space of reasons. As he states directly in the Second Letter,

My friends, the fight against dogmatism is waged with weak weapons if criticism rests its whole system merely upon the state of our cognitive faculty (*Erkenntnissvermögens*), and not upon our genuine essence (*unser ursprüngliches Wesen*).[38]

This evident distaste for a "noumenal ignorance/practical priority" thesis is, however, presented within a framework deeply committed to many founding Kantian and Fichtean assumptions, making quite complicated both the issue of how Schelling wants us to understand the status of his "original essence" question, and the right way to understand his allegiances and disagreements.[39] So, on the one hand, Schelling concedes that critical idealism has successfully established that "no absolutely objective cognition is possible," or that "the object is knowable only under the condition of the subject."[40] But he also concedes that this point does not "refute" dogmatism (treated throughout as equivalent to metaphysical realism) "theoretically." He makes this point by introducing some distinctly Schellingean worries about the way in which any synthetic unity in our experience must presuppose an original "absolute unity" inexplicable within the critical system. Pursuing this point would quickly take us deep into the Schellingean bog, not to mention important discussions in Hölderlin, Novalis, and the early Hegel. The important concession here, however, is just the point that there is no theoretical access to such an unconditioned absolute, and so, in what then appears to be a Fichtean move, Schelling also seems to insist on the priority of practical requirements in understanding such an "original essence," in our being practically committed to it.

Kant's First *Critique* is said by Schelling to have proved that "no system, whatever its name, is, in its consummation, an object of knowledge, but merely an object of an activity, a practically necessary but infinite activity."[41] And, " . . . no man can convince himself of any system except pragmatically, that is, by realizing either system in himself."[42] And, "The highest dignity of philosophy is to expect everything of human freedom. Hence nothing can be more detrimental to philosophy than the attempt to confine it in the cage of a system universally valid by theory."[43]

Yet in the Sixth Letter, Schelling begins to indicate why such Fichtean formulations do not express fully his own position. That is, he reformulates what he takes to be the central problem raised by a critical idealism and then begins to defend his characteristic claim that there can be no wholly idealistic (or practical) nor realistic (or generally theoretical) resolution of it, and certainly not the practical idealism he takes Fichte to be defending. (That is, he concedes the limitations of any theoretical resolution, and the appropriateness of the practical framework just invoked, but he denies the *ultimacy* of such a practical point of view; he insists that such a practical orientation just ultimately returns us to the theoretical or realism problem in a never-ending "circle." Idealism and what would become the philosophy of nature are *equiprimordial,* and the problem is to find a way to *state* this equiprimordiality in a way just both to its absolute and its metaphysically "indifferent" status.)

Now, understanding Schelling's Spinozistic formulations of the Basic Question at issue would require at least a full book. (For Schelling, the controversy in all philosophy is said to be: "the point from which the original opposition in the human mind" proceeds; or the "stepping-out," *Heraustreten,* "from the Absolute."[44] Or later: "how the Absolute could come out of itself and oppose to itself a world."[45]) This Schellingean reformulation of Fichte's problem (how the "I" could originally oppose itself to a "not-I"), itself a reformulation of Kant's *Grundproblem* (how are synthetic a priori judgments possible; how can the mind know a priori what is not-mind), does not, though, however eventually glossed, lead for Schelling to a Fichtean resolution. There can be no "priority" to the "I"'s self-determination, whether conceived theoretically or practically or even, to use the language adopted above, whether conceived in terms of the autonomy of the normative. Self-imposing a norm must always be treated as "conditioned," arising already within some understanding of the logic of finitude and opposition, an origin not a result or object of thought, an "absolute" not itself explicable in terms of reasons because the unconditioned "essence" or "source" of such a possibility.

Here is what appears to be Schelling's swipe at Fichte's final resolution of such an issue.

It would be vain to believe that the victory is decided by the mere choice of principles which are to serve as the basis of one's system, and that in order to save one system of another, it matters only what principle one has set up at the outset. For what matters is not a trick by which one finds at the end what one had prepared initially and cleverly for such eventual discovery . . . it is nothing but an inevitable circle if our theoretical speculation sets up beforehand what our freedom will maintain afterwards in the scrimmage of the contest . . . Consequently, no philosopher will imagine that he has done everything by merely setting up the highest principles. For those principles have only a subjective value as a basis of his system, that is, they are valid for him only inasmuch as he has anticipated his own practical decision.[46]

This is also the tone taken in the *Treatise on Idealism in the Wissenschaftslehre,* where Schelling expresses his distaste for "Kantians" who "guard themselves against atheism" by "invoking a moral necessity." He claims that "they fail to recognize that everything within ourselves remains petty if it is not effected by nature itself, and the moral sublime is progressively trivialized at the hands of man unless it is perceived as a necessity."[47] (I note that the reference to Kantians is ambiguous here because Schelling's comments on Fichte are also so favorable, and in fact, he refers to him as a coconspirator, as it were, in the attempt to formulate a conception of philosophy that relies on neither theoretical nor practical priority; Fichte becomes "the founder of a philosophy that can legitimately be called a higher philosophy because its spirit [note the qualification here] is neither theoretical nor practical alone but both at once."[48])

These passages raise many issues. But we are also returned to the general question of this essay: how Fichte is handling the question of the possibility of human freedom, or whether he can avoid a short argument (and unconvincing) solution (i.e., we needn't be concerned that the world in itself is thoroughly determined because such a world could only be the object of a subjectively self-determined representation) or a Kantian, noumenal ignorance/practical priority solution. Schelling's question again highlights the issue of nature or substance,[49] and has suggested again that just "having to think of ourselves as free" is little philosophical consolation.

VI

Fichte never responded directly to Schelling's interpretation and apparent criticism, but there is fairly widespread agreement, based both on close textual reading and on Fichte's letters, that he took himself to be responding to Schelling in his 1797 Introductions.[50] These passages give Fichte the opportunity to restate his understanding of the fundamental relationship between idealism and freedom. Throughout especially the Second Introduction, Fichte goes to great length to stress his Kantian bona fides and in the course of doing so, especially in Section 6, does briefly appear to shift his basic claim toward the "priority of the practical" interpretation discussed above and therewith to seize one of the horns of the dilemma offered idealism by Schelling. He had by now adopted the term introduced with so many complications by Kant in the *KU*, and taken up enthusiastically by Schelling, "intellectual intuition," as his designation for the "I"'s original self-relation. In a very compressed discussion, he differentiates himself from both Kant and Schelling.

This intellectual intuition of which the *Wissenschaftslehre* speaks is not directed to any sort of being whatsoever [this is the reference to Schelling which he will expand in Sections 7–10]; instead it is directed at an acting – and this is something that Kant does not even mention (unless perhaps under the name "pure apperception").[51]

It is at this point that Fichte claims that there *is* a point in the Kantian system where such an intellectual intuition, or pure self-determination, does make its appearance, though not appreciated properly by Kant. "Since Kant, we have all heard, surely, of the categorical imperative?" In the body of the text that follows, however, it is clear that Fichte is making use of Kant's moral philosophy in the service of a general point, and not at all as a reorientation of his project. In fact, that "perhaps" in the quotation above assumes very large importance as all of the succeeding discussion returns to the similarities between Fichte's project and Kant's founding claims about the apperceptive nature of experience.

Again, however, to return to the points made in the early sections here, Fichte does not formulate his view on the implications of such a foundation by arguing for the metaphysical distinctness of a spontaneous mind, nor does he invoke the general unrepresentability of nature in itself as a stage in an argument for freedom. His point is more comprehensive.

So what then is the overall gist of the *Wissenschaftslehre,* summarized in a few words? It is this: reason is absolutely self-sufficient; it exists only for itself. But nothing exists for reason except reason itself. It follows that everything reason is must have its foundation in reason itself and must be explicable solely on the basis of reason itself and not on the basis of anything outside of reason, for reason could not get outside of itself without renouncing itself. In short the *Wissenschaftslehre* is transcendental idealism.[52]

It is on the basis of this restatement "in a couple of words," that he formulates his response to Schelling's question, or what he regards as Schellingean "objections and misunderstandings." The heart of such misunderstanding is that,

Some people contend that every act of thinking must necessarily be directed at some being. Consequently if no being pertains to the I with which the *Wissenschaftslehre* begins, then this I is unthinkable, and the entire science constructed on the basis of something so thoroughly self-contradictory is empty and nugatory [*nichtig*].[53]

In dealing with this objection, Fichte again must explain the relevance of his idealism to the question of the possibility of freedom. And again, at the outset, his point seems very briefly stated, even dismissive (again, as if a "short argument"). He treats the question as if it asks whether I really am capable of thinking, as I seem to myself to be thinking, and Fichte responds that this all has the same status of M. Jourdain being able to be surprised that he had been talking prose all his life. (Or it is like believing that one needs to consult Aristotle's account of life to find out if one really is living or might actually be dead.) It is, in other words, an empty and unnecessary question.

But Fichte does not make this point by invoking any theory of representation or any problem of the representability of the in-itself. He takes the problem immediately to be one concerning the categorial issue of *explanation.* The question, he claims, concerns the possibility of some account which relied on an exogenous "restriction" on the "really efficacious, truly practical activity of the self." It is *this* notion of some claim to a matter of fact restriction on our normative self-regulation that would be an absurdity, or itself an instance of what it is trying to deny. It would itself *be* the giving of reasons and the undertaking of commitments. (The point is made again in Section 10, when Fichte insists that "the relationship between free beings is one of free interaction [*Wechselwirkung*]; it is by no means a relationship of mere causality operating through mechanical forces."[54] We have been looking for Fichte's defense of such a claim, and that has led us to the import of his own gloss on this assertion: that anyone "presupposing the thorough-going validity of the mechanism of cause and effect," would "directly contradict themselves. What they say stands in contradiction to what they do; for to the extent that they *presuppose* mechanism, they at the same time elevate themselves above it."[55])

There is a full theoretical statement of the position Fichte wishes to defend against Schelling in Section 7. Fichte freely concedes that in the *WL,*

. . . the concept of being is by no means considered to be a primary and original concept, but is treated purely as a derivative one, indeed as a concept derived through its opposition to activity, and hence as a merely negative concept. For the idealist, nothing is positive but freedom; and for him, being is nothing but a negation of freedom.[56]

In the remarks surrounding this passage, Fichte makes clear that he is worried about readers taking such claims in the "ordinary" rather than the "philosophical" sense, taking him to mean that the material existence of objects depends on the "I"'s activity, whereas he is restricting himself to the possibility of existence claims and to an account of the conceptual implications of any realist claims about an "existent" itself "determining" such a possible claim-making or norm-regulated, activity. *That* would be like relying on Aristotle to "prove" that one is alive.

What is going wrong, he states in Section 9, concerns "the concept of the concept" of the "I," not a dispute between interlocutors who share the same ground rules. (The implication throughout these remarks is, in effect, that Schelling has treated Fichte in a misleading, "Reinholdean" way, or has not appreciated the radicality of Fichte's move from *Tatsache* to *Tathandlung*.)[57] The realist thinks this way:

> The final goal of their acting is their own I (in the sense in which they understand this word, i.e., their own individual person), which thus also constitutes the limit of their ability to think clearly [*die Grenze ihres deutlichen Denkens*]. For them, their own individual I is the only true substance, and reason is merely an accident of this substance. Their own person does not present itself to them as a particular expression of reason; instead, reason is present simply in order to assist this person in making his way in the world, and if he were to manage equally well without reason, then we could dispense with it and it would not exist at all.[58]

The Fichtean idealist frames the problem differently from the outset (he does not answer the same question differently).

> The relationship between reason and individuality presented in the *Wissenschaftslehre,* is just the reverse: here the only thing that exists itself is reason, and individuality is something merely accidental; reason the end and personality is a means; the latter is merely a particular expression of reason, one that must be increasingly absorbed into the universal form of the same. For the *Wissenschaftslehre,* reason alone is eternal, whereas individuality must ceaselessly die off.[59]

If there is a "monism" emerging in the post-Kantian philosophical world, the kind proposed by Fichte (and that decisively influenced Hegel, as this passage especially reveals) is what might be called a normative monism, a claim for the "absolute" or unconditioned status of the space of reasons. Stated less grandly, I take such passages as the above, and the shape of Fichte's apparent response to Schelling, to confirm again the interpretation proposed here. To deny the possibility of things in themselves is only to state the "mythic" nature of "the given." It is to make a claim about the "concept of the concept" of the subject of experience, and so to deny, as a conceptual claim, the possible role of causes in thinkings and doings.[60]

VII

As noted at the outset, the question of the relationship between idealism and the problem of freedom (or the short argument issue) is only one of the two major problems raised by Fichte's response to the *Aenesidemus* review. The other is the systematic problem, and this has two forms. One concerns the possibility of some argument that would successfully derive determinate norms for thinking and acting that are "necessary" in the sense suggested by Fichte: necessary as strict conditions for the possibility of such a wholly self-authorizing self-legislation (Fichte's expanded, normative version of the apperception condition). The other concerns the nature of the systematic argument for the overall structure which would result from such an argument form, especially the argument for the distinct necessity of norms of explanation and norms of justification and for the proper way to understand the relation between such "laws."

These introduce vast problems, "determinacy" or "content" problems that must be faced not only by Fichte but by anyone generally dissatisfied with the "uncritical" nature of empiricism and the insufficiency of modern naturalism to account for its own normative status (*whence* our supposedly indispensable norms?). They also set the stage for an important, very well-known criticism of Fichte (the one that decisively established him as a "merely subjective idealist"), Hegel's charge in his *Differenzschrift* that these two issues cannot be resolved within Fichtean assumptions.

> The I remains a subjective subject-object because the subjectivity of transcendental intuition is held fast. This is most strikingly apparent in the relation of the I to nature.[61]

Hegel goes on to make a number of Schellingean points about the consequences of Fichte's treating nature, in effect like Kant, as the totality of objects of possible experience, as an "ideal result," an "object of reflection," or a "dead" and "lifeless" object (consequences especially apparent in Fichte's *Rechtsphilosophie*). This ends up meaning that any actual, living *subject* is also for itself some achieved unity of various acts of reflections, an object to itself, not the living natural unity we intuitively want to give expression to, not a true subject for itself, but only in itself.

Such a criticism would begin a new discussion here. I raise the Hegel problem only to conclude by noting how profoundly his own conception of the task of systematic philosophy was influenced by Fichte (and thus, in a roundabout way, to agree again with those who see the *Aenesidemus* review as a "watershed," at least as important in the development of the Idealist tradition as the Jacobi and pantheism issues and the influence of the *Kritik der Urteilskraft*), and especially to stress the influence on Hegel of the kind of idealist considerations in the early Fichte highlighted above. For Hegel frames the problem of Fichtean idealism in a way that stresses the normative, rather than the psychological or substantialist dimensions. He does invoke the language of "producing the objective world out of pure consciousness" and so forth, but he had already chastised Reinhold and others for confusing Fichte with any dogmatic idealism, and he goes on to stress that the problem in Fichte is the normative basis upon which the subject can be said to limit or constrain itself.

The "absolute positing" he is referring to is the "self-limiting of the I by itself," the constraint of reasons, not some representation-making.[62] Moreover, to frame the problem this way, as Hegel does throughout the discussion of Fichte in *DS,* as the problem of the subject's self-limiting (or the self-authorization of rational norms) might then help to reframe the systematic project in Hegel's own *Encyclopedia.* The insufficiencies, for example, of explanations which refer exclusively to the material properties of bodies might not then be understood as a result of some ontological divide in the universe, or the necessary existence of *geistige* beings. That limitation, and so the necessity of explanations which refer to purposes or eventually intentions, might also be explicable as a self-limitation, by reason of itself, or a limitation intelligible by reference to the norm of explanation itself and its necessarily manifold dimensions. Whether this would replace Hegel's own view of Fichte and Schelling as mere way stations on the way to him, and would make Hegel himself finally and basically a "post-Fichtean," is a much longer and much different story.[63]

Notes

1. Texts and Abbreviations:

A
> G. E. Schulze, *Aenesidemus, Or Concerning the Foundation of the Philosophy of the Elements Issued by Professor Reinhold in Jena together with a Defense of Skepticism Against the Pretensions of the Critique of Pure Reason,* trans. George di Giovanni, in *Between Kant and Hegel: Texts in the Development of Post-Kantian Idealism* (Albany: State University of New York Press, 1985).

Beyträge
> Karl Leonhard Reinhold, *Beyträge zur Berichtigung bisheriger Missverständnisse der Philosophie,* vol. I (Originally 1790) (Darmstadt: Wissenschaftliche Buchgesellschaft, 1963).

CCW
> J. G. Fichte, "Concerning the Concept of the *Wissenschaftslehre,*" in *Fichte: Early Philosophical Writings,* trans. and ed. Daniel Breazeale (Ithaca: Cornell University Press, 1988).

CS
> J. G. Fichte, "A Comparison Between Professor Schmid's System and the Wissenschaftslehre" in *Fichte: Early Philosophical Writings,* trans. and ed. Daniel Breazeale (Ithaca: Cornell University Press, 1988).

D
> G. W. F. Hegel, *The Difference between Fichte's and Schelling's System of Philosophy,* trans. H. S. Harris and Walter Cerf (Albany: State University of New York Press, 1977).

DC
> F. W. J. Schelling, "Philosophical Letters on Dogmatism and Criticism," in *The Unconditional in Human Knowledge: Four Early Essays (1794–1796),* trans. and comm. Fritz Marti (Lewisburg: Bucknell University Press, 1980).

DS
> G. W. F. Hegel, *Differenz des Fichte'schen und Schelling'schen Systems der Philosophie,* in *Gesammelte Werke,*

Bd. 4, Jenaer Kritische Schriften, ed. Hartmut Buchner and Otto Pöggeler (Hamburg: Felix Meiner Verlag, 1968).

Fundament   Karl Leonhard Reinhold, *Ueber das Fundament des philosophisches Wissens* (Originally 1791) (Darmstadt: Wissenschaftliche Buchgesellschaft, 1963).

GA   *J. G. Fichte, Gesamtausgabe der Bayerischen Akademie der Wissenschaften,* eds. Reinhard Lauth and Hans Joacob (Stuttgart: Frommann-Holzboog, 1965).

GW   *F. W. J. Schelling, Historisch-kritische Ausgabe,* ed. Michael Baumgartner et al. (Stuttgart: Frommann-Holzboog, 1976–).

In   J. G. Fichte, *Introductions to the Wissenschaftslehre and Other Writings,* trans. and ed. Daniel Breazeale (Indianapolis: Hackett, 1994).

NM   J. G. Fichte, *Foundations of Transcendental Philosophy (Wissenschaftslehre) nova methodo (1796/99),* trans. and ed. Daniel Breazeale (Ithaca: Cornell University Press, 1992).

Nova Methodo (H)   J. G. Fichte, *Wissenschaftslehre nach den Vorlesungen von Hr. Pr. Fichte, GA,* IV, p. 2.

Nova Methodo (K)   J. G. Fichte, *Wissenschaftslehre nova methodo. Kollegnachschrift Chr. Fr. Krause 1798/99,* ed. Erich Fuchs (Hamburg: Felix Meiner Verlag, 1982).

Rev   J. G. Fichte, *Review of Aenesidemus,* in *Fichte: Early Philosophical Writings,* trans. and ed. Daniel Breazeale (Ithaca: Cornell University Press, 1988).

SA   G. E. Schulze, *Aenesidemus, oder über die Fundamente der von Herrn Prof. Reinhold in Jena gelieferten Elementar-Philosophie* (Brussels: Culture et Civilization, 1969) (*Aetas Kantiana*).

SW   *Sämtliche Werke,* ed. I. H. Fichte (Berlin: de Gruyter, 1971).

TISK   F. W. J. Schelling, *Treatise Explicatory of the Idealism in the Science of Knowledge,* in *Idealism and the Endgame of Theory: Three Essays by F. W. J. Schelling,* trans. and ed. Thomas Pfau (Albany: State University of New York Press, 1994).

Versuch   Karl Leonhard Reinhold, *Versuch einer neuen Theorie des menschlichen Vorstellungsvermögens* (Originally 1789) (Darmstadt: Wissenschaftliche Buchgesellschaft, 1963).

2. *Schillers Briefe in zwei Bänden,* vol. II (Berlin and Weimar: Aufbau-Verlag, 1982), pp. 12ff.

3. Daniel Breazeale, "Fichte's *Aenesidemus* Review and the Transformation of German Idealism," *Review of Metaphysics* 34 (1981): 546.

4. In the short essay, "Concerning the Concept of the *Wissenschaftslehre,*" Fichte seems to confirm the wildness of this position by insisting that his "first principle" "includes all possible content," that the content of this principle is "content pure and simple, absolute content." *CCW,* p. 111; *GA,* I, p. 52.

5. Or at least one of the many streams of influence looks like this. The complexity of the controversies and disputes relevant to the formation of the Idealist project is well known. One would also have to include such issues as the influence of Kant's *Critique of Judgment,* and the role of theories of beauty and art; Jacobi's conservative challenge, and the pantheism and atheism controversies; and various political and theological controversies. Cf. Rolf-Peter Horstmann, *Die Grenzen der Vernunft*

(Frankfurt am Main: Anton Hain, 1991) and Frederick Beiser, *The Fate of Reason* (Cambridge, Mass.: Harvard University Press, 1987).

6. Reinhold defined a *"Grundsatz"* as a "proposition which determines several other propositions" with respect to their form. See his account of how a system of philosophy develops in *Beyträge,* I, pp. 91–164.

7. This apart from the fact that the formulation makes Kant sound like an empirical skeptic, confining our knowledge to sensations or impressions. Schulze was to charge that this was especially true of Reinhold's version of the *Restriktionslehre.*

8. Rolf-Peter Horstmann, "Zur Aktualität des Deutschen Idealismus," *Neue Hefte für Philosophie* 35 (1995): 3

9. *Versuch,* p. 200. See also the formulation in the *Beyträge,* I, p. 267: "in consciousness the subject distinguishes the representation from both the subject and the object and relates it to them both," and in *Fundament,* p. 78.

10. Reinhold did not believe the principle was analytic since its content was a "universally recognized fact of consciousness": see Breazeale's account, "Between Kant and Fichte: Karl Leonhard Reinhold's 'Elementary Philosophy'," *Review of Metaphysics* 35 (1982): 797. And he certainly thought a good deal followed from such a claim: "Only such a science can demonstrate, in a manner which is both universally valid and which will eventually be universally accepted, that space, time, the twelve categories, and the three forms of the ideas are originally nothing but properties of mere representations." *Fundament,* 72–73.

11. Since, thanks to the *Briefe,* Reinhold had become such a popularizer of Kant, and was so associated with "official Kantianism," Schulze was able, for rhetorical purposes, to conflate their positions in any number of indefensible ways. See Nicolai Hartmann, *Die Philosophie des deutschen Idealismus* (Berlin: de Gruyter, 1974), pp. 14–15. On the general intellectual ferment and the rather hothouse atmosphere within which positions were discussed more as slogans or in terms of their supposed "spirit" rather than their "letter," see Dieter Henrich, "Konstellationen. Philosophische und historische Grundfragen für eine Aufklärung über die klassische deutsche Philosophie," in *Zur Architektonik der Vernunft,* ed. L. Berthold (Berlin: Akadamie Verlag, 1990), p. 18, and Rolf-Peter Horstmann, *Die Grenzen der Vernunft,* op. cit., p. 74.

12. The air of paradox intensifies with Fichte's counter that if *this* were true, then Schulze would have no basis for calling himself a *skeptic,* for denying "there is" something we have no access to. (When formulated this way, the only consistent position would be Berkeley's unusual realism: we do know things in themselves, but *esse est percipi.*)

13. *A,* p. 98; *SA,* p. 107

14. *A,* p. 99; *SA,* p. 108.

15. *A,* p. 138, *SA,* p. 115.

16. *A,* p. 166; *SA,* p. 127.

17. *Rev,* p. 73; *SW,* I, p. 19.

18. Ibid.

19. *Rev,* p. 73; *SW,* I, p. 20.

20. *Rev,* p. 67; *SW,* I, p. 11.

21. *Rev,* p. 69; *SW,* I, p. 15.

22. *Rev,* p. 65; *SW,* I, p. 10.

23. Whereas Reinhold was worried that Kant's position on the "thinkability" but not "knowability" of the thing in itself might "leave open" Spinozist speculations about

the real nature of what might only appear to be our freedom, and so insisted on the complete impossibility of any representation of such a realm (*Beyträge*, p. 431), Fichte went the further, somewhat more consistent, step of eliminating entirely any such (even unrepresentable) reference.

24. I say "case" advisedly, since it is not that easy to isolate the actual argument that is supposed to establish, as its conclusion, that space and time are subjective forms of intuition. See my discussion in *Kant's Theory of Form* (New Haven: Yale University Press, 1981), pp. 54–87.

25. Karl Ameriks, "Kant, Fichte, and Short Arguments to Idealism," *Archiv für die Geschichte der Philosophie* 72 (1990): 63–85 (*KFS* hereafter); and "Reinhold and the Short Argument to Idealism," *Proceedings of the Sixth International Kant Congress*, ed. G. Funke, T. Seebohm (Washington, D.C.: University Press of America, 1989), pp. 441–55.

26. Ameriks, *KFS*, p. 68.

27. "He [Fichte] is simply rejecting the sheerly unrepresentable, while avoiding coming to grips with the grounds for the Kantian possibility of something beyond the spatio-temporal realm." Ameriks, *KFS*, p. 79.

28. Ameriks, *KFS*, p. 82.

29. *NM*, p. 78; *Nova Methodo (K)*, p. 4.

30. See his remarks in "Concerning the Concept of the *Wissenschaftslehre*" on the subsidiary or merely propaedeutic issue of representation, and the relation between that issue and his ultimate concerns, *CCW*, p. 133; *GA*, I, p. 80.

31. *Rev*, p. 69; *SW*, I, p. 15.

32. *CCW*, p. 126; *GA*, I, p. 71 (see translator's note).

33. *In*, p. 20; *GA*, I, 4, p. 195.

34. *NM*, pp. 105–6; *Nova Methodo (H)*, p. 25 (K, p. 27).

35. This is from the notes to the *Aenesidemus* review, *GA*, II, I, p. 287.

36. See the discussion in "A Comparison between Prof. Schmid's System and the *Wissenschaftslehre*," and Fichte's explanation there for the claim that "With its first proposition the *WL* succeeds in establishing not just philosophy in its entirety, but also the conditions for all philosophizing. This proposition serves to reject not only everything which, but also everyone who does not belong within the domain of the *WL*." *CS*, pp. 323ff.; *GA*, II, pp. 443ff.

37. I stress again the multiplicity of the strands of strategies Fichte was taking up and trying out in these early writings. One strategy in such an enterprise to which he was clearly attracted does go in the Kantian-Reinholdean direction. Room can be made for reference to actions and agents by insisting that nature is itself a result, a construct, a phenomena; that the nonultimacy of our claims about it leave such room. But I am trying to point to another strategy, wherein the insufficiency of lawlike explanations for thinkings and doings is argued for more directly, within some comprehensive account of the place of the categories of reason (*Geist*) and nature (*Natur*). In my view this would only finally become apparent in Hegel's formulation of the *Encyclopedia* project. But that is another story.

38. *DC*, p. 161; *GW*, I, p. 56. See also "The time has come, my friend, to destroy the delusion, and to state plainly and resolutely that criticism means to do more than merely deduce the weakness of reason and prove only this much, that dogmatism cannot be proved." *DC*, p. 162; *GW*, I, p. 58.

39. See especially Reinhard Lauth's discussion in *Die Entstehung von Schellings Identitätsphilosophie in der Auseinandersetzung mit Fichtes Wissenschaftslehre*

(Freiburg: Alber, 1975), pp. 9–55; and Daniel Breazeale's discussion at the conclusion of his "Editor's Introduction" to *J. G. Fichte: Introductions to the Wissenschaftslehre and Other Writings* (Indianapolis: Hackett, 1994), pp. xxiii–xxxii.

40. *DC*, p. 165; *GW*, I, p. 62. Also see "Dogmatism must admit that I cannot stand on my own shoulders in order to look beyond myself," ibid.

41. *DC*, p. 171; *GW*, I, pp. 72–3.

42. *DC*, p. 172; *GW*, I, p. 73–4.

43. *DC*, p. 172; *GW*, I, p. 74.

44. *DC*, p. 163; *GW*, I, p. 60. Cf. Manfred Frank's formulation of Schelling's "fundamental thought," that "being or absolute identity is irreducible to the happening of reflection." Manfred Frank, *Eine Einführung in Schellings Philosophie* (Frankfurt am Main: Suhrkamp Verlag, 1985), p. 8.

45. *DC*, p. 174; *GW*, I, p. 78.

46. *DC*, p. 176; *GW*, I, p. 81.

47. *TISK*, p. 66; *GW*, I, p. 350.

48. *TISK*, p. 108; *GW*, p. 409.

49. Schelling himself poses his question even more broadly. What he is claiming is: by giving itself norms, the Fichtean subject presupposes the possibility of *leading* its life or formulating its thoughts; of not merely existing or being, but "opposing" itself to itself, taking itself up and ruling itself in a way explicable neither as an original choice nor as a manifestation of nature conceived as law-governed. Such a self-opposing is thus neither free in the modern voluntarist sense (itself chosen) nor a manifestation of nature as conceived post-Newton; some prior "process" is evinced in such a self-opposing. Trying to account for such an absolute "stepping out from itself" will lead Schelling into ever more opaque realms of metaphysics and theology, but one of his most suggestive indications of the spirit of his enterprise occurs with his remarks, at the end of the Letters, about Oedipus and the problem of freedom and necessity.

50. Breazeale, *Introductions*, op. cit., p. xxvii.

51. *In*, p. 56; *GW*, I, p. 472.

52. *In*, p. 59; *GW*, I, p. 475.

53. *In*, p. 79; *GW*, I, p. 493.

54. *In*, p. 94; *GW*, I, p. 509.

55. *In*, p. 95; *GW*, I, p. 510.

56. *In*, p. 84; *GW*, I, p. 499.

57. Hegel clearly sees the difference in the *Differenzschrift*, and cautions readers not to think of Fichte's project as a dogmatic idealism: " . . . Reinhold overlooks the transcendental significance of the Fichtean principle which requires one to posit the difference of subject and object in I = I at the same time as their identity . . . " *D*, p. 127; *DS*, p. 41.

58. *In*, p. 90; *GW*, I, p. 505.

59. *In*, p. 90; *GW*, I, p. 505.

60. See *IN*, p. 86; *GW*, I, p. 501.

61. *D*, p. 135; *DS*, p. 48.

62. *D*, p. 131; *DS*, p. 44.

63. I am much indebted to Wayne Martin and Dan Breazeale for their comments on and criticisms of an earlier draft of this paper.

A version of this paper will also appear in Günter Zöller, ed., *The Cambridge Companion to Fichte* (Cambridge University Press, 2000).

8

The Spirit of the *Wissenschaftslehre*[1]

DANIEL BREAZEALE

"The letter killeth, but the spirit giveth life"

(2 Cor. 3:6).

"The letter kills, and this is especially true in the case of the *Wissenschafts-lehre*. Part of the reason for this lies in the nature of this system itself, but part of it may also lie in the particular form taken by the previous 'letter' of the same."

(J. G. Fichte to E. C. Schmidt, 1–6 September, 1798).

I. "Spirit" versus "Letter"

To distinguish the "spirit" from the "letter" of a philosophical text or system is always to ask for trouble, since this distinction can all too easily excuse an indifference to what a particular thinker may actually have *said* and *written* and often reveals an attitude of cavalier disregard for questions of documentary evidence. Yet it is equally true that a refusal to rise above the most literal construal of a text can all too easily transform the study of the history of philosophy into a lifeless exercise in "the history of ideas" or reduce it to a branch of philology that remains blithely indifferent to the philosophical *issues* at stake.

The hermeneutic problem that presents itself here is simply another way of describing the relationship between understanding a portion of a text and the text as a whole. Without an appreciation of the "spirit" of a philosophy or of a philosophical work, one can scarcely understand or appreciate the "letter" of the same, and yet it is equally true that there is, in this case, no path to the spirit except through the letter, just as there is no way to grasp "the whole" except by means of the parts. The proper response to this problem is the same in both cases: one must always bear in mind the intimate – and famously circular – relationship between whole and part, spirit and letter, and one must always strive to confirm one's interpretation of the whole by applying it to specific texts and to test one's understanding of the *spirit* of a particular work or philosophy against the author's own *literal presentations* of the same.

To be sure, there is no final closure to this process of interpretation, no point at which one can be sure that one's grasp of the spirit is immune from further revision in the light of a more careful scrutiny of the letter. Nor does the moment ever arrive when one can put aside all "interpretation" and simply allow a text to "speak for itself." Nevertheless, it is the inescapable responsibility of every philosophical interpreter to evaluate or even to criticize specific claims made by a particular author in the light of one's own grasp of the "spirit" that allegedly animates the work in question.

As Kant remarked, with respect to Plato: "It is by no means unusual, either in ordinary conversation or in the case of written works, to discover, upon comparing the various thoughts expressed by an author on a particular subject, to discover that one understands him even better than he understood himself."[2] Admittedly, Kant was less than delighted when certain of his own followers had the temerity to apply this same insight to his own writings and thus asserted that certain of *his* explicit claims – concerning, for example, the relationship between things in themselves and sensible intuition or the impossibility of "intellectual intuition" – would have to be *rejected* as incompatible with "the spirit of the Critical philosophy." One of those who reached such a conclusion was Johann Gottlieb Fichte, who never tired of insisting that, for all of their external or "literal" differences (and even despite Kant's eventual public disavowal of Fichte's philosophy), the underlying "spirit" of the Critical philosophy and the *Wissenschaftslehre* were one and the same.[3]

Few philosophers have ever been more insistent than Fichte upon the importance of distinguishing "the letter" of a philosophy from "the spirit" of the same. Not only did he endorse, as a general rule of philosophical interpretation, the principle that "when one is unable to make satisfactory progress in one's interpretation [of a philosopher] by appealing to the *letter,* then one certainly has to interpret in accordance with the *spirit,*"[4] but he deliberately adopted a form of presentation for his *own* philosophy that was virtually guaranteed to force his own desperate readers to look beyond the often bewildering "letter" of his writings and to seek to grasp the animating "spirit" of the same. Indeed, he boasted of his success in adopting a form of presentation "that shuns the fixed letter"[5] and thereby *compels* his readers to strive to discover, on their own, the overall "spirit" of his philosophy, in the light of which alone the particular technical presentations of the same can be properly understood.

This deep-seated conviction concerning the difference between the spirit of the *Wissenschaftslehre* and any literal presentation of the same also helps explain Fichte's puzzling – and, for a scholarly exegete, often infuriating – habit of adopting a radically new mode of presentation and technical vocabulary for each new exposition of his system, a practice he defended as an appropriate means of deterring readers who might think they could master the *Wissenschaftslehre* merely by memorizing a glossary of technical terms.[6] Instead, he maintained:

My philosophy should be expounded in an infinite number of different ways. Everyone will have a different way of thinking it – and each person must think of it in a different way, in order to think *it* at all. . . . I consider [my own presentation] to be most imperfect. Yes, I know that it gives off sparks, but it is not a *single* flame. This summer [i.e., 1796] I have completely reworked it for my lectures. . . . How many more times will I revise my presentation! Nature has made up for my lack of precision by granting me the ability to view things in a number of different ways and by endowing me with a fairly agile mind.[7]

As the years went by and as the misunderstanding and distortions of the *Wissenschaftslehre* multiplied, Fichte became more and more skeptical of the ability of mere words – and especially of printed ones – to convey the essence of his thought. (This, incidentally, seems to have been the chief reason why, once he arrived in Berlin, he resolved not to publish any of the newer versions of his *Wissenschaftslehre* and chose instead to confine himself to oral presentation of the same, so, as he put it, "that misunderstanding can thereby be detected and eliminated on the spot."[8]) Meanwhile, he professed to judge the success of his own presentations of his thought only by the standard of how well or how poorly each seemed to achieve its intended purpose of leading – or perhaps provoking – his listeners or readers to "think the *Wissenschaftslehre* for themselves."

The remarks that follow take Fichte at his word regarding the distinction between the letter and the spirit of his philosophy and are an attempt to summarize, in the broadest possible strokes, what one reader has found to constitute the spirit of *Wissenschaftslehre,* or rather, the spirit of the early (or Jena) *Wissenschaftslehre.* In pursuit of this goal, it will be necessary to ignore a number of internal problems within specific texts from this period and to minimize the sometimes significant differences between the various published and unpublished presentations and elaborations of the Jena *Wissenschaftslehre.* Instead, we will begin with a survey of Fichte's own (literal) presentation – or rather, presentations – of the Jena *Wissenschaftslehre,* followed by a brief discussion of the systematic structure of the early *Wissenschaftslehre.* Only after this excursion through the "letter" of his Jena writings will we attempt to characterize the overall "spirit of the early *Wissenschaftslehre.*"

II. The "Jena *Wissenschaftslehre*"

Though the term "*Wissenschaftslehre*" is widely taken to designate a specific text (usually the *Foundation of the Entire Wissenschaftslehre* of 1794/95), Fichte never actually published a work with this title. Instead, he employed the term "*Wissenschaftslehre*" (which might be rendered as "Doctrine of Science" or "Doctrine of Scientific Knowledge," though *not* as "Science of Knowledge") as the general name for his own *philosophical standpoint* or *system,* a system that he himself considered to be no more than a further elaboration and systematic development of the transcendental idealism adumbrated in Kant's *Critiques.*

Even when construed in this broad sense, however, the term *Wissenschaftslehre* remains ambiguous. To begin with, the system in question includes of several different parts or systematic subdivisions, the first or "foundational" portion of which is often, even by Fichte himself, designated by the same name as the larger system to which it is merely the first part. Moreover, this system did not remain static and unchanged. On the contrary, it continued to undergo almost constant development and evolution, from the moment of its conception in the winter of 1793/94, almost up to the hour of Fichte's death. No less than seventeen different versions or presentations of "the *Wissenschaftslehre*" are known to exist,[9] though only two of these – the *Foundation of the Entire Wissenschaftslehre* and the very brief *Wissenschaftslehre in its General Outline* of 1810 – were actually published during the lifetime of their author. The purely external differences, both in systematic form and technical vocabulary, between these various presentations are dramatic, though how much real difference there is between the actual *content* of the various *Wissenschaftslehren* remains a hotly disputed question. It is, therefore, always advisable, when speaking of "Fichte's *Wissenschaftslehre,*" to specify the specific text or texts to which one is referring or to identify in some other way that particular version or presentation of the *Wissenschaftslehre* one has in mind.

By declaring that this essay be concerned with "the spirit of the Jena *Wissenschaftslehre,*" I mean to indicate that it is an attempt to describe what I consider to be the most distinctive and characteristic features of that version of his philosophy which Fichte constructed and propounded in his lectures and writings during his tenure at the University of Jena, which began in the summer of 1794 and ended in the spring of 1799. (In fact, the term "Jena *Wissenschaftslehre*" is often employed a bit more broadly, to include the earliest "studies" for the *Wissenschaftslehre,* which date from the winter of 1793/94, when Fichte was still living in Zurich, as well as the writings of his first year in Berlin, 1799/1800, when he was still attempting to defend and to revise for publication the final version of his Jena system.[10])

Some experts in the field would object to my attempt to characterize the general spirit of the Jena *Wissenschaftslehre* on the grounds that there are significant systematic differences between Fichte's earlier and later Jena writings,[11] whereas others would challenge my tacit suggestion that the spirit of the Jena *Wissenschaftslehre* is in some significant way different from that of the later – Berlin, Erlangen, and Königsberg – *Wissenschaftslehren* of the period 1801–14. My own view, nevertheless, is that the differences between the earlier (Jena) and later versions of the *Wissenschaftslehre* are indeed large and significant, whereas the differences between the earlier and later Jena writings are relatively minor and superficial – more a matter of "the letter" than of "the spirit." With this warning, let us now turn to consideration of Fichte's own *presentations* of his early philosophy and to an examination of the *systematic structure* of the same.

In anticipation of his arrival in Jena for the Summer Semester of 1794 Fichte published a brief work entitled *Concerning the Concept of the Wissenschafts-lehre,*[12] which was intended to serve as a general introduction to or "prospectus" for his new system, though at the time he composed this work the system itself was still very much "under construction." By the time of his arrival in Jena, however, this process was sufficiently advanced to permit him not only to lecture upon but also to have printed "as a manuscript for his students" a detailed presentation of the first or foundational portion of his newly conceived system. This text, the *Foundation of the Entire Wissen-schaftslehre,*[13] was originally intended to be distributed only in fascicles to his own students, but it was quickly made available to the public at large. Parts I and II were published in 1794 and Part III, along with the closely associated *Outline of the Distinctive Character of the Wissenschaftslehre with Respect to the Theoretical Faculty,*[14] appeared the following year. No sooner did these texts begin to circulate, however, than their author began complaining loudly and publicly about what he claimed to be the well nigh universal misunderstanding of his philosophy, a misunderstanding that he attributed in large part to the deficiencies and peculiarities of the 1794/95 presentations, as well as to the incomplete character of the same.

Two tasks, therefore, occupied Fichte's attention for the rest of his career at Jena. First of all, he immediately set about thoroughly revising his exposition of the first principles or "foundation" of his system and quickly produced a completely new presentation of the same, according to what he described as a "new method." These lectures on "The Foundation of Transcendental Philosophy (*Wissenschaftslehre*) *nova methodo*"[15] were repeated three times between 1796 and 1799, and in 1797 a revised version began to appear in installments in Fichte's own *Philosophical Journal* under the title *An Attempt at a New Presentation of the Wissenschaftslehre.*[16] This "New Presentation" was discontinued following the publication of the two Introductions and the first chapter,[17] but in the fall of 1800 Fichte returned to the project of revising for publication his lectures on the *Wissenschaftslehre nova methodo,*[18] only to abandon it a few months later for the radically new approach – and, I believe, the genuinely new content – one finds in the *Wissenschaftslehre* of 1801/2 (which initiates the period of the "later *Wissenschaftslehre*").

The external differences between the *Wissenschaftslehre nova methodo* and the *Foundation of the Entire Wissenschaftslehre* are certainly striking. Instead of beginning with the logical proposition "A = A" and then pretending to derive therefrom the transcendental principle "the I simply posits itself," the new presentation begins with the simple injunction to "think about the wall, and then think about he who is thinking about the wall." Indeed, the entire First Part of the *Foundation of the Entire Wissenschaftslehre*, with its deeply confusing reference to "three first principles," is dropped entirely, as is the organization of the presentation into separate "theoretical" (Part II) and "practical" (Part III) portions. As we shall observe later, the latter was one of the most misleading features of the *Foundation of the Entire Wissenschaftslehre* and was – and, indeed, continues to be – largely responsible for the failure of many readers to appreciate Fichte's account of the relationship between theoretical and practical reason. Despite such significant differences, the underlying spirit of these two presentations of the first principles of the Jena *Wissenschaftslehre* remains basically the same.

In addition to recasting his presentation of the foundations of his system, Fichte also was busy developing and systematically articulating the various branches or subdisciplines of the same. In pursuit of this goal, he revised his lectures on political philosophy or "philosophy of right" and published them in 1796/97 under the title *Foundation of Natural Right according to the Principles of the Wissenschaftslehre*.[19] In 1798, his revised lectures on moral theory appeared under the title *System of Ethics according to the Principles of the Wissenschaftslehre*.[20] He then planned to lecture upon and to publish a work dealing with a third systematic subdivision of the *Wissenschaftslehre*, namely, philosophy of religion. This project, however, had to be abandoned – ironically enough – because of the eruption of the "Atheism Controversy" and Fichte's subsequent dismissal from his post at Jena.

III. Systematic Structure

The clearest and most detailed sketch of the overall organization and systematic structure of the entire Jena *Wissenschaftslehre* occurs in the concluding section of Fichte's lectures on "The Foundation of Transcendental Philosophy (*Wissenschaftslehre*) *nova methodo*," which provides the guide for the following description of the systematic structure of the early *Wissenschaftslehre*.

(A) The Foundation. The first portion of the system is devoted to *prima philosophia*, that is, to a presentation of the first principles or foundations of the system as a whole. The "first philosophy" in question turns out to consist entirely of a transcendental analysis of self-consciousness and a systematic deduction of the necessary conditions and a priori structure of the same. It includes an inventory of everything that we must necessarily encounter – that is, "posit" – within consciousness. This foundational portion of the system is thus intended to provide a complete account of everything we *must* do and experience in order to perform the act with which the system begins: the act of "thinking the I." Without pretending to summarize this elaborate inventory or description and without making any effort to adumbrate the complex argument (or transcendental deduction) through which it is compiled, two salient points deserve mention, the first of which is the *inseparability* of theoretical and practical activities and elements in Fichte's account of the transcendental constitution of experience. The conclusion of both the *Foundation of the Entire Wissenschaftslehre* and the *Wissenschaftslehre nova methodo* is that "cognition" is impossible without "willing" and that "willing," in turn, always presupposes "cognizing." Only on the horizon of free acting and striving (and only on the presupposition of a practical "check" upon the same) is any encounter with an "object" possible; and yet practical striving always presupposes theoretical cognition both of a goal to be accomplished and of a world within which this goal is to be realized.

Whatever the "primacy of practice" might mean for Fichte, therefore, it does not imply a Schopenhauerian exaltation of "blind willing" at the expense of knowing, nor does it warrant the widely accepted portrait of Fichte as a "ethical idealist," for whom the objective world is *nothing but* an arena for practical striving, a sort of moral gymnasium posited by the "I" simply so that it will have an arena within which to "work out" its practical projects.[21] With respect to his presentation of the foundation of the *Wissenschaftslehre,* Fichte's primary advance upon Kant's account of the constitution of experience is not to have *subordinated* theory to practice, but rather to have demonstrated the inseparability of the same, by showing, in his words, that "our freedom itself [is] *a theoretical determining principle of our world.*"[22]

A second (and closely related) point concerns the importance ascribed by Fichte's transcendental philosophy to the realm of sheer contingency, "otherness," or "giveness" in making experience – and therefore self-consciousness – possible. Though philosophers since Hegel have tended to dismiss Fichte as a "subjective idealist" who, in Russell's inimical words, "abandoned things in themselves and carried subjectivism to a kind of insanity,"[23] the actual upshot of his "foundational" analysis of self-hood is that the "I" can "freely posit itself" if and only if it is not, in fact, as free as it takes itself to be, but is instead, *originally limited* in a variety of ways. The limitations in question are of two sorts: first, there are those associated with sensible "feelings," which form the actual content of what is obscurely described in the *Foundation of the Entire Wissenschaftslehre* as the "check" or *Anstoß* that must occur if an "I" is to be possible at all. In addition, there is the very different sort of "limitation" (or rather, necessary self-limitation) that is implicit in the "I"'s recognition of itself as one rational individual among others: a recognition that occurs when the "I" recognizes itself to be "called" or "summoned" to limit its own freedom out of respect for the freedom of others. Though first introduced in Fichte's treatise on natural right, this doctrine of the "summons" or *Aufforderung* is subsequently fully integrated into the new presentation of the foundations of transcendental philosophy contained in the lectures on *Wissenschaftslehre nova methodo,* where it is demonstrated that the "I" can posit itself only as *one among many.*[24] Without the *Anstoß* and the *Aufforderung,* neither freedom nor consciousness would be possible at all: This much can be demonstrated by a transcendental analysis of the concept of the subject, but no mere philosophy can determine, in advance of experience, either the actual occurrence or the determinate content of either the check or the summons.[25]

The first portion of the Jena *Wissenschaftslehre* does not, therefore, attempt to establish a new "metaphysics of the absolute I." On the contrary, as befits a presentation of the "foundation of transcendental philosophy," it contains neither more nor less than an exhaustive analysis of the conditions necessary for the possibility of free self-positing. What this analysis reveals is that the "I" can be a freely self-positing subject only insofar as it is also (for itself) an originally limited object, and that willing is just as dependent upon knowing as knowing is upon willing. Only an "I" that encounters and posits an objective (intelligible) *realm* of free moral agents and an objective (sensible) *world* of material objects in space and time; only an "I" that encounters and posits *itself,* first, as a rational individual among others, that is, as a *moral* agent and a *social* self, and second, as a *materially embodied* agent within a sensible world: only such a *finite self* can be – and posit itself as – free and self-conscious. A genuinely unlimited or "absolute I" is either a philosopher's fiction (an explanatory hypothesis that eventually subverts itself, which is what happens to the "absolute I" with which the *Foundation of the Entire Wissenschaftslehre* commences[26]) or else it is a regulative idea of reason: an unobtainable goal of infinite striving, posited as such not by the transcendental philosopher, but by the ordinary, finite I that philosophy describes and analyzes.

(B) Systematic Subdivisions. In addition to its first or foundational portion, the entire Jena *Wissenschaftslehre* also comprises four "special philosophical sciences," which constitute the systematic subdivisions of the entire *Wissenschaftslehre.*

(1) Theoretical philosophy. First, there is a specifically "theoretical" portion devoted to philosophy of nature or "theory of the world," which would resemble Kant's *Metaphysical First Principles of Natural Science,* supplemented by a consideration of organic laws. The task of narrowly "theoretical" philosophy, as construed by Fichte, is simply to

develop and to analyze the concept of objectivity deduced in the first part of the system, until one has finally established – in as much concrete detail as is obtainable from the a priori standpoint of transcendental philosophy – *what experience, and hence "nature," necessarily is and must be.*

It is important to note, even if only in passing, the radical dissimilarity between Fichte's conception of the philosophy of nature and certain other projects that have gone by the same name. What is most striking about Fichte's concept of nature is how *little* he believed one can learn about nature from the a priori standpoint of philosophical reflection – which may explain why he himself showed so little interest in developing this branch of his system. In any case, the kind of "theoretical philosophy" envisioned (though not actually constructed) by Fichte would appear to have far more in common with what we today call the philosophy of science than with the a priori *Naturphilosophie* of Schelling and Hegel.[27]

(2) Practical philosophy. The second systematic subdivision of the *Wissenschaftslehre* is "practical philosophy" or "ethics," the task of which is not to explain how the world actually *is* and *must be,* but rather, how it *ought to be constructed by any rational being whatsoever,* without regard to the individual circumstances of such a being. As developed in the *System of Ethical Theory,* this branch of the *Wissenschaftslehre* begins with a deduction and analysis of the first principle of ethics (i.e., with the deduction of the categorical imperative – albeit in new, "Fichteanized" form). It also includes a deduction of the "reality and applicability" of the moral law (which constitutes the most original portion of Fichte's treatment of ethics), as well as a detailed derivation of specific duties from the principle of duty in general.

(3) Philosophy of the postulates. In addition to the specifically "theoretical" and "practical" subdivisions of the *Wissenschaftslehre,* there is also a third and more complex systematic subdivision, which Fichte calls "philosophy of the postulates" and further subdivides into (a) "theory of right" or "doctrine of law" (*Naturrecht*), which considers the demands that theoretical reason addresses to practical reason, and (b) "philosophy of religion," which considers the postulates that practical reason addresses to theory.

(3a) Philosophy of right. Whereas theoretical philosophy deals with "nature as such" or "experience in general" and practical philosophy deals with the categorical demands issued by "reason as such," philosophy of right or political philosophy is concerned with investigating, once again from the a priori standpoint of transcendental reflection, *how the freedom of rational individuals must be (hypothetically) limited*

if they are to coexist with one another. Accordingly, the first task of
Fichte's *Foundation of Natural Right* is to show that the individual "I"
cannot posit itself as a free subject unless it simultaneously posits and
recognizes the existence of *other* free subjects – which, in turn, requires
that the individual "I" freely *limit* its own freedom in recognition of the
freedom of others. This a priori "deduction of intersubjectivity," which
is repeated both in the lectures on *Wissenschaftslehre nova methodo* and
in the *System of Ethics* is, without question, one of the most important
and original features of Fichte's early philosophy. It was also the direct
inspiration for Hegel's better-known account of how individual self-
consciousness is constituted through mutual recognition.

The remainder of Fichte's political philosophy is devoted to the task
of "deducing" (occasionally in rather fanciful, even absurd detail) those
constitutional arrangements and juridical/political institutions that provide the necessary conditions for the possibility of a community of
freely acting, mutually recognized individuals. The thrust of such a
political philosophy is to provide a transcendental deduction of the
social contract as well as an a priori justification of a determinate
number of inalienable political rights. (A sharp distinction between the
categorical realm of moral obligations and the hypothetical domain of
juridical rights is one of the most distinctive – and important – features
of Fichte's political philosophy.)

(3b) Philosophy of religion. If political philosophy views the practical demands of morality from the standpoint of the actual world, then
philosophy of religion adopts the opposite perspective and describes
how nature itself must be thought of as a "moral world order." Some
idea of how this branch of the Jena *Wissenschaftslehre* might have been
developed may be gleaned from the essay that provoked the Atheism
Controversy, "On the Basis of Our Belief in a Divine Governance of the
World" (1798),[28] in which Fichte really does seem (despite his later
protestations to the contrary) to *identify* the deity with the moral world-
order. A rather different conception of God is already apparent in Book
3 of *The Vocation of Man* (1800), a difference that may presage the
impending shift from the "earlier" to the "later" *Wissenschaftslehre.*[29]

(4) Aesthetics. The final systematic subdivision of the Jena *Wissenschaftslehre* is "aesthetics," though the latter appears to bear a very
different and more ambiguous relationship to the system as a whole
than do any of the previously mentioned subdisciplines. On the one
hand, Fichte describes the aesthetic *standpoint,* from which one con-
templates the given world of natural necessity "just as if we had produced it," very much in the manner of Schiller's *Letters on the Aesthetic
Education of Man.* So construed, the aesthetic standpoint functions as a

useful *intermediary* between the ordinary standpoint, which it is the task of philosophy to "explain," and the transcendental standpoint, which is the standpoint occupied by philosophy. But "aesthetics" in this sense of the term is not a special "philosophical science" at all and is thus less a systematic subdivision of the *Wissenschaftslehre* than a useful propaedeutic to the same.

In addition, Fichte also characterizes aesthetics in more conventional terms, as a special philosophical science in its own right, a discipline that "describes the aesthetic way of looking at things and establishes the rules of aesthetics." He never, however, produced a systematic presentation of such a science.[30] (It is surely no accident that the two systematic subdivisions of his system that remained most undeveloped – namely, philosophy of nature and aesthetics – were the two fields in which Fichte himself had the least direct, personal interest.)

(C) "Critique." The preceding mention of the potentially propaedeutic role of aesthetics is a reminder that several of Fichte's most important and best-known writings of the Jena period do not, strictly speaking, belong to his systematic presentation of the *Wissenschaftslehre* at all. Instead, the writings in question, which include *Concerning the Concept of the Wissenschaftslehre* (1794)) the two "Introductions to the *Wissenschaftslehre*" (1797), and the plaintively titled *Sun-Clear Report to the Public at Large Concerning the Genuine Essence of the Latest Philosophy: An Attempt to Force the Reader to Understand*[31] (written in 1800 and published in 1801), belong to what Fichte himself called the "critique" of philosophy.[32] In these essentially metaphilosophical texts he reflects upon and attempts to explain the overall character of philosophy in general and of his own philosophy in particular. Here he presents his own account of the relationship between his transcendental project and other conceptions of philosophy, as well his own understanding of the relationship between the *Wissenschaftslehre* and other disciplines and between the standpoints of transcendental philosophy and of ordinary experience. A primary purpose of such discussions is, first, to distinguish "philosophical thinking" from all other forms of thinking and especially from the kind of thinking characteristic of the ordinary standpoint or natural attitude. Another, no less important purpose is to distinguish the kind of philosophizing characteristic of the *Wissenschaftslehre* from all other forms of philosophizing.

These published examples of philosophical critique have a parallel in the introductory lecture course on "logic and metaphysics" that Fichte repeated every semester he taught at Jena, beginning with the winter semester of 1795/96. It is revealing that the textbook he selected for this class (which might accurately be described as his "introductory course" in philosophy) was not one of his own books nor any work by Kant or Reinhold or any other "Critical" philosopher. Instead, he used Volume 1 of Ernst Platner's *Philosophical Aphorisms*. Platner, who is sometimes counted among the "popular philosophers"[33] of the period, is best described as a mitigated skeptic. His text surveys a variety of classical philosophical issues both from a systematic and an historical perspective and subjects each position it describes to a searching skeptical examination. It is indicative of the "spirit of the Jena *Wissenschaftslehre*" that Fichte should have considered a thorough acquaintance with modern skepticism to be the ideal preparation for the study of his own philosophy. Far from ignoring the skeptical challenge to the possibility of knowledge and philosophy, the Jena *Wissenschaftslehre presupposes* and largely accepts the skeptic's successful demolition of most if not all of the preceding philosophical systems and standpoints. Just as Fichte himself was first forced to construct his new system as a direct response to the skeptical challenge of Schulze/*Aenesidemus*,[34] so he believed that the best way to prepare people to "think the *Wissenschaftslehre* for themselves" was, as he put in a letter to Reinhold, "to make them frightened and uneasy in their own houses, to tear down their houses piece by piece, until they are left cringing in the open [– a method that] compels them to seek a shelter that has already been prepared for them elsewhere."[35]

Though he may successfully have terrorized his own students in this manner, Fichte's published introductions to the *Wissenschaftslehre* are less threatening and are largely devoted to hypothetical reflections upon the goals, the deductive strategy, and starting point of transcendental philosophy. In fact, very few philosophers have shown as much interest as Fichte in understanding and in explicating the distinctive character, tasks, and methods of their own speculative enterprise. These narrowly "critical" writings thus provide especially valuable testimony regarding "the spirit of the *Wissenschaftslehre*."

The primary *task* of philosophy, according to Fichte, is to answer the question, "Why do we assume that actual things exist, beyond and in addition to our representations?"[36] Since it is precisely through those same representations that we distinguish between "representations" and "things," then the latter distinction must itself be grounded in a distinction between freely-produced, merely "subjective" representation and other, "objective" ones, the distinguishing feature of which is that the latter appear to occur independently of our will – and to be in this sense "necessary." The question philosophy has to answer can thus be rephrased as "What is the foundation [*Grund*] of those representations of mine that are accompanied by a feeling of necessity?"[37] An awareness

of the distinction between freely produced and "necessary" representations – between "subjective" and "objective" *Vorstellungen* – is simply *assumed* to be an integral feature of what Fichte characterizes
variously as "the ordinary standpoint," "the practical point of view," or
"the standpoint of life." Philosophy's task is by no means to prove that
there is an objective or external world, but rather to *explain* why we
must assume (or "posit") that there is such a world. It attempts to
accomplish this task by discovering, within the a priori structure or
activity of consciousness itself, the transcendental *ground* or *foundation*
of the ordinary standpoint; and it purports to corroborate this hypothesis
by somehow "deriving" the latter from the former. The project of the
Wissenschaftslehre might therefore be described as that of explaining
the "feeling of necessity" that accompanies certain representations by
analyzing the necessary operations of the intellect itself, thereby explaining *psychological* in terms of *transcendental* necessity – and
neatly inverting the Humean strategy.

In order even to formulate such a project, however, one must first
have transformed the ordinary standpoint into an object of philosophical reflection. In Fichte's language, this means that the would-be philosopher must be capable of transporting himself or herself – however
temporarily and artificially – to a standpoint "higher than" the practical
standpoint one is trying to "explain." This new standpoint – which is
referred to by Fichte as the "philosophical," the "speculative," or the
"transcendental" standpoint – is, in contrast to the ordinary standpoint,
never forced upon anyone; instead, it can be attained only by virtue of a
freely initiated act of reflection, through which one, so to speak, sets
aside one's everyday, unexamined assumptions about the relationship
between necessary representations and external objects and treats these
same assumptions as standing *in need of explanation.* (Here again,
transcendental philosophy's debt to modern skepticism is plain.) From
this characterization of the task of philosophy it follows that any so-
called philosophy – whether the "popular philosophy" of Fichte's era or
any other variety of "commonsense philosophy" or epistemological
naturalism – that appeals directly to the *philosophical authority* of
ordinary experience has simply confused *explanans* and *explanandum*
and is thus, in Fichte's eyes, no "philosophy" at all.

Philosophy begins with a willful act of abstraction from the standpoint of ordinary experience and then proceeds to explain the latter by
deriving it from a hypothetically proposed ground or first principle.
Furthermore, according to Fichte, there are really only two basic explanatory strategies open to the philosopher at this point: One can either
attempt to derive ordinary experience from the pure "I" (the sheer

concept of free selfhood) or else one can attempt to derive it from the pure "not-I" (the sheer concept of determinate thinghood).[38] "Dogmatism" is Fichte's name for all philosophies that attempt to explain ordinary experience by postulating a realm of independently existing things in themselves that somehow affect the mind, whereas the strategy that tries to derive our quotidian consciousness both of the material world and of ourselves as empirically sensible individuals from the concept of pure subjectivity is called "idealism."

Since these two positions argue from diametrically opposed first principles, it follows that neither can directly refute the other. This, however, does not imply for Fichte (as it did for Schelling[39]), that these two opposing positions possess an equivalent speculative value. Even in advance of any effort to establish either system, the disadvantages of dogmatism are evident enough. First of all, the dogmatist will obviously have to explain representations themselves, as well as the consciousness that entertains them, as peculiar kinds of *things,* which, in Fichte's view, is just another way of saying that he will be unable to explain consciousness at all, since he deliberately ignores or denies the all-important heterogeneity between the realm of causally interacting things and that of intentional representations (which is precisely what he thought philosophy is supposed be explain).

Moreover, dogmatism must either *ignore* our (subjective) consciousness of our own practical freedom or simply *reject* it as illusory. A philosophy that takes the concept of bare thinghood as its highest explanatory principle will, on Fichte's view, be utterly unable to account for the possibility of genuine human freedom. Indeed, *no* philosophy can "account for freedom," in the sense of deriving freedom from something higher. Thus, the only way to provide freedom with any sort of philosophical warrant is to adopt the opposing, idealist strategy of *starting with freedom* (the reality of which is simply assumed by the *Wissenschaftslehre*) and then attempt to derive the possibility of representations of things therefrom.

Though idealism may possess a certain prima facie theoretical or speculative advantage over dogmatism, in the sense that it at least holds out the possibility of being able to explain the connection between representations and things,[40] its true superiority lies elsewhere and rests upon strictly *practical* or *moral* considerations: namely, its compatibility with our everyday view of ourselves as free and responsible moral agents. The possibility that our inner conviction concerning our own freedom is simply an illusion cannot, as Fichte freely admits, be rejected on purely *speculative* grounds; nevertheless, such a possibility will be simply *intolerable,* he maintains, to anyone with a firm sense of

his or her own moral obligations and vocation and with a lively awareness of his or her own freedom. This then is the gravamen of Fichte's
essentially *practical* case against dogmatism (as well as against skepticism): Idealism alone accords with our extraphilosophical moral (and
hence ontological) commitments, that is to say, with our practical conception of ourselves as *free agents*. The idealist's moral obligation to
affirm his or her own freedom gives the idealist a practical *interest*[41] in
favor of a theoretical conception of the self that at least holds out the
promise of explaining objective experience without denying human
freedom. (Our practical interest in a "system of freedom" does not, of
course, guarantee that any such system is actually possible. The *real
possibility* – that is, the truth – of the *Wissenschaftslehre* can be established only by successfully constructing and defending such a "universally valid" system.)

The celebrated "choice" between idealism and dogmatism thus
proves to involve no choice at all on the part of the idealist.[42] As Fichte
puts it in the "First Introduction" of 1797:

> I *cannot* go beyond this [idealistic] standpoint, because I am not *permitted* to go
> beyond it. With this, transcendental idealism simultaneously reveals itself to be
> the only type of philosophical thinking that accords with duty. It is the mode of
> thinking in which speculation and the ethical law are most intimately united. I
> *ought* to begin my thinking with the thought of the pure I, and I ought to think of
> this pure I as absolutely self-active – not as determined by things, but rather as
> determining them.[43]

No mere philosophy, including the *Wissenschaftslehre,* can actually
liberate human beings or improve their moral character. Nor can any
philosophy *prove* the reality of freedom. All that even the best philosophy can do is demonstrate that there is no necessary *conflict* between
belief in moral freedom and belief in the reality of causally interacting
material objects.[44] The latter belief, while inseparable from the natural
attitude, is not assumed but rather *explained* by the *Wissenschaftslehre;*
whereas the former belief – the practical conviction that one is free to
act morally – which is also part of the ordinary standpoint, at least for
the morally self-aware individual, is simply *presupposed* by the *Wissenschaftslehre,* for which it serves as the ultimate explanatory ground of
experience as a whole. Fichte's philosophy thus turns out to have at
least one important extra- or prephilosophical presupposition: for a
lively, practical awareness of one's own freedom is an absolute *prereq-
uisite* for entering into the chain of reflections that constitute the Jena
Wissenschaftslehre. Indeed, it is precisely because it proceeds *from*
an affirmation of practical freedom *to* an analysis of the conditions

necessary for the possibility of the same that Fichte could proudly
describe his early philosophy as "the first system of freedom."[45]

IV. The Spirit of the Jena *Wissenschaftslehre*

(1) Fichte's Practical Foundationalism. Our characterization of the "spirit of
the Jena *Wissenschaftslehre*" might well begin with the point just made:
namely, that the early *Wissenschaftslehre* is, above all, a system or
philosophy of *human,* which is to say, of *finite* freedom. As we have
now seen, transcendental philosophy can no more demonstrate the reality of freedom than it can demonstrate the reality of those practical
limitations that are apprehended as sensible feeling or prove the reality
of the categorical moral "summons" to self-limitation. Instead, it has to
begin with a practical conviction concerning the reality of moral responsibility and the nonillusory character of freedom. For Fichte then, as for
Kant, the celebrated "primacy of practical reason" thesis is first and
foremost a thesis concerning the primacy of certain *interests* over others,
not a claim concerning the constitutive primacy of practical over theoretical reason (or, in Fichte's technical language, the primacy of the
"real" over the "ideal" acts and powers of the "I"). On the contrary,
Fichte is strongly committed to what might be called an "equiprimordiality thesis" with respect to the relationship between theoretical and
practical reason.

This unflinching recognition that transcendental philosophizing, like
every other human activity, must ultimately be grounded upon a practical interest (and, more specifically, upon our interest in asserting our
own freedom) has a direct bearing upon Fichte's distinctive variety of
foundationalism. Fichte was a notorious and inveterate philosophical
foundationalist, one who believed that the task of searching for an
ultimate ground of experience is one that reason cannot escape because
it is a task contained within the concept of reason itself and who maintained that to call into question the possibility of "grounding" experience in some manner is simply to call into question the very possibility
of philosophy itself. On the other hand, his espousal of philosophical
foundationalism is frankly qualified by numerous admissions of the
unavoidably circular or self-referential character of every philosophical
deduction[46] and by a frank recognition of the indemonstrability and
speculative dubitability of any proposed first principle.

Philosophy must propose some ultimate ground of explanation, but
the proposed first principle of the Jena *Wissenschaftslehre* (i.e., the sheer
concept of "I-hood," which is supposed to be produced by the act of free
self-reflection that the student of the *Wissenschaftslehre* is called upon

to *perform*) is neither demonstrable nor self-evident. Instead, like the postulated freedom of the "I" itself, this first principle must be actively *posited* as the first principle of a transcendental deduction of the conditions necessary for the possibility of experience. In philosophy, as in everyday life, *im Anfang war die Tat.*[47]

(2) Fichte's Modest Transcendentalism. A "beginning" is only just that; and the "original act of consciousness" described in the Jena *Wissenschaftslehre* cannot constitute itself unless something is simply "given to" as well as simply "posited by" the self-positing "I": namely, its own *original limitations.* Though this point has already been mentioned several times, it is worth dwelling on, because it is at once so central a feature of the Jena *Wissenschaftslehre* and yet so widely ignored.[48]

In one sense, Fichte's doctrine of original "feeling" (which is simply a less abstract name for what is elsewhere characterized as a necessary *Anstoß* or "check" on the practical activity of the "I"[49]) plays the same role in the *Wissenschaftslehre* that the discredited doctrine of externally efficacious things in themselves plays in dogmatism and in vulgar Kantianism. An explicit and essential feature of experience is the sheer *contingency* or *giveness* of the same. Indeed, the argument of the Jena *Wissenschaftslehre* is that such a realm of contingency is among the conditions necessary for the possibility of freedom itself. Unlike things in themselves, however, the *Anstoß* is never external to the "I"; instead, it is neither more nor less than the "I"'s encounter with its own original limits. Feelings are, by definition, modifications of the subject, albeit *involuntary* and *contingent* ones. The term "feeling" does not, therefore, designate the *passive affection* of the "I" by something beyond itself. Instead, it designates "the most primordial interaction of the I with itself, [which] even precedes the Not-I . . . [in the I's feeling of itself] its activity and passivity are united in a single state."[50]

To be sure, no transcendental philosophy can ever explain *why,* in any particular case, we discover ourselves to be limited or *angestossen* in one determinate manner rather than another. Philosophy cannot tell me why I am the particular person that I am nor why my world has the determinate and contingent empirical properties that it does. These are questions to which no answer is ever possible. In order to find out who I am and what the world is like I have to keep myself *open to experience,* to the realm of what is purely contingent and merely empirical. Here, Fichte confesses, "we have arrived at the point where all deduction comes to an end."[51]

This frank recognition of the *limits* of a priori philosophizing accounts for the characteristic *modesty* of the Fichtean project, in comparison, at least, with the later systems of thinkers in the same tradition, such as Schelling and Hegel.[52] To criticize the *Wissenschaftslehre,* as Josiah Royce does, for its failure to explain why there is a belt of asteroids between Mars and Jupiter,[53] is simply to display one's failure to grasp the crucial difference between the Schellingian/Hegelian project – with its unbridled celebration of the autonomy of speculative reason and its enthusiastic embrace of an a priori *Naturphilosophie* – and its less pretentious and more purely transcendental Fichtean (and Kantian) rival.

Another way to express this point is to endorse Hegel's well-known description of the *Wissenschaftslehre* as "a philosophy of reflection." Unlike absolute idealists and speculative metaphysicians, the author of the Jena *Wissenschaftslehre* accepts the fact that *vorstellendes Denken* ("picture thinking") is the only kind of thinking there is, either in ordinary life or in transcendental philosophy. Philosophy is thus no more able than any other human (all-too-human) activity to transcend what Fichte often described as "the circle within which every finite understanding, that is, every understanding that we can conceive, is necessarily confined."[54]

What a transcendental deduction *can* demonstrate is that *if* there is to be any selfhood at all, and *if* the "I" is supposed to posit its own freedom for itself, *then* it must also discover itself to be, in some other sense, contingent and limited and thus *not free at all.* These original limitations or determinations of the "I" are certainly not external objects nor things in themselves. Yet it is undeniable that the "I" *does* experience "external objects." How is this possible? It is precisely this question that the *Wissenschaftslehre* claims to answer: Namely, by showing, in great detail, that the "I" *cannot* be an "I" at all (that is, that it cannot act freely and self-consciously) unless, in accordance with the necessary laws of its own acting and reflecting, it "posits" a realm of external objects as the "cause" of its own original limitations.

In order to move from the subjective realm of self-feeling to the objective realms of other persons and material things, the "I" must posit and reposit its own original limitations and must do so in accordance with the necessary and universal laws of its own acting (laws which it is the explicit task of transcendental philosophy to deduce and to analyze). Only through *thinking,* not feeling, are there any objects for the "I," and only if it posits such objects can the "I" posit itself.[55] Thus one could also observe that without material objects and other persons there could be no self-conscious "I." Fichte is not a whit less insistent than Kant that transcendental idealism is inseparable from empirical realism and must never be confused (as it so often is) with other, more extravagant varieties of "idealism."

Though Fichte, to this day, is widely associated with the claim that nothing is really real but the "absolute I" and that everything else is merely a free product or "posit" of the absolute "I," this claim is, in fact, quite incompatible with what is here taken to be the deepest spirit of his thought (or at least of his Jena system). What the Jena *Wissenschafts-lehre* purports to demonstrate is that though the "I" originally posits itself as or "takes itself to be" absolutely free, it can actually posit itself in this manner only if its freedom is, in fact, not absolute at all, but is narrowly constrained by the finitude of the "I" itself, both as an individual member of a moral community and as an embodied thing in a material world. Only a finite "I" can posit anything – including its own infinity. Nor can these "necessary limits" be simply posited by the "I" itself. To be sure, they are subsequently posited by the "I," but originally they must simply be *discovered.*

(3) Fichte's Dialectical Dualism. We have now had several opportunities to observe that though the *Wissenschaftslehre* begins with an assertion of freedom, it also demonstrates that mere (or "absolute") freedom is not only "not enough" but is not even *conceivable.* There can be no freedom without limitation; no self-hood without the other; no practical willing without theoretical cognizing. These dualities, along with the many others that are such a conspicuous feature of all of Fichte's early presentations of his thought, are simply variations on what he himself describes as "the duality that permeates the entire system of reason and which has its foundation in the original duality of subject and object."[56] Despite influential claims to the contrary, Fichte remained throughout his Jena period a *dualist* of a sort, a thinker for whom *difference* remains fundamental and philosophically irreducible and for whom pure unity can never be more than, on the one hand, a *philosophical hypothesis* or *fiction,*[57] produced by reflective abstraction for the purposes of a mere "thought-experiment," or, on the other, a necessary *goal* or *practical demand,* posited – but never achieved – by the finite "I," which finds itself compelled by the very structure of selfhood to maintain that it *ought* to be what it never *is:* namely, infinite in its freedom and unified in its nature.

Like Fichte's "idealism," his "dualism" is neither *metaphysical* nor *psychological* in character, nor is it a dualism of reality and appearance. It does not postulate the interaction of two sorts of substance, nor is it a description of how an independent reality ("the absolute") appears to a finite consciousness.[58] Nor does the *Wissenschaftslehre* pretend to recount the acts and passive states of some special sort of "mental object."[59] The dualism of the Jena *Wissenschaftslehre* is strictly *transcendental* and is implicit in the structure of consciousness itself, at least as that is characterized within this system. It is a dualism of infinity and finitude, of self-positing and feeling, of freedom and facticity, or, to employ the technical terminology of the *Foundation of the Entire Wissenschaftslehre,* of *Tathandlung* (Act) and *Anstoß* (check) – neither of which can be ultimately reduced to nor derived from the other and both of which are necessary for the possibility of ordinary consciousness and self-consciousness.

Though the preceding distinctions are made at the purely transcendental level, they nevertheless refer us to and are ultimately grounded upon distinctions encountered *within* experience, to the extent, at least, that a fundamental human experience is that of one's own, profoundly divided nature (*qua* "free thing"). In any case, it is certainly the presupposition of the Jena *Wissenschaftslehre* that to be an "I" at all is to be aware of oneself as simultaneously free and unfree, infinite and finite, absolutely self-positing and originally limited or determined. Hence one can aptly characterize the spirit of the early *Wissenschaftslehre* by noting that this is a philosophy of, by, and for "divided selves."

Though philosophy can deduce the reality neither of freedom nor of limitation, it can demonstrate the necessary *connection* between the two. Each of these elements – free self-activity and determinate limitation – can be "derived" from the other, in the specifically transcendental sense that each can be shown to be a condition necessary for the possibility of the other, and thus *both* can be shown to be conditions necessary for the possibility of any consciousness whatsoever and hence of experience in general. Fichte's conclusion, therefore, is that what we call a "world" is something that can exist only for a practically free and self-aware being. Conversely, such a self-positing "I" can exist for itself (and, since "being for itself" is a necessary feature of selfhood, can "exist" at all) only insofar as it is not, *malgre lui,* the absolute ground of its own determinate existence, but instead finds itself to be *inexplicably* and *incomprehensibly* limited on virtually every side.[60]

This recognition of the "original duality" of the self, however, is by no means the end of the story. Since freedom and limitation appear to cancel each other out, and since, as we have just seen, the *practical primacy* of freedom is a presupposition of the *Wissenschaftslehre* (in the sense that it *presupposes* that the "I" *ought to* determine the "Not-I"[61]), it further follows that the relationship between freedom and determination (limitation) cannot be conceived as one of mere equilibrium. On the contrary, it must be conceived of as an inherently unstable or *dialectical*[62] relationship, a relationship that gives rise to and expresses itself as an *ongoing temporal process* through which the original contradiction between the I's freedom and its original limitation is transformed into an endless struggle to subordinate the latter to the former: to transform every "ought" into an "is." (Of course, it also follows that were this process ever to be completed then consciousness itself would be immediately extinguished, since selfhood has been show to require and to presuppose *both* freedom and limitation. This is precisely why the struggle in question has to be conceived of as endless or "infinite.")

Before coining the name "*Wissenschaftslehre*" for his new system, Fichte considered several other possibilities, including *Strebungsphilosophie* or "philosophy of striving"[63]; and one might wish that he had retained this term, which is so much more evocative of the genuine "spirit" of his early system than is the innocuous "Theory of Science." In any case, the intimate connection between a *Strebungsphilosophie* and a *Wissenschaftslehre* is certainly demonstrated by Fichte's Jena system, according to which knowing is possible only for a willing creature. Fichte realized from the start that, for all of his misleading talk about the "pure I" and about the single, "absolutely first" principle of his system, any coherent and tenable system of freedom would have to be grounded upon a dialectical dualism, and grounded in such a way that freedom could express itself only as endless striving.

(4) Fichte's Theory of Finite Subjectivity. "System of freedom," "practical foundationalism," "modest transcendentalism," "dialectical dualism," "philosophy of striving": These are some of the terms I have employed in an effort to capture the spirit of the Jena *Wissenschaftslehre*. But perhaps the most straightforward way to characterize the spirit of this same philosophy is in terms of the theory of subjectivity presented in these early writings.

Despite occasional and misleading suggestions to the contrary on Fichte's part, the conclusions to be drawn from the account of subjectivity contained in his Jena writings are as follows: Philosophical concepts of "pure selfhood" or of the "absolute I" are just that: mere theoretical concepts posited for the purposes of transcendental explication. Such concepts are abstractions, constructions, or fictions. They refer to nothing that actually exists – in this world or any other. On the contrary, the only kind of "I" that actually exists and is conceivable as an "I" is *finite* and *divided*. Such a self is free, but not absolutely so. It is self-conscious, but it is also and necessarily conscious of what is manifestly *not* itself: a moral (noumenal) realm of other free selves and an empirical (phenomenal) realm of material objects, each governed by its appropriate laws. Though the laws governing each of these realms can be discovered by transcendental reflection upon the bare concept of the "I," the laws in question are certainly not products of the free activity of the "I." Nor can the contingent content of either of these realms be derived a priori[64]; instead, this content is originally *given* to the "I" along with its capacity to act freely and the requirement ("summons") that it actualize this capacity. The concept of a disembodied "I" – whether understood as a finite "spirit" or as an infinite one (God) – is self-contradictory and inconceivable. Equally inconceivable is the notion of an "absolute" or nonindividual "I." A fundamental lesson of the Jena *Wissenschaftslehre* is that the "I" cannot posit itself as a free subject at all – and thus cannot *be* an "I" at all – except insofar as it posits itself as a finite person: one among many, a material "I."

An *embodied* ego and a *social* self: this, not the "absolute I," is the real "I" of the early *Wissenschaftslehre*. An endless *striving* for unity, but a constant *struggle* with duality: this is the sum and substance of Fichte's conclusion concerning the human condition. What better way, then, to capture the "spirit of the *Wissenschaftslehre*" – and what better way to reveal the fundamental error of the still-prevailing, historical caricature of Fichte's philosophy – than to describe it as a "theory of finite subjectivity"?

Notes

1. The following abbreviations are employed in this essay:
   GA   *J. G. Fichte: Gesamtausgabe der Bayerischen Akademie der Wissenschaften,* ed. Reinhard Lauth, Hans Jacob, and Hans Gliwitzky (Stuttgart: Frommann-Holzboog, 1964–), cited by series, volume, and page number.
   WLnm   Fichte, *Foundations of Transcendental Philosophy (Wissenschaftslehre) nova methodo,* trans. and ed. Daniel Breazeale (Ithaca and London: Cornell University Press, 1992). This translation is a conflated edition of both the Halle and Krause transcripts of Fichte's lectures. The devices employed in this volume to differentiate between these two transcripts are not reproduced here.
   IWL   Fichte, *Introductions to the* Wissenschaftslehre *and Other Writings (1797–1800),* trans. and ed. Daniel Breazeale (Indianapolis and Cambridge, Mass.: Hackett, 1994).
   EPW   *Fichte: Early Philosophical Writings,* ed. and trans. Daniel Breazeale (Ithaca and London: Cornell University Press, 1988).
   All translations are my own.
2. *Critique of Pure Reason,* A 314/B 370. See, too, Kant's application of this method of interpretation "according to the spirit and intention" in his defense of Leibniz in his *On a Discovery According to Which Any New Critique of Pure Reason Has Made Superfluous by an Earlier One* (1790) in Henry Allison, *The Kant-Eberhard Controversy* (Baltimore, Md.: Johns Hopkins University Press, 1973), pp. 157–8.
3. See, for example, Section 6 of the "Second Introduction to the *Wissenschaftslehre*" (in IWL).
4. IWL, p. 63n. See too Fichte's explicit discussion of the "spirit/letter" distinction as it applies to philosophy: first, in his 1794 lectures "Concerning the Difference between the Spirit and the Letter within Philosophy" (in EPW, pp. 192–215), and then in his

essay "On the Spirit and the Letter in Philosophy, in a Series of Letters" (written in 1795 and published in 1800), trans. Elizabeth Rubenstein in *German Aesthetic and Literary Criticism: Kant, Fichte, Schelling, Schopenhauer, Hegel,* ed. David Simpson (Cambridge, U.K.: Cambridge University Press, 1984), pp. 74–93.

5. Second Introduction to *Concerning the Concept of the Wissenschaftslehre* (EPW, p. 100).

6. See the remark on this subject in the preface to the first edition of the *Foundation* (GA, I/2: 252). Even if a fixed "scientific terminology" could be established for the *Wissenschaftslehre,* Fichte considered this to be the *last* and least important task facing the founder of this system. Meanwhile, he remained content to revise and vary his own terminology from presentation to presentation, improvising along the way whatever terms seemed useful and appropriate in each particular context. See the note on the "provisional nature" of all of his own terminology in the second edition of the *Concerning the Concept:* "I will continue to make use of circumlocution and multiplicity of expression in order to give my presentations the clarity and specificity necessary to fulfill my intentions in each particular instance" (EPW, p. 106). See, too, the similar comments in the 1801 "Public Announcement of a New Presentation of the *Wissenschaftslehre*" (IWL, pp. 192 and 201).

7. Letter to K. L. Reinhold, March 21, 1797 (EPW, p. 417).

8. *Pro memoria* to the Prussian Cabinet of Ministers, 3 January, 1804 (GA, III/5: 223; trans. in WLnm, pp. 31–2). See too Fichte's letter to Reinhold, 2 July, 1795 (EPW, p. 398).

9. See Hans Gliwitzky, "Editor's Introduction" to Fichte, *Wissenschaftslehre 1805* (Hamburg: Felix Meiner Verlag, 1984), pp. lxxi–lxxii.

10. The first sketch of what eventually became the *Wissenschaftslehre* ("Eigne Meditationen über ElementarPhilosophie/Practische Philosophie," GA, II/2: 216–66) was drafted in Zurich during the winter of 1793–4, while Fichte was engaged in a systematic reconsideration of Kant's Critical philosophy and Reinhold's Elementary Philosophy and preparing to defend both against the skeptical attack of G. E. Schulze/Aenesidemus. The radically new philosophical strategy and standpoint that emerged from this reconsideration were first made public in Fichte's review of *Aenesidemus* (in EPW, pp. 59–79). By the spring of 1794, he was delivering his first public lectures on his new system of philosophy, for which he had by then coined the name "*Wissenschaftslehre.*" A partial transcript of these lectures has recently been discovered and published by Erich Fuchs: *Fichte, Züricher Vorlesungen über den Begriff der Wissenschaftslehre: Februar 1794; Nachschrift Lavater; Beilage aus Jens Baggesens Nachlass: Exzerpt aus der Abschrift von Fichtes Züricher Vorlesungen,* ed. Erich Fuchs (Neuried: Ars Una, 1996).

11. Max Wundt, for example, made a sharp distinction between the "spirit of the 1794/95 *Wissenschaftslehre*" and "the spirit of *Wissenschaftslehre* 1796/99" (*nova methodo*). See Wundt, *Fichte-Forschungen* (Stuttgart: Frommann-Holzboog, 1929), pp. 1–141. A convincing case for the "unity" of the Jena *Wissenschaftslehre* can be found in the recent work of Ives Radrizzani. See, especially, *Vers la fondation de l'intersubjectivité: Des Principes à la Nova Methodo* (Paris: Vrin, 1993) and "Der Übergang von der *Grundlage* zur *Wissenschaftslehre nova methodo,*" *Fichte-Studien* 6 (1994): 355–66.

12. In EWP, pp. 94–135.

13. Translated by Peter Heath as *Fundamental Principles of the Entire Science of Knowledge,* in *The Science of Knowledge,* ed. and trans. Peter Heath and John Lachs (Cambridge, U.K.: Cambridge University Press, 1982).

14. In EPW, pp. 233–306.
15. In WLnm, pp. 65–474.
16. In IWL, pp. 1–188.
17. For a discussion of the relationship between Fichte's lectures on "The Foundation of Transcendental Philosophy *Wissenschaftslehre* (*nova methodo*) and the published "Attempt at a New Presentation of the *Wissenschaftslehre*," as well as for an account of the survival of the former in the form of student transcriptions, see the Editor's Introduction to WLnm.
18. "Neue Bearbeitung der W.L. 1800" (GA, II/6: 331–402).
19. A new English edition of this text, edited by Frederick Neuhouser and translated by Michael Baur, is forthcoming from Cambridge University Press.
20. A new English edition of this text, edited and translated by Günter Zöller, is forthcoming from Cambridge University Press.
21. This characterization of Fichte was well articulated by Josiah Royce, who described Fichte's position as follows: "The deepest truth, then, is a practical truth. I *need* something not myself, in order to be active, that is, in order to exist. My very existence is practical; it is self-assertion. I exist, so to speak, by hurling the fact of my existence at another than myself. I limit myself thus, by a foreign somewhat, opaque, external, my own opposite; but my limitation is the free choice of my true self. By thus limiting myself, I give myself something to do, and thus win my very own existence. [. . .] The essence of his doctrine consists in identifying Kant's theoretical and practical reason, and in saying that all our assertion of a world beyond, of a world of things and of people, merely expresses, in practical form, our assertion of our own wealthy and varied determination to be busy with things and with people. Thus, then, each of us builds his own world. [. . .] No activity, no world; no self, no not-self; no self-assertion, no facts to assert ourselves upon" (*The Spirit of Modern Philosophy* [Boston: Houghton, Mifflin, 1892], pp. 157–8). For further discussion of this point, see my "The Theory of Practice and the Practice of Theory: Fichte and the 'Primacy of Practical Reason,'" *International Philosophical Quarterly* 36 (1996): 47–64.
22. GA, I/5: 77.
23. Bertrand Russell, *A History of Western Philosophy* (New York: Simon and Schuster, 1963), p. 718.
24. This incorporation of the doctrine of the summons (i.e., the deduction of intersubjectivity) into the "foundational" analysis of the possibility of self-positing is surely the most important and substantial innovation contained in the *Wissenschaftslehre nova methodo* (in comparison with the *Foundation of the Entire Wissenschaftslehre*).
25. For further discussion of this point, see my "Check or Checkmate? On the Finitude of the Fichtean Self," in *The Modern Subject: Conceptions of the Self in Classical German Philosophy*, ed. Karl Ameriks and Dieter Sturma (Albany: State University of New York Press, 1995), pp. 87–114.
26. The classic presentation of this immensely influential way of reading the *Foundation of the Entire Wissenschaftslehre* is to be found in Alexis Philonenko, *La liberté humain dans la philosophie de Fichte* (Paris: Vrin, 1966; 2nd ed., 1980).
27. The closest that Fichte ever came to developing this purely "theoretical" branch of the *Wissenschaftslehre* was in his 1795 work, *On the Distinctive Character of the Wissenschaftslehre with Respect to the Theoretical Faculty* (in EPW, pp. 243–306), though most of this text should really be considered a further elaboration of the

prima philosophia presented in the *Foundation of the Entire Wissenschaftslehre.* See Reinhard Lauth, *Die transzendentale Naturlehre Fichtes nach den Prinzipien der Wissenschaftslehre* (Hamburg: Felix Meiner Verlag, 1984).

28. In IWL, pp. 141–54.

29. On the other hand, the view of God and immortality found in Part III of *The Vocation of Man* was already anticipated in Fichte's lectures on "Logic and Metaphysics" during his last semester at Jena (see GA, II/4: 312–30). Admittedly, this new account of God and immortality, along with certain (closely related) aspects of the account of "pure will" presented in the second half of the *Wissenschaftslehre nova methodo,* are difficult to reconcile with the "spirit" of the early *Wissenschaftslehre* as here characterized.

30. In contrast to all of the other philosophical subdisciplines, which are described as generating their *content* along with the *concept* of the same (which is, according to Fichte, simply a corollary of the claim that these sciences describe certain necessary acts of the intellect), and can, for this reason, be described as "real [*reel*] philosophical sciences," aesthetics does not produce its object. Yet neither is it a purely "formal" science like logic. Instead, it occupies a distinctive middle ground in which freedom and necessity are joined, as it were, "naturally" and without the need for any additional postulates. The most explicit presentation of Fichte's views on aesthetics are to found in his unfinished "On the Spirit and the Letter in Philosophy, in a Series of Letters," originally written in 1795 for Schiller's *Die Horen,* but rejected by Schiller and finally published by Fichte in 1800.

31. Translated by John Botterman and William Rasch as "A Crystal Clear Report to the General Public Concerning the Actual Essence of the Newest Philosophy: An Attempt to Force the Reader to Understand," in *Philosophy of German Idealism,* ed. Ernst Behler (New York: Continuum, 1987).

32. The distinction between "critique" and "philosophy" (or "metaphysics") is explained in the new preface to the second edition of *Concerning the Concept of the Wissenschaftslehre* (1798, in EPW, pp. 97–100).

33. Regarding the "popular philosophy" movement in late eighteenth-century Germany, see Chap. 13 of Lewis White Beck, *Early German Philosophy: Kant and his Predecessors* (Cambridge, Mass.: Harvard University Press, 1969) and Chap. 6 of Frederick C. Beiser, *The Fate of Reason: German Philosophy from Kant to Fichte* (Cambridge, Mass.: Harvard University Press, 1987). For Fichte's own lecture notes for his course on Logic and Metaphysics, see GA, II/4, as well as the student transcript of these same lectures in GA, IV/1: 175–450.

34. See my "Fichte on Skepticism," *Journal of the History of Philosophy* 29 (1991): 427–53, and "Fichte's *Aenesidemus* Review and The Transformation of German Idealism," *Review of Metaphysics* 34 (1981): 545–68.

35. Letter to Reinhold, 4 July, 1797 (EPW, p. 421).

36. WLnm, p. 78.

37. WLnm, p. 88.

38. The reason that these are the only two options is because the philosopher's sole means of obtaining the concept of his explanatory ground is by reflective abstraction from the concept of ordinary experience, which always involves the presence of an object to a subject. So the philosopher has the choice of "abstracting" from this duality either the "subject in itself" or the "object in itself." Since these two options directly cancel each other, the third possibility – transcendent dualism – can be rejected in advance.

39. See F. W. J. Schelling, "Philosophical Letters of Criticism and Dogmatism," in Schelling, *The Unconditional in Human Knowledge: Four Early Essays (1794–1796)*, trans. Fritz Marti (Lewisburg, Pa.: Bucknell, 1980), pp. 156–218.

40. In contrast to dogmatism, idealism at least possesses the *potential* both to explain the "leap" from consciousness to things and to provide an account of objective experience which does not entail the denial of human freedom; for, unlike the dogmatist, who recognizes only the "single series" of mechanically interacting things, the idealist recognizes, within consciousness itself, a *dual* series of "things" and "representations." It is, after all, within consciousness itself that the distinction between consciousness of objects (things) and consciousness of one's awareness of objects (mere representations) is first posited. This "dual series of being and observing, of what is real and what is ideal" (IWL, p. 21) is present within the intellect itself, which thus already involves a synthesis of ideality and reality. From the mere fact that the transcendental idealist has access to both the ideal and the real series, however, it by no means follows that he will necessarily *succeed* in explaining the connection between these two series or that he will in fact be able to "derive" the latter from the former. That transcendental idealism can indeed account for our consciousness of representations accompanied by a feeling of necessity is a claim that can finally be established only by actually providing the detailed account in question.

41. See my "Kant, Fichte, and the 'Interests of Reason,'" Δαιμον, *Revista de Filosofia* 9, 1994: 81–98.

42. See my "How to Make an Idealist: Fichte's 'Refutation of Dogmatism' and the Starting Point of the *Wissenschaftslehre*," *Philosophical Forum* 19 (1987/88): 97–123.

43. IWL, p. 50. Ironically, as Fichte's philosophy clearly shows, though I *ought* to think of the "I" in this way and though I *can* begin my philosophizing with the concept of the purely self-determined "I," such a concept quickly proves to be self-contradictory. Or rather, it is gradually transformed in the course of Fichte's presentations of the foundations of his system into the concept of a finite, individual "I," endlessly striving to become the foundation of its own determinacy.

44. For an extended discussion of this point, see my "Philosophy and the Divided Self: On the Existential and Scientific Tasks of the Jena *Wissenschaftslehre*," *Fichte-Studien* 6 (1994): 117–47.

45. Letter to Jens Baggesen, April or May 1795 (EPW, p. 385). See, too, Fichte's letter to Friedrich David Gräter, 17 June, 1797 (GA, III/3: 125).

46. For a vigorous challenge to the usual "foundationalist" reading of Fichte, see Tom Rockmore's many writings on this subject, especially his "Antifoundationalism, Circularity, and the Spirit of Fichte," in *Fichte: Historical Contexts/Contemporary Controversies*, ed. Daniel Breazeale and Tom Rockmore (Atlantic Highlands, N.J.: Humanities Press, 1994), pp. 96–112. This same volume also contains two critical responses to Rockmore's thesis: Alain Perrinjaquet, "Some Remarks Concerning the Circularity of Philosophy and the Evidence of Its First Principle in the Jena *Wissenschaftslehre*" (pp. 71–95) and my own "Circles and Grounds in the Jena *Wissenschaftslehre*" (pp. 43–70).

47. Goethe, *Faust* I, l. 1,237. See my "Certainty, Universal Validity, and Conviction: The Methodological Primacy of Practical Reason within the Jena *Wissenschaftslehre*," in *New Perspectives on Fichte*, ed. Tom Rockmore and Daniel Breazeale (Atlantic Highlands, N.J.: Humanities Press, 1996), pp. 35–59.

48. "Forgetting to take into account the role of original feeling leads to an unfounded

transcendent idealism and to an incomplete philosophy that is unable to account for the purely sensible properties of objects" (IWL, p. 75).

49. Though the term *Anstoß* does not occur in the revised presentation of the Jena *Wissenschaftslehre* (that is, in the *Wissenschaftslehre nova methodo*), the doctrine itself is retained in the deduction of the necessity of "original feeling."
50. EPW, p. 274.
51. It is remarkable how many interpretations of Fichte have ignored his unambiguous insistence upon this point: "The *specific determinacy* of the limitation in question is, however, not something that can be derived. [. . .] because, as we can also see, such determinacy itself provides the condition for the very possibility of all I-hood. Consequently, we have arrived at the point where all deduction comes to an end. This determinacy appears to be something absolutely contingent and furnishes us with the *merely empirical* element in our cognition" (IWL, p. 75).
52. This also is reflected in Fichte's account of the essential differences between the kind of questions that can be explored by natural science (which adopts the standpoint of ordinary life) and transcendental philosophy. See, for example, the "Prof. Schmid" essay, in which Fichte asserts that the former begins just where the latter ends, and "its scope [unlike that of philosophy] is endless" (EPW, p. 334). Regarding the difference between the standpoints of life and philosophy, see my "The Standpoint of "The 'Standpoint of Life' and 'The Standpoint of Philosophy' in the Jena *Wissenschaftslehre,*" in *Transzendentalphilosophie als System: Die Auseinandersetzung zwischen 1794 und 1806,* ed. Albert Mues (Hamburg: Felix Meiner Verlag, 1989), pp. 81–104.
53. Josiah Royce, *The Spirit of Modern Philosophy* (Boston: Houghton, Mifflin, 1892), p. 167.
54. "Review of *Aenesidemus,*" EPW, p. 67.
55. Nor is mere thinking sufficient. In order to ascribe *reality* to the objects posited in this manner, they must, in turn, be connected to the I's original (prephilosophical) *belief* in its own freedom. This point, which is implicit in all of Fichte's Jena writings, is made most explicit in Book 3 of *The Vocation of Man.* It does not, however, represent any real advance in Fichte's thinking following his departure from Jena.

    The close relationship between *The Vocation of Man* and Fichte's Jena system is obscured by dramatic differences in *form* and *presentation.* Though the rhetorical strategy of *The Vocation of Man,* a work intended as a direct response to F. H. Jacobi's notorious *Open Letter Letter to Fichte,* is quite unlike that of any of Fichte's Jena writings, the basic doctrines presented in this text are, with the exceptions already noted, fully consistent with Fichte's Jena teachings. In other words, the differences between the Jena writings and *The Vocation of Man* are mainly a matter of "the letter" rather than "the spirit."
56. See "A Fragment" (1799), EPW, p. 435.
57. For a (frankly experimental) attempt to emphasize the purely fictional character of all transcendental explanations, see my "Fichte's Philosophical Fictions," in *Essays on the Later Jena Wissenschaftslehre,* ed. Daniel Breazeale and Tom Rockmore (Atlantic Highlands, N. J.: Humanities Books, forthcoming).
58. Such a dualism of "reality" and "appearance" does seem to characterize some of the later versions of the *Wissenschaftslehre,* such as those of 1804; and, admittedly, there are also some traces of it in the Jena system as well, particularly in those portions of the *Wissenschaftslehre nova methodo* in which Fichte characterizes the relationship between the "noumenal" and the "phenomenal" in terms that suggest

that the latter is simply the "appearance" of the former, viewed through the "colored glass" of time (see WLnm, pp. 364–9). Such claims are, of course, quite difficult to reconcile with the overall spirit of the Jena writings, as interpreted here. For further discussion of this important issue, see my "The *Wissenschaftslehre* of 1796/99 (*nova methodo*)," in *The Cambridge Companion to Fichte,* ed. Günter Zöller (Cambridge: Cambridge University Press, 2000).

59. For Fichte's rejection of "psychologistic" interpretations of the *Wissenschaftslehre,* see, for example, "From a Private Letter" (IWL, p. 174).

60. "The world is nothing more than our own inner acting (*qua* pure intellect), made visible to the senses in accordance with comprehensible laws of reason and limited by incomprehensible boundaries within which we simply find ourselves to be confined" ("On The Basis of Our Belief in a Divine Governance of the World," IWL, p. 149).

61. See Lecture One of *Some Lectures Concerning the Vocation of the Scholar* (in EPW, pp. 145–53).

62. This idea – that contradiction is the animating principle not only of consciousness and of human activity, but of philosophy itself (which can best be understood as an effort to overcome, at the level of transcendental speculation, the fundamental contradiction between moral freedom and scientific determinism, or between transcendent "idealism" and transcendent "realism") – is a fundamental and distinctive feature of the Jena *Wissenschaftslehre* and is an important feature of the "spirit" of the same. See Reinhard Lauth, "Der Ursprung der Dialektik in Fichtes Philosophie," in *Tranzendentale Entwicklungslinien von Descartes bis zu Marx und Dostojewski* (Hamburg: Felix Meiner Verlag, 1989), pp. 209–26.

63. "Eigne Meditationen über ElementarPhilosophie/Practische Philosophie" (GA, II/3: 265).

64. Once again, it cannot be denied that Fichte himself occasionally seems to violate flagrantly his own strictures concerning the limits of transcendental philosophy. The most notorious instances of this occur in his *Foundation of Natural Right,* with its "transcendental deductions" of such things as light, air, locking door latches, and the missionary position (see GA, II/3: 377 and II/4: 43 and 97; see too Fichte's all-too-misleading reply to early critics of these same passages, in "Annals of Philosophical Tone," in EPW, pp. 346–352.). Though it is usually – if not always – possible to interpret these passages in a manner consistent with what is here described as the spirit of the Jena *Wissenschaftslehre,* this does require a certain amount of ingenuity on the part of the interpreter.

9

The Beginnings of Schelling's Philosophy of Nature

MANFRED BAUM

Schelling's philosophy of nature is known to be the counterpart to his version of transcendental idealism which dominated his first writings from 1794 on (*Über die Möglichkeit einer Form der Philosophie überhaupt*). Only after he had left the *Tübinger Stift* and entered the university of Leipzig in 1796 in order to study mathematics, natural sciences, and medicine, did he become more interested in the field of physics and other sciences. His *Ideen zu einer Philosophie der Natur* of 1797 was the first of a series of books and articles that made him famous for being the inaugurator of the new, speculative "Naturphilosophie" that marked his place in the history of post-Kantian philosophy.

In light of the recent discovery and publication of his early commentary on Plato's *Timaeus,* the story of his philosophical development has to be rewritten. The early influence of Kant's and Leibniz's philosophy of nature can no longer be considered the main factors contributing to the new conception of a cosmology that could satisfy the conditions set by the revolution in philosophy due to Kant and Fichte. The text of Schelling's commentary also documents the great impact that Reinhold's early philosophy made on him, although for only a short time. Schelling's later reputation as the Plato of his time, which was ill-founded as long as his youthful attempts to interpret and transform Plato's thought were not taken account of, also now gains at least some plausibility. In light of the *Timaeus* commentary, we now see much more clearly how the unification of Kant's and Plato's ideas was the beginning of Schelling's original philosophy, and we can see the consequences of this for the conception of religion Schelling came to draw from this new position.

I. The Context

Schelling's commentary on Plato's *Timaeus* is dated by its editor, Hartmut Buchner, to the period between January and June 1794 (14).[1] Thus we are dealing with a treatise by an eighteen- or nineteen-year-old student, which clearly shows some traces of its origin in the spiritual atmosphere of the *Tübinger Stift*. This can be seen from the remark that Schelling adds to Plato's answer to the question why the world was created by its author. Plato's divine

creator of the world, because of his lack of envy and jealousy, wanted everything he created to become as similar to himself as possible. Such a motivation
is, according to Schelling, "an idea which never came to the mind of a Moses or
a Jew" (27). Compared to Plato's Demiurge, the god of the Old Testament is a
jealous and vengeful god. Schelling thus deals a blow to the traditional doctrine
of Judaism and Christianity.

The other passage of our text that should be interpreted against the background of the theological and political situation of the *Tübinger Stift,* is a long
footnote to a passage in Plato (*Timaeus* 29 A6) where the Demiurge is called
"the best of causes." Here, Schelling points to the fact that in the *Timaeus* there
is mention of only one creator of the world; the Demiurge is there spoken of
only in the singular. The cautious, obscure and ambiguous way in which Plato
speaks about this, his anxious way of securing his words and his claim to mere
probability for his story of the coming into being of the world – all this is,
according to Schelling, an indication of Plato's awareness of his offence against
the orthodoxy of his time (i.e., against polytheism and belief in demons). All of
this is also an indication of the fact that Plato tried to escape the suspicion of
asebeia directed towards his heretical thoughts. "He speaks exactly in the tone
which the oppressed friend of truth is still now urged to assume" (25). Schelling
comments in French on the alleged timidity of Plato's language: "C'est tout
comme chez nous" (25); and we may suppose that Schelling wants, in making
this footnote, to indicate that he himself is using a hidden way of speech in his
commentary on the *Timaeus.* For this commentary was written in a context of
religious and political oppression; its author speaks about Plato's dialogue as a
student on a scholarship from the local duke in a divinity school that is dedicated not to free research and teaching, but to the training of ministers and state
servants. In this school, a certain orthodoxy in theology and a particular confes-
sion of faith were required by state authority. Schelling would have endorsed
what Hegel wrote to him about the alliance between Storr's theology of revelation and Carl Eugen's absolutism: "Religion and Politics have operated in
conspiracy, the first has taught what despotism wanted it to teach: contempt of
the human race, its inability to any good, to be something through itself."[2]

This religious and political situation was projected backward by Schelling
onto Plato's *Timaeus:*

How similar is the language of truth at all times! I have mentioned what I said so far
because one thinks oneself so often to be doing a good (but certainly ill-placed) service
(which would better be called flattery) to revelation by either seeking to deny knowledge of the one god of all the philosophers of antiquity, or, if this cannot be done, by
repeating the old babble of the church fathers that they drew from revelation. But one
will not find one or the other opinion confirmed by this dialogue of Plato. (25f.)

In Schelling's view, Plato reached his conviction that the cause of the world is
one by means of reason alone. Plato put forward this philosophical insight in a

myth whose language is meant to at the same time disclose a philosophical theory and clothe it in an imagery that is easy to follow. Schelling's own understanding of this dialogue can be gathered from the remark used as a motto for his treatise: "Plato himself adduces the principle on which the manner of exposition in the Timaeus has to be judged: 'It is difficult to find the author and father of this universe, and it is impossible, after one has found him, to proclaim him to all' [*Timaeus* 28 C]" (23). The reason for this impossibility will be seen later.

The hermeneutic principle of Schelling's commentary is the disclosure of the necessarily esoteric meaning of Plato's dialogue. But Schelling faces this task in an historical situation that, similar to that of Plato himself, is overshadowed by an unholy alliance of church and state power. "The elevation of revelation at the expense of reason," Schelling writes, is today as irreconcilable "with the sincerity of an impartial historian" (26) as it was at the time of the church fathers. Not only the historian, but also and especially the theologian and philosopher at all times is witness to a forced insincerity.

It is a "daily" experience, he writes, "how often . . . *not conviction* by real *proofs,* but political superiority which has once for all privileged a certain opinion, forces the voice of opposition to be silent or at least to speak so softly that it can hardly be heard. This is an unfairness which is as great as the triumphant mockery of privileged teachers about dissenters who have no other power on their side than the power of truth or at least of conviction" (26).

It is obvious from Hegel's and Schelling's correspondence that what Schelling refers to is again the orthodox Tübingen school of theology that had recently made use of Kant's and Fichte's philosophy of religion in defending its claims, while at the same time allying itself with church and state power in order to preserve its traditional privileges. Hegel makes a very realistic assessment of the most recent "theological-Kantian course of the Tübingen philosophy": "Orthodoxy cannot be shaken as long as its profession has its worldly profits from being interwoven with the totality of a state."[3] Schelling's answer of 4 February, 1795 is rather optimistic when he alludes to his expectations about Fichte's philosophy: "then the last philosophical cobweb of superstition made by the *privileged* philosophers will totally rip apart."[4]

Within this context of contemporary and theological history, Schelling polemicizes against the "supremacy of such propositions," which according to the "*most scrupulous* conviction" of "dissenters" are false, against the "scornful clinging to privilege" and against the suppression by "the political yoke of hierarchy" that cries out for a second Luther in order to "shake it off" (26). This context will prove to be of great relevance for our understanding of Schelling's philosophical interpretation of Plato's *Timaeus.*

The second determining factor that needs to be mentioned here is of a directly philosophical character. Schelling wrote a dissertation (now lost) for his examination to become a "Magister" in the fall of 1792, which had as its title: *Über die Möglichkeit einer Philosophie ohne Beinamen nebst einigen Bemerkungen über die Reinholdische Elementarphilosophie.*[5] The title refers to the first volume of Reinhold's *Beyträge zur Berichtigung bisheriger Mißverständnisse der Philosophen* of 1790 and to his work *Über das Fundament des philosophischen Wissens* of 1791. It is possible that Schelling became acquainted with Reinhold's philosophy through a lecture by the Tübingen professor J. F. Abel, called *Prolegomena Metaphysices secundum theoriam Reinholdianam* in the summer semester of 1792.[6] The first volume of the *Beyträge* also, however, contains an argument with the Tübingen professor of philosophy and theology Flatt, who was one of Schelling's teachers, about Reinhold's *Versuch einer neuen Theorie des menschlichen Vorstellungsvermögens* of 1789. We are in any case entitled to assume that Schelling at the beginning of 1794 had been interested in Reinhold's version of Kant's Critical philosophy for a long time. The text of the commentary on the *Timaeus* shows, on the other hand, no trace of any engagement with Fichte's writings on the *Wissenschaftslehre,,* although Fichte was in Tübingen in May 1794 and in the same month published his work *Über den Begriff der Wissenschaftslehre* which played such a great role in Schelling's *work Über die Möglichkeit einer Form der Philosophie überhaupt,* completed on 9 September, 1794. We may, therefore, conclude that Schelling's commentary was written before May 1794. This conclusion explains why we often hear in the commentary about the *Vorstellungsvermögen,* and that only in the book *Über die Möglichkeit* do we find Schelling distancing himself from Reinhold's *Theorie des Vorstellungsvermögens.* Thus, it is very likely that Schelling's transition from Reinhold to Fichte occurred in the summer of 1794 and that the commentary on the *Timaeus* belongs to the period before this transition.

This can be confirmed by further evidence from Schelling's hand. In his letter of 6 January, 1795 to Hegel, he writes: "Philosophy has not yet reached its end. Kant has given the results: the premises are still lacking. And who can understand results without the premises?"[7] This definition of the task of a post-Kantian philosophy is evidently borrowed from Reinhold, whose *Theorie des Vorstellungsvermögens* is at this point (end of January 1795)[8] not yet known to Hegel. In this work Reinhold says about his *Briefe über die Kantische Philosophie,* that they were designed to draw attention to "those *results*" of Kant's philosophy "which spring from it with respect to the fundamental truths of religion and ethics." But since he wanted simply to inaugurate the "study and understanding" of Kant's work and could not presuppose this, "nothing was left to him [Reinhold] other than the attempt to establish these results independently of the Kantian premises."[9] For it was Reinhold's view that the premises required for the Kantian results are contained in his own *Theorie des Vorstellungsvermögens,* which in matter of fact provides the foundation for Kant's theory of knowledge and thereby makes it possible, and that "the essential results of the critique of reason" thereby receive confirmation and a new meaning independently of the Kantian writings.[10]

In the same letter in which Schelling adopts Reinhold's conception of the present task of philosophy, he also reports that he is acquainted with the first part of Fichte's *Grundlage der gesamten Wissenschaftslehre.* "I read and I found that my prophecies had not deluded me."[11] On his own efforts in philosophy we then read: "I am happy enough if I am among the first who welcome the new hero, Fichte, in the land of truth."[12]

This not wholly reliable report on the transition to the new hero Fichte as the man who has brought Kant's philosophy to completion is in agreement with Schelling's new assessment of Reinhold's achievements in his next letter to Hegel, which is written entirely from a Fichtean perspective. Reinhold's attempts to bring back philosophy to its ultimate principles and thereby to carry on the Kantian revolution were not successful. But, Schelling writes, "indeed even this was a step over which science had to pass and I do not know whether we do not owe it to Reinhold that we will now so soon . . . stand on the highest point."[13] Schelling now considers Reinhold's philosophy a preliminary step to the truly last stage of philosophy that consists in providing a new highest principle of all philosophy, that is, of practical philosophy too, namely "the pure, absolute I."[14] Accordingly, we read in Schelling's work *Vom Ich als Prinzip der Philosophie* (1795) that Reinhold has made the respectable, yet unsuccessful attempt to "elevate the empirically conditioned I (which shows up in consciousness) to be the principle of philosophy."[15] Reinhold's *Theorie des Vorstellungsvermögens* appears to be an example of his not coming to grips with Fichte's insight that only the absolute "I," and not the "I" of the *Vorstellungsvermögen,* can be the sought-for unconditioned principle. In light of this, even Schelling's own attempt in the commentary on Plato's *Timaeus* to verify Reinhold's *Vorstellungsvermögen* as the principle of theoretical philosophy or of the philosophy of nature in its oldest form is rendered obsolete.

II. Plato and Critical Philosophy

An interpretation of the *Timaeus* and even of the whole of Plato's philosophy from the standpoint of Reinhold's theory of the faculty of representation, taken as a systematization of Kant's Critical philosophy, is an enterprise that is not new. In his commentary, Schelling refers twice to Wilhelm Gottlieb Tennemann's treatise *Über den göttlichen Verstand aus der Platonischen Philosophie* in the first volume of *Memorabilien* (1791). This philosophico-theological journal was edited by the Jena professor Heinrich Eberhard Gottlob Paulus, who was a friend of the Schelling family and had printed in the fifth volume of the same year Schelling's treatise *Über Mythen, historische Sagen und Philosopheme der ältesten Welt.* Paulus had, in the *Preface* of the first volume of the new journal, declared philology to be the "only possible foundation for a system of enlightenment that was historically grounded."[16] As an example within the philosophical domain, he there mentions Tennemann's treatise, calling it "a psychological interpretation of Platonic ideas concerning the divine intellect that had only become possible through certain ideas of the critical philosophy" and that cast new light on the history of the word *logos.* Still earlier, Tennemann had published similar interpretations of the Platonic philosophy in the spirit of the Critical philosophy. In 1790, his treatise *Versuch, eine Stelle aus dem Timaios des Plato durch die Theorie des Vorstellungsvermögens zu erklären* appeared, and shortly afterward *Über die älteste Revolution in der Philosophie mit Hinsicht auf die neueste.* In the *Preface* to his work *Die Lehren und Meinungen der Sokratiker über Unsterblichkeit,* which appeared in 1791 but was written earlier, Tennemann expresses regret that he had become acquainted with Reinhold's *Briefe über die Kantische Philosophie* too late to make use of it in the present book: "They would have taught me that I needed to pay attention to Plato's conception of the faculty of representation . . . I would then have made this study the basis of my exposition of his system."[17]

Tennemann's four-volume work *System der Platonischen Philosophie* (1792–5), arguably the most distinguished achievement of Platonic studies in the eighteenth century, is the realization of this project. Its first two volumes had already appeared when Schelling wrote his own commentary. In the *Preface* to the first volume he announces the exposition of Plato's system: "First of all will come my treatise on Plato's conception of the faculty of representation by means of which I will endeavor to throw light upon the whole system."[18]

In Tennemann's contribution to *Memorabilien,* we find the same opposition of revelation and philosophical reasoning and the same polemics that we find in Schelling's text against the presumption of the church fathers that Plato's philosophy had derived its doctrines, as far as they agree with the Christian religion, from the sources of revelation. "A little more," Tennemann writes, "and Plato himself would have been a Christian."[19] And again, he writes that this "phantom" of the church fathers should have been expelled long ago "through sound exegesis." But Plato's philosophy had "up until now" never been exposed in its "true form,"[20] in which everything is understood to depend on the "concept of Logos and Nous." The genuine meaning of the latter could be derived from its role in the generation of the world.

Following the exposition in the *Timaeus,* we see that the world consists of a "basic stuff (or matter) and [the] form of a World," viz. on the one hand what is perceptible and on the other the combination and order of this stuff "according to certain intelligible laws and paradigms," which have been "imprinted on" matter in the process of its formation. Tennemann's explanation of this doctrine that, to his mind, contains nothing at all that could indicate an anticipation of Christian speculations about the Trinity, reads: "It can easily be shown that Plato was led to this conception by the constitution of the faculty of representation."[21] At the basis of Plato's exposition of the world's generation and his description of the world-soul, we thus have the two factors of the human "faculty of representation" which we know from Kant's philosophy.[22] The form of the world is grounded in "all that the understanding at first introduces into experience and comprehends out of itself," and the matter of the world consists in "what is given and is in itself incomprehensible, on the basis of which the comprehensible is perceived."[23] With this statement, Tennemann anticipates a main thesis of Schelling's commentary.

But Tennemann not only makes use of the ultimately Kantian conception of the human faculty of representation for his explanation of Plato's demiurgic intellect and its role in the generation of the world. He also justifies his understanding of the real meaning of Plato's theory of ideas by borrowing a specific feature of Reinhold's theory of the faculty of representation. Tennemann defends his thesis that Plato's ideas can only be understood as concepts in the divine intellect by making reference to the passage in the *Timaeus,* which we already know from Schelling's commentary. He translates: "since God is the highest good [*der Höchstgute*], who, being without any envy wants to translate into reality everything that is good, he sought to make everything as similar to himself as possible" (cf. *Timaeus* 29 E1–3).

Now in this passage Tennemann discovers evidence for his claims that the ideas can not be eternal entities existing outside the divine understanding, and that a second understanding existing outside God's understanding is not a possibility for Plato (although Christian speculation on the Logos hoped to find such a doctrine in Plato's text). According to Tennemann, Plato's god is "to himself his ideal and paradigm and he sought to make the world similar to it." This also means: "Since therefore the ideal of the world is in god, all the ideas must by the same token be in god. They are the purest concepts of reason of the supreme intelligence and are thus eternally unchangeable; the deity, being constantly aware of them, only acts according to them alone."[24] The Christian interpretation, according to which Plato's doctrine of the world-soul in the *Timaeus* "has made the understanding into a substance distinct from the deity: a substance which is thus eternal and ungenerated,"[25] must thus be false. For it implies that Plato had a doctrine of "a double understanding," "one in God, another outside himself, one as a predicate of the deity, the other as a substance."[26] But it is absurd not only to assume a reduplication of the understanding, but also to think of any understanding as a substance and to thereby give substantiality to its rational concepts or ideas. In particular, those assumptions stand in contradiction to the insight that "the understanding (nous) can only be thought as a predicate of a soul, that is, of a subject that is unknown in itself."[27]

This latter insight Tennemann has obviously borrowed directly from Reinhold's *Theorie des Vorstellungsvermögens*. There Reinhold writes,

Since the subject cannot represent itself as a mere subject, but only as an object, and
since it has for that purpose no other predicate than that of a being which represents [*des
Vorstellenden*], one can easily understand that the subject in so far as it is taken to be
something more than just the logical substratum of the predicate of representing
[*vorstellend*], (namely as a substance) must remain eternally incomprehensible to itself.
The *self* [*Ich*], in so far as by this notion more is to be conceived than the mere activity of
representing, is for itself a natural mystery, concerning those attributes which pertain to
it as a substance.[28]

This Reinholdian doctrine of the nonsubstantiality of the self and thereby of
the understanding as a mere faculty of representation combines Kant's critique
of the paralogisms of rational psychology with Locke's doctrine of the unknowability of all substances, and anticipates a fundamental element of Husserl's phenomenology. It is taken by Tennemann as the basis of his interpretation of all the passages in Plato in which we read: "understanding can only be
in a soul."[29] And since this Platonic Nous is taken to be "the faculty of rational
concepts or ideas,"[30] the divine reason has to be understood as a faculty of
representation which is at the same time an intelligence producing concepts
and ideas and a power of action that shapes matter according to those representations. Just as for Reinhold the self comprehends itself "in its *great predicate*,
the *faculty of representation*," which is "the clue to all its self-knowledge and
to everything knowable outside itself,"[31] so, in Tennemann's view, Plato's
Nous is "only a predicate of the deity."[32] This predicate can therefore make
intelligible the form of the world as an effect of the understanding; but such a
form is for Plato far from personified or made into a substance separated from
the deity. At the end of his treatise, Tennemann refers to Friedrich Victor
Leberecht Plessing,[33] whose interpretation of the Platonic ideas is opposed to
his own. In this opposition, too, Schelling follows Tennemann.

Plessing, in Ortloff's *Handbuch der Literatur der Geschichte der Philosophie* (1798), is included with Tiedemann, Meiners, and Tennemann among
the four leading historians of philosophy of that time. The controversy about
the proper understanding of the Platonic doctrine of ideas, in which Plessing
and Tennemann figure as the protagonists of two long opposing parties, is one
of the most important topics in the historiography of philosophy. To this
controversy also belongs the theory of the ideal numbers that Aristotle and his
commentators attributed to Plato. But this issue is far surpassed in its relevance
for the understanding of Plato and for his definition of philosophy by the
conception of Plato's ideas as the thoughts of God, a conception which can be
documented from the days of the platonism of the first century A.D. Philo of
Alexandria is the first author in whom the theory of ideas, understood in this
way, can be found.[34] In modern times we have among the historians of philoso-

phy two camps, which are led by Cudworth (1678) and Brucker (1723) respectively, and that claim that the ideas are either concepts of God (in agreement with neoplatonic doctrine), or (in agreement with the testimony of Aristotle) eternal substances existing for themselves and known only through pure thought. Among the followers of Cudworth we find his translator and commentator Mosheim (1733) and Meiners (1782), and among the followers of Brucker we have Monboddo (1773) and Gedike (1782). Plessing belongs to the followers of Brucker, but he by far surpasses him in exactness and historical judgment, at least as far as the Platonic theory of ideas is concerned. Of all the Plato scholars mentioned above he comes closest to the historical truth.

Although Plessing was an immediate student of Kant's, his conception of ancient philosophy and of Plato's theory of ideas in particular is free from any uncritical Kantianism. In his treatise *Über den Aristoteles* (1786), he says about the Eleatics, Plato and Aristotle: "Their pure concepts of the understanding were grounded in real substantial objects which were allegedly intuited immediately by the understanding: for they attributed to the latter an immediate power of intuition; but we, in our new philosophy, do not do that."[35] So Plessing is fully aware of the opposition between Platonism and Kantianism within theoretical philosophy. For his understanding of Plato's ideas, however, he relies on Kant's theory of the dependence on intuition of all knowledge. He takes the Ancients to have thought the same way about the origin of human knowledge: "They grounded it in certain original intuitions which they considered as the arch-principles on which all science and knowledge has to be based."[36] According to Plessing, then, there is a twofold meaning to Plato's "ideas": (i) they are "immaterial entities, which are called substances in the strictest sense," where substance means "something immovable, persistent and existing for itself," and these entities have been seen in a former state of the soul by means of the understanding's immediate faculty of intuition; (ii) they are the intuitions and representations of the understanding.[37] In short: Platonic ideas are substances as well as concepts. Plato is taken to have assumed "a separate existence of the universal as the original essence of things."[38]

Plessing claims to have discovered this account of Plato's ideas.[39] Both in his commentary and in the *Allgemeine Übersicht der neuesten Literatur* (1797), Schelling vehemently criticized this conception. In the latter work he says: "Plato strives hard to express in words that the ideas contain a being which surpasses all empirical existence by far. But nevertheless one can hear up to this day the proof of Plato's ideas being real substances, just as Kant's things in themselves."[40] Then follows a reference to Plessing's writings.

One can learn at least three things from this passage: (i) Schelling, as well as Hegel (even in the second edition of his *Wissenschaft der Logik*), is a follower of the middle- and neoplatonic conception of Plato's ideas that was revived in modern times by Cudworth; (ii) Schelling has mistakenly assumed that in assigning substantiality to the Platonic ideas, Plessing intended to attribute physical or empirical existence to them. This misunderstanding results from Schelling's view that substantiality as such is incompatible with the supersensible in general, although he never says this in so many words. But such a theory would not in any case justify a falsification in his report of Plessing's position; and (iii) The connection of the (in Schelling's view) false conception of Plato's ideas with an allegedly equally false conception of Kantian things-in-themselves can serve as a clue to our understanding of Schelling's own conception that (under the influence of Fichte) changes slightly by 1797 from what it was in 1794. A few pages later in his *Allgemeine Übersicht,* Schelling speaks of an "idea" that could not be understood by man "had he not (using Plato's language) intuited its model [Urbild] in the intellectual world (i.e., in himself, as a spiritual being)."[41] The Platonic idea is therefore, for Schelling, what the thing in itself is for Kant: something supersensible in the sense of being the ground or principle of the sensible in our representations. This means that the supersensible belongs to "that originally internal principle of all representing"[42] that we ourselves constitute. We ourselves are "that original self-determining of the spirit" of which we can be conscious as our "original spirituality"[43] whenever we are conscious of the moral law. This spirituality is that same intelligible entity that the Platonic idea, like the Kantian thing-in-itself, indicates as the ground of the world of the senses. It does so in an ambiguous and paradoxical way, because it suggests that the ground is itself a thing.

III. The Text

If we look for the beginnings of Schelling's philosophy in his commentary on selected passages of the *Timaeus* (as far as they are there present), we can find them in his interpretation of Plato's cosmogony that he takes in a literal sense, as did before him Aristotle and Plutarch[44] and the historians depending on them, Plessing and Tennemann. In what follows I will ignore the question of the adequacy of Schelling's interpretation.

Schelling understands Plato's sensible world as something quite heterogeneous vis-à-vis "everything formal" (27), and he takes this material aspect of objects of sensibility to be matter, which as such is without regularity and lawfulness. If there is a "form of the world," it cannot stem from sensible matter, that is, it can neither inhere in it, nor be produced by it. This form of the world did not originally belong to the world as sensible, but to the understanding. The combination of form and matter or of regularity and irregularity, which essentially exclude each other but are united within the world of experience, was in need of a third thing that "gave" to still unregulated matter "a form . . . which was a copy [Nachbild] of the original, pure form of the understanding" (27). This pure form of the understanding was given by the Demiurge to the unstable and irregularly moved original matter, in order to make the world, created in this way, as similar as possible to him. As we already know, the Demiurge's intention was to give it as much perfection, and consequently beauty, as possible: "The Demiurge had in his mind that no visible world . . . , if it did not partake in the form of the understanding, would be a work more beautiful than a world united with that form" (28 f.). More precisely, this means: The form that God shared with the world is a "form of movement through which the original motion that matter had independently of God, was brought into the limits of lawfulness" (28 f.). Thus the visible world was created as an imitation of an ideal world, grounded in the pure form of the Demiurge's understanding, that is, of a "*kosmos noetos*" (29 f.) or a world "in so far as it existed *in the idea.*" Within the ideal world, Schelling claims, there are two kinds of ideas: Some refer to single objects and are ideas of creatures (zoa) of the visible world, and others are the bases of this world in its formal aspect. They are "ideas in general" (30) such as "the idea of the good, of quantity, quality, causality and so on" (31).

This enumeration that combines an idea of pure practical reason with the most important of the pure concepts of the understanding in Kant's table of categories points to the philosophical intention of Schelling's interpretation of Plato's cosmogony. In two passages of his commentary Schelling declares as the "clue to the explanation of the whole of Plato's philosophy": "That he [Plato] everywhere transfers the subjective to the objective" (31). This "transfer [*Übertragung*] of the subjective to the objective governing the totality of Plato's philosophy" (38) is a procedure from which the Platonic (and even the pre-Platonic) metaphysics immediately follows. (Hence Schelling's statement "that the visible world is nothing but an imitation of the invisible" [31].) This central metaphysical theorem has its philosophical justification "in ourselves" (31), Schelling says, because it transfers the fundamental subjective principles of the representation of the world that are within us to this world itself as an objective relation of two worlds. The fundamental idea of young Schelling's philosophy of nature, which does not directly rely on Kant's transcendental philosophy but rather on Reinhold's theory of the faculty of representation, is contained in the one sentence:

[T]he whole of nature, as it appears to us, is not only a product of our empirical *receptivity,* but properly speaking [*eigentlich*] a work of our faculty of representation which contains pure, original forms (of nature) grounded in itself. Therefore the world in the representation belongs to a higher faculty than the mere sensibility, and nature is presented as a type [*Typus*] of a higher world, which expresses the pure laws of this world. (31)

To uncover the secret of Plato's philosophy of nature therefore means to achieve knowledge of the reason, lying "in man himself," why philosophy was already "early on" led to the "idea" "that the visible world [is] a type [*Typus*] of an invisible world" (131).

This "explanation" of a doctrine of two worlds, apparently so natural to human reason, which at the same time is an explanation of the rationality and truth of Plato's philosophy of nature, depends on the transfer of concepts and arguments from Kant's *Critique of Practical Reason*. Schelling's second dissertation of the year 1792 is entitled *Über die Übereinstimmung der Critik der theoretischen und praktischen Vernunft, besonders in Bezug auf den Gebrauch der Categorien, und der Realisierung der Idee einer intelligiblen Welt durch ein Factum in der letzteren.*[45] Although this work has not been preserved, we can gather from its title that in it Schelling must have dealt with the so-called categories of freedom with respect to the concepts of Good and Evil. After the passage in the second chapter of the first book of Kant's *Critique of Practical Reason* that outlines this theory, there immediately follows a *Typik der reinen praktischen Vernunft.*[46] Schelling's use of this piece of Kant's doctrine explains at once the strange combination of the idea of the good with the categories, which, according to Schelling's interpretation of Plato, is the basis of the two worlds "in formal respect." In the *Typik* Kant speaks of the "law of freedom" and of the "concept of the unconditioned good," and he holds that the understanding in his application of such an "idea of reason" cannot lay down as a basis "a *schema* of sensibility, but a law."[47] Such a law that can be exhibited in concreto in objects of the senses is "a law of nature, but only according to its form" and this could be called the "type of the moral law."[48]

Schelling obviously takes Kant's doctrine of types out of its context (which was the application of the formal moral law to given cases of maxims) and focuses on the metaphysics implied there. For Kant goes on to say that one is "allowed to think the nature of the sensible world as a type of an intelligible nature,"[49] "as long as I on no account transfer the intuitions . . . to the latter, but only refer the *form of lawfulness* in general . . . to it."[50] Schelling not only adopts the notion of "nature as type of a higher world" (31) – or the idea that the "visible world is a type of an invisible one" – from Kant's *Critique of Practical Reason* and incorporates it into a general theory of the faculty of representation; he also adopts Kant's concept of "enthusiasm" [*Schwärmerei*] and makes use of it in order to guard Plato against the charge of enthusiasm, that is, to portray Plato as a good Kantian.

"Enthusiasm" according to Kant's text consists in using "supersensible intuitions" as the basis of moral concepts instead of the type of practical judgment, that is, nature in its "pure form of the understanding."[51] For Schelling, enthusiasm means the procedure not of taking the visible world "merely with respect to the lawfulness of nature in general" as a type of an invisible one (for such a belief would well have "its ground in man himself"), but of extending this notion "also to the intuitions (according to their matter)" (31). Plato would only then have to be considered as an enthusiast if there were in his doctrine what one usually calls Platonic ideas, that is, substantial originals of single objects of the sensible world:

Had Plato taken for granted that every being in the world was objectively grounded in an invisible but physically existing original [*Grundwesen*] which contained the character of its whole species, that would have been enthusiasm, i.e., it would be a transfer of the merely sensible which belongs *only* to empirical intuition, to the supersensible. (32)

Thus it is true that in Plato there is a transfer of the subjective to the objective, that is, a transfer of what has its ground in man himself to the world, which thereby appears as a relation of two worlds, one being the type of the other; but this kind of transfer is justified as long as it is merely an objectification of a form of the faculty of representation, which includes both theoretical and practical reason: an objectification symbolized in the demiurgic activity of giving form to matter. This kind of objectification of the "lawgiving to nature prescribed through the pure understanding" (31) allows us to see nature as a type of the intelligible nature contained in the pure practical reason of man. Plato's transfer is therefore legitimate, because he did not assume ideas as objects of a nonsensible intuition, but only such ideas that made the human activity of understanding and reason thinkable as the form of the world: "Plato assumed ideas which underlie the worldly beings only *in so far* as these ideas could be object of pure thought, expressions of the pure form of the faculty of representation" (32). In thus proving Plato to be a Critical philosopher, Schelling at the same time unveils the secret of the Demiurge. The author and father of this world, who is so difficult to find and who, when found, cannot be revealed to the people, is nothing but the human faculty of representation itself.

In Plato's philosophy, however, this faculty of representation is not only the author of the universal lawfulness of nature, but, by means of that lawfulness and of preexisting matter, also the author of the "lawfulness of single products" of nature (32 f.). This second authorship came about when the form of the understanding produced specific kinds of worldly beings (ibid.). Schelling thus determines the relation between the two kinds of Platonic ideas that he distinguishes in such a way that the specific forms of natural beings are derived from the universal form of the understanding. Speaking the language of the *Timaeus,* this means that the Demiurge "let run together the universal laws of nature in order to produce single, regular products" (33). It cannot be overlooked that Schelling has here conceived of the relation between the universal and the particular as a relation of a whole to its parts. In doing so he makes use both of Plato's conception of the world as a living being [*zoon*], that is, as an organized being whose parts are only possible through the relationship to the whole, and of Kant's *Critique of Judgement* whose doctrine of natural purposes in §65 he quotes. In addition to this, however, Schelling makes use of a key notion from the *Introduction* to the *Critique of Judgement,* the transcendental principle of the purposeness nature in its particular laws. "Every single worldly being was thus not the work of *matter,* but, properly speaking, a *harmonizing* [*Zusammenstimmung*] *of single pure laws* into One whole, which means, it was the work of an idea . . . of a pure *form* of *unity,* the work of an *intelligence*" (33). Schelling refers without saying so to Kant's theory of the systematic unity of "particular empirical laws" of nature and his claim that they had to be regarded "as if they too" had been given by "an understanding (even though not ours)" and in such a way that they were purposive for our faculty of knowledge.[52] Schelling transfers this theory to the production of the singular worldly beings themselves through the "architect of the world [*Weltbaumeister*]" (32), and these beings *are* therefore nothing else but harmonizations of different "pure" laws into one whole. Schelling identifies the worldly beings so constructed with the "creatures" (30) or "Zoa" (32) of the visible world.

An examination of Schelling's rigorous Kantianization of Plato's philosophy in the *Timaeus* and *Philebus,* which includes his discovery of Kant's table of categories in the latter and of Kant's concept of substance from the first analogy of experience in the former, would be a rewarding task, although also a tiresome interpretation of an interpretation or a commentary of a commentary. Many hermeneutical snares would have to be faced. Although the surprising continuity in the development of Schelling's ideas makes it often possible to use later statements as a clue to the understanding of the notes of the youthful author, there still is the danger of overlooking the differences which his older and newer views nevertheless contain. Schelling's interpretation of Plato that was so fruitful for himself and yet so brutal, does not in principle differ from Tennemann's; and it is inconceivable without the model of Tennemann. This is in particular true of the polemics against the allegedly physical but in any case objective existence of the Platonic ideas, defended by Plessing. Schelling's elimination of the objectivity of the ideas and of the world-soul, too, for the benefit of their origination in the human subject and its faculty of representation is nothing but an undoing of that Platonic transfer of the subjective to the objective, viz. of Plato's identification of the human understanding with the understanding of the Demiurge, a transfer and identification that reveal their meaning only in the Critical philosophy.

According to Schelling, Plato is the discoverer of "a supersensible principle of the form and harmony of the world [which lies] in ourselves" (34), and the only supersensible element that he could discover is the so-called faculty of representation as a unity of theoretical and practical reason. In Plato's view, as seen by Schelling, the divine understanding has shared its pure, original form with the human understanding, and Schelling takes this, with Kant's *Critique of Judgement,*[53] to mean that the "ideas of a divine understanding had become possible in [human] understanding . . . by way of an intellectual community of man with the origin of all beings" (37). But just this Platonic conception is only due to a characteristic transfer of the subjective to the objective, as can be seen in the idea of the unity of the world: "For the world is, properly speaking, a unity only as a *representation in us*" (38), Plato's philosophizing started out from a "kind of procedure of our reason" (38); reason has "subjectively produced" (38 f.) the idea of the world, and this is also true of the efficacy of the rational world-soul: "it is quite analogous with the efficacy of human reason" and with the human soul (42).

　　Finally, for Plato the existence of the ideal originals in the divine reason can only be either a "pure" or a "physical" one. Because of the indestructability of the originals, the latter is, however, impossible, and a third kind of existence is not thinkable for Schelling. But the pure existence of the ideas has a merely logical meaning. "The idea of an existence of supersensible (real) *objects,*" which correspond to the ideas and are therefore called ideals, "coincides with the idea of the existence of mere *ideas*" (44). Therefore, as Schelling says using a Kantian phrase[54] (which, however, Kant intended in an entirely different way), the concept of existence when applied to the idea of God is "an abyss for human reason – either it gives itself over to the most excessive enthusiasm, or it does not even go one step over the limits of the idea," that is, of the representation (44). If one tries to make the logical meaning of the concept of existence into a real one, this being posited outside of the representation can mean, according to Schelling, only physical existence. In ideas and ideals (such as god and the human soul), their existence coincides with their logical or ideal existence: "there is no existing object of the supersensible world" outside the ideal, i.e., of existence in mere thought (45). The existence of God is therefore necessarily indeterminable and impredicable, and the existence of the faculty of representation itself is only given in the consciousness of its representing. "We can think of no concept existing outside the representation which is not at the same time tied by us to a physically existing object" (72). Therefore, the concept of God as well as that of the human soul is either the concept of a thing that exists "somewhere," which is out of question in both cases, or it is the concept of something "which is not present in any location" and which, for that reason, we can "not" represent at all "as present" (74). Schelling's intentionally ambiguous manner of expression makes it impossible to decide whether he thinks the concept of existence, because of its alleged (and un-Kantian) connectedness with natural and localizable beings, can simply not be applied to god and the human soul, or whether the interpretation of Plato's philosophy of nature and its theological foundations, being an objectification of the subjective, means what Henry Allison has called a "transcendental humanism,"[55] which, though inspired by Kant and Reinhold, already clearly anticipates the views of Feuerbach.

Notes

1. Page numbers in the text refer to F. W. J. Schelling: *Timaeus (1794)*, ed. Hartmut Buchner (Stuttgart: Frommann-Holzboog, 1994). All translations, except of the *Critique of Pure Reason*, are mine.
2. 16 April, 1795 in *Briefe von und an Hegel. Band I: 1785–1812*, ed. Johannes Hoffmeister, (Hamburg: Felix Meiner Verlag, 1969), p. 24.
3. January 1795 in *Briefe von und an Hegel*, p. 16.
4. Loc. cit., p. 21.
5. See Wilhelm G. Jacobs, *Zwischen Revolution und Orthodoxie?* (Stuttgart: Frommann-Holzboog, 1989), p. 284.
6. Loc. cit., p. 74.
7. *Briefe von und an Hegel*, p. 14.
8. Loc. cit., p. 16.
9. Karl Leonhard Reinhold, *Versuch einer neuen Theorie des Vorstellungsvermögens* (Prag and Jena: Widtmann und Mauke, 1789), p. 57.
10. Reinhold: *Versuch*, pp. 67f.
11. *Briefe von und an Hegel*, p. 11.
12. Ibid.
13. February 4, 1795 in *Briefe von und an Hegel*, p. 21.
14. *Briefe von und an Hegel*, p. 22.
15. Friedrich Wilhelm Joseph Schelling *Historisch-Kritische Ausgabe. Werke 2*, eds. Hartmut Buchner and Jörg Jantzen (Stuttgart: Frommann-Holzboog, 1980), pp. 98f.
16. No pagination.
17. Wilhelm Gottlieb Tennemann, *Lehren und Meinungen der Sokratiker über Unsterblichkeit* (Jena: Akademische Buchhandlung, 1791), p. VIII.
18. Wilhelm Gottlieb Tennemann, *System der Platonischen Philosophie. Erster Band* (Leipzig: Barth, 1792), p. XXVI.
19. Wilhelm Gottlieb Tennemann, "Ueber den göttlichen Verstand in der Platonischen Philosophie," in *Memorabilien. Eine philosophisch-theologische Zeitschrift der Geschichte und Philosophie der Religionen, dem Bibelstudium und der morgenländischen Literatur gewidmet von Heinr. Eberh. Gottlob Paulus*, vol. 1 (Leipzig: Crusius, 1791), p. 36.
20. Loc. cit., p. 37.
21. Loc. cit., p. 40.
22. See *Critique of Pure Reason*, (London: Macmillan, 1973), B 132.
23. Tennemann, *Ueber den göttlichen Verstand*, p. 41.
24. Loc. cit., p. 45.
25. Loc. cit., p. 47.
26. Loc. cit., pp. 47f.
27. Loc. cit., p. 48.
28. Reinhold, *Versuch*, p. 338.
29. Tennemann, *Ueber den göttlichen Verstand*, p. 48.
30. Ibid.
31. Reinhold, *Versuch*, p. 338.
32. Tennemann, *Ueber den göttlichen Verstand*, p. 53.
33. Loc. cit., p. 64.
34. Cf. Paul Oskar Kristeller, *Die Ideen als Gedanken der menschlichen und göttlichen Vernunft* (Heidelberg: Winter, 1989), p. 13.

35. Friedrich Victor Leberecht Plessing, "Ueber den Aristoteles," in *Denkwürdigkeiten aus der philosophischen Welt,* vol. 3 (Leipzig: Müller, 1786), p. 50.
36. Friedrich Victor Leberecht Plessing, "Untersuchungen über die Platonischen Ideen, in wie fern sie sowohl immaterielle Substanzen, als auch reine Vernunftbegriffe vorstellten," in *Denkwürdigkeiten,* vol. 3, p. 116.
37. Loc. cit., p. 112.
38. Loc. cit., p. 127.
39. Loc. cit., p. 115.
40. Schelling, *Historisch-Kritische Ausgabe. Werke 4,* p. 133.
41. Loc. cit., p. 142.
42. Loc. cit., p. 134.
43. Loc. cit., p. 142.
44. Cf. Harold Cherniss, *Aristotle's Criticism of Plato and the Academy,* (New York: Russell & Russell, 1962), pp. 421ff.
45. Jacobs, *Zwischen Revolution und Orthodoxie?,* p. 284.
46. *Kants gesammelte Schriften,* Akademie-Ausgabe, vol. V (Berlin: Reimer), p. 67.
47. Loc. cit., p. 69.
48. Ibid.
49. Loc. cit., p. 70.
50. Ibid.
51. Loc. cit., pp. 70f.
52. Loc. cit., p. 180.
53. Loc. cit., p. 363.
54. *Critique of Pure Reason,* B 641.
55. Cf. his "Kant's Transcendental Humanism," *The Monist* 55 (1971): 182–207.

10

The Nature of Subjectivity:
The Critical and Systematic Function of Schelling's Philosophy of Nature

DIETER STURMA

I

It is well known that transcendental idealism for Kant simply represents a critical idealism, one that draws the limits of knowledge in terms of the distinction between phenomena on the one hand and things in themselves on the other. According to Kant, the transcendental idealist can also be understood as an empirical realist who refuses to dissolve the duality between our experience and objects of our experience, and concedes the existence of objects independent of the subject.[1] The Kantian doctrine of transcendental idealism, irrespective of its various possible forms and modifications, is specifically characterized by a fundamental dualist structure with regard to the distinction between the "given" and the "constituted." It was precisely this dualism that represented the *skandalon* of philosophy for the post-Kantian idealists, one that had at all costs to be overcome, despite their recognition of the positive aspects of Kant's contribution.

The early German idealist attempts to articulate a philosophical system are all essentially monistic in character, expressly designed to translate the Kantian dualism into the terms of a monist theoretical model. Nonetheless, with his *System of Transcendental Idealism* of 1800 – conceived at a time when that dualism was already widely regarded as having been transcended – Schelling took up and modified the question concerning the relative opposition between idealism and realism. For according to Schelling, the concept of transcendental idealism is capable of opening up a perspective from which the opposition between realism and idealism can be seen to derive from a third moment or dimension. In his *System of Transcendental Idealism,* Schelling writes:

If I reflect solely upon the ideal activity, I am presented with idealism, or the claim that the limit [Schranke] is posited solely through the ego. If I reflect solely upon the real activity, then I am presented with realism, or the claim that the limit is itself independent of the ego. If I now reflect on both of them together, then I am presented with a third moment that arises from both, something which one could call ideal-realism, or what we have previously described as transcendental idealism.[2]

Schelling's own third path toward transcendental idealism pursues the optimistic program of avoiding both the supposed bifurcation of Kantian dualism and the one-sided perspective of Fichte's theory of subjectivity in the *Science of Knowledge,* without falling back into the dark night of an undifferentiated monism. At the beginning of his development, Schelling believed that the project of a philosophy of nature was merely filling in an area that Kant and Fichte themselves had left undeveloped. But now Schelling no longer assumes that subjective idealism – whether in the form of transcendental idealism or the Fichtean *Science of Knowledge* – and the philosophy of nature can merely be conceived in a complementary correspondence to one another.

A number of contemporary authors, especially Reinhold, Jacobi, and Fichte, were influential in prompting Schelling's new conception of transcendental idealism. But by 1800 Schelling had already completed his own turn toward the philosophy of nature. The figures of Plato, Spinoza, Kant of the *Third Critique,* and, last but not least, Hölderlin, had all been significantly involved in this development. And it was essentially the philosophy of nature that gave Schelling his distinctive philosophical profile toward the end of the 1790s. Nonetheless, very little is known about what effectively and decisively prompted Schelling's original attempt to revise idealism in terms of a philosophy of nature. While we can certainly identify a number of relevant influences here, they are quite insufficient on their own to explain Schelling's specific accomplishment in the philosophy of nature, or the particular role that it plays in his thought. We cannot really argue that his desire to develop the general pantheistic approach of early German idealism and romanticism played an important part in this. But Schelling's own approach is uniquely characterized by the distinctive attempt to connect these speculations on the philosophy of nature directly with the empirical scientific knowledge of the time.[3]

Apart from examining the sources in the cultural and philosophical background of the age, we could also attempt to clarify the emergence of Schelling's philosophy of nature by identifying the possible systematic reasons for this development.[4] This approach has the advantage of allowing us to evaluate the divergence between Schelling's earlier conception of transcendental idealism and his later position. In the following I shall therefore pursue this second option, and attempt both to outline the motivating systematic reasons behind the formulation of Schelling's philosophy of nature with particular attention to the fundamental criticism of idealism that is involved, and to reconstruct the systematic significance of his philosophy of nature itself.

II

In the overall context of classical German philosophy, the systematic significance of Schelling's philosophy of nature, despite its undeniably speculative intentions, lies preeminently in its essentially critical function.[5] The attempt to overcome the narrow epistemological limits of transcendental philosophy continues to animate all the numerous modifications and revisions that Schelling would subsequently make in the project of his philosophy of nature. In spite of the fact that his project was explicitly directed against the Kantian version of transcendental philosophy, Schelling nonetheless found encouragement in Kant's *Third Critique* in particular. Yet the general critical impetus which Schelling shared with other younger contemporaries – especially with Novalis and Hölderlin – still does not suffice to explain his characteristic path in constructing a philosophy of nature in order finally to translate transcendental idealism into another theoretical context altogether.

It is still regarded today as Schelling's original achievement to have introduced the idea of a philosophy of nature into classical German philosophy in the form of a "prehistory" of reason. Even at a time when he was still much impressed by Fichte's influential *Science of Knowledge,* Schelling was already beginning to sketch a theory of self-consciousness in terms of the self-development of nature:

(. . .) what the soul intuits is always its own self-developing nature (. . .) Thus through its own products the soul reveals the pathway, imperceptible for common eyes but clearly and distinctly visible to the philosopher, along which it gradually travels towards self-consciousness. The external world lies open before us in order that we may rediscover the history of our own spirit. (SW I, 123)

Schelling develops in terms of the philosophy of nature the basic idealist concept that having a relation to oneself is only possible through simultaneously having a relation to something else. For Schelling, that which is distinguished from consciousness itself belongs to the "history of self-consciousness."[6] With this idea he initially only takes up Fichte's project of a "pragmatic history of the human spirit." But the theoretical perspective assumed by the philosophy of nature soon led Schelling toward positions that far transcend the domain of idealism as it was articulated by Fichte.

It is Schelling's fundamental thesis, and one defended at every stage of his intellectual development, that subjectivity can never become transparent to itself as long as it remains within the immanence of reflection. That is why he attempted to extend the history of self-consciousness in a naturalist direction. In contrast to the epistemological implications of transcendental philosophy, what is given in external reflection does not simply stand opposed to subjectivity, but emerges rather as the visible manifestation of subjectivity's own history. For Schelling, therefore, self-consciousness is at the very least the provisional culmination of nature's process of self-development.[7]

But Schelling did not regard some such thesis of mere externalization as sufficient to accomplish the transition from transcendental philosophy to the philosophy of nature. For this thesis initially only sets the given of external reflection over against self-consciousness. From this perspective, the only thing that can be said of nature is that it constitutes a structural element in the self-relation of subjectivity. In the theoretical context of transcendental philosophy, this constructive reductionism is unavoidable, something that is also clearly revealed in the fact that such a philosophy can only provide purely negative determinations for the externality of subjectivity.

According to Schelling, the fundamental deficiency of every epistemologically conceived philosophy of subjectivity lies in the fact that it is not interested in the character of that to which self-consciousness relates in external reflection. As a result of this, the effects that are exercised upon self-consciousness by the natural dimensions of human beings are overlooked. In the last analysis, such an approach also generates difficult problems for the theory of reflection itself, because this approach must at least implicitly assume that subjectivity has to do only with itself. But the assumption of a pure self-relation on the part of subjectivity is justified in neither foundational-theoretical nor in phenomenological terms.

Schelling provides a simple explanation for the problem of the circularity of subjectivity and self-consciousness that appears insoluble within the narrow limits of epistemological theory. There is absolutely no need to discover ever new metaphorical ways of supposedly overcoming the logic of immanent circularity that attaches to self-consciousness.[8] In Schelling's eyes, all that is required is to interpret the transcendental conditions of subjectivity in a developmental and historical fashion. If it is indeed possible to grasp the given and the conditions of subjectivity in terms of a systematic and developmental prehistory of the fact of subjectivity itself, then there can be no pure self-relation on the part of subjectivity in the first place. According to this perspective, human subjectivity is not condemned ceaselessly to move solely within a closed circle of its own.

The systematically pressing task of any philosophy of nature consequently consists in reformulating Kant's refutation of idealism in such a way that the relata of self-relation appear as simultaneously independent and structurally identical. The immanent circularity of subjectivity can only be broken and an actual relation only be established if the relata are recognized in both their independence and their affinity. The speculative thrust of Schelling's attempt to extend Kant's refutation of idealism in the shape of the philosophy of nature consists in the claim that we can only conceive the possibility of self-relation by stepping out beyond the limitations of immanent subjectivity. This model of reflection is characteristic of Schelling's theory of subjectivity and it reappears in every phase of Schelling's thought. It is an approach explicitly intended to establish a position in which the limits of subjectivity have already been surpassed. The task of demonstrating precisely how this position is possible in detail is fundamental in Schelling's philosophy of nature.

This project of transcending the purely negative determinations of transcendental philosophy in terms of a philosophy of nature nonetheless takes its point of departure precisely from the basic foundations of that philosophy. From the interpretative perspective of early German idealism, these transcendental-philosophical foundations are essentially governed by the idea of self-positing unconditioned subjectivity. In the so-called *älteste Systemprogramm des deutschen Idealismus,* these foundations are emphatically celebrated as the only possible way of conceiving the thought of a creation *ex nihilo:*

The first Idea [*Idee*] is naturally the representation [*Vorstellung*] of myself as an absolutely free being [*Wesen*]. Along with the free, self-conscious being there simultaneously emerges – out of nothing – an entire world – the one true and conceivable creation out of nothing.[9]

Over thirty years later, that is, after passing through every stage of his protean philosophical development, Schelling is still describing this thought just as emphatically as before:

With this act of self-positing: I am, the world commences for every individual; in every individual this act is at once the eternal and timeless inauguration of itself and of the world. Every human being begins, as it were, in an eternal manner (*modo aeterno*), and with this human being its entire past, present and future are posited for its representation. (SW X, 90)

It is clear, therefore, that Schelling does not simply repudiate the idealist concept of self-positing even in the later phases of his thought. But he qualifies the concept by arguing that it cannot actually accomplish what Fichte and the other early idealist thinkers expected to accomplish, namely, to resolve the problem of the transition from the immanence of subjectivity to the objectivity of subjectivity. As far as the recognition of the idea of an objectivity independent of subjectivity is concerned, Fichte's *Science of Knowledge* in Schelling's eyes even represented a decisive regression in comparison with Kant's thought. When he compared the two positions directly, Schelling attributed more objectivity to the Kantian critique of knowledge than he did to the post-Kantian project of the *Science of Knowledge.*

For all its objective intentions the concept of self-positing still harbors a number of egocentric connotations. In Schelling's view, it is particularly well-suited to flattering our self-centered attitudes. The concept in question could not redeem its promised access to the unconditioned, since subjective idealism was incapable of providing an argument to prove that the world of objects as given in experience exists only for and on the basis of human subjectivity. The unconditioned domain that was promised reveals itself, on the contrary, as an admission of dependency, since the reflecting consciousness constantly experiences with regard to itself that it does not dispense with the spatiotemporally given objects of its perception. Once the theoretical context of the philosophy of nature is provided, the self-certainty of the subject loses all appearance of being something entirely without presuppositions. Anyone who attempts to derive the dependency of the objects of outer reflection from the supposedly unconditional character of self-certainty fails, according to Schelling, to think through the problem of self-consciousness to the very end:

But it is immediately revealed here that although indeed the external world is only there for me insofar as I am also there and conscious of myself (and this is obvious), it is also true on the other hand that while I am there for myself, and am conscious of myself, that with this explicit affirmation that I am, I also find the world already – there – in being, and thus that the already conscious ego cannot possibly produce the world. (SW X, 93)

The fact that an external world exists for me does not mean that there is an external world only for me or only through me. The immanence of subjectivity that appeared so indestructible for Fichte is, according to Schelling, simply the result of a far-reaching mistake in the argument itself. It is because idealism is incapable of grasping its own presuppositions that it supposes it contains these presuppositions solely within itself. Only an idealism that has failed to understand itself properly sets itself up in opposition to a naturalist realism.

Schelling's version of transcendental idealism in effect overcomes the immanence of subjectivity. In this regard his approach essentially concurs, at least as far as its results are concerned, with Kant's refutation of idealism. And it is a historical irony of German idealism that it finally reformulates the very argument with which Kant originally hoped to dispel problematic and dogmatic idealism, and the argument that the early German idealists had striven so hard to challenge.

Although Schelling's version of transcendental idealism approaches the Critical philosophy in many ways, it should not be overlooked that it also diverges from it in essential respects. In particular, Schelling regarded Kant's refutation of idealism as a rather half-hearted and therefore inadequately explicated attempt. Schelling emphatically showed that the immediate consciousness of the existence of other things outside myself does not really suffice to overcome the immanence of subjectivity. The half-heartedness of Kant's approach could be seen not least in the concessions that he made to problematic idealism. For Schelling, the immanence of subjectivity may only actually be broken if subjectivity is capable of recognizing itself precisely in that which it is not. Unlike Kant, who drew the limits of self-consciousness from within, Schelling recognised in self-consciousness a manifestation of what it itself is not:

But nothing would prevent this ego that I am now conscious of in myself from reflecting upon a moment when it was not yet conscious of itself – from assuming a region beyond the consciousness now present to itself and an activity which no longer enters consciousness in its own right but solely as a result. (SW X, 93)

According to this view, subjectivity stands neither merely opposed to the given contents of the world nor does it first have to pass over into something other than itself. On the contrary, subjectivity comes to self-consciousness in what is other precisely *as* "the other of itself."

Schelling derived a decisive stimulus for his completion of the refutation of idealism from the third *Critique*. Whereas Kant had determined the idea of the totality of nature, as a connected system of ends, in a regulative but not in a constitutive sense, Schelling grasped the analytic of teleological judgment[10] in particular as the preparatory ground for a deduction of the objective teleological character of nature. Whereas Kant had spoken cautiously of the legitimacy of supposing inner purposiveness with regard to the organic products of nature in general, Schelling assumed the necessity of conceiving nature in its entirety as absolutely purposive in character. The defining feature of this approach consists in the fact that the resulting concept of the organism, in spite of all the implicit speculative intentions, is mediated in the first place by epistemological considerations. According to Schelling, nature itself cannot just contingently happen to cohere with the human principles of knowledge. Rather, our knowledge of nature can only arise *because* nature is an organism and because the principle that lies at the basis of nature is the same as that which lies at the basis of ourselves. The concept of organism thereby becomes the model of an original unity of nature and spirit that immediately constitutes our human experience of nature and of ourselves.

The other of self-consciousness for Schelling is no longer therefore simply an external impact [*Anstoß*], but rather the extension of self-consciousness. In his early philosophy of nature, Schelling had already emphasized the fundamental structural correspondence between nature and spirit: "The system of nature is at the same time the system of our own spirit."[11] Nature is understood here as an organic totality of matter and spirit that unfolds in various complex processes and stages of development. Schelling proceeds on the assumption that such a concept of nature, according to its very constitution, does not allow the opposition between mechanism and organism, the opposition that had been so problematic for the post-Kantian idealists, even to arise at all; for his concept of nature presupposed a principle that constitutes organic and inorganic nature alike.[12] If we assume the structural identity of nature and spirit, then the dualism between what is given and what is made can be transcended. We can then conceive an organic unity of producer and produced that in turn also allows us to grasp the site of subjectivity in nature as a point of departure for an expanded understanding of ourselves and of nature: "As long as I am myself identical with nature, then I can understand what living nature is as easily as I can understand my own life itself."[13]

According to Schelling's history of self-consciousness articulated in the context of the philosophy of nature, then, self-consciousness is not merely anchored in nature but must preeminently be regarded as its expression. From the earliest version of his philosophy right through to his later thought, Schelling continued to describe this idea in terms of the Platonic metaphor of a "connecting bond." On the basis of this "mysterious bond,"[14] which holds the opposed moments together, nature can be grasped as "visible spirit" and spirit can be grasped as "invisible nature." The equation "Nature = Visible Spirit" and "Spirit = Invisible Nature" clearly reveals the characteristic features of a monist theory of identity that treats differences in the world as perspectival distinctions. Such a theory finds exemplary expression in the *System of Transcendental Idealism* of 1800.

III

It must be admitted that great difficulties are involved in providing theoretical justification for Schelling's various systematic attempts to develop a philosophy of nature. Nonetheless, the critical problematisation of idealism that prepared the way for Schelling's speculations on the philosophy of nature remains highly significant in itself. This problematization was intrinsically determined by considerations all of which represented constructive reactions to the narrowly focused analysis of subjectivity characteristic of the Critical philosophy and of Fichte's *Science of Knowledge.* For Schelling, that which is given independent of consciousness and that which is posited in and through consciousness are essentially one and the same. If some such identity thesis is not presupposed, according to Schelling, both the nature within myself and the nature outside of me must continue to remain utterly incomprehensible. But since nature is temporally prior, then subjectivity itself, quite apart from the question concerning the underlying principle of both, acquires the form of an intrinsically altered nature. The constructive advantage attaching to the naturalist derivation of subjectivity consists above all in the fact that all the externalization and correspondence problems which beset transcendental philosophy and subjective idealism appear to be resolved in a single stroke.

Schelling perspicuously formulated the problem involved in the externalization of subjectivity, and his interpretation of the "I am" goes beyond merely identifying the unconditioned character of self-certainty. For he also attempted to show that "even presupposing Fichte's proposition that everything only is through and for the ego, it is still possible to comprehend the objective world."[15] What Schelling had already emphatically invoked in his *Letters on Dogmatism and Criticism,* as the human striving toward an unchangeable selfhood,[16] reappeared transformed in the context of the philosophy of nature as the "labor of self-awareness" [*die Arbeit des "Zu-sich-selbst-Kommens"*]:[17] It is only in and through this labor that the authentic capacity of subjectivity is revealed, which essentially consists in nothing else but discovering itself in the nature that lies beyond it and the nature that develops within it. Schelling summarises this idea 1827 in *On the History of Modern Philosophy:*

I therefore attempted, in a word, to explain that indissoluble connection between the ego and the external world which it necessarily represents to itself by recourse to a transcendental past of this ego that precedes our actual or empirical consciousness, an explanation which thereby led me towards the idea of a transcendental history of the ego. (SW X, 93/94)

For Schelling, this "transcendental past" of the ego was no mere extravagant flight of speculation that transfigured the time before the ego came to consciousness of itself. If the fundamental proposition of Cartesian thought is only properly understood, it is seen to lead toward the idea of the transcendental past:

For the "I am" is simply and precisely the expression for the process in which the ego comes to awareness of itself as such – this coming to awareness of itself, that is expressed in the "I am," thus presupposes an self-exteriority [*ein außer- und von-sich-Gewesensein*] and pastness of itself. For only that which was already external to itself can possibly come to subsequent awareness of itself. The first condition of the ego, therefore, is a self-exteriority. (SW X, 94)

The concept of the transcendental past is a metaphorical expression which results from combining a temporal and an epistemological determination. The construction of the concept thereby connects the systematic conditions of the possibility of self-consciousness with the presuppositions of its own developmental history. The constructive connection between epistemology and developmental history thus extends the meaning of the basic Cartesian thesis of the "I am." For it now expresses an idea of self-certainty that determines the instantaneous intuition of one's own existence as a result rather than simply as an entirely self-sufficient point of departure.

Schelling's fundamental claim, namely that the "I am" is already an expression of the process of "coming to awareness" of the ego, does not attempt to grasp self-consciousness from the perspective of its psychological self-evidence or familiarity with itself. It attempts rather to demonstrate that self-consciousness is not exclusively a question of self-certainty or self-familiarity, and that a series of conditions *within* self-consciousness must already be fulfilled if the latter is to arise at all. What distinguishes this basic claim from the epistemologically structural history of self-consciousness already developed in Kant's Critical philosophy and in Fichte's *Science of Knowledge,* is the assumption that the reconstructed conditions of self-consciousness must be at least partly identical in structure to the *phenomenon* of self-consciousness.

The idea of the ego's "coming to awareness of itself" in the "I am" possesses a decentering function: The subject of self-consciousness sees itself as a reflective instantiation of a dimension that is not itself egocentrically structured.

To that extent, the phenomenon of self-consciousness takes on the significance of a process of coming to awareness through which nature becomes partially transparent to itself in the form of the rational individual. In evaluating this idea of "coming to self-awareness" in the "I am," we must also take care to distinguish between the subjective standpoint of the finite individual and that transindividual objectivity that Schelling calls Ego or *"Geist."* The idea of "coming to self-awareness" implicit in the "I am" is thus subject to further differentiation. The path from self-exteriority to self-awareness is a movement from impersonal to personal subjectivity: I can only become conscious of myself if I encounter an external world in a manner that itself stands under the conditions of a transindividual and impersonal subjectivity.

With this concept of coming to self-awareness in the "I am," it is striking just how close Schelling comes to Kant's epistemology of self-consciousness. For the latter is also constructed from combining transcendental determinations and concepts that relate essentially to the actually occurring phenomena of consciousness. According to Kant, the identity of self-consciousness can only be maintained over time because the synthesis of the given manifold, of the data of consciousness, stands under the condition of the transcendental unity of apperception.[18] As a typical post-Kantian philosopher, Schelling takes a further step. He subjects Kant's epistemologically negative determinations, such as "the transcendental unity of apperception" or the "given of sensible intuition," to a naturalist extension of meaning. The idea of a genetic isomorphism of nature and spirit as derived from the real existence of finite self-consciousness is particularly significant in this context:

That which is thought of as beyond consciousness is the same for all individuals, since the individual has not yet exercised an influence here, and it is this which explains why for my own representation of the external world I must unconditionally count upon the agreement of all other human individuals, and this without having any experience of the same myself (even the child who shows me an object already presupposes that this object must exist for me as well as for the child itself). (SW X, 94)

The fact that the referential character and the coherence of human experience cannot be grasped exclusively from the subjective standpoint lends an initial plausibility to the position of problematic idealism. It is only a more penetrating analysis of human experience that can bring the decisive presupposition to the focus of philosophical attention: namely, that genetic isomorphism of nature and spirit in which finite subjectivity participates. If no such isomorphism had developed in the first place, then there could never be any consciousness either of inner or outer nature. In that case, there could be no practical reciprocal action between subjectivity and nature, and the sensible perception of objects and events of nature could never arise.

The circumstance that the genetic isomorphism of nature and spirit represents the condition of the possibility of our experience and interaction with natural processes and events does not itself signify, however, that acting and knowing subjects could exercise cognitive mastery over this isomorphism. We are certainly capable of responding to it practically, but as such it remains opaque to us. According to Schelling, our every representation of the external world is as blind as it is necessary.

Schelling's deduction of the objectivity of subjectivity is based upon the thesis that finite subjectivity is itself involved in the developmental history of this isomorphism of nature and spirit. What might initially appear as nothing but speculative flights of natural philosophy are actually derived from fundamental considerations that are not formally unlike those that support Kant's transcendental deduction of the pure concepts of the understanding. Schelling, too, attempts to derive and justify the referential character and coherence of human experience in a single step. The important distinction between Kant's and Schelling's deduction consists in their differing interpretations of the fact that the conditions of the possibility of self-consciousness cannot themselves be correlated with experiential states. Whereas Kant is content, with typical critical modesty, to point out that I am not explicitly conscious of the original unity of my representations under self-consciousness in general,[19] Schelling entertains the possibility of deriving the conditions of the referential character and coherence in human experience from the ways in which nature manifests itself:

But insofar as the ego now becomes an individual ego – something which indeed immediately announces itself in the "I am" – insofar as it has now arrived at this "I am" with which its individual life commences, it no longer recalls the path which it has traversed up to this point, but since consciousness only emerges precisely at the end of this path, the (now individual) ego has traversed the path towards consciousness itself quite unconsciously and unknowingly. This is what explains the blindness and necessity of its representations of the external world, as well as the identity and universality of the same in all individuals. The individual ego now finds in its consciousness nothing but the monuments, the memorials as it were, of the path rather than the path itself. (SW X, 94/95)

This metaphor of the monuments and memorials of the path that leads to consciousness cannot simply be explained as an extravagant expression of the philosophy of nature. It actually helps Schelling address the ambitious task of rendering the exteriority of the self accessible to consciousness in a different form. For the concrete labor of "coming to self-awareness" is essentially concerned with nothing else but this prior exteriority on the part of consciousness.

It might seem plausible to suspect the presence of some form of subjective idealism still lurking behind the image of the process of "coming to self-awareness," to interpret the latter simply as a continuation, albeit it a highly complicated one, of the idealist conception of self-creation. Such an interpretation, however, would certainly fail to grasp the specific character of Schelling's argumentation as opposed to that found in Fichte. As far as Schelling is concerned, it is an unshakable fact of finite existence that the latter does not simply possess the external and inner conditions of its own "coming to self-awareness" at its own disposal. Our various forms of theoretical and practical dependence upon inner and outer nature impose narrow limits on the possibility of self-knowledge. By virtue of the naturalist incorporation of subjectivity, these forms of dependency continue to exercise their effects and do not simply lose their influence when rational individuals enter into the domain of explicit consciousness and self-consciousness. This circumstance is the reverse side, as it were, of the various gradated levels involved in nature, spirit, and subjectivity. If the boundaries here are fluid ones, then the various dispositions and characteristics of human individuals cannot rigidly be detached from these contexts. All processes of self-knowledge must therefore also recognize the possibility that those determinations that we identify as the motivating reasons for our own attitudes, perspectives, and modes of behavior are not necessarily the true causes of the latter.

As for Kant, for Schelling self-knowledge in the strict sense of the word is impossible. Whereas Kant in this connection points to epistemological reasons for this, and to the limited discursive means at the disposal of rational individuals, Schelling regards the natural history of subjectivity as representing the decisive obstacle to a fully cognitive self-relation. In accordance with this account, self-knowledge must be grasped as a process that must transpire in some harmonious relation to that natural history. But that is certainly a task that dramatically exceeds the powers of the individual. From a naturalist perspective the life of persons represents nothing but an "eternal fragment," and our cognitive relationship to ourselves must likewise remain a fragment.[20]

Schelling's notion of the process of "coming to self-awareness" was originally motivated by the fundamental thought: "no relation to the self without a relation to nature." It is precisely the truth of this thought that prevents us from ever finally concluding this process either practically or cognitively. Of course it is also true in a quite trivial sense that self-knowledge is ultimately a never-ending process, but Schelling was able to go further than this and reveal that self-knowledge is inconclusive not only on the basis of the finitude of reflective life itself, but also by virtue of those naturally determined components from which that life is first composed.

According to Schelling, the conception of the process of "coming to self-awareness" through the movement from a prior self-exteriority toward a reconstructed self-exteriority only finds its ultimate completion in a theory of the self-limitation of reason itself. Schelling first began to elaborate this theory in his *Treatise on the Essence of Human Freedom* in 1809, which marked a decisive break with idealist conceptions of freedom in particular and indeed with typically idealist strategies of argumentation in general.[21] Schelling's theory of the self-limitation of reason ultimately and effectively culminated in the diagnosis that human reason in itself is groundless and can only find its essence in something outside or beyond itself.

IV

It would certainly seem promising to expect further clarification of these issues from Schelling's recently published commentary on Plato's *Timaeus* (see above). And in fact the *Science of Knowledge* does indeed contain some extremely valuable indications as far as the understanding of Schelling's philosophical development is concerned. But the understanding of the later developments of Schelling's thought is not essentially made that much easier after all, since the relevant basis for further interpretation is now more complex in character and throws a distinctive light upon that phase of Schelling's thought that was particularly concerned with articulating the philosophy of nature. If the editor's dating of the text is correct, the commentary was composed during the first half of 1794, namely *prior* to Schelling's extensive engagement with Fichte's *Science of Knowledge*.

In this respect, the commentary on the *Timaeus* appears fairly irrelevant for a systematic understanding of Schelling's philosophy of nature. But although the *Timaeus Commentary* is far too early a piece to furnish any immediate systematic contribution to the understanding of Schelling's philosophy of nature, it is nonetheless informative about the original sources of his thought, and provides insight into his later writings, in particular the *Treatise on the Essence of Human Freedom*.

In the commentary, Schelling shows that he is closely indebted to Plato's *Timaeus* insofar as he principally dedicates his energies to the question concerning the origin and the essential forms of the world. On the other hand, the terminology and methodological approach clearly reveals the still insufficiently assimilated influence of Kant and Reinhold. To a certain extent, the commentary attempts to map Kant's doctrine of categories onto Plato's doctrine of ideas.[22]

It is also striking that the *Timaeus Commentary* places a considerable emphasis upon the perspective of the philosophy of nature that in this form is not actually followed up in Schelling's subsequent writings. Schelling's early engagement with Plato leads him to ask after the "becoming of being,"[23] and his intentions are clearly directed toward the idea of nature even "before the origin of the world." Anticipating Hegel's speculative logic here, one could already regard this formulation as an attempt to discover the thoughts of God before the creation in terms of a philosophy of nature. But Schelling only addresses himself to such far-reaching questions much later in the *Treatise on the Essence of Human Freedom.* This dimension is conspicuously and entirely absent in his early philosophy of nature.

Schelling concerns himself in his *Timaeus Commentary* with metaphysical questions that he attempts to elaborate decisively in the later stages of his thought. It is only with the *Treatise on Freedom* that the concept of the "becoming of being" receives an impressive if also thoroughly enigmatic interpretation, which opens up a fundamental abyss between the being insofar as it exists and the being that is merely the ground of existence.[24] This is a concept that has very little to do with the pantheistic position of Schelling's early philosophy of nature that was so heavily influenced by Spinoza's naturalist monism.

Traces of the *Timaeus Commentary* are nevertheless to be found in Schelling's early philosophy of nature, and particularly in his project for a "speculative physics."[25] Schelling's critical forays against the intellectual climate of the age also may be understood as manifestations of the same revolutionary spirit in which the project of a speculative physics was conceived. But it seems rather more important to recognize that his *Timaeus Commentary* already harbored the speculative potential that he would explicitly develop only in the later phases of his thought.

After 1800, the path of Schelling's philosophical thought became increasingly radical and this in turn also forced him to advance far beyond the concepts of externalization that he had explored in his philosophy of nature. The culminating products of this radical development are the *Treatise on the Essence of Human Freedom* and the *Philosophy of Revelation,* which both oppose the position elaborated in *The System of Transcendental Idealism* a new philosophy in which existence and the ground of existence can no longer be brought into systematic connection with one another.

Schelling's later works undertake to engage the question concerning the very ground of existence from which nature and man alike first emerge. But he no longer seeks the answer to this question within a closed idealist system. He now accepts the seemingly inevitable impossibility of such philosophical and systematic closure. This progressive radicalization of Schelling's speculation in these works thereby departs decisively from the general monist perspective shared by the other representative thinkers of German idealism. In this sense, Schelling's *Treatise on the Essence of Human Freedom* must really be seen as the great alternative project to Hegel's *Phenomenology of Spirit.*

The *Timaeus Commentary* reveals a specific aspect of the history of German idealism that has been largely concealed from the reception of Schelling's thought because of the powerful influence that Fichte's *Science of Knowledge* began to exert upon Schelling almost immediately after the composition of the earlier work. Even before his early attempts to formulate a philosophy of nature, Schelling had begun to pursue questions that he would only properly take up again after 1800. It looks as though the overwhelming encounter with

Fichte's *Science of Knowledge* diverted him to the kind of considerations that he could only address again once he had recognized that Fichte's project and his own early philosophy of nature had proved a failure. From the perspective of reception history, this rather suggests the need for a theory of distraction or deflection that could grasp the successive phases of Schelling's unfolding philosophy as a system of fractures, one that relinquishes any claim for coherent developmental unity and simply pursues its own original insights without reserve. Schelling's early philosophy of nature and the *System of Transcendental Idealism* of 1800 accordingly represented monist periods in his thinking that respond systematically to a range of fundamental dualist problems. But they also in turn provided the stimulus – together with the extremely influential formulation of Hegel's monist position – to develop a theory of the self-limitation of reason that would decisively repudiate the very idea of a unified system so characteristic of idealism in the first place.

Notes

1. Cf. Immanuel Kant, *Kritik der reinen Vernunft* (Hamburg: Felix Meiner Verlag, 1956), A 369f./B 518ff.
2. Friedrich Wilhelm Joseph von Schelling, *Sämmtliche Werke* (Stuttgart and Augsburg: J. G. Cotta'scher Verlag, 1856–61) [henceforth cited as SW], vol. III, p. 386. This and all translations, including the translation of the author's original text, are by Nicholas Walker.
3. Cf. Wolfgang Wieland, "Die Anfänge der Philosophie Schellings und die Frage nach der Natur," in *Materialien zu Schellings philosophischen Anfängen,* ed. Manfred Frank and Gerhard Kurz (Frankfurt am Main: Suhrkamp Verlag, 1975), pp. 237–79; Friedrich Wilhelm Joseph von Schelling, *Ergänzungsband zu Werke, Band 5 bis 9. Wissenschaftshistorischer Bericht zu Schellings Naturphilosophischen Schriften 1797–1800* (Stuttgart: Frommann-Holzboog, 1994).
4. In the context of a historical reconstruction of philosophy, much is to be learned from the recent edition of Schelling's early commentary on Plato's Timaeus: *F. W. Schelling, "Timaeus" (1794),* edited by Hartmut Buchner (Stuttgart: Frommann-Holzboog, 1994). See Section IV of the present essay. For further interpretation of Schelling's *Science of Knowledge,* also see Manfred Baum's contribution in this volume.
5. See my essay, "Schellings Subjektivitätskritik," in *Deutsche Zeitschrift für Philosophie* 44 (1996): 429–46. Cf. Andrew Bowie, *Schelling and Modern European Philosophy* (London and New York: Routledge, 1993), pp. 30–44.
6. SW I, p. 382. For the concept and overall idea of a history of self-consciousness in the context of a philosophy of nature, see SW I, pp. 382ff. and III, pp. 395ff. Cf. my essay, "Die Odyssee des Geistes. Schellings Projekt einer naturphilosophischen Geschichte des Selbstbewußtseins," in *Philosophie der Subjektivität? Zur Bestimmung des neuzeitlichen Philosophierens,* vol. 2, ed. H. M. Baumgarter and W. G. Jacobs (Stuttgart: Frommann-Holzboog, 1993), pp. 580–90.
7. See SW I, p. 383.
8. As is well known, it was Fichte who explicitly attempted to realize this project. According to Dieter Henrich, it was this that led him toward his "original insight"

into the nature of self-consciousness; see Dieter Henrich, "Fichtes ursprüngliche Einsicht," in *Subjektivität und Metaphysik,* ed. D. Henrich and H. Wagner (Frankfurt am Main: Klostermann, 1966), pp. 188–232. Cf. my *Kant über Selbstbewußtseins. Zum Zusammenhang von Erkenntniskritik und Theorie des Selbstbewußtseins* (Hildesheim: Georg Olms, 1986), pp. 107–27.

9. See "Das sogenannte Älteste Systemprogramm des Deutschen Idealismus," in *Materialien zu Schellings philosophischen Anfängen,* ed. M. Frank and G. Kurz (Frankfurt am Main: Suhrkamp Verlag, 1975), p. 110.

10. See Immanuel Kant, *Kritik der Urteilskraft,* "Akademie" edition, vol. IV (Berlin: de Gruyter, 1968), §§62–68.

11. SW II, p. 39.

12. See SW II, pp. 347ff.

13. SW II, p. 47.

14. See SW Il, p. 55, 359; SW X, p. 229.

15. SW X, p. 95.

16. See SW I, p. 335.

17. SW X, p. 93.

18. See Kant, *Kritik der reinen Vernunft,* B 131 ff. [§16]; cf. Dieter Sturma, *Kant über Selbstbewußtsein: Zum Zusammenhang von Erkenntniskritik und Theorie des Selbstbewußtseins* (Hildesheim: Georg Olms, 1985), pp. 30–106.

19. See Kant, *Kritik der reinen Vernunft,* B 132 f.

20. SW III, p. 608. Cf. my *Philosophie der Person. Die Selbstverhältnisse von Subjektivität und Moralität* (Paderborn: Schöningh, 1997), pp. 232–40.

21. See my essay, "Präreflexive Freiheit und menschliche Selbstbestimmung," in *F. W. J. Schelling: Über das Wesen der menschlichen Freiheit,* ed. Ottfried Höffe and Annemarie Pieper (Berlin: Akademie Verlag, 1995), pp. 149–72.

22. See Dieter Henrich, *Konstellationen. Probleme und Debatten am Ursprung der idealistischen Philosophie (1789–1795)* (Stuttgart: Klett-Cotta, 1991), pp. 116–20; Hermann Krings, "Genesis und Materie – Zur Bedeutung der 'Timaeus' – Handschrift für Schellings Naturphilosophie," in *F. W. J. Schelling: "Timaeus,"* pp. 123–4; Rüdiger Bubner, "Die Entdeckung Platons durch Schelling," in *Neue Hefte für Philosophie* 35 (1995): 32–55.

23. *F. W. J. Schelling: "Timaeus,"* p. 63.

24. SW VII, p. 357.

25. See Rüdiger Bubner, "Die Entdeckung Platons durch Schelling."

11

Substance, Causality, and the Question of Method in Hegel's *Science of Logic*

STEPHEN HOULGATE

I

In the eyes of many, Hegel's *Science of Logic* appears to be a monstrous anachronism – a work, written thirty years after Kant's *Critique of Pure Reason,* that revives precisely the kind of naive metaphysics Kant had shown to be illegitimate. For Hegel, by contrast, the *Logic* represents the culmination of a philosophical development that Kant himself set in motion. Kant's great achievement, in Hegel's view, was to place at the center of philosophical attention the *categories* through which philosophers had traditionally understood the world. Philosophers from Aristotle to Spinoza and Leibniz employed various categories, such as "substance" and "causality," to understand what there is, but, according to Hegel, they never examined with sufficient rigor whether it is actually legitimate to employ them in the way they did. Kant's merit is to have focused specifically on those categories themselves and to have undertaken an extensive and thorough enquiry into their source and range of validity.[1]

In the course of his enquiry, Kant recognized that the source of the categories was not empirical experience or divine revelation but the spontaneity of thought itself and that the true character of the categories could thus be discovered by examining the distinctive activity of thought. This Kantian insight above all others is the one that Hegel embraces most keenly in his *Logic.* From Hegel's perspective, however, Kant's own attempt to discover the categories in the Metaphysical Deduction in the *Critique of Pure Reason* falls short of what a truly *critical* philosophy should deliver: Kant simply took it for granted that the basic activity of thought is that of using concepts in judgments and read off the categories from what he saw as the primary logical functions of judgment.[2] It is true that in the Transcendental Deduction Kant went on to argue that judgment itself presupposes the transcendental unity of apperception or the thought of the unity of the "I."[3] But he never demonstrated that the very nature of apperception as such, in abstraction from its relation to intuition, requires that we use concepts or that we make judgments. From Hegel's point of view, therefore, Kant's claim that "understanding may . . . be represented as faculty of judgment" – indeed, that understanding is fundamentally discursive – remains ultimately ungrounded.[4]

Fichte improved on Kant, according to Hegel, by explicitly *deriving* the categories and the activity of judgment from what he took to be the most fundamental and universal activity of thought: the fact that (as Fichte saw it) the "I" "posits" both itself and what is not itself. In Hegel's view, however, even Fichte took too much for granted in his derivation of the categories, because we may not simply *assume* that thought is ultimately the self-positing of the "I." After all, such self-positing might itself be generated by a more fundamental, impersonal activity of thinking, as, for example, Spinoza would have claimed. This is not to say that Spinoza would necessarily be right; it is merely to point out that Fichte was much less cautious than he ought to have been in identifying his starting point.[5]

The task facing the modern philosopher, for Hegel, remains that set out by Kant in the Metaphysical Deduction, namely, to derive the basic categories of thought from the spontaneous activity of thought itself. If that task is to be carried out in a genuinely critical way, however, we may not proceed from the assumptions made about thought by either Kant or Fichte. The aim of Hegel's own *Science of Logic* is thus to derive the categories from thought *without* assuming in advance either that understanding is equivalent to judging or that thinking is the self-positing of an "I." Indeed, as Hegel insists in the *Encyclopedia Logic*, "all . . . presuppositions or prejudgments must equally be given up when we enter into Science, whether they are taken from representation or thinking; for it is this Science, in which all determinations of this sort must first be investigated."[6] For Hegel, therefore, the *Logic* must begin by abstracting from all that we normally take thought to be and by holding only to the quite abstract thought that thought *is,* that it is simple immediacy or *being* – being whose sense to begin with is wholly indeterminate and unspecified. From this somewhat inauspicious beginning, Hegel believes, the categories of thought are to be derived.[7]

What I propose to do in this essay is not to discuss the merits of the *Science of Logic* as a whole, but to examine the accounts of two categories to which Hegel is led by his presuppositionless analysis of thought: the categories of substance and causality. In so doing I hope to shed light on the distinctive *method* that Hegel believes presuppositionless philosophizing requires one to follow. In particular, I hope to show that such a method involves, not "regressing" in a quasitranscendental way from one concept to its "condition," but demonstrating how one concept transforms itself immanently *into* another.[8] Indeed, I hope to show that – at least in the analysis of substance and causality – Hegel's *Logic* seeks to do precisely what one commentator, Robert Pippin, thinks it does *not* do: namely, establish "that 'in thinking' one Notion one would really *be* 'thinking its other'."[9] At the end of the essay, I will suggest that the distinctive method followed in the *Logic,* in particular the form it takes in the analysis of substance and causality, underlies one of the most significant differences between Hegel and Kant. For, whereas Kant holds that the categories of substance and causality are logically distinct (though epistemically interdependent), Hegel claims that the category of substance turns out logically *to be* the concept of causality itself. In carrying out the Kantian project of a Metaphysical Deduction of the categories in what he considers to be a thoroughly critical and presuppositionless manner, Hegel is thus led to a new and decidedly un-Kantian understanding of those categories themselves.[10]

For the purposes of this essay, by the way, I shall accept Hegel's claim that the *Science of Logic* is both a logic and an ontology – that it provides an account both of the primary categories of thought and of the constitutive determinations of being itself. I will not try to defend this claim here, though I have tried to do so elsewhere.[11]

II

Let us turn now to Hegel's conception of substance and causality in the *Science of Logic.* In Chapter 3 of Section 3 of the "logic of essence," Hegel declares substance to be, not "*being* as such, but *being* that is *because* it is, being as the absolute mediation of itself with itself."[12] Substance is being that does not merely happen to be, therefore, but that is *by virtue of* or *through* itself – being that, as W. T. Stace puts it, is "self-grounded, . . . determined by self and not by another."[13] Such self-grounding, substantial being, according to Hegel, is not just to be found in one kind of entity rather than another (for example, in gods rather than mortals), but is to be found in all entities: it is "the being in *all* being" by virtue of which things *are* at all. Substance is thus not itself one thing amongst other things, for Hegel, but is what being itself – the being in all things – ultimately is: "immediate actuality itself."[14]

As several commentators have pointed out, Hegel's position is very close to that of Spinoza: Substance, for both philosophers, is neither simply a bearer of properties, nor a Leibnizian monad, but being itself, understood, in Spinoza's words, as "what is in itself and is conceived through itself."[15] Although Hegel is very close to Spinoza, however, his conception of substance is by no means exactly the same. One of the subtle differences between the two philosophers is that, whereas Spinoza stresses that substance is primarily the indwelling ground or "free cause" of finite things, Hegel puts more emphasis on the idea that substance is the self-grounding being or subsisting *of* the things themselves – the very *Bestehen* or *Subsistieren* of things.[16] The fact that Hegel chooses to define substance as *being* that is because it is, is thus not merely a linguistic idiosyncrasy on his part, but indicates an important feature of the concept: namely, that substance is above all the very being of beings as such, rather than their logically distinct ground.

Yet, we should remember that substance is not just being, for Hegel, but being that is *because* it is – being that is (to use the Fichtean terminology employed by Hegel) self-*positing*. Indeed, Hegel insists that substance "*is* only this self-positing" and is nothing beyond that.[17] The moment of positing and originating may well be submerged in the idea of substance as being, but it is not obliterated by that idea altogether. Furthermore, Hegel notes that this idea of substance as the activity of positing necessarily places substance in *relation* to that which is posited by it. Such being that is posited, or brought about, by substance is called by Hegel, following an ancient tradition, *accidentality.* The very idea of substance as the activity of positing thus necessarily introduces a logical distinction between substance itself and the accidents that are dependent upon it.

But does this not conflict with what has been said so far? For how can we understand substance, not just as being, but as the explicit activity of positing, without setting substance *ahead* of finite, "accidental" things and so losing sight of the fact that it constitutes the very being *of* finite things themselves? Substance, it seems, demands to be thought both as positing or giving rise to all that there is and as the very being of all that there is. Yet how is that to be done? Hegel's answer is simple: This can only be done by understanding the process of substance's posit*ing* to be identical with the unfolding of that which is posit*ed* by it, that is, with *Gesetztsein.*[18] The strange conclusion to which Hegel is led by his analysis is thus that the realm of accidentality – which we are required by the very idea of substance to regard as posited by, dependent upon, and to that extent different from, substance – must at the same time be understood to be *one and the same being* as substance itself:

substance, as this identity of the reflective movement, is the totality of the whole and embraces accidentality within it, and accidentality is the whole substance itself.[19]

This means that the movement of accidentality – the events and occurrences that take place among the finite things that exist – is not to be thought of as pointing back to a substance that would serve as its logically prior ground or cause, but is to be thought of as the very movement, "actuosity" or "tranquil unfolding" of substance itself. The movement of accidentality *is* the movement of substance itself for Hegel, because accidentality is simply that which substance in its self-positing posits *itself* to be: it is substance itself *as* posited being.[20] The concept of substance as the activity of positing necessarily implies a distinction between itself and the realm of posited or accidental being; but, by virtue of being the thought of the very being of beings themselves, that concept also requires us to identify substance and accidentality with one another. To the extent that the thought of substance is inevitably the thought of a difference or relation between substance and its accidents, therefore, it is, as Hegel puts it, just as inevitably the thought of that "relation as immediately vanishing."[21] Substance, for Hegel, thus constitutes one being and one world – the world of finite things and processes that we see about us, regarded as a single, unfolding unity.[22]

Yet, is it enough to understand substance to be simply unfolding as the realm of finite, accidental things? Do we not need to conceive of substance as more active than that – as truly *generating* and *giving rise to* what occurs in the world? Equally, however, do we not still need to keep in mind that substance is one with, and so does not simply precede (or, indeed, lie "beyond" or "beneath"), what occurs in the world? Hegel thinks that we must conceive of substance in both these ways at once, and that we can meet this requirement if we think of substance as the *changing* of one accident into another, as *der Wechsel der Akzidenzen*. There is an ambiguity in the word *Wechsel* that Hegel exploits at this point in his analysis: for it indicates both the activity of bringing about change and the occurring of change itself (which is why I have translated it as "changing" rather than "change"). To think of substance as the actual changing of the accidents into one another is thus to think of it precisely as we are required to do: namely, as the active producing (and destroying) of things that is one with the coming into being (and passing away) *of* those things themselves.

When substance is understood in this way, it is understood, according to Hegel, as *power* (*Macht*). To conceive of substance as power is thus not to conceive of it as an entity or force (*Kraft*) preceding or underlying events in the world, but rather as the actual *changing* and *turning* of one thing into something else. Substance, for Hegel, proves to be nothing other than this turning of one thing into another – a turning that provides the unity and continuity *of* the realm of accidentality itself, or the "*form-unity* of accidentality." In contrast to Kant, therefore, Hegel does not conceive of substance as merely having power, but as *being* nothing but power. Moreover, he conceives of power itself, not just as potency or capacity – as mere *Vermögen* – but as actual, active *Macht*.[23] At this point, of course, the line between Hegel's concept of substance and that of Spinoza becomes very fine indeed.

If Hegel's analysis is correct, we are required by the very concept of substance itself to think of it – not unlike Nietzschean will to power – as creative (and destructive) power operating *in* the very movement of finite things themselves. This is to understand substance as more active with respect to accidentality, and in that sense more distinct from accidentality, than is the case when the two are understood simply to constitute one unfolding or "actuosity." Yet, this is clearly still to understand the difference between substance and its accidents to be a disappearing difference.

On the one hand, to think of substance as power is necessarily to think of *it* as changing the accidents from being into nonbeing and from nonbeing into being. The accidents themselves are thus not thought to exercise any power of their own, but to be posited, or brought into being (and destroyed), by substantial power itself.[24] On the other hand, however, the idea of substance as the being *of* all beings at the same time prevents us from conceiving of substantial power as anything distinct from the sphere of accidentality itself. This means that the substantial power creating and destroying things can in fact be nothing other than the very being or subsisting *of* things themselves: "one accident, then, expels another only because its own *subsisting* is this totality of form and content itself in which it and its other equally perish."[25]

This latter idea cannot mean that substance is to be equated with the *sheer* accidentality of things as such, since substance *rather than* accidentality is the power of creating and destroying. It must mean, therefore, that substantial power is to be equated with the *true* or *inner* being of the accidents themselves, with the *Inneres der Akzidenzen*. Substance as power is thus not altogether reducible to accidentality, but it is not really anything of its *own* either, since it is simply the inner being of things conceived as *changing* them into something else – the inner being of things themselves in the form of power over them. Conceived in this way, substance is thus not conceived as *real*, but rather as *formal*, power – that is, power that has no determinate identity of its own over against the things it changes, creates, and destroys. "On account of this *immediate identity* and presence of substance in the accidents," Hegel remarks, "no *real* difference is as yet present."[26]

As we have seen, the very idea of substance establishes a difference between the positing that substance is and the accidental being that is posited by it. We have also seen, however, that the concept of substance undermines the very difference it establishes. Substance has thus been conceived (i) as one and the same process or "actuosity" as the movement of its accidentality, and (ii) more specifically, as the actual changing of accidents into one another, or power – power that is identical with the inner nature or subsisting of things themselves. The difference between substance and accidentality has been understood constantly to disappear, because substance has been understood always to be the being *of* or *in* beings themselves, rather than their prior ground. Yet, as Hegel reminds us at the end of his discussion of substance, substance "is just as much reflection" as it is being, just as much the active *positing* of posited being as it is the subsisting of things. And as such, he points out, the idea of substance necessarily *sustains* the very difference between substance and accidentality that it undermines. That is to say, the idea of substance establishes a difference between itself and its accidents that is in fact just as much determinate and irreducible as it is disappearing. This is not rendered fully explicit by the idea of substance as the power *within* things themselves;

but, according to Hegel, it needs to be rendered fully explicit if we are to do justice to all that is implied by the concept of substance. Consequently, what must now be seen to follow from the very idea of substance is that "substance is power, and power that is *reflected into itself* and does not merely pass over [into its other], but that posits *determinations* and *distinguishes them from itself.*" When substance is conceived in this way, it is understood to be a real, determinate power of its own after all.[27]

And yet – as one will now have come to expect – Hegel insists that, in moving to this idea of substance as real power, we cannot lose sight of the fact that substance is nothing other than the very *being* of beings. Such power thus cannot be thought of as determinate power prior to or behind the realm of finite things as such, because that conflicts with the very idea of substance. Substance must be conceived as determinately distinct from what it posits, therefore, but at the same time as nothing other than the realm of finite things themselves. For Hegel, this can only mean one thing: that substance can only be thought as the real, determinate power of positing and determining when such power is recognized to be identical with the very being of finite, determinate things, that is to say, when finite things are themselves understood to *be* such determinate, determining power. In other words, substance can only be conceived as real determining power, which is nothing prior to or beyond determinate things as such, when it is understood to constitute the realm of finite, determining *causes*. With this move, Hegel goes clearly beyond Spinoza and shows that the one substance that there is, is in fact individuated into a plurality of finite, causal substances.

What should be noted about Hegel's analysis here is that he understands substance to be causality because he understands the idea of substance both to undermine and to sharpen the difference between substance and accidentality at one and the same time. In the idea of substance as formal power, the difference between substance and its accidents almost disappears altogether, since substance is conceived, in Charles Taylor's words, as the "power over them, which is also their power."[28] Yet the accidents are in fact only thought to have power *within* them, and so are not thought of as exercising determining power through the whole of their being, as being truly substantial and powerful *themselves*. With the idea of substance as constituting the realm of finite causes, however, the lingering difference between substance and its finite accidents finally disappears completely, because now "accidentality, which *in itself* is substance, is . . . also *posited* as such."[29] That is to say, substance is now truly thought to be the being of all beings, because all finite beings are recognized to be nothing other than determinate instances *of* explicit substantial power.

But do we not lose the very idea of accidentality as such if finite things are no longer understood to be mere accidents of substance, but causal substances of their own? Hegel thinks not, because along with the idea of finite things as causes comes the idea of finite things as *effects;* and when finite things are understood as effects, Hegel thinks that their difference from, and dependence on, substantial power is actually sharpened and their accidental character reinforced. When finite things are conceived as merely *accidental* to substance, they are regarded as dependent on and as posited by substance, but also as having within them the very power of substance itself. When finite things are conceived as mere *effects* of causal substance, however, they are regarded as utterly dependent and as lacking any inner power of their own at all. When it is understood as the effect of a cause, therefore, "the accident is *posited* as this, that it is only something *posited.*" Thus, just as a cause is substance conceived as a finite, determinate member of the world of things, so an effect is an accident that has been deprived of its inner power or substantiality. Or, as Hegel himself puts it, "sublated (*aufgehoben*) substantiality, that which is merely posited, [is] *effect;* but substance which is for itself is *cause.*"[30]

Conceiving of the relation between substance and accidents more precisely as that between cause and effect thus allows us to conceive of what is accidental more properly *as* accidental and dependent on substance, and it also allows us to conceive of substance more properly *as* substantial. It thus allows us to conceive of a genuinely irreducible and determinate *difference* between "substance" and its "accidents," which the concept of substance as such implies but does not render fully explicit. But it also allows us to conceive of a genuine *identity* between "substance" and "accidentality," which the concept of substance as such implies but does not render fully explicit, either. For substance can only be thought as real, determining, causal power, when it is thought as the power *of* precisely those finite, determinate things that were previously understood to be mere accidents of substance.

Although the concept of substance is the concept of the very being of beings, it initially requires us to think of such being as merely the power *within* things. Once substance is understood as causality, however, not only is substance more clearly distinguished from that which it posits, but the idea that substantial power merely resides "within" finite things is also left behind, because substance is now thought to *be* finite thinghood itself. This is not to say that substantial power is no longer to be conceived as residing within things at all; it is to say that such power does not *merely* reside "within" things but constitutes what things themselves *are* — the substantial power *of* things themselves. To conceive of being as the realm of causality is thus to conceive of it much more clearly as a world with *one* dimension to it, than is to conceive of being as substance. But, paradoxically, this means that conceiving of being as causality is to think what is required by the concept of substance — namely, the unity of being and reflexive positing (of *Sein* and *Setzen*) — more appropriately than is done by the concept of substance itself. Hegel arrives at the concept of causality, therefore, by recognizing that, when it is conceived properly, there is nothing substance can be but the causality of finite things themselves.[31]

III

We can see from the above account of substance that, in Chapter 3 of Section 3 of the "logic of essence," Hegel employs a distinctive method of philosophizing. He begins with a minimal definition of a concept, derived from the analysis of more primitive concepts, and shows, by rendering explicit all that is implied by that concept, that what we are considering turns out in the end not *merely* to be what we initially understand it to be. Hegel thus begins with the idea of substance as self-positing being and shows that such substance turns out in fact to be nothing other than the process of finite causality. The same process of conceptual transformation occurs in Hegel's analysis of causality itself: He begins with the idea of a cause as that which brings about an effect and shows that such causality turns out in fact to be nothing other than reciprocal causality. Hegel's claim is thus not just that substance, causality, and reciprocal causality entail or presuppose one another, but that substance turns out *to be* causality and causality turns out *to be* reciprocal causality, when they are properly understood.

In his analysis of causality Hegel considers first of all the very form or idea of being a cause – what it is to be a cause as such – and he notes that a cause is minimally the positing of an effect.[32] Furthermore, the manner in which Hegel arrives at the concept of cause requires him to understand a cause as causal substance, that is, the power of positing an effect *by itself*. A cause, for Hegel, is thus a "*self-subsistent source of production from out of itself*"; or, as he puts it in the *Encyclopedia,* a cause (*Ursache*) is an original and originary thing (*ursprüngliche Sache*).[33]

Now, if being a cause is nothing but the actual posit*ing* or produc*ing* of an effect, this means that "in so far as the cause has not yet acted, or if it has ceased to act, then it is not cause." A cause as such thus cannot be a cause before positing its effect, nor is it a cause any longer once its effect has been produced. It is only a cause as such in the very *producing* of the effect. Similarly, an effect is only an effect in *being* produced or caused and does not continue to count as an explicit effect once the process of producing or causing it has been completed. If a cause is indeed the positing of its *effect,* however, then it is necessarily the process of passing over into its posit*ed* state and so is actually the disappearing of its posit*ing* – of its causality – as such. Consequently, a "cause is *extinguished (erlischt)* in its effect; and with it the effect, too, is extinguished, for it is only the determinateness of the cause." What finally results from the process of causality is thus not an explicit effect as such, but what

Hegel calls an "indifferent actuality," that is to say, *something* that simply is what it is and is quite indifferent to its status as effect.[34]

One should remember here that Hegel does not begin by considering the causal activity of things that are anything beyond being causes. He begins by considering only what it is to be a finite cause as such; and he claims that such causal activity is essentially transitory – activity that occurs and in occurring ceases. Furthermore, he claims that once a cause has extinguished itself in the producing of its effect, it leaves something that is no longer effect or cause as such but just "an *immediacy* which is indifferent to the relation of cause and effect."[35] We know from Hegel's analysis of substance that the realm of the finite is necessarily the realm of causality. What we have now discovered, through considering the very movement of causality itself, is that this realm is in fact composed of finite things that are not just causes and effects, but that also exhibit an *immediate* character of their own – a character which by itself makes them neither cause nor effect as such.

Hegel thus shows through his analysis that the specific form of "being a cause" or "being an effect" is actually separable from – and in that sense, external to – the immediate character or quality of things. In making this claim, however, he is not denying that finite things can and must give rise to certain effects or themselves be effects of other causes. He is simply noting that the specific, immediate character of something – its being this stone or this body of water – does not by itself mark that thing as a cause rather than an effect or as an effect rather than a cause, but is equally compatible with either form. Or, to put it another way, he is pointing out that *what* something is does not suffice by itself to explain *why* that thing should now be a cause or now be an effect. The fact that this stone has an effect on something, or that this water now falls as rain and now forms a pool on the ground, must thus be explained by – and so be contingent upon – something beyond the stone's and the water's simply being the things they are. Indeed, Hegel believes that the form of causality must actually be given to a thing – or placed in it – by other things to which it relates. A cause, for Hegel, is thus what a given thing is *posited* by another to be: "this water has the determination of being rain and cause as a result of this determination being posited in it by another."[36]

Since the power of positing is being understood here as the power of causality, this means that a thing must be *caused* by another to be the cause that it is. Like Spinoza and Kant, therefore, Hegel understands causality to entail an infinite regress in which one thing points back to *another* that serves as its cause. And he takes this view because he thinks that the form of being a cause or being an effect is by its very nature separable from – and so external to – simply being a specific thing, and is thus a form that any given thing can only be caused by something else to exhibit.

Yet, although a thing has to be caused to be a cause by something other than itself, the causality it exercises is, in Hegel's view, in every case its *own* causality (*seine eigene*).[37] This is so for two reasons: (i) because something can only be said to exercise causality at all to the extent that it is a "*self-subsistent source of production from out of itself*," and (ii) because the quality or form by virtue of which a thing exercises causality belongs to that specific thing, not to any other thing, even if it has been given to that thing by something else. To say that a thing is caused by another to exercise causality, is thus not to deny that that thing *is* indeed a cause; it is not to deny the originary character of each cause. It is simply to point out that each thing is empowered to manifest originary power of its own by the work of another, just as people often have to be *given* their independence. Real causality, for Hegel, is thus "*originativeness* which is equally in its own self *positedness* or *effect*."[38]

To the extent that a thing is not merely the effect of another, but is indeed caused by another to be a genuine cause, it must, of course, produce effects of its own on other things, and in fact cause them to be causes of their own in turn. The infinite regress from one thing to another is thus at one and the same time an infinite progress in which one thing points forward to another in which its effect is exhibited. The causality of any particular cause may well cease with the production of its effect, therefore; but causality does not cease altogether, since what is brought about by the causality of the first thing is precisely the further causality of the second.[39]

Hegel has shown that causality must take the form of an infinite regress and progress in which each thing is empowered to be the cause that it is by other things and in turn empowers further things to be causes themselves. Hegel now goes on to show, however, that the actual causal action of one thing on another is not just a matter of one-way dependency, but in fact involves two-way dependency. For whatever depends upon the causality of another for its causal power, also plays a role of its own in making it possible for that other to exercise causality in the first place. The reason for this is that a thing can only exercise causality in having an effect *on* something and so can only come to be the cause that it is in *relation* to that which it affects. Thus, even though one thing, B, is indebted to another thing, A, for its causal power, A could not act as a cause in the first place (and so empower B to be a cause of its own) were it not for the fact that B is there to be affected. One should not think of causal power as something that is simply transferred *from* one thing *to* another, therefore (as if it were somehow immediately present in the former at some point), but rather as something that the first thing only comes to exhibit in the first place *in* encountering the second.[40] Causal power only arises in an encounter.

This is not to deny that things are caused to be causes by the actions of other *things* that precede, or stand apart from, them. But it is to point out that those other things cannot act as *causes* as such apart from, or prior to, the things they affect − that they cannot be causes immediately in themselves, but only in relation to, and so by means of, the things they affect. After all, although the rain causes the ground to be wet, it only does so *on reaching the ground.* Causality thus does not merely imply that things form a regressive or progressive sequence in which one points to another, but – more important – that things form relations of coexistence *together.*[41] (It should be noted, by the way, that causes that are remote from their effects in space or time are not really causes at all, for Hegel, but rather belong to the conditions of a thing.[42])

If one thing is actually to exercise causality, it thus requires the presence of a second thing as its condition, just as the further causality of the second thing requires as its condition the presence of something which it can affect in turn. Although the causality of the second thing derives from the action of the first upon it, therefore, it does not arise directly from the effect of the first but must await the presence of a third before it occurs. As Hegel puts it, "causality is *presupposing* activity; the cause is *conditioned.*"[43] The condition of all causal activity, however – the thing that is in each case acted upon – is itself a potential cause. The condition of the causal activity of any thing is thus the presence of another thing that is potentially a cause itself and that is open to being determined by the one that acts to exercise explicit causality of its own (when the conditions are right). When a thing is open to being determined by another in this way, it is understood, according to Hegel, as passive. A thing can thus only act as a cause and so be an *active* substance in relation to another, *passive* substance.

To the extent that something is passive in relation to another, Hegel says, the latter is able to exercise external power or force (*Gewalt*) over the former. Hegel points out, however, that the power of acting on another does not belong to the active substance simply through itself, but also by virtue of the passivity and weakness of the other. That is to say, a thing may only act on, and exercise real power over, another, because the nature of the latter itself *allows* the former to do so. But this means that when a thing is acted upon, it is not just forced into an alien mold by the sheer power of something else, but is in fact given a form to which it is itself open by virtue of its own passivity. In this sense, Hegel says, "what it receives as something *alien,* namely, to be determined as a *positedness,* is its own determination. . . . Its *being posited* by another, and its own *becoming,* are one and the same thing."[44] The butter is thus not simply cut into by the knife, but *allows* the knife to cut into it because of its own constitution.

But, since the passive substance codetermines the outcome of the action of the other upon it in this way, it is in fact itself an *active* partner in the relationship. Indeed, the constitution of the passive thing is to be regarded as a contributory *cause* of what happens to it, together with the active substance.[45] Thus, in any causal relation in which one thing acts upon another, not only does the presence of the latter serve as a condition of the action of the former, but the latter also serves as a contributory cause of the action of the former in that its own constitution actually *enables* or *empowers* the former to act in the way it does. And, of course, to the extent that the active substance is empowered to act in a certain way by the passive substance, one can say that the active substance displays a certain passivity of its own with respect to the passive substance. *Because of* the nature of butter, therefore, the knife *cannot but* cut through it when it is applied to it.

But if the knife acts on the butter in a certain way because the butter empowers the knife to do so, it is also true that the butter in turn can only empower the knife to act in that way because the knife itself is able to be so empowered. The knife is thus itself responsible for the fact that the butter empowers it to act on the butter in the way it does. That is to say, the butter only empowers the knife to cut through it because the latter is indeed a knife and not a feather.

There is much more that can be, and needs to be, said about causality than this. What has been said suffices, however, to show that Hegel regards all causal activity as involving the *reciprocal* determination of things by one another. Causal activity thus does not merely involve an endless regress or progress from one thing to another thing, but is at the same time "bent round" (*umgebogen*) by its very nature into "infinite *reciprocal action*" or *Wechselwirkung*.[46] As I noted above, this is not to deny that things owe what they are to other things that stand apart from, or precede, them; but it is to assert that one thing only *causes* an effect in another with which it coexists in a relation of reciprocal determination. It is thus to recognize that the causal power that each thing exhibits – indeed, which each thing *is* – in relation to others, never belongs to that thing alone, but only arises *in* that relation itself. In so far as things enter into causal relations, therefore, they do not have unambiguous logical priority over one another, but rather become moments of a single process of change. In the "logic of the concept," Hegel will analyze the rational structure of any such process, and will go on to show that what we initially understand to be simply the causal action of one thing on another, is in fact the combined activity of mechanical and chemical objects working together.[47]

IV

The account I have given of Hegel's analysis of substance and causality has been highly abbreviated and simplified. My aim here is not, however, to explore every nook and cranny of Hegel's analysis, nor indeed to provide a comprehensive defense of that analysis, but merely to give an idea of how Hegel's philosophy proceeds. What has become apparent is that, at least in Chapter 3 of Section 3 of the "logic of essence," Hegel proceeds by showing that certain concepts – and the dimensions of being to which they refer – turn out on reflection not *merely* to be what they present themselves as being. Substance, for example, is initially conceived as the being of all beings; but this very being turns out in fact to be nothing other than the causal activity of things, and such causal activity itself turns out to be nothing other than recipro- cal action. This is not to say that there is no such thing as substance at all – no such thing as that being *by virtue of which* beings are what they are. Rather, it is to say that we underdetermine the character of such being if we conceive of it *merely* as the substance "within" all things and not as the very acting, determin- ing, changing, and developing that is constitutive *of* things themselves. Equally, it is not to say that there is actually no causality in the world – no active determining of one thing by another – but rather that we only give a surface description of such determining activity if we conceive of it *merely* as one-way causality and fail to appreciate the reciprocity and cooperation be- tween things that it involves. Such concepts as substance and causality are not simply to be dismissed, therefore, but are to be recognized as *underdetermina- tions* of what they refer to; or, to put it another way, they are to be understood as capturing mere abstract moments of what is actually going on.[48]

To conceive of mechanism and chemism *merely* as the substance "within" things rather than the concrete activity of objects themselves, or to conceive of such activity in turn *merely* as one-way causal activity, is thus, in Hegel's view, profoundly reductive. For, by themselves, such conceptions imply that what occurs in the world is simply determined by a universal indwelling power or by a series of individual origins, rather than constituting a single, complex process of development.

It is important to note that the method of the last part of the "logic of essence" is not itself the single governing method – or "substance" – of Hegel's whole philosophy. It is not exactly the method of the "logic of being," for example: For, although Hegel shows there that quality turns into quantity, what emerges from his analysis is not that quality turns out in fact to be *nothing other than* quantity, but rather that quality turns out to be *both* quality *and* quantity as well. The method we have been explaining is not quite the method of the "logic of the concept," either: For mechanism does not turn out in fact to be *nothing other than* chemism, but rather *develops* through its own logical structure *into* chemism, just as chemism *develops* through its own logical structure *into* teleological activity and life. Thus, although Hegel is led to conclude that substance and causality are never to be encountered immediately *as such,* he is led to conclude that quality, quantity, mechanism, and chemism *are* to be encountered immediately as such, even though they will also be seen to pass, or develop, into other modes of being.

Although, from the point of view of the whole, all the categories in the *Logic* capture "moments" of what there is, what is thought through the categories of substance and causality – as, indeed, through all the categories in the "logic of essence" – is thus much more radically "momentary" or partial than what is thought through any other categories of the *Logic*. The reason for this is that nonreflexive moments of the whole, such as quality and quantity, or mechanism and chemism, enjoy a degree of immediacy or independent identity over against one another which reflexive moments, such as substance and causality, never enjoy.[49] The fact that water changes its constitution with certain changes in temperature shows that quantity "passes over" into quality and that the two are not wholly independent. Nevertheless, there is a difference between quantity and quality and, within a certain range, quantitative changes have no bearing at all on a thing's qualitative makeup. Within certain limits, therefore, quantity can be said to be nothing but quantity, and quality nothing but quality; and the same can be said of mechanical and chemical activity. By contrast, what is thought as substance and causality can *never* be said just to be that, but is only ever conceivable as *aufgehoben* in a structure that includes more than itself. Substance is never *just* substance or indwelling power, therefore, but is always the process of actual causality. Similarly, causality is never *just* one-way causal activity, but is always reciprocal interaction between things.

Yet, despite these subtle differences between the various parts of the *Science of Logic,* the last part of the "logic of essence" does exhibit an important characteristic common to Hegel's philosophy as a whole: namely, that it is moved forward, not (as Schelling thought)[50] by any desire on the part of the philosopher to reach some tacitly anticipated goal, but by nothing other than the immanent, presuppositionless *self-transformation* of the concepts under consideration. It is this idea, that concepts transform themselves into further, more complex conceptions of what there is, that constitutes logical or philosophical necessity for Hegel and that most obviously distinguishes his philosophy from Kant's. To conclude, I would like further to clarify the difference between Kant and Hegel by briefly comparing their respective conceptions of substance and causality in particular.

V

The first thing that strikes us when we undertake such a comparison is that many of the conclusions reached by Kant and Hegel are in fact remarkably similar. Like Hegel, Kant understands substance to be both one and many, since he believes that substance in nature is universal matter, but that "all parts of matter will likewise be substances."[51] Like Hegel, Kant thinks that all substances determine one another reciprocally.[52] And, like Hegel, Kant thinks that causality occurs in nature as mechanical and chemical activity.[53]

In spite of these similarities, however, there are also considerable differences in the ways in which the two philosophers think about substance and causality. First of all, whereas Hegel is led to his conclusions by developing a purely *logical* account of those categories, Kant is led to his conclusions by trying to establish the *epistemic* role that the categories play in making possible objective experience in time. Second, whereas Hegel argues that substance turns out logically *to be* causality, and that causality turns out logically *to be* reciprocal causality, Kant argues, in Paul Guyer's words, that "substance, causality and community are three separate concepts" which "can be *used* only in conjunction with one another."[54] The concepts of causality and reciprocal causality are thus epistemically interdependent, in Kant's view, but they are nevertheless logically distinct concepts. Similarly, though causality is always the causality of a substance, being a substance does not simply amount to being a cause.

Kant makes this last point clear in a comment he makes on what he understands to be the causal relation of substance to its own accidental states. He maintains that motion is an accident or condition of material substance that must be caused in part by some prior condition of matter. But he also maintains that the cause of motion is "moving force" within material substance itself.[55] Material substance thus stands in a twofold relation to motion: It is the substance of which motion is merely an accidental state or condition, but at the same time it in part grounds or causes accidental motion by virtue of the force it harbors within itself. The danger Kant sees is that we will be led by our recognition of this latter relation simply to equate substance with causal force. Indeed, he accuses Spinoza of doing just that; and he would surely have accused Hegel of doing the same. To follow Spinoza, however, is in Kant's view to lose sight of what it means for substance to be *substance* as such rather than a cause. That is to say, it is to lose sight, not just of the different epistemic roles played by the concepts of substance and causality, but of what he sees as the clear *logical* difference between them.

The proposition: "the thing (substance) *is* a force," rather than the quite natural one, "substance *has* a force," is a proposition that is . . . in its consequences very disadvantageous for metaphysics. For the concept of substance is thereby basically lost: namely, the concept of inherence in a subject, in place of which that of dependence on a cause is posited. . . . A substance *has* indeed, apart from its relation as *subject* to its accidents (and their inherence), also the relation to the same as *cause* to effects; but the former relation is not one and the same as the latter.[56]

It should be pointed out, of course, that although Kant thinks equating substance with causality entails losing the concept of substance as he understands it, Hegel thinks it actually involves gaining the true concept of substance itself.

There are, in my view, two reasons why Kant's conception of the relation between substance and causality (and reciprocal causality) differs in this way from that of Hegel: (i) Kant derives the categories, not from the indeterminate thought of being, but from what he understands to be the different "functions" of judgment; and (ii) he understands a category to entail the thought of something "as determined in respect of one of the logical functions of judgment."[57]

The categories are thus regarded as logically distinct by Kant, first of all, because they are derived from quite distinct judgment forms: Substance is conceived as that in which accidents *inhere* (or as that which finds itself positively determined in its accidents), whereas a cause is understood to be that which *grounds* its effect.[58] Second, the categories are regarded as distinct because the primary term in each case (substance or cause) is fixed in its relation to the secondary term (accident or effect). This means that substance for Kant "must always be considered as subject and never as mere predicate," and so can never be simply *equated* with the movement of its causally connected accidents.[59] Similarly, a cause must always be conceived as logically *prior* to its effect, and so is not to be understood as only being a cause in the first place by means of its effect or by being empowered to be a cause by the thing it affects.[60]

Hegel, by contrast, begins his search for the proper conception of the categories, not with the functions of judgment, but with the indeterminate thought of being. Such being eventually reveals itself, in Hegel's account, not just to be immediate, but to be constituted in its immediacy by reflexivity and negativity, indeed to be the process of constituting or "positing" *itself* (*dies reine Herstellen aus und in sich selbst*).[61] Since Hegel is led to his concept of substance simply by continuing to render explicit what is implied by this thought of being, it should be clear why he understands substance to be being that is because it is, rather than that in which accidents "inhere," and why – in marked contrast to Kant (but like Spinoza) – he understands the idea of positing or originating to be built into the idea of substance from the very start. It should also be clear that Hegel is actually clarifying, rather than simply losing, the concept of substance as he understands it, when he goes on to show that substance in fact amounts to nothing but causality.

Despite certain similarities between them, Kant and Hegel have very different conceptions of substance and of the logical relation between substance and causality. For Kant, these two concepts are epistemically interdependent but logically distinct, whereas for Hegel the concept of substance turns out logically *to be* the concept of causality when it is properly understood. What I have tried to show in this essay is that Hegel is led to his view by his distinctive *method* of philosophizing – a method that involves not regressing from one concept to its precondition or criticizing concepts by reference to some anticipated *terminus ad quem,* but rather allowing concepts to transform themselves into new concepts and so, as Alan White puts it, to "make their own way."[62] Hegel is committed to this method because he believes that a truly critical philosophy should not just take for granted how thought is to be conceived, but should let thought determine itself and its categories immanently and presuppositionlessly. Kant would no doubt have criticized Hegelian method for leading to the confusion of categories with one another. But Hegel's rejection of Kant's own procedure for deriving the categories is, in my view, quite justified. For it seems to me that, by assuming that the categories must be derived from the functions of judgment, Kant does indeed *prejudge* the issue of how they should be conceived and thereby also of how philosophy itself should proceed; and that is something that a truly critical philosopher should not do.

Notes

1. G. W. F. Hegel, *The Encyclopaedia Logic. Part I of the Encyclopaedia of Philosophical Sciences with the Zusätze,* trans. T. F. Geraets, W. A. Suchting, and H. S. Harris (Indianapolis: Hackett Publishing, 1991), §41 and Addition 1. I have occasionally modified translations.
2. Hegel, *Encyclopaedia Logic,* §§41–2. For Kant's Metaphysical Deduction, see I. Kant, *Critique of Pure Reason,* trans. N. Kemp Smith (London: Macmillan, 1929), B 91–113. Kant refers to his derivation of the categories from the logical functions of judgment as a "metaphysical deduction" on B 159.
3. Kant, *Critique of Pure Reason,* B 141–2.
4. Kant, *Critique of Pure Reason,* B 94.
5. Hegel, *Encyclopaedia Logic,* §42. See also G. W. F. Hegel, *Science of Logic,* trans. A. V. Miller (Atlantic Highlands, N.J.: Humanities Press, 1989), pp. 75–8, and *Werke in zwanzig Bänden,* ed. E. Moldenhauer and K. M. Michel, 20 vols. and Index (Frankfurt am Main: Suhrkamp Verlag, 1969–), p. V [*Wissenschaft der Logik* I], 76–9. Further references to the *Science of Logic* will be given in the form: Hegel, *SL,* 75; *WL* I, 76 or *SL,* 555; *WL* II, 219. For Fichte's derivation of the categories from the self-positing of the I, see J. G. Fichte, *The Science of Knowledge,* trans. P. Heath and J. Lachs (Cambridge, U.K.: Cambridge University Press, 1982).
6. Hegel, *Encyclopaedia Logic,* §78.
7. Hegel, *SL,* 69–70; *WL* I, 68–9.
8. On Hegel's "immanent" method in the *Science of Logic,* see S. Houlgate, *Freedom, Truth and History. An Introduction to Hegel's Philosophy* (London: Routledge, 1991), pp. 41–76; A. White, *Absolute Knowledge: Hegel and the Problem of Metaphysics* (Athens: Ohio University Press, 1983), p. 57; and R. Winfield, *Reason and Justice* (Albany: State University of New York Press, 1988), pp. 118–35.
9. R. Pippin, *Hegel's Idealism. The Satisfactions of Self-Consciousness* (Cambridge, U.K.: Cambridge University Press, 1989), p. 255.
10. For a further comparison of Hegel and Kant, see S. Houlgate, "Hegel, Kant, and the Formal Distinctions of Reflective Understanding," in *Hegel on the Modern World,* ed. A. B. Collins (Albany: State University of New York Press, 1995), pp. 125–41.
11. See S. Houlgate, "Thought and Being in Kant and Hegel," *The Owl of Minerva; Biannual Journal of the Hegel Society of America* 22 (1991): 131–40, "A Reply to Joseph C. Flay's 'Hegel's Metaphysics'," *The Owl of Minerva* 24 (1993): 153–61, "Hegel and Fichte: Recognition, Otherness, and Absolute Knowing," *The Owl of Minerva* 26 (1994): 3–19, and *Freedom, Truth and History,* pp. 69–74. See also Hegel, *SL,* 49; *WL* I, 43. I would thus argue, against Robert Pippin, that Hegel can indeed legitimately claim that a thing's not being something else is part of what makes it what it is, and that he is not limited to claiming that things simply have to be *characterized* contrastively; see Pippin, *Hegel's Idealism,* p. 188.
12. Hegel, *SL,* 555; *WL* II, 219.

13. W. T. Stace, *The Philosophy of Hegel* (1924) (New York: Dover Books, 1955), p. 216.
14. Hegel, *SL,* 555; *WL* II, 219.
15. *A Spinoza Reader. The Ethics and Other Works,* ed. and trans. E. Curley (Princeton: Princeton University Press, 1994), pp. 85, 93–4 [*Ethics,* I. Def. 3, and I. Prop. 14, Dem.]. See also H. Allison, *Benedict de Spinoza: An Introduction* (New Haven: Yale University Press, 1987), p. 48.
16. *A Spinoza Reader,* pp. 97, 100, 105 [*Ethics,* I. Prop. 16, Cor. 1, I. Prop. 18, Dem., and I. Prop. 29, Schol.], and Hegel, *SL,* 555, 557; *WL* II, 219, 221.
17. Hegel, *SL,* 554; *WL* II, 218.
18. See Hegel, *SL,* 555; *WL* II, 219: "The reflective movement is the reflective movement that is *self-related* . . . "
19. Hegel, *SL,* 556; *WL* II, 220.
20. Hegel, *SL,* 556; *WL* II, 220. On the term, "actuosity," see also Hegel, *Encyclopaedia Logic,* §34 Addition.
21. Hegel, *SL,* 557; *WL* II, 222.
22. The fact that the idea of substance itself implies a difference between itself and its accidents leads representational thinking, or *Vorstellen,* to construe substance as "the simple identity of being" beyond or beneath finite things. But, according to Hegel, the idea that substance is *simply* distinct from its accidents is actually an illusion or *Schein* projected by substance itself. For substance and its accidents are in fact not ultimately distinct, but form one and the same reality or "actuosity." See Hegel, *SL,* 556; *WL* II, 220.
23. Hegel, *SL,* 556–7; *WL* II, 220–1. See I. Kant, *Schriften zur Metaphysik und Logik* I, ed. W. Weischedel (Frankfurt am Main: Suhrkamp Verlag, 1968), pp. 340–1 [*Über eine Entdeckung nach der alle neue Kritik der reinen Vernunft durch eine ältere entbehrlich gemacht werden soll,* BA 73]. See also K. Düsing, *Das Problem der Subjektivität in Hegels Logik* (Bonn: Bouvier Verlag, 1976), p. 228.
24. Hegel, *SL,* 556–7; *WL* II, 221: "The accidents as such . . . have no power over one another. . . . In so far as such an accidental seems to exercise power over another, it is the power of substance which embraces both within itself."
25. Hegel, *SL,* 557; *WL* II, 221.
26. Hegel, *SL,* 557; *WL* II, 221–2.
27. Hegel, *SL,* 558; *WL* II, 222. See B. Lakebrink, *Kommentar zu Hegels "Logik" in seiner "Enzyklopädie" von 1830. Band I: Sein und Wesen* (Freiburg and Munich: Verlag Karl Alber, 1979), pp. 376–7.
28. C. Taylor, *Hegel* (Cambridge, U.K.: Cambridge University Press, 1975), p. 288.
29. Hegel, *SL,* 557; *WL* II, 222.
30. Hegel, *SL,* 558; *WL* II, 222–3.
31. The problem with the concept of substance taken by itself, as with all the concepts in Section 3 of the "logic of essence" (including "the absolute" and "necessity"), is thus that it represents the *imperfect* fusion of being and essence.
32. Hegel, *SL,* 559; *WL* II, 224: "Cause is nothing but this determination, to have an effect, and effect is nothing but this, to have a cause."
33. Hegel, *SL,* 559; *WL* II, 224, and *Encyclopaedia Logic,* §153. See also J. Biard, et al., *Introduction à la lecture de la science de la logique de Hegel II. La doctrine de l'essence* (Paris: Aubier Montaigne, 1983), p. 351.
34. Hegel, *SL,* 559–60; *WL* II, 225.
35. Hegel, *SL,* 560; *WL* II, 225.
36. Hegel, *SL,* 564; *WL* II, 230. See also: "The stone's movement and the causality

attaching to the stone in its movement are present in the stone only as a *positedness* (*Gesetztsein*)."

37. Hegel, *SL,* 564; *WL* II, 230.
38. Hegel, *SL,* 564; *WL* II, 231.
39. Hegel, *SL,* 566; *WL* II, 233: "The outcome of the movement of the determinate causal relation is this, that the cause is *not merely extinguished* in the effect and with it the effect, too, as in formal causality, but that the cause *in being extinguished becomes* again in the effect, that the effect *vanishes* in the cause, but equally *becomes* again in it."
40. Hegel, *SL,* 566; *WL* II, 233: "What is present here is not an *external transition* of causality from one substrate to another; on the contrary, this *becoming-other* of causality is at the same time its own *positing.*"
41. An early anticipation of Hegel's view is to be found in Plato's *Theaetetus* 157a: "There's neither anything affecting before it comes together with that which (gets) affected, nor anything affected before it comes together with that which affects" (trans. S. Bernadete, Chicago: University of Chicago Press, 1986). I am grateful to Wendell Kisner for pointing this out.
42. See Hegel, *SL,* 561–2; *WL* II, 227.
43. Hegel, *SL,* 566; *WL* II, 233.
44. Hegel *SL,* 568; *WL* II, 235–6. See *SL,* 125; *WL* I, 134: "The determining from outside is at the same time determined by the something's own, immanent determination."
45. Hegel, *SL,* 568; *WL* II, 236: "Passive substance is *in itself* positedness . . . and consequently receives within it an effect through the other substance; but this positedness is, conversely, the passive substance's *own* in-itself; this is thus its *own* effect, it itself displays itself as cause."
46. Hegel, *SL,* 569; *WL* II, 237.
47. See Hegel, *SL,* 712; *WL* II, 410–1 on the idea of mechanical objects as themselves "composite" or *zusammengesetzt.*
48. See, for example, Hegel, *Encyclopaedia Logic,* §28 Addition: "In the same way, finite things behave as 'cause' and 'effect' . . . and when they are grasped according to these determinations, they are known in their finitude."
49. See, for example, Hegel, *SL,* 123; *WL* I, 133: "In the sphere of quality, the differences in their sublatedness [as moments] also retain immediate, qualitative being over against one another (*gegeneinander*)."
50. F. W. J. von Schelling, *On the History of Modern Philosophy,* trans. A. Bowie (Cambridge, U.K.: Cambridge University Press, 1994), p. 138. See also Pippin, *Hegel's Idealism,* p. 236.
51. I. Kant, *Philosophy of Material Nature,* trans. J. Ellington (Indianapolis: Hackett, 1985), Book II [*Metaphysical Foundations of Natural Science*], p. 49.
52. Kant, *Critique of Pure Reason,* B 257–62.
53. Kant, *Metaphysical Foundations of Natural Science,* p. 87.
54. P. Guyer, *Kant and the Claims of Knowledge* (Cambridge, U.K.: Cambridge University Press, 1987), p. 213.
55. See Kant, *Critique of Pure Reason,* B 230, and *Metaphysical Foundations of Natural Science,* p. 42.
56. Kant, *Schriften zur Metaphysik und Logik* I, pp. 340–1 [*Über eine Entdeckung,* BA 73], my translation. See also I. Kant, *Schriften zur Naturphilosophie,* ed. W. Weischedel (Frankfurt am Main: Suhrkamp Verlag, 1968), pp. 165–6 [*Über den Gebrauch teleologischer Prinzipien in der Philosophie,* A 130], and D. Henrich,

The Unity of Reason: Essays on Kant's Philosophy, ed. R. Velkley (Cambridge, Mass.: Harvard University Press, 1994), p. 21.

57. Kant, *Critique of Pure Reason,* B 128–9.
58. Kant, *Critique of Pure Reason,* B 230, 112.
59. Kant, *Critique of Pure Reason,* B 129, 186.
60. Kant, *Critique of Pure Reason,* B 112: in the causal relation "the consequence does not in turn reciprocally determine the ground, and therefore does not constitute with it a whole." Kant certainly believes that substances in space reciprocally determine one another (B 257–62) and that the parts of an organism "combine into the unity of a whole because they are reciprocally cause and effect of their form" (*Critique of Judgment,* trans. W. S. Pluhar (Indianapolis: Hackett, 1987), §65). But he does not believe, as Hegel does, that the very idea of causal influence as *such* entails reciprocal determination.
61. Hegel, *SL,* 411; *WL* II, 39.
62. White, *Absolute Knowledge,* p 57.

12

Point of View of Man or Knowledge of God:

Kant and Hegel on Concept, Judgment and Reason

BÉATRICE LONGUENESSE

There is something quite paradoxical in Hegel's presentation of Kant's Critical system in the first part of his 1802 article "Faith and Knowledge." On the one hand, Hegel praises Kant for having expressed the "true idea of reason" in his *Critique of Pure Reason* and his *Critique of Judgment*. On the other hand, he describes the so-called pure practical reason expounded in the second *Critique* as resulting from a "complete trampling down of reason."[1] More surprising still, it seems that in effect, Hegel sees an anticipation of his own notion of reason in those explanations of *judgment,* in Kant's first and third *Critiques,* where our discursive abilities are presented as inseparable from sensibility (synthetic a priori judgments in the first *Critique,* aesthetic and teleological judgments in the third *Critique*). By contrast, he considers as a destruction of reason what Kant took to be its purest and highest use: its practical use in the autonomous determination of the will, as described in the *Groundwork for the Metaphysics of Morals* and in the second *Critique.*

What is the motivation for this peculiar appropriation of Kant's Critical system? The beginning of an answer to this question can be found already in Hegel's early theological writings, most notably, "The Spirit of Christianity and its Destiny." There Hegel proclaimed the superiority of the moral teaching of Jesus (whose principle was love as the expression of life) over Kantian morality that teaches the bondage of inclinations and sensibility by reason and the moral law. Hegel's subsequent effort, in the Jena period to which "Faith and Knowledge" belongs, was to sustain his opposition to Kantian moral and metaphysical dualism. But now he would do this not by appealing to feeling or religious belief, but by developing a philosophical system that reaped the benefits of the Kantian Copernican revolution while unifying what Kant divides: reason and sensibility, thought and being, freedom and necessity.

It is important to keep in mind this initial motivation in order to understand the apparent reversal in the conception of reason that I have just described. When Hegel finds "the true idea of reason" announced in Kant's explanation of synthetic a priori judgments or in Kant's analysis of teleological and aesthetic judgments, it is because he sees in these elements of the Critical system the beginning of what is needed to correct Kant's false conception of reason, a false conception that is most apparent in Kant's characterization of *practical* reason. This means, in turn, that the demands Hegel makes on practical philosophy and the fundamental mistake he wants to overcome in Kant's practical philosophy, are what govern his reading of Kant's theory of judgment in both the first and third *Critiques*. If this is right, even though Hegel devotes very little time to Kant's *Critique of Practical Reason* in his exposition of the Critical system in "Faith and Knowledge" (his criticism of Kant's practical philosophy is in fact developed more fully in the part of this chapter devoted to Fichte), coming to terms with it is at the heart of every one of his moves with respect to the other two *Critiques*.

My first goal in this paper is to show just this: One can understand Hegel's appropriation and transformation of Kant's philosophy only if one considers Hegel's relation to all three *Critiques together.* One should not consider separately Hegel's reading of Kant's theoretical philosophy, *on the other hand* Hegel's reading of Kant's practical philosophy, and *finally* his reading of Kant's theory of reflective judgment. Hegel's reading is a reorganization of the Critical system as a whole. It starts with a demand for a new type of moral philosophy. It goes on with a search for the relevant metaphysics, for which Hegel finds the key concepts in Kant's third *Critique*. And it is crowned by a reinterpretation of Kant's *magnum opus:* the *Critique of Pure Reason*. This is admittedly not the order in which the Critical system is presented in "Faith and Knowledge": with only a few exceptions, Hegel's exposition mainly follows the chronological sequence of the three *Critiques*. Nevertheless, I hope to show that following the systematic order I have indicated is the best way to understand what exactly Hegel does with Kant's system.

As it happens, following this order also helps clarify Hegel's appropriation of three key terms in Kant's general logic and in his transcendental logic, which become key terms in Hegel's speculative logic: concept, judgment, and reason. In "Faith and Knowledge," Hegel calls *concept* what Kant called *pure reason* and most notably, pure *practical* reason. He calls *reason,* on the other hand, Kant's *intellectual intuition* as expounded in the *Critique of Judgment*. And he calls *judgment,* or "absolute judgment," what Kant called, in the first *Critique,* synthetic a priori judgment, meanwhile giving a very idiosyncratic interpretation of Kant's question: "How are synthetic *a priori* judgments possible?"[2]

Of course, it would be a mistake to think that "Faith and Knowledge" gives us a definitive view of Hegel's appropriation of the Kantian vocabulary. What it does give us, however, is an indispensable indication of the shifts in context and meaning that Hegel imposes upon Kant's logical terms. Keeping these shifts in mind is of primary importance for understanding Hegel's mature philosophy, and most of all, for assessing the change of scenery when one moves from Kantian (transcendental) to Hegelian (speculative) logic. I shall argue that we should take Hegel at his word when he claims to have used Kant against Kant, and to have built upon those aspects in Kant's philosophy that pointed the way toward restoring a "knowledge of God" over the mere "point of view of man." But I shall also argue that Kant's philosophy provided grounds to make the reverse move: to use Kant against Kant and make it the goal of philosophy to come to terms with the "point of view of man" rather than with "knowledge of God." These grounds can be found in those very aspects of Kant's thought on which Hegel built his own case: Kant's theory of judgment, and the unity of sensibility and intellect in the first and third *Critiques.*

So, my paper is built around an elucidation of the three terms: concept, reason, and judgment, in Hegel's confrontation with Kant in "Glauben und Wissen." I then propose some tentative conclusions about the overall import of this confrontation.

I. Hegel's Concept, and Kant's Pure Reason

Kant, Jacobi, and Fichte, the three leading characters of "Faith and Knowledge," have in common, according to Hegel's presentation of their philosophies, that they hold thought and reality to be insuperably divided. They are, however, dissatisfied with this division, and each of their philosophical systems is a particular expression of the need to overcome it. For each of them, this need should be answered by reaching beyond the empirical given to a higher reality where thought and being are one. But for all of them, such a task is in the end impossible, or at least reserved for feeling and belief rather than knowledge and reason. Reality remains a given that is ultimately opaque to knowledge and resistant to self-determining, free agency.

Kant was the first to have expressed this opposition in its purest form. He defined as *pure reason* thought insofar as it is completely independent from the empirical given (it does not owe either its form or its content to it) and is even opposed to it (in its practical use, it determines ends for action which demand the overcoming of empirical desires and motivations). But his "pure reason" should really be called *concept,* according to Hegel's terminology:

The concept has presented itself in its highest abstraction as so-called pure reason. (292: 59)

[In Kantian philosophy], the absolute concept, which is simply for itself as practical reason, is the highest objectivity in the realm of what is finite [*im Endlichen*], postulated absolutely as ideality in and for itself. (296: 62)

[Kantian philosophy] gives the name *reason* to the *concept.* (301: 67)

[Kantian philosophy] makes of this empty concept absolute reason, theoretical as well as practical. (303: 68)

It is clear from these texts that Hegel gives a very unusual meaning to the term *concept.* First, he seems to be calling *concept,* indifferently, the so-called faculty of reason, its activity, and the intentional correlate of this activity: for instance, practical reason *as* the activity of moral reasoning *that is manifested as* the moral law. Or perhaps, theoretical reason *as* the activity of system-building *which is manifested* in a system of objective knowledge.[3]

Second, if *concept* is to be identified with Kant's "pure reason," it is a holistic mode of thinking. This was apparent in Kant's own presentation of practical reason: thinking the moral law is all at once thinking (willing) the law, thinking (willing) each individual human being as "not only a means, but also an end in itself," and thinking (willing) the world as a kingdom of ends.[4] Similarly, the specific function of reason in the theoretical domain is to produce for the "distributive use" of understanding in cognition the form of a system: of a complete whole of interrelated cognitions.[5] Hegel's concept, then, takes up this holistic function of Kant's pure reason. In this sense, it should be distinguished both from what was called *concept* in Kant's general logic ("general and reflected representation"), and from Kant's categories. These are defined in relation to the logical functions of judgment.[6] Hegel's concept, as it appears in "Faith and Knowledge," is related to what Kant would have called *the form of a system.*

Now, according to Hegel, Kant only introduced confusion by naming the concept so considered "reason." It does not deserve the name. Why is that, and what does deserve the name of reason?

Kant provides three main definitions of reason: It is a logical or discursive capacity to form mediate inferences. It is a faculty of principles. It is a faculty of the unconditioned.[7] This last characterization concerns more specifically "pure" reason, reason as not merely ordering empirical or mathematical concepts and propositions, whose meaning is provided by sensibility, but as generating its own concepts and principles.

Reason in its practical use is most properly the "faculty of the unconditioned." First, it is the source of the highest principle under which all rules of determination of the will should be subsumed: the moral law.[8] Second, it is the source of our positive concept of freedom as autonomy, therefore the source of the only positive concept we have of a cause which is unconditioned by an antecedent cause: the autonomous will. Third, this practical use is what drives reason in its theoretical use to attempt to reach the unconditioned (unconditioned knowledge, which means also knowledge of the unconditioned).[9]

But practical reason is also the faculty of the unconditioned in another, more fundamental sense: it is *itself,* in formulating its principle and postulating its objects, *unconditioned.* There is no further ground for formulating the moral law than reason itself as determining the will. This is how, from being described as the faculty of *thinking* the unconditioned, reason becomes described as being *itself unconditioned:* It is not determined by anything but itself.

Now, Hegel recognizes this character of Kantian practical reason. This is why he calls the concept "infinite":

In Kantian philosophy the infinite concept is posited in and for itself, and is that alone which is acknowledged by philosophy. (296: 62)

The concept is "infinite" in the sense in which Spinoza defined what is "infinite in its own kind": it is not limited by anything else belonging to the same kind as itself.[10] By contrast, empirical reality is always finite: Any empirical reality is limited, or conditioned, by another empirical reality. Hegel complains, however, if the concept (Kant's pure reason, as primarily practical reason) is opposed to empirical reality, if it has a causal relation to it, as it does in the moral determination of the will, and empirical reality (instincts and empirical motivations) resists its causal action, then it is finite rather than infinite. It is limited, albeit not by something "of the same kind," but by something "of another kind":

Infinite concept is simply opposed to what is empirical, and the sphere of this opposition, consisting of what is empirical and what is infinite, is absolute (but when infinite and finite are so opposed, the one is just as finite as the other) – and beyond the concept and the empirical, lies what is eternal. (297: 63)

If we express Hegel's complaint in Kantian terms, we can say that Kant's reason, far from being "unconditioned," is irrevocably conditioned. Being a "mere concept" in the sense explained above, it in fact depends for its actualization on conditions external to itself (the empirical existence of living beings, with their empirical abilities and impulses to act). Worse yet, these conditions are not only external, but also, on Kant's own account of them, foreign and opposed to it. This being so, Kantian practical reason is bound to become "tyranny and the tearing apart of ethical life and beauty" (383: 143).[11]

Now, Kant himself acknowledged that pure reason, and even pure practical reason, is in a sense *conditioned*. For instance, he wrote:

It depends . . . upon the subjective constitution of our reason, that moral laws must be represented as commands (and the actions conforming to them as duties), and reason expresses this necessity not as an *is*, but as an *ought:* this would not happen if reason were considered, with respect to its causality, independently of sensibility (as the subjective *condition* [my emphasis] of its application to objects of nature).[12]

This text is from §76 of the third *Critique,* where Kant then goes on to contrast our "conditioned" reason with "intellectual intuition": Only an intellectual intuition, or an intuitive intellect, would be unconditioned in the sense of spontaneously generating its own objects. According to Hegel, Kant had there "the true notion of reason."

So, to sum up: Hegel despises Kant's practical reason because of its opposition to sensibility. He finds in Kant himself the germs of a higher notion of reason, in fact the only true notion of reason (understood as "faculty of the unconditioned"). This true notion of reason is what Kant defines, in the *Critique of Judgment,* as "intellectual intuition." This is what we now need to consider.

II. Hegel's Reason, and Intellectual Intuition in Kant's Third *Critique*

The idea of an intellectual intuition, in §§76–7 of the *Critique of Judgment,* is part of Kant's effort to clarify what he meant when he said earlier (§75) that the concept of a natural purpose provides only a principle for the reflective use of our power of judgment. In this context, Kant assigns the idea of intellectual intuition a mainly negative role: It is contrasted with our own discursive intellect in order to make clear in what sense both mechanism and teleology, as heuristic principles for the study of organisms, should be considered as subjective principles, holding only for our limited capacity of knowledge. But the negative role of the idea of intellectual intuition is inseparable from a positive one. Its supposition serves to warrant that nature is so constituted that our subjective principles can successfully regulate our cognitive efforts: that we shall find nature conforming to the expectations generated by our discursive mode of thinking. We need briefly to consider these two roles in order to understand what Hegel does with Kant's idea.

(1) Our understanding is discursive or, to recall a disconcerting phrase from the first *Critique,* it "can only think."[13] This means that it can only form *general* concepts (general and reflected representations), and has to depend, for their reference to particular objects, on sensible intuitions. This means also that merely thinking a concept does not give any indication as to the existence of any object corresponding to it. Even less does *thinking* a concept generate its *object.* Objects are given, their actuality is attested only by empirical intuition, that is, perception.[14]

There is, however, one way in which our concepts actually function as the cause of the existence of particular objects. This is when they do not have a merely cognitive function (as rules for recognizing given objects), but function as determinations of the will (as rules for producing objects, in technical activity). Such concepts are called purposes (*Zwecke*). Objects produced according to such concepts can themselves be called "purposes."

Reason . . . is the capacity to act according to purposes (a will); and the object which is represented as possible only from such an action would be represented as possible only as a purpose.[15]

All man-made objects are of course purposes in this sense. Technical activity is a particular type of natural causality: causality according to concepts, or purposeful causality. But some empirical objects given in nature present such characteristics as also to be considered as purposes, "by a remote analogy with our own causality according to purposes."[16] They are then called "natural purposes" (*Naturzwecke*). Organisms are such "natural purposes." What characterizes them as such is that in them

we have to judge (*beurteilen*) a relation of cause and effect which we find ourselves able to consider as law-governed only by making the representation of the effect the underlying condition of the causal efficiency of the cause.[17]

In other words: In investigating the causal laws governing the formation, growth, and reproduction of an organism, we need to suppose that the organism, as a purpose to be achieved, is the cause of the combination of material elements that has as its effect the production of the organism. The organism is thus the cause and effect of itself. The constitution of the organism as a whole is what has causally determined the specific combination of its parts. This does not mean, however, that we should give up the possibility of explaining organisms according to strictly mechanical principles: principles of the science of motion of material substances, which proceeds by composition of parts into wholes (composition of masses, of directions, of moving forces . . .) and excludes all consideration of intentionality and purposiveness from the science of nature.[18] But we know from the first *Critique* that we have and can have no access either to ultimate causes or to the complete determination of individual things. We therefore have no option but to preserve both mechanism and teleology: both the maxim that all objects in nature (including organisms) are to be investigated according to strictly mechanistic laws, and the maxim that some objects (organisms) should be investigated by appealing to final causes. The conjunction of these maxims is no contradiction if one remembers that they are mere regulative principles for the reflective use of our power of judgment. As such, they are not objective, but merely subjective principles.

The question is: in what sense are they subjective? This is where the notion of an intellectual intuition comes into the picture. But it should first be said – although this is not quite clear in Kant's explanation – that there is a sense in which our two maxims should be deemed subjective quite independently of any contrast with another type of intellect. They are subjective as opposed to our own *determinant* judgments, which are objective. Mechanism and teleology would be objective if they could be asserted as principles accounting for the complete determination of organisms, for the existence of organisms as fully determinate individual objects. On the contrary, a merely regulative principle for the reflective use of the power of judgment makes both mechanism and teleology mere heautonomous rules, rules that the power of judgment sets for itself in its empirical use.

Now, the very fact that determinant and reflective uses have to be distinguished in this way is a characteristic of our own finite, discursive understanding. In this sense (which is then a second sense of "subjective"), *both* determinant and reflective uses of our power of judgment are "subjective." Their principles (for instance, the second Analogy of experience for the determinant use, mechanism and teleology for the reflective use) hold for us, not for all possible intellects we may think of. If we suppose an intellect for which concept and intuition are not distinct, an intellect that unlike ours does not depend on receptivity for the reference of its concepts to objects, then neither determinant judgment (which has to find the particular objects for a given general concept) nor reflective (which has to find universal concepts for given particular objects) have any use at all. "Subjective," in this second sense, does not distinguish rules for reflective judgment from principles for determinant judgment, but characterizes both as *ours,* holding "from the point of view of man." And the idea of an intellectual intuition is meant to stress just this: It is characterized in a strictly negative sense, as that intellect that, not being dependent upon a receptivity for the provision of its objects, would not be discursive, and therefore would be in need of no power of judgment, whether determinant or reflective.

Although he introduces intellectual intuition as a merely negative notion, Kant nevertheless gives a vivid account of what the world might be like, as known by such an intellect. There would be no distinction between the possible and the actual: Every object of thought would, by the mere fact of being thought, also be actual. There would therefore be no *contingent* existence: No object which, while recognized as existing, could also be thought as not existing. Therefore, there would be no distinction between contingent and necessary existence. In fact, the whole set of modal categories would disappear.[19] And this would hold for the practical standpoint as well as the theoretical. For intellectual intuition, what we think of as an imperative imposed upon our sensible desires just is the law according to which we act as intelligences. Indeed, it is not even a law, in the sense of *law* we know, because it is not a universal principle distinct from its particular instantiations. It just is, as universal, identical to its complete instantiation, as one whole. We see, then, why the distinction between mechanism and teleology has no more raison d'être. The rule of mechanism is imposed upon our reflective power of judgment by the understanding in its distributive use, which proceeds from parts to whole. The rule of teleology is imposed upon our power of judgment by consideration of particular empirical objects, which have to be understood from whole to parts. Both depend upon the discursive nature of our understanding. Both would be useless for an intellectual intuition, which would reveal their common ground.[20]

Finally, not only is the notion of an intellectual intuition "merely negative." It is also, itself, merely "relative to us." This is because we can think it, and think the features of the world as thought by such an intellect, only by contrast with our own understanding. The supposition of an intellectual intuition that escapes the distinctions of our own intellect (most notably, the distinction between possible and actual) is itself a supposition proper to an intellect such as ours.[21]

(2) But given these limitations in its status, the idea of an intellectual intuition also has a positive role. It is not merely an idea that our reason forms in contrast to our own intellect, in order to think its limitations. It is also a supposition that allows us to assume the ability of our intellect, in its discursive character, to produce adequate knowledge of the world. This is because it provides the ground for the affinity of appearances, so that our discursive effort at their complete determination by concepts can meet with ever improved success. It thus grounds what Kant calls the "subjective purposiveness" of nature, the fact that we can suppose nature to be so constituted that our efforts at forming empirical laws and empirical concepts will succeed. And this holds not merely for our investigation of organisms according to the concept of a natural purpose, but for all of our efforts at exhaustively determining nature under a unified system of empirical laws.[22]

So considered, intellectual intuition plays the same role as the Transcendental Ideal in the first *Critique*. And indeed, it is described in very much the same terms. In the first *Critique,* the Transcendental Ideal or the idea of a whole of reality, which ultimately becomes identified with the idea of an *ens realissimum* as the ground of all reality, is described as a concept that has not merely "under it" but "in it" the totality of positive determinations or realities by limitation of which all empirical things could be completely determined.[23] In the third *Critique,* intellectual intuition is contrasted with our own discursive intellect as thinking (and thus generating by its very act of thought) the whole of reality from a "synthetic universal." Such a "synthetic universal" has the features of an intuition: It is described as "the intuition of a whole as such."[24] But it also has the features of a concept: It is a universal, and universality is, according to Kant's *Logic,* the form of a concept.[25] Two points need to be particularly stressed here. First, both the idea of a whole of reality (*KdrV*) and the "synthetic universal" (*KdU*) thus combine features of representations that had been carefully distinguished in the Transcendental Aesthetic of the first *Critique:* there Kant had distinguished concepts *under which* particular representations are contained, from intuitions (in this case, space and time as pure intuitions) *in which* particular representations are contained (*KdrV* A 25/B 39). The relation between universal and particular, characteristic of concepts, was in this way distinguished from the relation between whole and parts, characteristic of intuitions. But the *totum realitatis* (*KdrV*) and the *synthetic universal* (*KdU*) relate to particulars both as *universal* and as *whole.* Second, in the *Critique of Pure Reason* the *totum realitatis* is grounded in an *ens realissimum* (that itself becomes *ens originarium, ens summum, ens entium,* before being even *personified* on moral grounds: cf. A 578–9/B 606–7, A 583/B 611n, A 696–701/B 724–9*).* Similarly the "synthetic universal" is the thought of an intuitive intellect that generates the whole of reality while thinking it. This is what "knowledge of God" is: the genitive is both subjective and objective, knowledge is God's knowledge and knowledge for which the object is inseparably God as the ground of all reality, and the whole of finite realities so grounded.[26]

I have shown elsewhere that in the Analytic of the *Critique of Pure Reason* (in the Appendix on the "Amphiboly of Concepts of Reflection"), Kant argued in favor of substituting for the rationalist idea of an *ens realissimum* as the ground for the complete determination (individuation) of empirical objects, the critical recognition of the transcendental role played by our forms of cognition: our (intuitive) forms of sensibility on the one hand (which provide the form for the relation whole/parts, characteristic of intuition), our (discursive) forms of spontaneity on the other hand, and here most notably the forms of infinite and disjunctive judgment and the form of a continuous hierarchy of genera and species (which provide the form for the relation universal/particular, characteristic of concepts).[27] In analyzing Kant's view, I argued that the reason why in the Dialectic the Ideal was nevertheless maintained as a problematic concept (which therefore still has a role to play in cognition, but as a merely regulative idea) was its necessary postulation in practical philosophy (in the context of the Postulates of practical reason). If I am right in my identification of the *intellectus archetypus* and the *ens realissimum,* then the *intellectus archetypus* in the third *Critique* also could have been critically reduced to (as it were, dismantled into) the transcendental role played by our forms of intuition on the one hand, and our discursive forms on the other hand (to which should be added, however, in the investigation of organisms, the analogy provided by our own technical activity). But here, too, Kant maintains the idea of an intuitive intellect as an indispensable regulative concept, again in view of the role it is called upon to play in moral theology.[28]

So, to sum up: Intellectual intuition is for Kant a negative counterpart to our own (conditioned) reason, both theoretical and practical; it is, as such, the regulative idea of a common ground for mechanism and teleology, as well as a ground for the "subjective purposiveness" of nature; this regulative idea becomes a support for a moral proof of the existence of God; as such it is an object not of knowledge, but of ethical faith.

We now have what we need to understand and evaluate Hegel's reception of Kant's intellectual intuition. Hegel inherits from Kant the representation of intellectual intuition as unconditioned, as thought thinking itself while generating everything it thinks. He inherits from Kant the representation of it as the supersensible ground of the world. He inherits from Kant the idea that such an unconditioned ground is a necessary assertion of reason. He differs from Kant in that for Kant, the "reason" that asserts intellectual intuition differs from the intellectual intuition it asserts, and thus asserts it as it were "from outside," or from the point of view of man. As a result, the assertion remains, in its cognitive use, a merely regulative maxim for both determinant and reflective judgments; and in its practical use, it is a postulate or belief. For Hegel, on the other hand, the "reason" that asserts intellectual intuition is intellectual intuition itself: God's knowledge. This means that God's knowledge is accessible to finite consciousness. Hegel's anti-Kantian claim is that Kant knew this, explicitly acknowledged that he knew it, but did not have the courage to follow up on his discovery. It is this last, anti-Kantian claim, or, perhaps, Kantian-against-Kant claim that we need to examine.

Kant, protests Hegel, has nothing more than empirical psychology to support his claim that the human faculty of knowledge consists in what it appears to be: the ability to proceed discursively from general to particular and from particular to general. In reality, not only has he reached the idea of another type of knowledge, but he has given a very vivid description of it. In spite of this, Kant chose empirical psychology against reason.

Kant has here both in front of him, the idea of a reason in which possibility and actuality are absolutely identical, and the appearance of this reason as faculty of knowledge where they are separate; he finds in the experience of his thinking both thoughts; in the choice between them, however, his nature has despised the necessity, the rational, which is thinking an intuitive spontaneity; and he has decided in favor of the appearance. (326: 89–90)

The idea (of an intuitive intellect) is something absolutely necessary but nevertheless problematic; for our faculty of knowledge nothing is to be acknowledged except the form of its own appearance in its exercise (*Ausübung*) (as Kant calls it), in which possibility and actuality are separate. This appearance is an absolute essence, the intrinsic nature (*das Ansich*) of knowledge, as if it were not also an exercise (*eine Ausübung*) of the faculty of knowledge, when it thinks and knows as a necessary idea an understanding for which possibility and actuality are not separate, in which universal and particular are one, whose spontaneity is intuitive. (325: 89)

The argument seems quite lame. To imagine what a knowledge would be which escaped the limitations of our own is not to assert such a knowledge, or to determine any object by means of it. What does give some ground to Hegel's complaint, however, is that Kant goes further than to merely form the problematic concept of an intuitive intellect. When Hegel says that Kant "found in the experience of his thought" the idea of such an intellect, we need to think not only of the thought-experiment of thinking a nondiscursive understanding, but also of the "fact of reason" of the categorical imperative, and of the moral theology to which the critique of teleological judgment and its concept of an intuitive intellect subsequently gives its support.

Moreover, when Hegel argues that Kant had found intellectual intuition "in the experience of his thought," he can rest his claim not only on Kant's detailed characterization of what an intellectual intuition would be, but also on Kant's explanation of aesthetic judgments and their relation to a supersensible ground. This is a very important point. Indeed, Kant's analysis of aesthetic judgments is perhaps where the choice between remaining strictly within the "point of view of man," or somehow finding within this point of view a way to reach "knowledge of God" is most directly offered. We therefore still need briefly to consider this analysis before proceeding with the evaluation of Hegel's position.

In the Analytic of Aesthetic Judgment, Kant describes the peculiarities of judgments in which the predicate is "beautiful." The paradoxical feature of such judgments, according to him, is that they call for universal assent like cognitive judgments, although their claim to universal assent cannot be sustained by concepts and proof. On the contrary, the only ground for claiming everybody's assent to our own aesthetic judgment is the feeling of pleasure that accompanies the apprehension of a given object. If I say: "This liquid freezes at zero degrees Centigrade" and expect everybody to agree, it is because I know that this particular judgment is deducible from a universal rule: "All liquid which is water freezes at zero degrees; this liquid is water; therefore, this liquid freezes at zero degrees Centigrade." In this case, the subjective universality of my judgment depends on its objective universality: the recognition of the subject of the judgment as falling under a concept which provides the universal ground for the attribution of the predicate.[29] In an aesthetic judgment, on the other hand, subjective universality (I expect all others to agree with me, I am indignant if they do not, I endeavor to convince them and I condemn them as inept if they don't) does not rely on proof, but on a feeling of which everybody is capable and that I try to awaken in others and to confirm in myself by an indefinitely pursuable process of description and interpretation.

Kant's explanation of this peculiar feature of aesthetic judgments is the following: The reason why we claim the same degree of universal assent for them as we do for our cognitive judgments is that the very faculties, with the very a priori features that are put into play for the latter, are also put into play for the former. Cognitive judgments are made possible by an agreement between imagination and understanding that finds expression in an empirical concept. In aesthetic judgments, we recognize an agreement between imagination and understanding that no conceptual characterization can exhaustively analyze. The pleasure we feel, and that is expressed in the predicate "beautiful" applied to the object occasioning it, is a pleasure in feeling this agreement *and* the impossibility of fully analyzing it into concepts, as well as the pleasure we take in the a priori certainty that every human being is capable of taking part in this pleasure, by virtue of the same a priori capacities which provoke it in us.[30]

Now, given this explanation, it comes as somewhat of a surprise that in the Dialectic of Aesthetic Judgment, Kant should take up the matter all over again, in the form of an antinomy. The paradoxical character of the judgment of taste, as expounded in the Analytic, can be expressed, he says, in the form of two contradictory propositions:

(1) Thesis. The judgment of taste is not grounded upon concepts, for otherwise one could dispute about it (determine by proof).

(2) Antithesis. The judgment of taste is grounded on concepts, for otherwise, despite its diversity, one could not quarrel about it (one could not claim for this judgment the necessary agreement of others).

Kant's solution is then to defuse the contradiction by showing that thesis and antithesis are not using "concept" in the same sense: the thesis is really saying: "The judgment of taste is not grounded upon *determinate* concepts" (such as would be a concept of the understanding which would ground a cognitive judgment). The antithesis is saying: "The judgment of taste is grounded on a concept, but an *indeterminate* one" (the concept of the supersensible ground common to the object of our sensible intuition and to ourselves as intuiting it).[31]

From the Analytic, it appeared that the ground for the aesthetic judgment was the harmonious activity of imagination and understanding in the apprehension of a sensible object, an activity that strove toward a completely determined concept without ever reaching it (hence, the qualification of the aesthetic judgment as "merely reflective"). Now, it seems that the Antinomy could have been solved by sticking to these terms. The thesis would then have been interpreted as saying that the aesthetic judgment is not grounded on a determinate concept, that is, on a discursively specified concept, of which the object judged "beautiful" could be recognized as the instantiation. The antithesis would have been interpreted as saying that the aesthetic judgment is nevertheless grounded on the agreement of the intuition (produced by imagination) with an activity of conceptualization that it encourages without allowing it to exhaust what the sensible intuition is teaching us.[32] This would make Kant's interpretation of aesthetic judgment the epitome of his Copernican revolution: The source of the aesthetic pleasure is the activity of the mind that produces the unity of sensible intuition and with it, the inexhaustible terrain for all concepts.

But instead of building on this, Kant makes sensible intuition the mere appearance of a supersensible ground. The solution to the antinomy does not consist in referring us back to the Analytic. The "undetermined" concept of the antithesis is not the free play of imagination and intellect in its concept-producing activity. It is the concept of the supersensible, which is indeterminate because it is indeterminable in the forms of our discursive activity.

Not surprisingly, it is this side of the Kantian explanation that Hegel finds interesting. According to him, the intuition of the beautiful was one of the "experiences" of intellectual intuition that Kant had hit upon.

When Kant reflects upon reason as conscious intuition, upon beauty, and upon reason as intuition deprived of consciousness, upon organisms, what is expressed is the idea of reason, in a more or less formal fashion. (322: 86)

Kant recognizes in beauty another intuition than sensible intuition, and describes the substrate of nature as an intelligible substrate, as rational and identical with all reason. (328: 91)[33]

It should be kept in mind that "reason" here is intellectual intuition as described in the Critique of Teleological Judgment. If one takes seriously the idea that in aesthetic judgment the feeling of pleasure expressed in the predicate "beautiful" is universally grounded in the concept of the supersensible as the common ground to the object and to ourselves, it then makes some sense to say that intuiting beauty is consciously intuiting intellectual intuition, as inseparably manifested in the form of the object and in our activity of producing (apprehending) this form.

Of course, Hegel is well aware that this is certainly not a formulation Kant himself would have accepted. Even here Kant is careful to maintain an insuperable breach between the concept of the supersensible (which the critique of teleological judgment identifies as the problematic concept of intellectual intuition) and our sensible intuition of the beautiful. The first is an idea of reason, and as such incapable of adequate sensible presentation; the second is an aesthetic idea, as such incapable of being "exponiated" (*exponiert*) namely reflected under an adequate concept.[34] As if, Hegel objects, it did not result from what Kant has said that the idea of reason was the exponiation of the aesthetic idea, and the aesthetic idea the presentation (*Darstellung*) of the idea of reason. Kant refuses to see this because he can think of the presentation of the idea of the supersensible only as a sensible synthesis on the model that he expounded for what he calls concepts of the understanding, and he can think of the "exponiation" of the intuition in the idea only on the model of discursive reflection. In other words, he is guilty of exactly what he denounces in the mathematical antinomies of the first *Critique*. As Hegel puts it,

Kant demands precisely what grounds the mathematical antinomy, namely an intuition for the idea of reason in which the idea would be expanded as finite and sensible and at the same time as supersensible, as a beyond for experience, not the sensible and supersensible intuited in absolute identity; and an exponiation and knowledge of the aesthetic [namely, the sensible, B.L.] in which the aesthetic would be exhaustively reflected by the understanding. (323: 87)

This is an interesting objection. It shows that Hegel accepts Kant's point in the mathematical Antinomies, according to which no successive synthesis in intuition can generate an object to match Kant's idea of the unconditioned or Hegel's "infinite concept"; and no discursive concept can match space and time as "infinite given magnitudes."[35] What we can and do have, however, according to Hegel, is another kind of match, a prediscursive match, in fact an immediate identity between sensible intuition, as intuition of the beautiful, and intellectual intuition: "the sensible and supersensible intuited in absolute identity."

If this is so, the *concept,* or Kant's pure practical (and theoretical) reason, should be understood against the background of this prediscursive identity: against the background of Hegel's *reason.* This is how Hegel's reorganization of Kant's Critical system finds its culmination in a reinterpretation of Kant's first *Critique* and of the question which for Kant initiated the Critical system: "How are synthetic *a priori* judgments possible?"

Before turning to this last point, let me recapitulate again what we have so far. Hegel criticizes Kant's reason (especially Kant's practical reason) for being irreducibly divided from sensibility, and thus divided from the sensible world. He thinks he can find in Kant's explanation of aesthetic judgment the solution to this division. In aesthetic judgment, we experience the identity of the sensible and supersensible in ourselves and in the world. In interpreting Kant's conception of aesthetic judgment in this way, however, Hegel focuses on Kant's solution to his Dialectic of Aesthetic Judgment, rather than on Kant's Analytic of Aesthetic Judgment. My own question has been: Why does Kant seem to ignore the solution to the Dialectic that his own Analytic might have provided? I shall to leave this question aside for now, and turn to Hegel's reception of Kant's question: "How are synthetic *a priori* judgments possible?"

III. Kant's Synthetic a priori Judgments and Hegel's "Absolute Judgment"

The nature of Hegel's opposition to Kant should now be clear: Hegel chastises Kant for not adopting the point of view that Kant himself has defined as the only true one. The consistent line of Kant's philosophy, according to Hegel, is to forbid us access to this higher point of view whenever he encounters it, as he does in his critique of teleological and of aesthetic judgment. It is significant, in this regard, that Hegel should begin his presentation of the Kantian philosophy by denouncing Kant's treatment of the idea of God: Kant, says Hegel, criticizes this idea as empty in his first *Critique,* posits it in the end as a necessary postulate of practical reason and an object of faith, but nowhere gives it its true status: that of the beginning and only content of all philosophy.

The highest idea which [Kantian philosophy] happened upon in its critical occupation, and which it treated as an empty lucubration and an unnatural scholastic trick which consists in extracting reality from concepts, it then posits, but at the end of philosophy, as a postulate which is supposed to have subjective necessity, but not the absolute objectivity which would lead us to begin philosophy with it and acknowledge it as the only content of philosophy, instead of ending with it, in faith. (302: 67)[36]

Acknowledging this idea as "the beginning and only content" of philosophy would have meant acknowledging that the task of philosophy is not to elaborate the opposition between "spirit and world, soul and body, I and nature," but to expound the absolute identity which is their common ground. This is what true idealism is: the recognition of the merely phenomenal character of *both* sides of the opposition. *Both* concept and sensible reality, I and nature, Kantian reason (and more particularly, Kant's most pure, i.e., practical reason) and sensibility, are merely phenomenal, which means that they are nothing in themselves, and have as their common ground the absolute identity which is Kant's suprasensible or intellectual intuition, i.e., Hegel's absolute.

Hegel's interpretation of Kant's question: "How are synthetic *a priori* judgements possible?" consists in reformulating it – and reformulating the answer to be given to it – in terms of the "true standpoint": the point of view of identity that he has gathered from the third *Critique*. This standpoint, Hegel argues, was already present in the first *Critique,* although there as elsewhere it was blurred by Kant's Critical, that is, Lockean-psychological, preferred standpoint.

> The true idea of reason finds itself expressed in the formula: "how are synthetic *a priori* judgments possible?" This problem does not express anything else but the idea that in the synthetic judgment subject and predicate, that the particular, this the universal, that in the form of being, this in the form of thought, – this heterogeneous is at the same time *a priori*, i.e., absolutely identical. The possibility of this positing alone is reason, which is nothing but this identity of the heterogeneous. (304: 69)

This text has justifiably been the object of many commentaries.[37] What has been insufficiently perceived, I think, is that Hegel's reading of Kant's question is a retrospective reading, a reading from the point of view of the completed Kantian system: the holistic point of view of the Transcendental Ideal, of the Postulates of practical reason, and of the third *Critique*. So, the effort we have to make in assessing Hegel's interpretation is twofold: We have to consider Kant's notion of synthetic a priori judgments in the light of the Critical system as a whole; and we have to see how Hegel reinterprets it in the terms of a philosophy whose "beginning and sole content" is the concept of God, or the absolute identity of thought and being in intellectual intuition. Such a reading helps better to understand some of the most difficult and important points in Hegel's treatment of judgment. I shall briefly consider three of these points: (i) subject and predicate in synthetic a priori judgments, (ii) identity, and (iii) the nature and role of transcendental imagination.

(i) Subject and predicate. Hegel characterizes subject and predicate in synthetic a priori judgments as "the particular [and] the universal, that in the form of being, this in the form of thought." This is puzzling. In Kant's analysis of the logical form of categorical judgments, both subject and predicate are *concepts* (and of course, "particular" and "universal" do not qualify subject or predicate, but the judgment itself. A judgment can be, as to its quantity, universal, particular, or singular. Concepts, as "general and reflected representations," are always universal).[38] When Kant analyzes the difference between analytic and synthetic judgments, however, he introduces into the form of judgment the object of intuition, subsumed under the concepts that are themselves subordinated to one another in the judgment: "x, which I think under concept A, I also think under concept B." Or: "to x, to which pertains A, also pertains B." When the form of judgment is so considered, its subject is always ultimately x, the object of intuition, and the concepts related to one another in judgment are predicates of this x.[39] This holds for all objective judgments, and therefore also for the Principles of Pure Understanding, as synthetic a priori judgments. They have the form: "Every A is B." For instance: "Every A [thing that happens] is B [such that it presupposes something upon which it follows according to a rule]" (Second Analogy of Experience). Or "All A's are B": "All A's [appearances] are B [extensive magnitudes]" (Principle of the Axioms of Intuition). In both cases (as in all other Principles of Pure Understanding), the subordination of concept A to concept B is made possible by the subsumption under concept B of all xs subsumed under concept A. The xs so subsumed are pure manifolds of space and time, synthesized by productive imagination; and therefore, they are also any empirical manifold given in forms of space and time that have been so synthesized.[40]

Hegel's claim, I think, is that in each of Kant's "principles of pure understanding" (synthetic a priori judgments) and subsequently, in each and everyone of our empirical judgments, what is really subsumed is the whole of what is given in intuition, under "the concept," namely the act of thinking, that is, the whole of interrelated discursive concepts, whether these concepts are already determined or to be determined in relation to intuition.[41] This is certainly a sustainable point for Kant himself. Indeed, he makes just such a claim in the Transcendental Ideal of the first *Critique,* when he shows that knowledge of any empirical object is achieved under the regulative idea of a totality of positive determinations within the framework of the whole of space and time as formal intuitions.[42]

The whole of what is given in intuition is what Hegel here calls "the particular." It could perhaps be better described as "the realm of the particular": the given manifold within which any particular object is delimited. The "universal," on the other hand, is the unitary act of thought that generates the representation of a totality of fully determined, interrelated concepts. The particular is "in the form of being" and the universal is "in the form of thought." Being and thought are just this: intuitive and discursive forms for one and the same presensible and prediscursive "absolute."

This last point, however, is not Kant's any more, but Hegel's. It is for Hegel that both intuition and concept, particular and universal, being and thought are mere appearances of an original identity that is that of intellectual intuition, or the *intellectus archetypus,* or the *ens realissimum.* For Kant, this could certainly not be asserted from a theoretical standpoint, but only postulated from a practical standpoint. Because he did not give full due to this view, says Hegel, Kant fell victim to the very same fate he attributed to Hume: He remained within the limits of too narrow a conception of his problem.[43] I think that one possible way of understanding this charge is the following. According to Kant, Hume's narrowly psychological method prevented him from seeing that the perception of any objective temporal succession depends upon the implicit assumption that "everything that happens presupposes something else upon which it follows according to a rule"; it also prevented him from discovering that other concepts, besides that of cause, are a priori conditions of our experience of objective temporal relations. According to Hegel, Kant's own subservience to the standpoint of empirical consciousness prevented him from seeing that his own a priori principles presupposed the judgment: The particular is the universal, the whole of intuition is the whole of thought.

The task of philosophy is to develop this last judgment. But this means that contrary to what Kant thought, there was a third positive answer to the question: "How are synthetic a priori judgments possible?" It is not just mathematical judgments (Kant's first positive answer), and not just the principles of pure understanding as foundations of a metaphysics of nature (Kant's second positive answer), that are possible.[44] In fact, these are poor subjective substitutes for what alone is the truly synthetic *a priori* judgment: the proposition in which "subject and predicate, that the particular, this the universal, that in the form of being, this in the form of thought, – this heterogeneous is at the same time *a priori,* i.e., absolutely identical." This proposition alone is sufficient to restore the metaphysics that Kant eliminated in the Transcendental Dialectic of the first *Critique.* It is what the Preface to the *Phenomenology* will call "der spekulative Satz" ("the speculative proposition"), and what the chapter on judgment in the Subjective Logic will expound as the self-developing, self-correcting "judgment" present in any particular empirical judgment.[45]

(ii) Identity. It would be implausible to suppose that when Hegel says: "in synthetic *a priori* judgments subject and predicate are *a priori,* i.e., absolutely identical," he is confusing synthetic judgment with analytic judgment. Hegel's point is rather that Kant's question about synthetic a priori judgments, and his answer to it, find their full development only in the assertion of identity in the sense which Hegel, after Schelling, thinks he inherits from the third *Critique:* the particular (intuition), and the universal (concept, i.e., the pure systematic form of Kant's reason), are "identical" in that they are the two sides of our discursive mode of apprehending what is originally one: what an intellectual intuition would apprehend as thought and being all at once. This is why Hegel also says: "The possibility of this positing is alone reason, which is nothing but this identity of the heterogeneous." What he calls here "positing" is the form of predication which relates "the particular" and "the universal." The ground of such a "positing" is Hegel's reason, or Kant's intellectual intuition "which is nothing but this identity of the heterogeneous."

But this does not answer the main question: How can Hegel pretend that the *assertion* of such an identity was even hinted at – that Kant "confusedly recognized [this] idea" (301–2) in his explanation of synthetic a priori judgments? Hegel's answer is that this idea was present in Kant's conception of transcendental imagination. This is an interesting point: Indeed, Kant's solution to his question ("How are synthetic *a priori* judgments possible?") lies entirely in his theory of imagination.[46] In order further to understand Hegel's "identity," and its relation to Kant's own solution to his question, we need to consider their respective conceptions of imagination.

(iii) Imagination. Hegel praises Kant for having introduced the idea of identity in his transcendental deduction of the categories: first as transcendental unity of apperception, then as the figurative synthesis of imagination which is, according to §26 of the Transcendental Deduction in the B edition, the source of the unity of space and time.

This again is a point, in Hegel's reading of Kant, which has been the object of much debate. My thesis is that Hegel's account of the role of transcendental imagination and of its relation to the transcendental unity of apperception on the one hand, to the unity of intuition on the other hand, is accurate. The only issue between him and Kant is: How should we interpret *the unity of apperception* itself? I shall consider each of these two points in turn: (a) imagination, (b) the unity of apperception.

(a) What we find in the transcendental deduction of the categories, according to Hegel, is the idea that the transcendental unity of apperception is the source of both the unity of intuition and the unity of concept. In the former capacity, it is transcendental imagination. In the latter capacity, it is that unity of consciousness that accompanies all general concepts: what Kant called the "analytic unity of apperception." That the synthetic unity of imagination is the source of the unity of intuition means that space and time, which according to the Transcendental Aesthetic were merely forms of receptivity, are in fact also products of spontaneity.[47]

It has been charged that this interpretation of the relation between imagination and intuition gives too much to spontaneity, and "collapses" the distinction between intuition and concept. Hegel's reading of Kant's theory of imagination, so the charge goes on, is therefore not immanent, but introduces presuppositions that are foreign to Kant.[48] In fact, I do not think that this is the case *on this precise point.* Hegel's reading of the relation between unity of apperception, transcendental imagination, and forms of intuition is supported not only by the "second part" of the Transcendental Deduction (the explanation of figurative synthesis in §26), but also, among other texts, by the metaphysical deduction of the categories itself, where Kant already states that "the same function, which gives unity to various representations in a judgment, also gives to the mere synthesis of various representations in one intuition a unity which, expressed universally, is called pure concept of the understanding."[49] This "same function" is the transcendental unity of apperception. As "giving unity to various representations in a judgment," it is the analytic unity of apperception, or discursive understanding; as "giving unity to the mere synthesis of various representations in one intuition," it is transcendental imagination. It is therefore perfectly accurate to say that for Kant, one and the same transcendental unity of apperception is at work on the one hand as transcendental imagination (which is the source of space and time as formal intuitions), on the other hand as discursive understanding.

(b) But the disagreement between Kant and Hegel concerns the question: What *is* the unity of apperception? For Kant, it has no other possible status than that of the act of a finite consciousness: a consciousness that is not the source of its own empirical objects, but merely generates the forms according to which these objects are perceived and conceptualized. These forms themselves, whether they are forms of figurative synthesis (space and time) or forms of intellectual synthesis (judgment, discursive thought) have and can have no other status than that of forms of finite, because receptive, consciousness: space and time are forms in which multiplicities are *given,* forms of judgment are forms in which these multiplicities are *reflected upon,* in order to form concepts or "general and reflected representations."

For Hegel, the unity of apperception is much more than this. It is the same "reason," or intellectual intuition, which Hegel found in Kant's account of aesthetic and teleological judgment. Now, to interpret the transcendental unity of apperception in these terms is to say that it is the source not only of the form but also of the matter of appearances. It is to say that it is that unity for which there is no distinction between form and matter, between possible and actual, between concept and intuition, which Kant defined in the third *Critique* as intellectual intuition. This is certainly not an assertion Kant would have accepted. And Hegel knows this: Unfortunately, he says, Kant acknowledged his discovery in the transcendental deduction of the first *Critique* even less than he did in the *Critique of Judgment.* In both cases, Hegel concludes, Kant ultimately lost the benefit of his great discovery, and his idealism remained mere subjective or formal idealism.

IV. Concluding Remarks: Kant *Contra* Kant

Hegel's main effort, in subsequent years, is to show how the development and self-criticism of the point of view of finite consciousness and discursive thought supersedes itself into the recognition of the superior standpoint, that of the absolute identity between thought and being, or reason, or the idea. This is what leads to logic assuming the position, not of a mere preparation to metaphysics, but of metaphysics itself; to the emergence of dialectic as an essential aspect of this logic; to the invention of a "science of the experience of consciousness" as the introduction to philosophy; and to the statement, in the mature Subjective Logic, that unity of apperception and concept are one and the same. Now this is quite a remarkable statement if one remembers that in "Faith and Knowledge," *concept,* identical with Kant's pure (theoretical and practical) reason, and *unity of apperception,* identical with Kant's intellectual intuition, were sharply distinguished.[50] So, certainly, the mere consideration of "Faith and Knowledge" is not enough to come to an assessment of Hegel's argument against Kant. Why did I nevertheless announce that I would argue in favor of using Kant against Kant not, like Hegel, to advocate the ascent to "knowledge of God," but rather to elucidate "the point of view of man?"

According to Hegel, on several occasions Kant "met in the experience of his thought" the idea of an intellectual intuition. It is this "experience" that Hegel intends to develop to its full extent; and it is the immanent relation of finite, discursive consciousness to this experience that his mature system will intend to prove and develop – meanwhile giving up the expression "intellectual intuition" in favor of "absolute knowing" (in the *Phenomenology*) or "absolute idea" (in the *Science of Logic*). But this "experience" is in fact highly questionable in its very starting point, in Kant's philosophy. For the benefit of practical reason, in Kant's first *Critique* the idea of God is not only problematically admitted, but also apodeictically asserted or posited in the Appendix to its Transcendental Dialectic, even though the Appendix to the Analytic had seemed to reject it, and asserted that instead, our forms of sensibility and discursivity alone are the transcendental principles for the individuation and universal affinity of appearances. In the third *Critique,* the idea of the supersensible is assumed as the solution to the antinomy of the critique of taste even though the Analytic of Aesthetic Judgment had seemed already to provide such a solution with the "free play" of our sensibility and intellect; and finally, in the Dialectic of Teleological Judgment intellectual intuition is presupposed as the common ground to both natural teleology and mechanism for the ultimate benefit of ethicotheology. Practical reason is thus the true ground, in Kant, for the assertion of intellectual intuition. But Hegel argues (and this is, I think, one of the most remarkable statements of "Faith and Knowledge") that Kant's practical reason is just as phenomenal as his theoretical reason ("phenomenal" in the sense Hegel gives to this word: it belongs to the standpoint of finite consciousness, where intuition and concept, being and thought, are divided). Indeed, in the third *Critique,* Kant himself recognized that practical reason belongs just as much as theoretical reason to the discursive, conditioned use of our intellect, albeit intellect as will and not simply as cognitive power. I would then suggest that if such is the case, instead of pushing the results of Kant's dialectic, in all three *Critiques,* toward a reconciliation of "point of view of man" and "knowledge of God," another, more defensible option is to retreat once and for all into the Analytic of all three *Critiques* and further elucidate the "point of view of man": the nature of the ever more complex intertwinings of sensibility and discursivity, passivity and activity, by means of which our access to the world is achieved.

This does not mean that nothing is to be gained from Hegel's endeavor. Even listing only those of its promising aspects that are already present in "Faith and Knowledge," one would have to mention the holistic approach to Kant's theory of concept and judgment, the recognition of the centrality of judgment for the elucidation of the nature of discursive thought, the inseparability of Kant's theoretical and practical reason, and the retrospective reading of the Critical system from the standpoint of its completed results. But it is helpful to keep in mind the exact nature of the difficulty we face when trying to reap the benefit of Hegel's insights: they are expounded within the context of a supposedly achieved or achievable standpoint to which Kantian philosophy itself, even while severely restricting access to it, gave more weight, or so I have tried to show, than its own critical findings were able to warrant.

One may object that it is misleading to extend to the mature Hegel the defense of intellectual intuition, or intuitive intellect, which is characteristic of his early Jena period and his collaboration with Schelling. After all, the *Phenomenology of Spirit* is opened by a resounding attack against Schelling's identity philosophy and Jacobi's intuition of God, and as I pointed out, the expression 'intellectual intuition' is not much used in Hegel's mature texts. Is it not misguided, then, to think that the discussion of Kant in "Faith and Knowledge" brings any light at all on Hegel's mature philosophy?[51]

In answer to this objection, it should first be noted that indeed the Preface to the *Phenomenology of Spirit* shows that Hegel did not want any confusion between his own philosophical standpoint and Jacobi's or even Schelling's "Absolute." I think this is a major reason why he mostly gave up the expression "intellectual intuition" in favor of that of "absolute knowledge" or, in the Logic, "absolute idea." Another reason is his denunciation of the illusions of "immediate" knowledge: The whole purpose of the *Phenomenology of Spirit* is to show that reaching the standpoint of "absolute knowledge" is a result, not an immediate given. Nevertheless, the discussion with Kant is taken up again in the introduction to the mature Subjective Logic in terms very similar to those of "Faith and Knowledge," and there again Hegel chastises Kant for having ignored the standpoint he had himself defined as the only true one: that of intellectual intuition.[52] I think that this reference to Kant's intellectual intuition, and the careful consideration of what this reference amounts to, what role it plays first in Kant's system, and then in Hegel's, helps clarify what Hegel means when he claims that his logic is "the presentation of God, as he is in his eternal essence before the creation of nature and of a finite spirit,"[53] or his ever-renewed insistence that he means to reinstate metaphysics as knowledge of God. What my discussion has not considered at all is how and whether Hegel actually shows, in the *Phenomenology* and after, that finite consciousness and (practical and theoretical) discursivity can supersede themselves into such a standpoint. This would need an altogether different and much more developed study. Here I have only tried to show how the relation between Hegel's project and its Kantian ancestor might help clarify its import and plausibility.

Second, one striking aspect of the discussion of intellectual intuition in "Faith and Knowledge" is that despite the dichotomy stressed by Hegel between "concept" (Kant's practical and theoretical, discursive reason) and "reason" (Kant's intellectual intuition), already what interests Hegel is the mediation between discursive and nondiscursive intellect by means of judgment (his "absolute judgment") and syllogism. Judgment is said to be the "appearance of reason," and Hegel calls for the mediation, by syllogism, between judgment and reason (intellectual intuition, with the conceptual articulations which Kant has already begun to expound for it). So, Hegel's interest is already quite different from either Schelling's "point of indifference" or Fichte's intellectual intuition as intuition of the moral self. The logical/conceptual aspect, the distinctive type of universal (Kant's "synthetic universal") and therefore the new laws of thought it entails, the unity of possibility and actuality and the collapsing of the concept of necessity into that of unconditioned freedom, are already at the center of Hegel's interest in Kant's intellectual intuition. They will be further developed in his mature *Logic*.

This interest in the mediation between discursive and nondiscursive thought is even more apparent if one considers, as I have done, not just Hegel's reinterpretation of "reason," but also the overall shift from Kant's *categories* to Hegel's *concept* and from Kant's *synthetic a priori judgment* to Hegel's *absolute judgment*. Here, too, "Faith and Knowledge" helps us understand the use of these terms in the mature *Logic*, as a detailed examination of the latter would, I think, confirm.

Finally, the more general concern of my paper was the relation between Kant's and Hegel's endeavors. My view is that Hegel is right in seeing a tension within Kant's philosophy between "point of view of man" and striving toward "knowledge of God." Hegel is also right in claiming that the resolution of this tension depends on an interpretation and development of Kant's theory of judgment. But I have tried to defend the view that Kant's Critical philosophy offers the tools for a resolution symmetrically opposed to the one Hegel is attempting: a systematic development of the "point of view of man" which is quite different from the Lockean "empirical psychology" Hegel is charging Kant with. Elements for such a development can certainly be found in Hegel's philosophy itself – in his *Phenomenology of Spirit,* but also in his mature *Science of Logic* and *Encyclopedia of Philosophical Sciences.* Showing this, however, is beyond the ambition of the present paper.

Notes

1. On the "true idea of reason," see "Glauben und Wissen," in G. W. F. Hegel, *Werke in zwanzig Bänden, Theorie Werkausgabe* (Frankfurt am Main: Suhrkamp Verlag 1970), vol. 2, p. 304; *Faith and Knowledge,* trans. Walter Cerf (Albany: State University of New York Press, 1977), p. 69. On the "trampling down of reason" that is presupposed in Kant's conception of practical reason, op. cit., p. 321; Eng. trans. p. 85. The "trampling down of reason" is achieved, according to Hegel, in Kant's criticism of the ontological proof. I shall return to this point later.

   Works of Hegel will be quoted from the Suhrkamp edition, with indication of volume and page, followed by reference in the relevant English translation. In order to avoid an excessive number of endnotes, references to "Glauben und Wissen" will be given in parentheses within the main text, with only indication of page number (from Volume II of Suhrkamp), followed by indication of the corresponding page number in the English translation. All translations in the present essay, however, are mine.

   I use the following abbreviations:

   GW   "Glauben und Wissen."
   FK   "Faith and Knowledge."
   PG   *Phänomenologie des Geistes.*
   PS   *Phenomenology of Spirit,* trans. A. V. Miller (Oxford: Oxford University Press, 1977).
   WL   *Wissenschaft der Logik,* Suhrkamp edition, vols. 5 and 6.
   SL   *Hegel's Science of Logic,* trans. A. V. Miller (New York: Humanities Press, 1976).

2. Quotes in support of this claim will be given in the course of this paper, in parts I (concept), II (reason), and III (judgment).

3. Cf. *GW,* p. 333; *FK,* p. 96: "The purity of the infinite concept . . . is posited at the same time in the sphere of understanding as the objective, but here in the dimensions of the categories; and on the practical side as *objective law.*" Hegel also uses the term "understanding" (*Verstand*) and "what belongs to understanding" (*das Verständige*) instead of "concept" to describe Kant's "pure reason" (cf. for instance *GW,* pp. 302, 305, 307; *FK,* pp. 67, 70, 72). On the other hand, as we shall see, Hegel calls "reason"

Kant's intellectual intuition, or his own transformation of it. This shift in vocabulary is essentially maintained all the way into the mature period of Hegel's philosophy (see concluding remarks of this paper).

4. Cf. the three formulations of the categorical imperative: *Grundlegung der Metaphysik der Sitten* Ak. IV, pp. 402, 428, 431–2; *Groundwork of the Metaphysics of Morals,* trans. H. J. Paton (New York: Harper, 1964), pp. 70, 96, 98–9.

All references to Kant's writings, except references to the *Critique of Pure Reason (KdrV)*, are given by volume and page number of the Akademie edition of *Kant's Gesammelte Schriften* (Berlin, 1902–98), followed by references in a current English translation. *KdrV* is quoted with the usual reference to A and B editions.

Translations and abbreviations used:

KdpV   *Kritik der praktischen Vernunft,* Ak.V.

CPrR   *Critique of Practical Reason,* trans. Mary Gregor (Cambridge, U.K.: Cambridge University Press, 1997).

KdrV   *Kritik der reinen Vernunft, Critique of Pure Reason.*

KdU   *Kritik der Urteilskraft,* Ak.V.

CJ   *Critique of Judgment,* trans. Werner Pluhar (Indianapolis: Hackett, 1987).

L   *Logik* (Ak. IX).

JL   *The Jäsche Logic,* in *Lectures on Logic,* trans. J. Michael Young, The Cambridge Edition of the Works of Immanuel Kant, (Cambridge, U.K.: Cambridge University Press), pp. 521–640.

Refl   *Reflexionen* (cited with volume and page of the Akademie Ausgabe).

5. Cf. *KdrV,* A 582/B 610; A 647/B 675.
6. *L,* §1, p. 91; *JL,* p. 589; *KdrV,* A 70/B 95–A 83/B 109.
7. For an explanation of these definitions and their relation, cf. *KdrV,* A 298/B 356–A 309/B 366.
8. Cf. *KdpV,* §§5, 6, and Remark, pp. 28–30; *CPrR,* pp. 26–8.
9. "Unconditioned knowledge," namely knowledge expressed in a proposition that provides the condition for its own truth, either expressed in its subject (in a categorical judgment), or in its antecedent (in a hypothetical judgment) or in the divided concept (in a disjunctive judgment). Therefore "knowledge of the unconditioned," namely knowledge of an object that can be thought as a subject providing a sufficient ground for its synthetic predicates, or that can be thought as the complete totality of antecedent conditions for a given event, or that can be thought as the object whose concept is sufficient ground of all positive determinations of things. See *KdrV,* A 333/B 390.
10. Cf. Spinoza: *Ethics,* Book I, Definition 2: "That thing is said to be finite in its own kind *(in suo genere finita)* that can be limited by another of the same nature." See *The Collected Works of Spinoza,* ed. and trans. Edwin Curley (Princeton: Princeton University Press, 1985), vol. 1, p. 408.
11. I borrow this striking charge against Kant's moral philosophy from the part of the paper that is devoted to Jacobi. But see similar complaints in the exposition of Kant's philosophy: *GW,* p. 318, *FK,* p. 81. In expounding Kant's Third Antinomy of Pure Reason, Hegel denounces Kant's view of reason, characterized as free but plagued with opposition. This opposition, Hegel says, becomes destructive contradiction when the emptiness wants to give itself a content and becomes a doctrine of duties.
12. *KdU,* §76, p. 403; *CJ,* pp. 286–7.
13. *KdrV,* B 135.

14. Cf. *KdrV,* Postulates of Empirical Thought in General, A 219/B 266 .
15. *KdU,* §64, p. 370; *CJ,* p. 248.
16. *KdU,* §65, p. 375; *CJ,* p. 255.
17. *KdU,* §63, p. 366–67; *CJ,* p. 244.
18. On mechanism according to Kant, see Henry Allison: "Kant's Antinomy of Tele-ological Judgment," in *System and Teleology in Kant's Critique of Judgment,* Spindel Conference 1991 ed. Hoke Robinson (Memphis: Memphis State University Press, 1992), p. 26–8.
19. As Düsing has pointed out, this does away with Leibniz's distinction between possible, represented in God's intellect, and actual, brought into existence by God's will (see Klaus Düsing: "Ästhetische Einbildungskraft und intuitiver Verstand. Kants Lehre und Hegels spekulativ-idealistische Umdeutung" in *Hegel-Studien* 21 (1986): 106n.6). One might then be tempted to say that Kant's intellectual intuition, or intuitive intellect, is more like Spinoza's *deus sive natura* than like Leibniz's infinite intellect. It should be noted, however, that not only the distinction between possible and actual but *all* modal categories (including that of necessity) disappear from knowledge of objects in an intuitive understanding: cf. *KdU,* §76, p. 403; *CJ,* p. 286. Why does Kant nevertheless persist in describing the intuitive intellect itself as an "absolutely necessary being" (*KdU,* p. 402; *CJ,* p. 285)? Perhaps because it is a representation formed by *our discursive* reason, for which modal categories of course hold even in its consideration of an intellect for which there would be none. This transition from discursive reason to intuitive intellect and the annihilation, in intuitive intellect, of all modal consideration in favor of absolute freedom of self-determination, is, I think, a major source for the transition, in the mature *Science of Logic,* from Hegel's exposition of modal categories in the last chapter of the Logic of Essence, to the Logic of Concept where necessity gives way to freedom. *WL* 6, pp. 200–217, 239–240; *SL,* pp. 541–43, 570–71. I shall have more to say, at the end of this paper, on the ways in which Hegel's confrontation with Kant in "Faith and Knowledge" helps clarify major aspects of his mature system.
20. Cf. *KdU,* §78, pp. 410–15; *CJ,* pp. 294–300.
21. "It is not necessary to prove that such an *intellectus archetypus* is possible, but only that we ourselves, in the opposed consideration of our own discursive, image-dependent understanding (*intellectus ectypus*), and in considering the contingency of its being so constituted, are led to this idea (of an *intellectus archetypus*) and that it does not entail any contradiction" (*KdU,* §77, p. 408; *CJ,* pp. 292–3). See also: "The concept of an absolutely necessary being is an indispensable idea of reason, but a problematic concept for the understanding. But it does hold for the use of our faculties of knowledge, according to their specific constitution, and therefore not of objects and therefore for all knowing beings: because I cannot presuppose in all thinking and intuition as two different conditions of exercise of their faculties of knowledge, and therefore of the actuality and possibility of things" (*KdU,* §76, pp. 402–3; *CJ,* pp. 285–6).
22. "In order to be able at least to think the agreement of things in nature with our faculty of judgment (which we think as contingent, and therefore possible only through a purpose directed towards it) we must think at the same time another understanding, in relation to which and before any end set to it, we can represent as necessary this agreement of natural laws with our faculty of judgment, which for our understanding is thinkable only by the mediation of ends" (*KdU,* §77, p. 407; *CJ,* p. 291).
    The role of the supposition of an intellectual intuition in grounding the unity of

nature under empirical laws is announced in the Introduction to the *Critique of Judgment: KdU,* p. 180; *CJ,* p. 19. There Kant, however, merely mentions "an intellect (even if it is not ours) . . . [which makes possible] a system of experience according to particular laws of nature." Intellectual intuition is not mentioned before §76, in the course of the solution to the dialectic of teleological judgment.

23. Cf. *KdrV,* A 577/B 605: "The transcendental major premise which is presupposed in the complete determination of all things is therefore no other than the representation of the sum of all reality; it is not merely a concept which, as regards its transcendental content, comprehends all predicates *under itself;* it also contains them *within itself;* and the complete determination of any and everything rests on the limitation of this *total* reality." This idea of a "sum of all reality" in turn leads to that of the *ens realissimum* as the *ground* of all reality or positive determination in finite things: "All possibility of things (that is, of the synthesis of the manifold in respect of its content) must therefore be regarded as derivative, with only one exception, namely, the possibility of that which includes in itself all reality. . . . All negations (which are the only predicates through which anything can be distinguished from an *ens realissimum*) are merely limitations of a greater, and ultimately the highest, reality" (A 578/B 606). I analyze these difficult texts in detail in "The Transcendental Ideal, and the Unity of the Critical System," *Proceedings of the Eighth International Kant-Congress* (Milwaukee: Marquette University Press, 1995), vol. I-2, pp. 521–39.

24. *KdU,* §77, p. 407; *CJ,* p. 291.

25. *L,* §2, p. 91; *JL,* p. 589.

26. This is of course a Leibnizian heritage, although many features in Kant's elaboration of the concept of God are *not* Leibnizian (most notably, the collapse of the modal categories). Hegel will remember all of this in his mature *Science of Logic.*

27. Cf. my "The Transcendental Ideal," op. cit.

28. On the Transcendental Ideal, cf. *KdrV,* A 571/B 599–A 583/B 611. On the relation between the critique of teleological judgment and moral theology ("*Ethikotheologie*") cf. *KdU,* §§86–7.

For a different view of the relation between the first and third *Critique,* see Burkhard Tuschling: "Intuitiver Verstand, absolute Identität, Idee. Thesen zu Hegels früherer Rezeption der *Kritik der Urteilskraft,*." in *Hegel und die Kritik der Urteilskraft* ed. H.-F. Fulda and R.-P. Horstmann (Stuttgart: Klett-Cotta, 1990). Tuschling's view is that the supposition of an intellectual intuition was an essential innovation of the third *Critique* and an indispensable tool to ground (i) the unity of empirical laws, (ii) the possibility of knowledge of organisms, (iii) the unity of theoretical and practical reason. He moreover argues that this "speculative" move (in the Hegelian sense) is confirmed and expanded in Kant's *Opus postumum.* See also his contribution: "The System of Transcendental Idealism: Questions Raised and Left Open in the Critique of Judgment," in *System and Teleology in Kant's Critique of Judgement* ed. Hoke Robinson. I disagree with Tuschling in that I think the problem of the unity of empirical laws and affinity of appearances is already handled in the first *Critique.* The novelty of the third *Critique* is (i) to relate the solution to this problem and the explanation of our "merely reflective" (aesthetic and teleological) judgments, and (ii) to make this relation a new tool for thinking the articulation between the legislation of reason by the concept of freedom, and legislation of understanding by the concept of nature. As I said earlier, I also think the first *Critique* offered a viable critical reduction of the Transcendental Ideal and the idea of an intuitive intellect. Cf. "The Transcendental Ideal, and the Unity of the Critical System," op. cit.

29. The objective universality is itself grounded in reflection under logical functions of judgments, and application of the categories. This point cannot be developed here. Cf. Béatrice Longuenesse: *Kant and the Capacity to Judge* (Princeton: Princeton University Press, 1998). Also "Kant et les jugements empiriques: jugements de perception et jugements d'expérience," *Kant-Studien* 86 (1995): 278–307.

30. Cf. *KdU,* §38, §40.

31. The antinomy of taste: cf. *KdU,* §56, pp. 338–39; *CJ,* p. 211. Its solution: *KdU,* §57, pp. 340–1; *CJ,* pp. 211–14.

32. Indeed, Kant sometimes calls "concept" this very activity. Cf. *KdrV,* A 103 (On the Synthesis of Recognition in Concept): "The word 'concept' could already lead us by itself to this remark. Indeed, it is this consciousness which unifies in a representation the manifold which has been successively intuited, and then reproduced."

33. Here Hegel's debt to Schelling is most apparent. Cf. Düsing: "Aesthetische Einbildungskraft und intuitiver Verstand," op. cit.

34. Cf. *KdU,* §57 Anm. I, p. 343; *CJ,* pp. 216–17.

35. This is Kant's characterization of space and time in the Transcendental Aesthetic: cf. A 25/B 39, A 32/B 48.

36. "Unnatural scholastic trick" is a loose quote from Kant's criticism of the ontological proof. Cf. *KdrV,* A 603/B 631.

37. Cf. Klaus Düsing, *Das Problem der Subjektivität in Hegels Logik* (Bonn: Bouvier, 1976), pp. 109–112. Manfred Baum, *Die Entstehung der Hegelschen Dialektik* (Bonn: Bouvier, 1986), pp. 199–200. Robert Pippin, *Hegel's Idealism* (Cambridge, U.K.: Cambridge University Press, 1989), pp. 80–86. Béatrice Longuenesse, "Hegel, Lecteur de Kant sur le Jugement," *Philosophie* 36 (1992): 42–70.

38. Cf. *L,* §1.

39. Cf. *L,* §36, p. 111; *JL,* p. 606–7. *Refl,* 3042, Ak. XVI, 629. *Refl,* 4634, Ak. XVII, 616. *KdrV,* A 68–9/B 93–4. See also Longuenesse, *Kant and the Capacity to Judge,* op. cit., pp. 86–8; pp. 108–11.

40. Cf. *KdrV,* A 162/B 202; A 189/B 232.

41. This also means that "subsumption" acquires in this context a new meaning, since the traditional relations between *Umfang* and *Inhalt* are superseded. Cf. Klaus Düsing, *Das Problem der Subjektivität in Hegels Logik,* op. cit., p. 161. See also Hegel's remarks on this point in his mature *Subjective Logic: WL* 6, pp. 308–9; *SL,* pp. 628–9.

42. Cf. A 581–82/B 609–10. "An object of the senses can be completely determined only if it is compared with all the predicates of appearances, and is represented positively or negatively by means of these predicates. But because that which constitutes the thing itself (in the appearance), i.e., the real, must be given, because otherwise it could not be thought, but that in which the real of all appearance is given is one all-embracing experience, the matter of the possibility of all objects of the senses must be presupposed as given in a complete whole (*in einem Inbegriffe*) on the limitation of which alone all possibility of empirical objects, their differences among one another and their complete determination can rely . . . " I have given a detailed commentary of this passage in "The Transcendental Ideal, and the Unity of the Critical System." See also *Kant and the Capacity to Judge,* pp. 306–10. On space and time as formal intuitions, cf. *KdrV,* B 161n., A 430/B 457n.

43. p. 304; p. 69: "What happened to Kant is what he reproached Hume for, namely he

was far from thinking the task of philosophy with sufficient determination and universality, but remained within the *subjective* and external meaning of this question ["How are synthetic a priori judgments possible?"], and believed that he had exhibited the impossibility of rational knowledge; according to his conclusions everything called philosophy would end up being a mere folly of illusory rational insight."

44. As the *Science of Logic* will confirm, Hegel has a very poor opinion of Kant's analysis of mathematical judgments as synthetic *a priori*. See *WL* 5, p. 237; *SL*, pp. 207–08. As for the Analogies of Experience, in "Faith and Knowledge," he chastises Kant for having reduced his principles of pure understanding to mere subjective principles (*GW,* p. 311; *FK,* pp. 75–6).

45. Cf. *PG,* pp. 59, 61; *PS,* pp. 38, 40–1. *WL* 6, pp. 301–51; *SL,* pp. 622–63.

46. For a long time, this has not been a very fashionable thing to say in anglophone Kant-commentary. Kant's theory of imagination and the whole "imaginary topic of transcendental psychology" (Strawson) was to be excused from the table of serious philosophy. But the fact is, understanding Kant's theory of imagination is an essential condition for understanding his relation to his idealist successors as well as to his empiricist predecessors.

47. "The original synthetic unity of apperception comes to the fore in the transcendental deduction of the categories, and is recognized as being also the principle of the figurative synthesis, or of the forms of intuition, and space and time themselves are conceived as synthetic unities and productive imagination: spontaneity and absolute synthetic activity are conceived as the principle of sensibility, which before had been characterized merely as receptivity. This original synthetic unity (. . .) is the principle of the productive imagination, of the unity which is blind, drowned in difference and not distinguishing itself from it; and of the unity positing identically the difference, but differentiating itself from it, as understanding." (*GW,* pp. 304–5; *FK,* p. 70) On Kant's "analytic unity of apperception," cf. B 134n.

48. See Sally Sedgwick, "Pippin on Hegel's Critique of Kant," *International Philosophical Quarterly* XXXIII, no. 3 (September 1993): 273–83.

49. A 79/B 105.

50. Cf. *GW,* pp. 307–8; *FK,* p. 73. *WL* 6, p. 254; *SL,* p. 584. On the evolution of Hegel's thought between the early Jena period and the *Phenomenology of Spirit,* cf. Rolf-Peter Horstmann: "Probleme der Wandlungen in Hegels Jenaer Systemkonzeptionen," *Philosophische Rundschau* 19 (1972): 87–118; H. S. Harris, *Hegel's Development, II: Night Thoughts (Jena 1801–1806)* (Oxford: Clarendon, 1983); Manfred Baum, *Die Entstehung der Hegelschen Dialektik,* op. cit.; Bernard Bourgeois, *Le Droit Natural de Hegel* (Paris: Vrin, 1986).

51. I thank Ken Westphal for pressing me on this point.

52. Cf. *WL* 6, p. 264; *SL,* pp. 591–2. See also my "Hegel, Lecteur de Kant sur le Jugement," op. cit.

53. Cf. *WL* 5, p. 44; *SL,* p. 50.

13

Kant, Hegel, and the Fate of "the" Intuitive Intellect

KENNETH R. WESTPHAL

I

Kant's remarks on intellectual intuition captivated Schelling, Fichte, and Hegel, and the theme of intellectual intuition has entranced many Hegel scholars. Hegel's early Jena writings on Kant are complex, compressed, and cryptic. Nevertheless, I have become convinced that much of Hegel's interpretation of Kant at that time is in fact quite sophisticated and subtle, although often obscure and still developing.[1] Understanding and learning from Hegel's early writings, however, requires overcoming widespread unclarity about the nature of "the" intuitive intellect. It is widely assumed that, because it is nondiscursive, an intuitive intellect is aconceptual. That is how Schelling understood it, and that is often the view of the early Hegel, too. Most commentators – whether sympathetic or critical – have followed them in this assumption.[2] This is *not*, however, how Kant understood an intuitive intellect. As Moltke Gram has shown, Schelling and Fichte each have different accounts of "intellectual intuition," their accounts differ from Kant's, and indeed Kant discusses three distinct views under the heading "intellectual intuition."[3] Kant's three accounts of an intuitive intellect are these: (i) an intellect that knows things in themselves independent of any conditions of sensibility, (ii) an intellect that creates its own objects, and (iii) an intellect that intuits the sum total of the whole of nature. Gram points out that these accounts are logically independent of each other. The first account only requires knowledge *sans* sensibility; it does not require that objects are created in the act of knowing them, which is the hallmark of the second account. Moreover, neither the first nor the second accounts specify whether the object known is nature as a totality, which is the hallmark of the third account. Conversely, the third account is defined in terms of a certain kind of understanding, rather than the lack of sensibility, and it is silent about whether the object of knowledge is created in the act of knowing it. The one case in which these three accounts would be compatible is the case of God's divine intuition of creation as a whole. Indeed, Kant insists that God is the only plausible example of an intuitive intellect.[4] Kant's three accounts share one point in common: Each of them concerns knowledge of an object or objects other than the intellect. Fichte's account of intellectual intuition concerns immediate knowledge of the self.[5] Schelling's account of intellectual intuition concerns the identity of concept and object in absolute knowledge, in which both universal and particular and finite and infinite are united.[6] Indeed, on Schelling's view these supposed contrasts are indistinguishable because they are undifferentiated; in the absolute everything is simply one and the same. This "pure absolute identity" is supposed to be evident in pure intellectual intuition.

In the *Science of Logic,* Hegel acknowledged that Kant's philosophy formed the basis and point of departure for modern German philosophy, and his early writings show that from the outset this is true for Hegel's own philosophy.[7] Consequently, it is worth examining Kant's notions of an intuitive intellect more closely, to see that, in Kant's view, intellectual intuition (in any of the three versions distinguished by Gram) is not aconceptual. Kant does indeed say that if our understanding were intuitive, it would lack both concepts and intuitions − concepts, that is, "which concern merely the possibility of an object" and intuitions "which give us something, without thereby allowing us to know it as an object."[8] This is to say, an intuitive intellect would not have *our* kind of discursive concepts and sensible intuitions. Kant does call it an intuitive *intellect* (*Verstand*), however, not a power of intuition (nor an archetypal power of intuition).[9] The intellect (*Verstand*) is the power of concepts, and an intuitive intellect is an understanding "in the most general sense of the term."[10] Thus in Kant's view, intuition and concept are not eliminated, instead they are *identical* for an intuitive intellect. This identity of concept and intuition also holds for an intuitive intellect in Gram's other two senses. An intuitive intellect in Gram's second sense, according to Kant, is an *intellectus archetypus* − an intellect that creates objects by knowing them. If the creations of an intuitive intellect are *objects* and not just bare or indeterminate particulars then they have characteristics and are of kinds. A discursive intellect (like ours) represents such characteristics and kinds through general concepts that are distinct from sensory intuitions of the objects that instantiate them. An archetypal intuitive intellect does not represent objects or their kinds in this way. That does not mean that such an intellect, however, on Kant's view, dispenses altogether with any or all kinds of concepts by which to identify objects and their characteristics. Here, too, concept and intuition would be identical in, not absent from, an intuitive intellect. Kant insists in the third *Critique* that an intuitive intellect (in Gram's third sense) "proceeds from the *synthetically universal* (the intuition of a whole as a whole) to the particular, i.e., from the whole to the parts," and this, Kant immediately adds, requires that such an intellect have a "presentation of the whole" (*Vorstellung des Ganzen*).[11] In connection with an intuitive *intellect,* this *Vorstellung* cannot be simply a sensory intuition, but must be some kind of concept. This way of putting the point comes from the first *Critique,* to which Kant refers directly in this connection.[12] In the first *Critique,* Kant describes an intuitive intellect as one that, through its self-consciousness, supplies itself the manifold of intuition and thus as one "through whose presentation (*Vorstellung*) the objects of the presentation at once exist."[13] Though we cannot very well understand what sort of "concepts" or "presentations" – *Vorstellungen* – an intuitive intellect has, Kant is quite clear that an intuitive intellect is *an intellect,* that is, a power of *concepts,* though "in the most general sense of the term." Here, again, we must understand concepts to be identical with, rather than to be absent from, such intuitions. We will seriously misunderstand Hegel's better reasoning if we mistakenly assume that Kant's intuitive intellect dispenses altogether with concepts.

II

Unfortunately, Schelling and the early Hegel encourage this misunderstanding because their models of intellectual intuition are nondiscursive and aconceptual. Klaus Düsing has argued very persuasively that Schelling and Hegel did not hold exactly the same views about "intellectual intuition," "speculation," or the "absolute identity" that they supposedly reveal.[14] Before 1801, Schelling conceived "absolute identity" as an absolutely simple, undifferentiated unity. This ultimate undifferentiated unity simply cannot be known through philosophical reflection. Philosophy can only approach the absolute through a negative theology, although the absolute can be made manifest in art. Late in 1800, Schelling opted for a distinctive "philosophy of identity." In this view, speculative reason is superior to reflective understanding; the absolute is completely knowable through reason; this knowledge constitutes "metaphysics," the first and primary part of philosophy; and the absolute is conceived (like Hegel's) as an internally differentiated unity (although Schelling also retained his earlier notion of an undifferentiated absolute). Most important for our present purposes, Schelling claimed that knowledge of the absolute is constructed in pure intellectual intuition, which is altogether divorced from reflective thought. Philosophical reflection does not and cannot prepare us for intellectual intuition; one must simply have intellectual intuition of the absolute, and on that basis recognize its possibility and its achievement. Schelling's retention of an undifferentiated absolute and his claim that pure intellectual intuition has nothing to do with reflective thought show that Schelling's philosophy of identity is committed to a nondiscursive, nonconceptual account of knowledge.[15]

Hegel, in contrast, learned already in Frankfurt from Hölderlin to conceive "absolute identity" in terms of the ultimate and essential integration of all differences. In his 1801 philosophy of identity, Hegel held that speculation is the synthesis of intellectual intuition and reflective thought. Although Hegel still gave reflective (i.e., discursive, conceptual) thought a subordinate role, its role is nevertheless constitutive of speculative knowledge. The constitutive role of reflective thought is restricted, however, to demonstrating (in "logic") the ultimate inadequacy of finite reflective concepts for grasping the absolute. This demonstration, Hegel claimed, prepares us for speculative knowledge of the absolute via intellectual intuition. Hegel's account of knowledge at this time is completely ahistorical. Because intellectual intuition transcends reflective thought, it is nondiscursive. Because Hegel conceived the absolute as internally differentiated, it is possible that he did not view intellectual intuition as aconceptual, though if it involves concepts, they cannot be the familiar kind of "finite" discursive concepts found in ordinary thought and in philosophical reflection. However that matter may be settled (if it can be settled), Hegel simply assumed the possibility of such intellectual intuition, and he simply assumed that we indeed can have such intellectual intuitions of the absolute.

I shall now highlight the very important problems intellectual intuition caused Hegel, an important cause of his rejection of intellectual intuition, and some very important ways in which Hegel's mature epistemology built on Kant's account of discursive judgment in articulating the possibility and defending the legitimacy of a conceptual grasp of the totality of the world. Even if (somehow) Hegel's notion of intellectual intuition allows a role for some kind of nondiscursive concepts, that role is so meager that it cannot solve, indeed it cannot even address, the problems confronting intellectual intuition, all of which stem from the fact that it supposedly transcends discursive, reflective, conceptual thought. The first problem is revealed by Hegel's attitude toward Kant's arguments for the transcendental ideality of space and time.

III

The troubling point about Hegel's early view of Kant is his disregard of Kant's direct arguments for transcendental idealism in the Transcendental Aesthetic. In *Faith and Knowledge* Hegel notes, obliquely and in passing, that Kant holds that space and time are only forms of human intuition.[16] Hegel's stress on the role of the understanding in integrating our formal intuitions of space and time does not respond to this crucial set of Kant's arguments.[17] We know that in his mature writings and lectures Hegel accepted the standard objection to those arguments, the problem of the neglected alternative.[18] We know that this objection was commonplace among Hegel's immediate predecessors.[19] I have argued elsewhere that, properly formulated, this objection is sound.[20] It can even be shown that this objection follows on grounds internal to Kant's first *Critique* (see below, §VI). We do not know, however, when Hegel first considered or accepted the objection to Kant's arguments for transcendental idealism based on the neglected alternative. Perhaps that information was lost with

Hegel's 1789 notes on Locke, Berkeley, Hume, and Kant; but that is a mere possibility.[21] We do know that in 1795 Schelling wrote to Hegel that Kant had provided the proper results, but not their premises.[22] From that, along with Hegel's remarks about Kant in his early writings, we can be sure that Hegel was unpersuaded by Kant's arguments for transcendental idealism. Finding Kant's arguments unpersuasive, however, does not meet the general philosophical obligation to provide their detailed critical assessment and, potentially, refutation. As it stands, Hegel flatly begged the question against Kant in his early publications, including *Faith and Knowledge,* by disregarding Kant's direct arguments for the transcendental ideality of space and time.[23]

IV

This is a genuine problem for Hegel's treatment of Kant. It is only an instance, however, of a graver problem. Hegel's bold appropriation and transformation of Kant's description of an intuitive intellect is astonishing. The problem with Hegel's contention is far more serious than has been noticed. The problem is that the very model of an intuitive intellect is a model of a kind of knowledge in which there is no distinction between thinking and knowing. Because Hegel not only espoused this model, but was enthralled by it, he (mistakenly) assumed that the ability to conceive or to think this model shows that the model is true and is known to be true. These assumptions flatly beg the question against Kant and indeed against anyone who rejects the idea of an intuitive intellect as a model for human knowledge. By committing himself to the model of an intuitive intellect, Hegel committed himself to an account of knowledge to which question-begging is in principle endemic. In this regard, I suggest, Hegel's initial disregard of Kant's arguments for the transcendental ideality of space and time is no accident.[24] Nor is it an accident that the early Hegel, like Schelling, shows much more enthusiasm and conviction than proof or evidence for the absolute speculative standpoint supposedly attained by intellectual intuition.[25]

V

In his early publications, Hegel was quite willing to raise the problem of question-begging in general, as well as to press it against Reinhold,[26] and once in passing he mentioned the Dilemma of the Criterion classically formulated by Sextus Empiricus. That dilemma is the following:

[I]n order to decide the dispute which has arisen about the criterion [of truth], we must possess an accepted criterion by which we shall be able to judge the dispute; and in order to possess an accepted criterion, the dispute about the criterion must first be decided. And when the argument thus reduces itself to a form of circular reasoning the discovery

288   KENNETH R. WESTPHAL

of the criterion becomes impracticable, since we do not allow [those who make knowledge claims] to adopt a criterion by assumption, while if they offer to judge the criterion by a criterion we force them to a regress *ad infinitum*. And furthermore, since demonstration requires a demonstrated criterion, while the criterion requires an approved demonstration, they are forced into circular reasoning.[27]

This dilemma concerns question-begging at a very fundamental level, namely, regarding the very criteria for settling either substantive or methodological disputes. In the *Skeptizismus* essay, Hegel dismissed this problem because he thought it only concerns discursive, conceptual knowledge, which he called "reflection." He thought that he escaped this problem through intellectual intuition of the absolute, which he called "speculation."[28] Not until the summer of 1804 did Hegel recognize that his own philosophy, too, must avoid begging the question against alternative philosophical views.

An important stimulus to Hegel's reconsideration of intellectual intuition has been identified by Kurt Rainer Meist, namely, G. E. Schulze's brilliant anonymous satire and critique of Schelling and Hegel in his "Aphorismen über das Absolute" (1803).[29] Among much else, Schulze showed that Schelling's and Hegel's appeal to intellectual intuition is indistinguishable from Jacobi's appeal to "feeling" (something for which Hegel roundly criticized Jacobi in *Faith and Knowledge*), in part because in the Absolute nothing is distinct from anything else, and in part because (certainly) Schelling's and (probably) Hegel's intuitionism repudiated concepts, which are required to distinguish, differentiate, or otherwise identify the characteristics either of things or of knowledge. Schulze also expressly raised the problem involved in providing mere assurances that one knows the truth, along with the issue of how ordinary people are supposed to ascend to the absolute. In this connection he uses the metaphor of a ladder – a key problem and metaphor in Hegel's description of the aim and role of the *Phenomenology*.[30] Like the Dilemma of the Criterion, these concerns about the question-begging involved in mere assurances (i.e., mere assertions) and finding a ladder to genuine knowledge stem directly from Pyrrhonian skepticism.[31] In brief, Schulze's "Aphorisms" prompted Hegel to recognize that his speculative idealism cannot evade, but rather must address Pyrrhonian skepticism.

Following the publication of Schulze's "Aphorismen" Hegel clearly recognized in "Zwei Anmerkungen zum System" (probably written in Summer 1804) that the problem of question-begging is especially acute for any philosophy, such as his own, that recognizes the holistic character of knowledge and justification.[32] These two Remarks are only fragments of drafts, and they are characteristically compressed and difficult. Nevertheless, they reward careful scrutiny. In the first Remark, Hegel contends that a philosophy has only one idea, and this idea must be one and the same at the beginning and the end of a circularly organized philosophical system. Only in this way, he contends, can a philosophy avoid having an initial proposition that would require either a prior and independent starting point or subsequent mediation (*via* articulation in subsequent propositions). Either prospect would inevitably result in something other than absolute, that is, unconditioned knowledge.[33] The implication, pretty clearly, is that in order to be absolute, philosophical knowledge must avoid the problem of infinite regress posed by Sextus Empiricus, but also avoid the incompleteness involved in a progress of knowledge. Hegel's emphasis on completeness and circularity strongly suggests the holistic character of his conception of philosophy, and, in particular, Hegel's holistic conception of philosophical justification.[34]

Hegel's second Remark consists of four paragraphs. In the first paragraph he addresses the distinction between knowledge and its object. He acknowledges the common presumption that knowledge and its supposed objects are at best only contingently related, but he denies that such a distinction between knowledge and its object is tenable because these two moments must become one.[35] In the second paragraph (quoted below), Hegel acknowledges that it is hard to convince common sense not to view the relation of knowledge and its supposed object as anything other than contingent or accidental. In the third paragraph, Hegel claims already to have shown that the commonsense distinction between knowledge and its objects is null and void.[36] What remains of the fourth paragraph is the beginning of one incomplete sentence. In it Hegel again acknowledges that others regard the relation of knowledge to its supposed object differently than he does.[37] In a marginal note to this last paragraph (also incomplete), Hegel acknowledges that of course the "reality" of these two "components" (*Glieder*) of the opposition – that is, knowledge and its object – must be recognized, although this distinction must be philosophically reconstructed.[38]

This progression of topics in the second remark suggests rather clearly that Hegel is quite aware of his profound disagreement with commonsense, potentially skeptical ways of viewing the relation between knowledge and its objects, of his obligation to give the commonsense experiential distinction between knowledge and object its philosophical due, and of the variety of ways in which this distinction is construed. This awareness suggests that Hegel now recognizes that he, too, must avoid begging the question. When these remarks are contrasted with Hegel's earlier optimistic confidence about intellectual intuition placing him beyond the problem of question-begging, and when they are taken in connection with the holistic character of philosophy stressed in the first of Hegel's two Remarks, this suggestion is significantly reinforced.

This suggestion is further reinforced when the second paragraph of the second Remark is considered in its entirety. There Hegel states:

However, it is difficult to bring ordinary thought away from the fixing of this being for itself of knowledge and of its object. The *distinct knowledge,* that such a *being* for self of *diverse* [moments] destroys *itself,* underlies the habit of ordinary knowledge to reify the opposed [moments], and thereby to give them each a semblance of a particular subsistence for itself, so that it *posits* the *certainty* as the *knowledge of such a being for itself,* but connects the certainty with the form of *abstract being for itself* in such a way that *it* separates *that knowledge* [of that being for itself] *from it* [from that being for itself], and then again it divides within itself this knowing [*gewisse*] and known, as if there were a lot of such certainties.[39]

In this paragraph, Hegel explicitly discusses the supposed "certainty" that knowledge and its object are distinct and independent, and (at the end) Hegel notes that there are many ways in which this idea may be conceived and held to be "certain." He claims to have a deeper knowledge of this relation (enunciated in the first two clauses of the second sentence), and both of his two Remarks are dedicated to refuting in principle such cognitively opaque distinctions between knowledge and its object, by showing that knowledge and its object are not merely contingently or accidentally related. At the end of the first Remark, Hegel quite explicitly acknowledges that such refutations must not only be "for us" as absolute philosophers, but must be provided by philosophy from within itself in order to show (*zeigen*) that its claims are valid.[40] Between that point and his marginal comment regarding the importance of accounting for the commonsense distinction between knowledge and its object,[41] it appears that Hegel is well on his way to recognizing that absolute idealists, too, must avoid begging the question. This realization prepares Hegel to reconsider Sextus's Dilemma of the Criterion as *the* central methodological problem addressed in the Introduction to the *Phenomenology.*

If there was any lingering doubt in Hegel's mind about his rejection of all brands of philosophy of identity, recognizing that even absolute idealists must avoid question-begging and must address Sextus's Dilemma of the Criterion seals the fate of intellectual intuition in Hegel's theory of knowledge.[42] Accordingly, the Dilemma of the Criterion becomes *the* central methodological problem posed in the Introduction to Hegel's *Phenomenology,* where he develops a very subtle and powerful response to it.[43] His response involves an unqualified commitment to a discursive, conceptual model of human knowledge, a commitment he retains to the end of his career.[44] Although Hegel's mature epistemology distinguishes reason and understanding (or intellect, *Verstand*), he always insists that reason can only function by reintegrating conceptual distinctions made by the intellect. In the *Science of Logic,* on those very few occasions where he mentions intellectual intuition in connection with his own views, Hegel stresses as strongly and as clearly as possible that such supposed intuitions are definite and determinate – and thus genuinely contentful or significant – only insofar as they are articulated conceptually.[45] Hegel's mature account of absolute knowledge repudiates the aconceptual accounts of knowledge that are central to Schelling's and Hegel's own earlier accounts of the intuitive intellect. Hegel criticizes aconceptual intuitionism decisively, both with regard to empirical knowledge (in "Sense Certainty") and with regard to philosophical knowledge generally (in connection with Jacobi in the "Third Attitude of Thought Toward Objectivity").[46] His objections to aconceptual intuitionism are quite general, quite powerful, and by no means hold only against Jacobi.[47] In particular, they also hold against Schelling, whose intellectual intuition plays no role in the *Phenomenology* – other than as a position criticized internally and refuted by *reductio ad absurdum,* especially in "Observing Reason."[48] Indeed, in his *Lectures on the History of Philosophy* (1825), Hegel formulates the main problem with Schelling's philosophy in a way that makes plain the weakness it shares with Jacobi's "immediate knowledge" (i.e., intuitionism): "Nothing could be more convenient than to posit cognition on the basis of immediate knowledge, of what pops into one's head." Schelling's esoterism – some people have intellectual intuition of the absolute, some don't – only discredits his "standpoint of speculation" and its "pure intellectual intuition" further; retreating to a defensive esoterism abandons the project of accounting for *human* knowledge in general.[49] Hegel's remark from his history lectures directly recalls his parallel criticism of Jacobi in the *Encyclopedia,*[50] and directly recalls the remark with which he first introduces the problem of question-begging in the Introduction to the *Phenomenology:* "*one* barren assurance counts as much as another."[51] Only a discursive form of knowledge involving justification and critical assessment can avoid the crucial problem of question-begging.

VI

Hegel's mature epistemology incorporates several important points from Kant's Transcendental Ideal into his reinterpretation of Kant's Transcendental Deduction and Refutation of Idealism. By incorporating these points, Hegel's mature discursive and conceptual account of "absolute knowing" performs some of the functions Kant assigned to the intuitive intellect. Hegel suggests this line of thought already in *Faith and Knowledge* and elaborates it in the very important remark in the *Science of Logic,* "On the Concept of General."[52]

In *Faith and Knowledge,* Hegel recognized that Kant did and must hold that things in themselves are the source of sensory affection.[53] Moreover, Hegel also recognized that, on Kant's account, the contents of our sensations must be both varied and regular enough that we are able to bring them to intuition under concepts in determinate cognitive judgments about experienced objects. Kant called this variety and regularity of the content of our sensations the "transcendental affinity of the manifold of intuition"; for brevity I shall refer to it as "transcendental affinity." I have formulated this issue more precisely than Hegel did. Nevertheless, this is a point to which Hegel returned frequently in his Jena publications, and he was right that Kant's philosophy faces a grave problem accounting for it.[54] Transcendental affinity is a constitutive condition of the possibility of experience, and it is a formal condition of the possibility of experience. (Formal conditions allow particulars to be ordered, including such ordering as similarity or frequency.) This condition is fulfilled, however, neither by the a priori conceptual conditions of experience set out in the Transcendental Analytic nor by the a priori intuitive conditions set out in the Transcendental Aesthetic. Transcendental affinity is a constitutive, a priori necessary, formal, and yet also *material* condition of the possibility of experience. Although Kant repeatedly tries to account for the satisfaction of this condition by appeal to transcendental idealism, his arguments on this head all fail because he conflates the *ratio cognoscendi* of this condition with its *ratio essendi*. We can know on the basis of Kant's Transcendental Analytic that there must be a certain minimal (yet a priori indeterminable) degree of variety and regularity among the contents of our sensations in order for us to be able to subsume them under our concepts in cognitive judgments and thus to distinguish ourselves from objects and thus to be self-conscious.[55] Kant's transcendental idealism, howver, cannot account for the satisfaction of this condition at all. Human understanding can only function, and can only afford unified self-conscious experience, if – independently of us and our cognitive structure and activity – the objects and events we sense display sufficient variety and similarity for us to form judgments about them. This case shows that transcendental analysis of the necessary a priori conditions of unified self-conscious experience can demonstrate a priori that objectively real, mind-independent structures are necessarily required by a certain kind of subject in order for it to be self-conscious. This is precisely the prospect exploited by the neglected alternative, by Hegel's internal critique of Kant's idealism, and by Hegel's regressive quasitranscendental arguments for realism.[56]

It is worth examining briefly how the neglected alternative exploits this prospect. Seeing that this case parallels the case of transcendental affinity relieves at least some of the onus on Hegel's disregard of Kant's arguments in the Transcendental Aesthetic for transcendental idealism; the parallel between these two cases shows that Hegel at least recognized the relevant principles for effective criticism of those arguments.

Briefly, Kant argues as follows: Our concept of space is a priori. Our concept of space can be a priori only if its content is (or is based on) space as a form of our (human) sensibility. If this premise is true, transcendental idealism follows.[57] This key premise is defended by arguing by elimination against three possible alternatives: Our representation of space is innate, our representation of space is a posteriori, or we have direct acquaintance with space itself.

Even if our concept of space is a priori, however, and even if Kant's objections to those three alternatives are sound, there is a fourth possibility. On this (possible) view, our concept of space is a priori because its content is based on the spatial form of our outer sensibility, where that "spatial form" is understood as a receptivity or a sensitivity only to objects located in and occupying some region of (mind-independent) space.[58] On this view, only objects that in fact have spatial characteristics can affect or stimulate our outer sensibility, but those objects are spatially located, extended, and (potentially) moveable, regardless of whether we intuit them. Kant objects to the innateness hypothesis because it is arbitrary and explains nothing. The idea that an a priori concept of space could be based on a spatial form of outer intuition (in the sense just specified) is not arbitrary and is explanatory if thought and knowledge are based in action, if action is required for life, and if human life, action, and thought transpire in a world of objects and events that occupy (mind-independent) space. (Although I have not been able to identify this line of thought clearly in Hegel's early writings, it is central to his theory of knowledge in the *Phenomenology*.[59]) This is a possibility that Kant does not consider (nor does Allison). Hence this is a possibility that Kant does not argue against (nor does Allison). Thus Kant's argument by elimination is a non sequitur because he does not consider all the relevant alternatives. The neglected alternative proposes another candidate for an a priori, transcendental, formal condition of unified self-conscious experience (for any being with a form of outer receptivity that is only sensitive to spatial objects) that is nevertheless fulfilled by mind-independent facts about objects located in and occupying (mind-independent) space.

As noted above, the affinity of the manifold of sensory intuition is a transcendental condition of the possibility of self-conscious experience. The fact that this affinity of the manifold must be fulfilled by the transcendentally real, noumenal source of sensory affections provides yet another important reason why Hegel thought Kant had more knowledge of the supersensible ground of experience than he admitted.[60] Given Kant's distinction between appearances and things in themselves as objects of discursive and intuitive intellects respectively, this provides yet another important reason why Hegel thought Kant came closer to the actual experience of an intuitive intellect than he admitted. Bearing this point in mind helps to show that in *Faith and Knowledge* Hegel in fact did what he claimed to do. He identified a problem in Kant's theory of judgment that arguably arises both in Kant's theoretical and in his practical philosophies: Hegel contends that Kant does not have an adequate account of the relation between discursive concepts and the particulars subsumed under them, whether our judgments involve sensations or inclinations.[61]

Kant held that the synthetic unity of apperception is the highest point reached in the *Critique of Pure Reason*.[62] Hegel seized upon this idea and pointed out that Kant thus gave priority to the synthetic unity of apperception over the analytic unity of apperception, the "I think" that must be able to accompany each of "my" representations. The analytical unity may have priority over the synthetic unity as its *ratio cognoscendi,* but the synthetic unity of apperception takes priority over the analytic unity as its *ratio essendi,* precisely because actual instances of self-consciousness only occur on the basis of actual cognitive judgments by which we both identify objects and distinguish ourselves from them. This is the highest point of "synthetic judgments *a priori,*" in Hegel's view.[63] In this point what there is, what characteristics it has, what is thought about it, and what is judged true of it are identical – identical in content, and in at least one sense identical in number: The existing object is one and the same as the object known.[64] Even in *Faith and Knowledge,* Hegel clearly suggested the difference in form between them that he made explicit in the *Phenomenology:* the particular extant object known is "in the form of being," and the predicate truly ascribed to it is "in the form of thought."[65] (I do not claim that Hegel clearly maintained this distinction in *Faith and Knowledge;* quite the contrary. Even in that early essay, however, Hegel generally insisted on some sort of mediated – complex rather than "empty" – identity.[66])

VII

The two points I have sketched – Hegel's ultimate rejection of aconceptual or intellectual intuition and his reinterpretation of Kant's deduction of synthetic judgments a priori – are related. Although Hegel regarded Kant's account of the Table of Judgments as inadequate, he also regarded it as extremely instructive.[67] In his third remark on his Table of Judgments, Kant noted that a proper disjunctive judgment divides up the whole of a specific range ("sphere") of predicates relevant to a particular possible cognition.[68] Denying one predicate of the relevant kind of subject entails that another predicate within that range must be true of that subject; conversely, affirming a predicate of a relevant subject is tantamount to denying of that subject the other predicates within that range. I think Hegel seized upon this idea and recognized that singular categorical judgments and hypothetical judgments both presuppose disjunctive judgments. Hypothetical judgments require disjunctive judgments because establishing any judgment of the form, "If A then B," requires judging that no relevant alternative to B results (or follows) from A. Such conjoined hypothetical and disjunctive judgments are, in fact, central to Kant's Analogies of Experience.[69] If this is correct, then the categorical judgments required to identify objects in synthetic judgments a priori about them – judgments that are required for us to be self-conscious – also require disjunctive judgments whereby we discriminate any one object from other objects. If such disjunctive judgments require a grasp of the whole of the relevant range of alternatives within a class ("sphere"), then singular cognitive judgments about objects are possible only on the basis of holistic judgments about the relevant class of objects and predicates (i.e., about the relevant alternatives). This requires (within any "sphere") a complete set of mutually exclusive categories, at least some of which are in fact instantiated. This may (and likely will) differ significantly from a complete set of logically possible categories, such as the traditional "sum of all [logical] possibility," or taken as instantiated, the traditional *ens realissimum* – the topics of Kant's Ideal of Pure Reason.[70] (Is it logically possible that we could perceive more colors than are found in the standard spectrum of visible light?) Hegel's point is that actual hypothetical and categorical judgments are codetermined, and they are codetermined only in connection with extant things and events.[71] Note that this way of making Hegel's point decouples it from intellectual intuition, and thus suggests how Hegel could retain this view in his mature philosophy without relying on any kind of intuitionism.

In brief, Hegel held that hypothetical and categorical judgments are codetermined, that they can be codetermined only within a complete set or "sphere" of contrasting predicates, and that they can be codetermined only in connection with extant things and events. For brevity, I shall call this Hegel's "codetermination thesis."[72] This thesis has several important implications: (i) If Hegel is right about the codetermination thesis, then he detected a tension between Kant's account of (categorical) synthetic judgments a priori about objects and his denial of a discursive grasp of the totality of the world: Ultimately, local wholes or sets of predicates can be determined, for analogous reasons, only in relation to the whole set of such local wholes or spheres of predicates. This would have led Hegel, I suspect, to read a good deal into Kant's remark in the Third Analogy that "all appearances lie and must lie, in one nature, because without this *a priori* unity no unity of experience is possible, and therefore no determination of objects within it, would be possible," and would have led Hegel to recognize the constitutive importance of the regulative principles expounded in Kant's Transcendental Dialectic.[73] (ii) The codetermination thesis suggests how Hegel appropriated the Spinozistic slogan, *omnis determinatio est negatio:*[74] The determination of any single individual (or any particular group of individuals) as having a particular property is possible only on the basis of a disjunctive judgment that distinguishes that individual (or group) from other individuals (or groups) falling within the relevant class of alternative predicates (or kinds of groups).[75] (iii) The codetermination thesis suggests why Hegel did not worry about Sextus' Tropes of Relativity: according to Hegel's ontological holism, things in fact are what they are only in their relations to other things, including their relations of mutual contradistinction. This is one doctrine the mature Hegel retained and developed from the early *Skeptizismus* essay.[76] (iv) Given Kant's claim that only an intuitive intellect could grasp the whole, the codetermination thesis would seem to give enormous impetus, both to ascribing to Kant more reliance on such an intellect than he allowed, and to developing such an account of human knowledge. (v) Hegel came to realize, however, that judgments, including disjunctive judgments, are determinate only insofar as they are articulate, that is, only insofar as they are specified conceptually. This insight, along with the problem of question-begging, posed a central problem for Hegel's mature philosophy: establishing both the legitimacy and the actuality of a conceptual grasp of the totality. (vi) Cognitive judgments, whether disjunctive or categorical, require (*inter alia*) that the conceptions (predicates) they involve are in fact instantiated in the world. Hegel's criticism of Kant's idealism based on transcendental affinity and his regressive, naturalistic reconstruction of Kant's Transcendental Deduction and Refutation of Idealism provide strong grounds for showing that the conceptions involved in our cognitive judgments are in fact instantiated in the world. Finally, (vii) the problems involved in establishing that a range of instantiated predicates forms an exhaustive and mutually exclusive set lead directly to Hegel's fallibilism and his doctrine of determinate negation, according to which (in part) a positive thesis is justified only through an internal critical evaluation and rejection of its alternatives. This thesis holds, according to Hegel, both in philosophical and in empirical theory.[77]

VIII

I fully recognize that many important themes in Hegel's mature philosophy are sounded in his early writings. Due to the prominent role they give to an untenable, soon-to-be-rejected intellectual intuitionism, even when disambiguated, however, Hegel's early writings provide only very incomplete guides to interpreting his mature philosophy, especially his epistemology.[78]

Notes

1. See Klaus Düsing, "Ästhetische Einbildungskraft und Intuitiver Verstand: Kants Lehre und Hegels spekulativ-idealistische Umdeutung," *Hegel-Studien* 21 (1986): 87–128; Béatrice Longuenesse, "Point of View of Man or Knowledge of God," in this volume; and my essays, "On Hegel's Early Critique of Kant's *Metaphysical Foundations of Natural Science*," in *Hegel and the Philosophy of Nature*, ed. S. Houlgate (Albany: State University of New York Press, 1998), pp. 137–66, and "Kant, Hegel, and the Transcendental Material Conditions of Possible Experience," *Bulletin of the Hegel Society of Great Britain* 33 (1996): 23–41.

2. This assumption is also shared, for example, by Werner Pluhar, who in his translation glosses an "intuitive" intellect as one that is not "discursive, i.e., conceptual" (Kant, *Critique of Judgment*; Indianapolis: Hackett, 1987, p. 248). I shall refer to Kant's works by the initials of his German titles and by volume:page.line numbers of *Kants gesammelte Schriften*, ed. Königlich-Preußische [now Deutsche] Akademie der Wissenschaften, (Berlin: G. Reimer [now de Gruyter], 1902 –), usually referred to as

"Akademie-Ausgabe." I also use the standard designations of the two editions ("A" and "B") of Kant's first *Critique*.

3. Moltke S. Gram, "Intellectual Intuition: The Continuity Thesis," *Journal of the History of Ideas* 52 (1981): 287–304. Gram does not discuss Hegel's views in this article.

4. Reflexion 6048; Ak 28:433 (not cited by Gram). Gram contends further that these three accounts are incompatible. According to Gram, the first and second accounts are incompatible because the first excludes, while the third requires, the creation of the object known. The first and second accounts are incompatible with the third because they exclude any distinction between phenomena and noumena, whereas the third specifically concerns knowledge of "phenomena." Gram overstated the case, however. In fact, Kant's discussion of the third account (*KdU* §77) does not mention "phenomena" (or "noumena"); it only discusses nature as a totality and the "synthetically universal . . . intuition of a whole as a whole." Things in themselves, as objects of an intellectual intuition *sans* sensibility (*per* the first account) are only independent of the act of knowledge for finite, nondivine intellects. Kant is perfectly happy to countenance God creating things in themselves. The problem with Gram's account, I believe, results from his interpreting these three accounts from within Kant's transcendental idealist account of human understanding.

5. Actually, Fichte had at least four distinct senses of "intellectual intuition," each of which concern various aspects of self-knowledge. See Daniel Breazeale's excellent discussion, "Fichte's *Nova Methodo Phenomenologica*," *Revue internationale de philosophie* 206 (1998): 587–616.

6. Gram summarizes these points (op. cit., pp. 288–9) and documents and analyzes them thereafter. Gram initially claims, however, that Schelling's account of intellectual intuition involves direct acquaintance with our own mental *acts*, and that such acquaintance involves the knowing subject creating its object (ibid., p. 289). This characterization does not, however, quite fit either the passages Gram quotes from Schelling, or Gram's analysis of those passages (ibid., pp. 301–2).

7. *WL* I, *GW* 11:31 note; *GW* 21:46 note. Hegel's works are cited by abbreviations of the German title according to volume:page.line numbers of the critical edition of H. Buchner and O. Pöggeler, eds., *Gesammelte Werke* (published by the Rheinisch-Westfälische Akademie der Wissenschaften in association with the Deutsche Forschungsgemeinschaft; Hamburg: Felix Meiner Verlag, 1968–; abbreviated "*GW*"). The pagination from this edition has been reproduced in the recent translations of Hegel's early writings referred to here and below, viz., *Between Kant and Hegel: Texts in the Development of Post-Kantian Idealism* trans. and ed. G. di Giovanni and H. S. Harris (Albany: State University of New York Press, 1985); *The Difference Between Fichte's and Schelling's System of Philosophy*, trans. and ed. H. S. Harris and W. Cerf (Albany: State University of New York Press, 1977); *Faith and Knowledge*, trans. and ed. W. Cerf and H. S. Harris (Albany: State University of New York Press, 1977). Occasionally I also refer to *Werke in zwanzig Bänden*, ed. E. Moldenhauer and K. M. Michel (Frankfurt am Main: Suhrkamp Verlag, 1971), abbreviated "*MM*."

8. "Wäre nämlich unser Verstand anschauend, so hätte er keine Gegenstände als das Wirkliche. Begriffe (die bloß auf die Möglichkeit eines Gegenstandes gehen) und sinnliche Anschauungen (welche uns etwas geben, ohne es dadurch doch als Gegenstand erkennen zu lassen) würden beide wegfallen" (*KdU* §76, 5:402.1–5).

9. Most directly: "a power of complete spontaneity of intuition . . . would be an understanding in the most general sense of the term" (*KdU* §77, 5:406.20–24).

10. *KdU* Einleitung §VII, §§15, 23, 29, 35, 39, 62, 77; 5:190.7, 228.34–6, 244.16–18, 266.2–3, 287.26–7, 292.28, 365.27–8, 406.16–17; see preceding note and *KdrV* B 138, 3:112.20–1.

11. *KdU* §77, 5:407.19–25.

12. *KdU* §77, 5:405.27–32.

13. *KdrV* B 138–9, 3:112.23–5; cf. B 145, 3:116.13–16.

14. See Klaus Düsing, "Spekulation und Reflexion: Zur Zusammenarbeit Schellings und Hegels in Jena," *Hegel-Studien* 5 (1969): 93–128; "Vernunfteinheit und unvordenkliches Daßsein. Konzeptionen der Überwindung negativer Theologie bei Schelling und Hegel," in *Einheitskonzepte in der idealistischen und in der gegenwärtigen Philosophie,* ed. K. Gloy and D. Schmidig (Bern: Lang, 1987), pp. 109–36; and especially "Die Entstehung des spekulativen Idealismus. Schellings und Hegels Wandlungen zwischen 1800 und 1801," in *Transzendentalphilosophie und Spekulation: Der Streit um die Gestalt einer Ersten Philosophie,* W. Jaeschke (1799–1807) (Hamburg: Felix Meiner Verlag, 1993), 2:144–63.

15. Düsing notes that Schelling's later philosophy retreats from this account of knowledge in his philosophy of identity to a view much like his earlier idealism, that reason cannot know the absolute, the absolute must simply be presupposed ("Die Entstehung des spekulativen Idealismus," p. 162).

16. G&W, *GW* 4:323.10–14.

17. G&W, *GW* 4:327.6–29, referring to *KdrV* B 160 and note.

18. Cf. *Vorlesungen über die Geschichte der Philosophie* III, *MM* 20:341; *Hegel's Lectures on the History of Philosophy,* trans. E. S. Haldane and F. H. Simson (New York: Humanities, 1955) 3:434; *Enz.* §254 Anm. (1817: §197), §448 *Zusatz.*

19. Vaihinger cites the following figures who, before Hegel, insisted on the problem of the neglected alternative: Lambert, Pistorius, Lotze, Fries, Maass, the anonymous author of "Ueber Raum und Zeit," Flatt, Tiedemann, Schwab, G. E. Schulze (Aenesidemus), Selle, Ouvrier, Brastberger, Platner, J. G. Schultz, Maimon, Bardili, Schleiermacher, and Beneke. See H. Vaihinger, *Commentar zu Kants Kritik der reinen Vernunft* (Stuttgart, Berlin and Leipzig: Union Deutsche Verlagsgesellschaft, 1892), 2:142 note 2, 143, 144 note 1, 307, 312ff., esp. 323. He concludes that the objection is sound (ibid., pp. 148, 389–90, 310).

20. *Contra* Henry Allison's attempt to defend Kant's arguments in *Kant's Transcendental Idealism: An Interpretation and Defense* (New Haven: Yale University Press, 1983), abbreviated "*KTI*"; see my book, *Hegel's Epistemological Realism: A Study of the Aim and Method of Hegel's Phenomenology of Spirit* (Dordrecht and Boston: Kluwer, 1989), abbreviated "*HER*", pp. 39–43.

21. Rosenkranz reports that Hegel attended Flatt's course in 1789 on Locke, Berkeley, Hume, and Kant. In this connection, Hegel evidently wrote notebooks (which Rosenkranz had in hand) full of extensive excerpts from their writings. See *Georg Wilhelm Friedrich Hegels Leben* (Berlin, 1844; Darmstadt: Wissenschaftliche Buchgesellschaft Darmstadt, 1963), p. 14. Unfortunately, these notebooks are now lost.

22. "Kant provided the results; the premises are still missing. And who can understand results without premises? Perhaps a Kant, but what is the great crowd to make of it? *Fichte,* the last time he was here, said that one must have the genius of a Socrates to fathom Kant. I find this truer every day." Schelling to Hegel, 6 January, 1795. J. Hoffmeister, ed., *Briefe von und an Hegel* (Hamburg: Felix Meiner Verlag, 1952) 1:14; *Hegel: The Letters,* trans. C. Butler and C. Seiler (Bloomington: Indiana

University Press, 1984), p. 29, translation emended. Hoffmeister notes that Fichte visited Tübingen in May 1794 (op. cit., 1:435 note 3).

23. This question-begging is not alleviated by ascribing to Hegel an argument parallel to that sometimes heard against skepticism about commonsense objects, namely that we do have commonsense knowledge of perceptible things around us, so that skepticism consequently is false. The parallel would be that Hegel insists he has intuitive knowledge of the absolute, so that Kant's restriction of human knowledge to phenomena is consequently false. Neither argument recognizes that skeptical or Kantian positions are supported by arguments that require critique, and not merely rejection *via* a contentious *modus tollens*. See §V below concerning Hegel's dawning awareness that even absolute idealists are obliged not to beg the question.

24. I would like to offer a conjecture regarding a related point. It is also troublesome that Hegel claims that Kant promulgates merely "empirical psychology" (e.g., G&W, *GW* 4:322.1–8, 341.21–24). Hegel regards Kant's philosophy as "psychological" insofar as it tries to explain the content and structure of our experience in terms of our nature as sentient beings (cf. *WL* II, *GW* 12:22.33–23.1; A. V. Miller, trans., *Hegel's Science of Logic* (New York: Humanities Press, 1976), abbreviated "*SL*"; p. 589. I suspect he calls it "empirical" psychology because Kant had refuted, or at least rejected, rational psychology in the Paralogisms (cf. G&W, *GW* 4:336.32–337.6) and because Kant (supposedly) does not derive his account of our cognitive abilities systematically from a single principle. Such a derivation would be required for his account of our abilities to count as rational rather than historical – that is, empirical – knowledge. (Both Hegel and Kant take over this medieval distinction; cf. *KdrV* A 835–36/B 863–4.) Cf. Hegel's remark in his *Lectures on the History of Philosophy:* "Now Kant goes to work [in his critique of theoretical reason] psychologically, that is, historically" (*MM* 20:339, my trans.; *Lectures on the History of Philosophy: The Lectures of 1825–1826,* ed. R. F. Brown, trans. R. F. Brown and J. M. Stewart (Berkeley: University of California Press, 1990), 3:222.

25. Schelling flatly begged the question against opponents and dissenters by charging that anyone who doesn't understand or accept his views lacked the relevant capacity or "organ" of intellectual intuition. *System des transcendentalen Idealismus: Schelling's Werke,* ed. M. Schröter (Munich: Beck, 1927), 2:369–70, 376; *System of Transcendental Idealism (1800),* trans. P. Heath (Charlottesville: University Press of Virginia, 1978), pp. 27–28, 33; cf. Schelling's explications of his *Darstellung meines Systems der Philosophie* in the Summer of 1801, in *Schellings und Hegels erste absolute Metaphysik,* ed. K. Düsing (1801–1802), ed (Cologne: Dinter, 1988), 43.29–44.1). Near the end of the 1800 *System*, Schelling claims that the "universally acknowledged and altogether incontestable objectivity of intellectual intuition is art itself. For the aesthetic intuition simply is the intellectual intuition become objective" (*Werke*, 2:625; trans. Heath, op. cit., p. 229). As an aesthete and occasional artist I recognize the power and richness of aesthetic experiences that give rise to this impression, yet as aesthetician and occasional art critic I can testify that this impression does not help at all to justify Schelling's claims about intellectual intuition.

26. See "Ueber das Wesen der philosophischen Kritik überhaupt . . . ," *GW* 4:118.21–119.12; and the *Differenzschrift, GW* 4:83.34–84.26.

27. Sextus Empiricus, *Outlines of Pyrrhonism* in *Works* I; Rev. R. G. Bury, trans. (Cambridge, Mass.: Harvard University Press, 1933), II §20; cf. I §§116–117.

300   KENNETH R. WESTPHAL

Hegel mentions the Dilemma of the Criterion in passing; *Skeptizismus*, GW 4:212.9. (I overlooked his mention of it in *HER*, 219 note 54.)

28. *Skeptizismus*, *GW* 4:215.26–31, 220.8–27.
29. G. E. Schulze, "Aphorismen über das Absolute," in *Neues Museum der Philosophie und Literatur* 1, ed. F. Bouterwek (Leipzig, 1803): 107–48; reprinted in *Transzendentalphilosophie und Spekulation*, op. cit., Quellenband 2.1, pp. 337–55; see K. R. Meist, "'Sich vollbringender Skeptizismus.' G. E. Schulzes Replik auf Hegel und Schelling" (ibid., 2:192–230).
30. See Schulze, op. cit., pp. 346–50; Hegel, *Phänomenologie*, *GW* 9:23.3–4; cf. 47.34–48.4; 55.18–24; *Hegel's Phenomenology of Spirit*, trans. A. V. Miller (Oxford: Clarendon Press, 1977), pp. 14–15, 42–3, 49.
31. See my discussion, "Hegel, Harris, and Sextus Empiricus," *Owl of Minerva* 31, no. 2 (2000).
32. See "Zwei Anmerkungen zum System," *GW* 7:343–7. I follow the dating suggested by Henry Harris, *Hegel's Development: Night Thoughts (Jena 1801–1806)* (Oxford: Clarendon Press, 1983), p. 580 (entry 210).
33. *GW* 7:343–4.
34. This *Anmerkung* shows Hegel's recognition that he must solve the problems of circularity that confronted Fichte, rather than escape them through Schelling's style of intellectual intuition. On Fichte's concern with circularity, see Daniel Breazeale, "Circles and Grounds in the Jena *Wissenschaftslehre*," in *Fichte: Historical Contexts/Contemporary Controversies*, ed. D. Breazeale and T. Rockmore (Atlantic Highlands, N.J.: Humanities Press, 1994), pp. 43–70. Also see his article, "Certainty, Universal Validity, and Conviction: The Methodological Primacy of Practical Reason within the Jena *Wissenschaftslehre*," in *New Perspectives on Fichte*, ed. T. Rockmore and D. Breazeale (Atlantic Highlands, N.J.: Humanities Press, 1996), pp. 35–59.
35. *GW* 7:345.2–11. I do not profess to understand Hegel's reason for this supposed "must." The relation between one and many that supposedly leads to unity (*GW* 7:345.8–11) is obscure and implausible.
36. *GW* 7:346.1–21.
37. *GW* 7:346.22–347.4.
38. *GW* 7:346.28–347.5–10.
39. *GW* 7:345.12–21; my trans. Hegel wrote: "Von dem Fixirn aber dieses Für sich seyns des Erkennens und seines Gegenstandes ist das gemeine Denken schwer abzubringen; die *deutliche Erkenntniß*, daß ein solches für sich *seyn Verschiedener sich* zerstört, unterliegt der Gewohnheit des gemeinen Erkennens, die Entgegengesetzten zu substantiiren, und ihnen dadurch den Schein eines besondern für sich Bestehens zu geben, so daß es die *Gewissheit*, als das *Wissen um ein solches für sich seyn setzt*, aber die Gewißheit an die Form des *abstracten Für sich seyns* so knüpft, daß es *das Wissen um dasselbe von ihm* trennt, und dann ebenso auch wieder dieses gewisse und gewußte so in sich theilt, als ob es eine Menge solcher Gewißheiten gebe."
40. *GW* 7:344.22–27. Hegel makes this remark specifically about the circular character of a proper philosophical system, which must show (*zeigen*) that it has no beginning, and so does not begin with a mere assumption, due to the mutual implication of its "first" and "last" elements.
41. *GW* 7:344.28–347.5–10.
42. This also adds to Hegel's reasons to differentiate his philosophy more fully and explicitly from Schelling's. Düsing notes that, after 1804, Hegel rejects the idealist

metaphysics of substance, modeled on Spinoza and central to his philosophy of identity, in favor of a different kind of speculative idealism based on the self-knowledge of absolute spirit, a view he retains to the end of his career ("Die Entstehung des spekulativen Idealismus," pp. 162–3). It is worth noting that Hegel's marginal comment on the passage quoted above from his "Zwei Anmerkungen zum System" shows that these remarks already belong to his new conception of absolute spirit, which is designed to resolve the problem about the relation between concepts and their contents (*GW* 7:345.23–8).

Henry Harris dates Hegel's philosophical break with Schelling circa late 1804, though on the basis of other evidence. See *Night Thoughts,* op. cit., pp. 397–8 and note 1, and *Hegel's Ladder* (Indianapolis: Hackett, 1997; 2 vols.), 1:280–1, 311 note 24. Harris there calls Hegel's attitude toward Schelling "at best ambivalent." I think this is incorrect. Any philosopher committed to determinate negation, that is, to constructive *Aufhebung* of alternative views, must appreciate the insights and suggestions found in other philosophies, while criticizing shortcomings and errors. (See *HER,* Chapters 6–9.) That is not ambivalence; it is critical appraisal. It may *look* ambivalent, but only if one disregards Hegel's method of internal criticism, and fails to recognize or to address the substantive details of Hegel's critical assessment of other views. I argue elsewhere that Harris does not adequately appreciate the point, purpose, or structure of Hegel's critical phenomenological method (see "Harris, Hegel, and the Spirit of the *Phenomenology,*" *Clio* 27 [1998]: 551–72). Harris's belief that I regard Hegel's *Phenomenology* "as a negative 'introduction' to speculative logic" ("L'etica del sapere," *Clio* 27 [1998]: 615–32; 626) rests on his disinterest in and misunderstanding of issues of philosophical assessment, criticism, and justification that are central to Hegel's *Phenomenology.* Hegel's rejection of Schelling's model of intellectual intuition is likewise the rejection of any merely negative introduction to his logic.

43. Cf. *HER,* Chapters 1, 6–9. For a briefer discussion of some main points, see my essay, "Hegel's Solution to the Dilemma of the Criterion" (revised version in *The Phenomenology of Spirit Reader: A Collection of Critical and Interpretive Essays,* J. Stewart [Albany: State University of New York Press, 1998], pp. 76–91). Michael Forster discusses only two of the five problems Hegel inherits from Sextus in *Hegel and Skepticism* (Cambridge, Mass.: Harvard University Press, 1989). See Förster's summary in *Hegel's Idea of a Phenomenology of Spirit* (Chicago: University of Chicago Press, 1998), Chap. 3; cf. *HER,* 11–16. The two problems he discusses, equipollence and concept-instantiation, fit his reconstruction of Hegel's early writings very well (*Hegel and Skepticism,* Part II). He overlooks the Dilemma of the Criterion, howeer, and so overlooks Hegel's radical epistemological reorientation in his mature writings. Thus it is no surprise that he finds Hegel's presentation of the problem of skepticism more convincing than Hegel's (supposed) solution to it (ibid., p. 5) and that he doesn't explain the supposed "self-contradictions" found in the finite forms of consciousness examined in the *Phenomenology* (ibid., pp. 108, 115). In the *Phenomenology* the problem of concept-instantiation is solved *en passant* by defending epistemological realism, in particular, through the internal critique and refutation of subjective idealism and skepticism (cf. *HER,* Chap. 11). Also see the review of *Hegel and Skepticism* by Willem de Vries, *Philosophical Review* 101 (1992): 401–4.

44. Regarding Hegel's rehabilitation of the correspondence theory of truth, which is required by his mature discursive account of knowledge, see my essay, "Harris, Hegel, and the Truth about Truth," in *The Phenomenology of Spirit: A Reappraisal,*

302   KENNETH R. WESTPHAL

ed. G. Browning (Dordrecht: Kluwer, 1997), pp. 23–9. (My criticisms of Harris there no longer pertain to his views in *Hegel's Ladder,* where Harris also retracts most of his criticism of *HER.*)

45. *WL* I, *GW* 11:38.12–40.29; 2nd ed. *GW* 21:62.12–65.26; *WL* II, *GW* 12:41.29–42.14; cf. 226.18–24. Similarly, on those very few occasions where he mentions "subject-object identity" in his mature writings, Hegel stresses the conceptually mediated character of that identity (e.g. *Enz.* §162 and Remark; *WL* II, *GW* 12:176–8; cf. *SL* 75–8, 610–11, 758–9; cf. 813: " . . . through intuition no science is produced; instead [it is produced] only *through thought*"; my trans.)

46. See my essays, "Hegel's Internal Critique of Naïve Realism," *Journal of Philosophical Research* 25 (2000): 173–229; and "Hegel's Attitude Toward Jacobi in the 'Third Attitude of Thought Toward Objectivity'," *The Southern Journal of Philosophy* 27 (1989): 135–6.

47. In view of Hegel's reconstruction of Kant's Transcendental Deduction in Hegel's mature writings, it is not surprising that he comes to equate the transcendental unity of apperception with the concept (cf. Longuenesse, "Point of View of Man or Knowledge of God," Section IV).

48. See *HER,* 164–9. Henry Harris's magnificent commentary on Hegel's *Phenomenology* (*Hegel's Ladder,* op. cit.) details many of Hegel's philosophical disagreements with Schelling, and in particular, with his intuitionism. In his attempt to rehabilitate Schelling, Andrew Bowie conveniently overlooks the problems Hegel points out in intuitionism, including intellectual intuitionism, See Bowie's *Schelling and Modern European Philosophy* (London: Routledge, 1993) pp. 18–19, 23–7, 46, 55–8, 83–4, 154–5. He also does not recognize the significance of Hegel's objection that the "identity" alleged to be found in intellectual intuition cannot be presupposed as an unmediated beginning (ibid., pp. 160–2; cf. *HER,* 150–5).

49. *MM* 20:428; Brown, ed., 3:260–1.

50. "There is nothing quicker or more convenient than to have to make the mere assurance, that I find a content in my consciousness with the certainty of its truth and that therefore this certainty doesn't belong to me as a particular subject, but rather to the nature of spirit itself" (*Enz.* §71 Remark; my trans.). For discussion, see "Hegel's Attitude Toward Jacobi . . . ," op. cit., §VII.

51. *PhdG* Introduction para. 4, *GW* 9:55.18–24; *HER,* 191; my translation.

52. G&W, *GW* 4:365.12–366.6; *WL* II, *GW* 12:11–28; *SL,* 577–95.

53. G&W, *GW* 4:330.34–7. See H. J. Paton, *Kant's Metaphysic of Experience* (London: George Allen & Unwin, 1936), 1:139–40; Allison, *KTI,* 250; and in greater detail my essay, "Noumenal Causality Reconsidered: Affection, Agency, and Meaning in Kant," *Canadian Journal of Philosophy* 27 (1997): 209–45.

54. I develop this point in "Kant, Hegel, and the Transcendental Material Conditions of Possible Experience," op. cit.

55. Although Kant occasionally formulates "affinity" with regard to connections among phenomena (*KdrV* A 766/B 794–5), I concentrate here on the most basic level of affinity, which concerns simple variety and repeatability among the contents of sensations (*KdrV* A 90–1/B 122–3, A 100–1, A 121–3, A 653–4/B 681–2, A 657/B 685). This is a more basic kind of affinity than those discussed by Allison in his contribution to this volume.

56. See *HER,* Chap. 11.

57. See Allison, *KTI,* 104–9; *HER,* 39–43; and "Affinity, Idealism, and Naturalism . . . ," op. cit.

58. I formulate the alternative this way in order to keep it as close to Kant's views as possible. One might instead drop reference to "forms of intuition" and simply insist that the concept of space is a priori because it cannot be defined in accord with concept empiricism, and that we are only capable of sensing outer objects that are unto themselves spatial.

59. This theme is central to Hegel's analysis of "Self-consciousness"; see *HER*, 160–4.

60. G&W, *GW* 4:340.26–341.34. The ground for Hegel's claim I cite here supplements those cited by Longuenesse in "Point of View of Man or Knowledge of God," Sections II and IV.

61. Cf. G&W, *GW* 4:346.5–26, 395.23–396.21. Here I report the point of Hegel's objection without endorsing it. On Hegel's mature critique of Kant's theory of moral judgment, see my articles, "Hegel's Critique of Kant's Moral World View," *Philosophical Topics* 19 (1991): 133–76; §§VIII, IX; and "How 'Full' is Kant's Categorical Imperative?," *Jahrbuch für Recht und Ethik/Annual Review of Law and Ethics* 3 (1995): 465–509, esp. §5.

62. *KdrV* B 134 note.

63. G&W, *GW* 4:328.7–29; cf. Kant: " . . . the *analytic* unity of apperception is only possible under the presupposition of some sort of synthetic [unity of apperception]" (*KdrV* B 134). Cf. Hegel's rejection of both "dogmatic" idealism and "dogmatic" realism in the *Differenzschrift* (*GW* 4:40.32–41.22).

64. See *HER*, 152–3.

65. G&W, *GW* 4:327.3–6; cf. *HER*, 164–5. In this regard, at least, Hegel's characterization of the relation of subject and predicate in synthetic judgments a priori is not so puzzling as Longuenesse suggests in "Point of View of Man or Knowledge of God," Section III.

66. Cf. G&W, *GW* 4:327.17–328.6. This is to say, alongside the model of "identity philosophy" according to which some sort of original undifferentiated unity comes to differentiate itself (cf. G&W, *GW* 4:328.23–9), in *Faith and Knowledge* there are significant traces of the sense of "idealism" characteristic of Hegel's mature sense of the term, according to which something is "ideal" if it exists, or is what it is, only as an integral member of a complex whole (cf. G&W, *GW* 4:325.30–326.2, 327.3– 29 (re: *KdrV* B 150–3, 160–1); *Differenzschrift*, *GW* 4:63.36–64.15, 82.3–14). On Hegel's mature sense of "idealism," see *HER*, Chap. 10.

67. Cf. *Enz.* §171 *Zusatz*.

68. *KdrV* A 73–4/B 98–9. For discussion of Kant's Table of Judgments, see Michael Wolff's outstanding study, *Die Vollständigkeit der kantischen Urteilstafel* (Frankfurt am Main: Klostermann, 1995), and the critical discussion of it in *Zeitschrift für philosophische Forschung* 52 (1998):406–59; also see Wolff's *Nachtrag*, in the same journal (2000).

69. On the joint role of such judgments in Kant's Analogies, see my essay, "Does Kant's *Metaphysical Foundations of Natural Science* Fill a Gap in the *Critique of Pure Reason?*," *Synthese* 103 (1995): 43–86; §§7, 9. Some such conjoint judgments seem to be at least part of Hegel's understanding of disjunctive judgments already in the Jena logic manuscript, though not in any obvious connection with Kant's Analogies (*GW* 7:87.10–93.27; *The Jena System, 1804–5: Logic and Metaphysics*, trans. and ed. J. W. Burbidge, G. di Giovanni, and H. S. Harris (Kingston: McGill-Queen's University Press, 1986), pp. 91–7. (Showing that this is in fact Hegel's understanding of the relation among the forms of judgment would require an extensive commentary on his *Logic*, and can only be suggested here.) The parallels between Hegel's treatment of disjunctive judgment in the 1804 Logic

304   KENNETH R. WESTPHAL

manuscript with his mature treatment in the *Encyclopedia* and *Science of Logic* suggest that he is already grappling with Kant's Table of Judgments in 1804 (see Hegel's explicit reference to Kant's Table of Judgments in *Enz.* §171 *Zusatz*). In view of his attention to Kant's remarks about the systematic character of the Table of Categories (e.g. G&W, *GW* 4:334.18–27, referring to *KdrV* §11, B 109–113), it is not surprising that Hegel would also pay close attention to Kant's Table of Judgments during his years in Jena.

70. Cf. *KdrV* A 571/B 599ff.

71. This requires a modal version of the material conditional, in order to avoid the absurd result that determining the truth values of all the conditional (hypothetical) propositions ipso facto determines the truth values of all the elementary (categorical) propositions. See Robert Brandom, "Semantic Paradox of Material Implication," *Notre Dame Journal of Formal Logic* 22 (1981): 129–32.

72. Béatrice Longuenesse ("Point of View of Man . . . ," Section III) shows that this thesis has good Kantian pedigree (A 581–82/B 609–10). I call this *Hegel's* codetermination thesis because it makes all the difference in the world that Hegel purports to defend this thesis without recourse to Kant's transcendental idealism and its distinction between phenomena and noumena – that is, without Kant's distinction between the human and the divine points of view. Longuenesse claims (op. cit., sec. IV) that Hegel resolves the tension in Kant's philosophy between the "point of view of man" and "knowledge of God" (where this "of" is both a subjective and an objective genetive; op. cit., sec. II) by striving toward "knowledge of God" by developing a positive account of "intellectual intuition," even if not under that name. In this connection, she further claims that Kant's philosophy provides the "tools" for the opposite resolution of this tension, "a systematic development of the 'point of view of man'," and that elements of this development can be found in Hegel's philosophy.

Even if Hegel's logic is (in Heidegger's term) an "onto-theology" (see Clark Butler, *Hegel's Logic: Between Dialectic and History;* Evanston: Northwestern University Press, 1996), however, Hegel's mature views are in fact a systematic development of the point of view of man, in which God and God's point of view turn out to be a human construction. See *HER passim*, Harris *HL passim* (I summarize the relevant points from *HL* in "Harris, Hegel, and the Spirit of the *Phenomenology*," op. cit., pp. 552–4, 560–1), Justus Hartnack, *An Introduction to Hegel's Logic* (Indianapolis: Hackett, 1998), and Pirmin-Stekeler Weithofer, *Hegel's Analytische Philosophie: Die Wissenschaft der Logik als kritische Theorie der Bedeutung* (Paderborn: Ferdinand Schöningh, 1992). Hegel's mature treatment of modal categories as merely subjective neither requires nor involves appeal to any form of intellectual intuition (see Harnack, pp. 73–8; Stekeler-Weithofer, pp. 288–303).

73. *KdrV* A 216/B 263, cf. A 581–82/B 609–10.

74. Spinoza, Letter 50.

75. Hegel's appropriation of this slogan is facilitated by Fichte's substitution of "determination" for Kant's "limitation," a key Kantian term concerning those disjunctive judgments that exclude a subject from a particular sphere of predicates. See the third principle of Fichte's *Wissenschaftslehre* (in *J. G. Fichte – Gesamtausgabe*, ed. R. Lauth and H. Jacob [Stuttgart: Frommann-Holzboog, 1965]) 2:282; *The Science of Knowledge with the First and Second Introductions*, trans. P. Heath and J. Lachs (Cambridge, U.K.: Cambridge University Press, 1982), p. 119. Cf. *KdrV* A 80/B 106, and Kant's remark that "[a]ll true negations are nothing but limitations – which

they could not be called, if the unlimited (the All) were not their basis" (A 576/B 604).

76. *Skeptizismus, GW* 4:215.26–31, 220.8–27; cf. *HER,* 162–3.
77. See *HER,* Chapters 7–9, 11. Hegel's account of justification is still of great philosophical interest. Frederick L. Will develops it in a pragmatist vein in *Beyond Deduction* (London: Routledge, 1988) and *Pragmatism and Realism* (Lanham, Md.: Rowman & Littlefield, 1997).
78. This paper originated as comments on Professor Longuenesse's paper at the Dartmouth College Conference, "The Idea of a System of Transcendental Idealism in Kant, Fichte, Schelling and Hegel" (August 1995), organized by Sally Sedgwick. I am grateful to Béatrice Longuenesse for several extended, informative, and enjoyable discussions of these issues and my attempts to grapple with them. I am grateful to the editor and to anonymous readers for the Press for allowing and encouraging me to revise and expand my comments into the present essay. I also thank Klaus Düsing for his interest and suggestions. Finally, I am grateful to the Alexander von Humboldt-Stiftung for a generous research fellowship in Heidelberg in the spring of 1995, during which this essay was begun.

14
Metaphysics and Morality in Kant and Hegel

SALLY SEDGWICK

Even for those who have struggled with Hegel long enough to discover that he is neither a positivist nor a communitarian, nor (at the other end of the spectrum) a Platonist, the fact that he also insists upon distinguishing his appproach to practical philosophy from Kant's may seem deeply puzzling. After all, the two philosophers share in common the same principal opponents. Both set out to undermine the skeptic's doubts about the possibility of objective practical judgments and requirements; both in addition reject positivist derivations of law, exclusively empiricist accounts of human behavior, and intuitionist forms of justification. The two philosophers furthermore seem to share the same conception of the conditions of human freedom. For Hegel as well as Kant, a theory of morality and political right devoted to advancing the cause of freedom must require more than just the absence of obstacles preventing the satisfaction of our animal passions. For Hegel as well as Kant, freedom requires in addition the respect of the ends we have as *rational* natures. We achieve this kind of freedom when our actions are motivated by the legislation of reason and when the social norms that constrain us are norms we can rationally endorse.

Despite these similarities, Hegel tells us in the *Philosophy of Right* that the conception of freedom he associates with Kant and discusses under the heading of "Moralität" must give way to the more adequate conception of "Sittlichkeit" or "ethical life." It is clear that Hegel finds unacceptable what he calls the "empty formalism" of Kant's practical philosophy; it is also clear that he thinks that Kant's practical philosophy is "formal" because its supreme law or categorical imperative is an a priori law of reason.[1] But this doesn't yet tell us why, for Hegel, these features of the Kantian approach are objectionable. In my view, we do his critique little justice if we say that it is aimed at a consequence that presumably follows from Kant's preoccupation with providing an a priori foundation for law and morality: namely, the failure to give sufficient moral weight to the empirical particulars that individuate persons and situations and need to be taken into account in the practice of moral assessment. As I shall argue below, the suggestion that Kant's formalism requires us to ignore empirical content in this way is neither plausible as a critique of Kant nor accurate as a representation of what troubles Hegel about Kant. We go more to the heart of the matter, I believe, if we say instead that Hegel is out to challenge the very distinction between the "empirical" and the "pure" or "a priori" so fundamental to both Kant's practical and theoretical philosophy. Hegel's critique of Kant's practical philosophy is an instance of his critique of Kant's idealism more generally, and of the assumptions about reason and nature upon which that idealism rests. Or so I shall argue here.

This is a paper, then, about what we could call the metaphysical foundations of Hegel's critique of Kant's practical philosophy. My objective is to demonstrate how the two different forms of idealism yield distinct conceptions of moral subjectivity and of the source of practical laws. In comparing the idealisms of the two philosophers, I draw attention to features of Hegel's conceptions of practical agency and freedom not also defended by Kant. And I argue that these are features we are likely to miss if we read the *Philosophy of Right* in abstraction from the larger aims of Hegel's idealism.[2]

I

Since this is a paper about the metaphysical foundations of Hegel's critique of Kant's practical philosophy, I begin my discussion with a currently unpopular topic: the metaphysics of Kant's metaphysics of morals. The place to start is the Third Antinomy of the *Critique of Pure Reason,* where Kant introduces the idea of transcendental freedom. Kant tells us there that transcendental freedom implies "absolute spontaneity" or independence from the causality of laws of nature. Absolute spontaneity, he claims, is a "special kind of causality": a power to initiate the "absolute" beginning of a series of events, a beginning that is neither itself in time nor caused by any prior condition in time. Although this idea of spontaneity contradicts our concept of nature as the series of antecedently determined events, it nonetheless is required by our concept of nature, according to Kant. This is because we necessarily think of nature, he argues, as a *completed* versus indefinitely regressive series – as having a "first" versus a merely "relative" beginning. We in other words necessarily suppose that in nature, "nothing takes place without a cause *sufficiently* determined a priori."[3]

Not only is the idea of transcendental freedom required by our concept of nature, Kant goes on to argue that it also must be presupposed in order to ground a particular understanding we have of our own behavior. When we consider our behavior merely empirically, we consider it as determined by natural laws over which we have no control. For any action, empirically considered, we expect to discover its causal conditions in, for example, natural predispostion or character, social environment and education. From this point of view, we do not suppose our behavior to come about "completely unconditioned" by any preceding state (A 555/B 583). But this is not the only perspective we bring to bear on our own actions, according to Kant. We in addition ascribe to ourselves and others the capacity of genuine agency: We assume that we can be held responsible for our actions and that we have not merely an "empirical" but also an "intelligible" character. We assume, in other words, that we possess the faculty of reason that is completely free and a special causal power.

Kant never wavers in his commitment to the following thesis: If we restrict our attention to the empirical character of the agent, we leave ourselves no way to ground moral laws and no basis for moral imputation. "Everyone must admit," he writes in the opening passages of the *Groundwork*, "that if a law is to count as moral, that is, as the ground of an obligation, it must be absolutely necessary . . . Accordingly, the ground of obligation . . . must be sought *a priori* . . . in concepts of pure reason . . ."[4] How may we be justified in contradicting our concept of nature as the series of causally determined events and in positing as the ground of obligation the idea of transcendental freedom? Kant's answer, of course, is transcendental idealism. Transcendental idealism permits us to think of objects in a "twofold sense": as given in perception via our a priori forms of intuition space and time (i.e., as appearances), and as independent of those a priori conditions (as things in themselves) (B xxvii). The subject as appearance is determined by natural causal laws and has no freedom. Considered in abstraction from the conditions of appearances, however, the subject may be thought to have an "intelligible" character and therefore a capacity of spontaneity that is "absolute." Although, according to this doctrine, we have theoretical knowledge only of appearances and not of things in themselves, Kant argues that we can nonetheless legitimately think of ourselves as having an intelligible character and as therefore free. We can and do think of ourselves in this way, he claims, as a condition of the possibility of morality.[5]

So the idea of transcendental freedom implies absolute spontaneity and is required, in Kant's view, in order to complete our understanding both of nature and of our own behavior. Its legitimacy, as we have just seen, depends upon the transcendental idealist distinction between objects of theoretical knowledge and objects of thought, between appearances and things in themselves.

It might seem that, in insisting upon transcendental idealism as the sole means of grounding obligation, Kant asks us to accept far too much. Not only must we be willing to challenge a deterministic account of human behavior, we also need to be persuaded that the only adequate way to do so requires that we suppose that our freedom is "transcendental" and our spontaneity "absolute." We, in other words, have to accept the idea that we are subjects capable of initiating actions from outside time, subjects that have in addition to an "empirical" character an "intelligible" character.

The situation could be worse. Kant could be requiring us to grant not merely the *idea* of the intelligible subject but its existence and theoretical knowability as well. But at least on one widely accepted interpretation of it, transcendental idealism does not require us to accept this much. According to the so-called deontologized or two standpoint interpretation, transcendental idealism permits no such assertions about objects independent of the a priori conditions of space and time.[6] It permits only that we adopt a conception of ourselves as capable of transcending those conditions, as capable of the kind of freedom required to ground our sense of ourselves as agents. Kant warns us not to give in to the temptation to try to know or understand how laws grounded in our intelligible nature can have a causal influence on our empirical or phenomenal nature. He frequently reminds us that "reason would overstep all its bounds if it undertook to explain how pure reason can be practical." Rather than try to explain how we can, as intelligible subjects, be moved by the idea of freedom, he tells us in the *Groundwork* that the "concept of an intelligible world is . . . only a point of view outside appearances which reason recognizes that it must take in order to think of itself as practical . . . "[7]

II

Surely there can be no question about whether it is possible to find passages in both Kant's theoretical and practical writings that provide support for the two standpoint interpretation.[8] But there of course *is* a question – a much debated one – about how consistent Kant is in his adherence to it. That is, there is the worry that he sometimes seems to commit the fallacy of (what he calls) "transcendental illusion" in claiming knowledge of the unknowable, of things in themselves (A 295/B 352).

Although Hegel is among those who raise this charge against Kant, what I am more interested in exploring here are his objections to Kant's distinction between appearances and things in themselves, between empirical and intelligible characters, which apply even assuming that Kant is consistent in adhering to the two standpoint view. That is, I am interested in Hegel's critique of the very *idea* of an intelligible versus empirical form of subjectivity. So in what follows I will be concerned with the following question: What, if anything, is unacceptable about Kant's conceptions of the practical standpoint and of practical agency once we set aside the worry that he sometimes seems to commit transcendental illusion in trying to theoretically explain or know them? Otherwise put: What, if anything, is unacceptable about Kant's conception of practical agency once we assume that he is not committed to an extravagant metaphysical thesis about the existence of the intelligible or noumenal self?

In answering this question we need to bear two points in mind: First, the thesis that the intelligible character is theoretically unknowable because not an object in space and time should not be understood to imply for Kant that its features are either eliminable or substitutable. The actions of the intelligible character are in his view *necessarily* "spontaneous" and therefore *necessarily,* in his words, "not subject to the form of time, and thus also not to the conditions of temporal succession . . . " (A 551/B 579). Kant never, in other words, suggests that it is merely contingently true that the intelligible character is, as he puts it, "free from all influence of sensibility and from all determinations through appearances" (A 541/B 569).

Second, the thesis that the intelligible character is theoretically unknowable should not be understood to imply for Kant that the idea of the intelligible character or of an absolute form of spontaneity plays anything less than an *essential* role in providing for the possibility of both his philosophy of nature and his account of practical agency. As we saw above, the idea of absolute spontaneity is in his view required to complete our understanding of nature as well as of our own behavior. Regarding the latter, he claims that we need to suppose that we have an intelligible character in order to ground our conception of ourselves as agents.[9] Even though it is not theoretically knowable because not an appearance in time, we nonetheless know with necessity that we have pure reason "as a purely intelligible faculty." We know this, Kant argues, because in matters of conduct we hold ourselves and others morally responsible (A 551/B 579, A 547/B 575). The fact of moral imputation implies that reason must have causality and that we have, in addition to an empirical character an intelligible character, because, as he puts it, "when we have in view merely the course of nature, *'ought' has no meaning whatsoever*" (A 547/ B 575; my emphasis).

So although our reason as an intelligible faculty is not itself an object of theoretical knowledge, we nonetheless have a priori and therefore necessary knowledge of its essential features and of its role in grounding morality. Just as we know with necessity that the "I think" or "original synthetic unity of apperception" is a condition of the possibility of all cognition, according to Kant, so we know with necessity that the intelligible character is a condition of the possibility of practical agency and moral imputation. We furthermore know, Kant reminds us again and again, that the laws of both forms of subjectivity contain nothing empirical.[10]

III

To return to our central question: What does Hegel find unacceptable about Kant's idea of the intelligible subject or of practical agency? The answer, briefly put, is that even a deontologized or two standpoint distinction between empirical and intelligible characters, between the subject as appearance and as thing in itself, presupposes in Hegel's view an untenable dualism. We now need to consider why he believes this is so.

Kant's distinction between empirical and intelligible subjects presupposes an untenable dualism because it depends on the assumption of what Hegel calls "original heterogeneity" or "absolute opposition."[11] One thing Hegel does *not* mean by this is that it is Kant's view that the ends of the intelligible subject and the ends of the empirical subject must always conflict. Rather, the intelligible subject is "absolutely opposed" to the empirical subject just in the sense that, on Kant's definition, the intelligible subject is supposed to contain nothing empirical: Its activity proceeds from a standpoint outside time and its laws are a priori. Likewise, the empirical subject or subject *qua* appearance is "opposed" to its intelligible or transcendental counterpart because on Kant's conception it is without form or law: It must rely for form or law on the a priori contributions of pure intuition and understanding. Neither space and time nor the laws of nature which determine the behavior of empirical subjects are given in the a posteriori content of sensation, according to Kant; this is why he identifies them as a priori forms of experience.

In the same way, empirical and rational motives are originally heterogeneous or absolutely opposed, on Hegel's reading of Kant. Although desire can be brought under the governance of reason, desire can never itself be rational, can never give rise to rational (i.e., categorical) imperatives – hence Kant's insistence that morality cannot rest on an empirical foundation. Nature itself cannot be the source of law. Law must the product of reason, and reason is a faculty that legislates from outside the realm of nature.

But how warranted is Hegel's charge of original heterogeneity? After all, objects of nature for Kant, rather than bare or unformed contents "absolutely opposed" to reason, seem more accurately described as unities of form and content. Every object of perception, he writes in the first *Critique,* "stands under the necessary conditions of synthetic unity of the manifold of intuition in a possible experience" (B 197/A 158). Every object of perception, in other words, is given via our a priori forms of intuition and thought through the categories. We know nature, according to Kant, as an already formed content.

Hegel was aware that, as appearance, nature cannot be known as a bare content, on Kant's conception. That is, he was aware of the role Kant awarded the a priori forms of subjectivity in making nature possible as the object of empirical knowledge. What is more, he thought that Kant's idea of the object as a unity of form and content was a profound discovery – profound enough to inspire the development of his own form of idealism.[12] Hegel nonetheless charges Kant with dualism because he believed that, for Kant, nature as appearance is a unity of parts supposed to be originally heterogeneous: the content or matter of nature is given a posteriori in sensation; the form of nature, on the other hand, derives from a subject that is transcendental and thus free of or "absolutely opposed" to that given empirical content. So although aware that in Kant's view we know nature only as a unity of form and content, Hegel characterizes form and content on Kant's conception as an original hetero-geneity, because in his view Kant assumed that the contributions of form and content are independent or separable. It is this thesis of separability, then, which is the main target of Hegel's critique.[13]

IV

Whatever verdict we may finally reach about the accuracy of this portrayal of Kant, it is not difficult to see why Hegel was persuaded by it. After all, what are we to conclude from the Kantian conceptions of reason and nature reviewed above if not that, for Kant, the contributions of form and content are indepen-dent or separable? This is certainly suggested by his insistence upon the "pure" or nonempirical nature of reason and the a priori status of its laws. It seems to underlie his assertion in the Antinomy that, "Reason is present and the same in all the actions of men and in all situations; it is not itself in time and does not fall into a new state in which it was not before" (A 556/B 584). The thesis of original heterogeneity furthermore seems responsible for Kant's view that the given a posteriori content of nature can never yield form or law, can never (as Hegel might put it) determine itself as rational.

But even should we grant that this dualism or "opposition" is as "absolute" as Hegel portrays it, why must we also conclude that it is objectionable? Hegel clearly believes that it is objectionable; but thanks to recent efforts to clarify the implications of this dualism for Kant's philosophy, it is far from obvious that he should. Turning our attention, now, to Kant's practical philosophy: Commentators have taken great pains to argue that Kant's dualism does not entail the undesirable features commonly associated with it. Most notably, it does not entail that his practical philosophy is an empty formalism. The fact that Kant draws a sharp distinction between our empirical and our rational or intelligible natures does not imply, these commentators point out, that in his view we can realize morality by relying on the faculty of pure practical reason alone. There is in other words no reason to suppose that it follows from the formal character of Kant's supreme moral law that his practical philosophy is a formalism in the sense that it awards no essential role to empirical content.

There is clearly something correct about this effort to cast Kant's dualism in a sympathetic light. Empirical content indeed plays an essential role in his practical philosophy, and in several respects. A good Kantian, for example, must not only test her maxims against the supreme law of practical reason or categorical imperative; she must also formulate her maxims properly. To do so, she needs to give careful attention to the specific facts of her case; she needs to apply good judgment in identifying what Barbara Herman has called its "mor-ally salient features."[14] She needs, that is, to be a good empiricist.[15]

Kant in addition argues that we cannot expect to realize morality without the help of social institutions and practices. Although the categorical imperative on his account is itself given by the nature of reason, he writes in his 1784 essay, "Idea for a Universal History With a Cosmopolitan Purpose," that reason itself requires, "effort, practice and instruction in order to progress gradually from one level of insight to the next." Reason and its supreme law is given as an "innate capacity," but this does not by itself secure for reason a governing role in our lives. The respect for and reliance upon reason, Kant claims, is something that education must encourage in us. Moreover, the right kind of education is possible only in a civil society capable of guaranteeing freedom under external laws. Moral enlightenment therefore cannot be achieved except in a society governed by a just constitution, in his view. And the security of any particular civil society furthermore depends on the existence of a law-governed federation of states. This is why, on Kant's account, enlightenment is not possible for the individual; we may hope for its realization, he says, only for the species.[16]

So moral character is unachievable in isolation from the right kind of social environment and institutions, according to Kant. It is also unachievable, in his view, without the help of natural inclination or feelings. In the absence of feelings of happiness or contentment, he says in the *Groundwork,* we are not likely to do what morality requires; this is why we have at least an "indirect" duty, he tells us there, to secure our own happiness.[17] In "Idea for a Universal History" he furthermore argues that we have our natural inclinations to thank for the very fact that our rational capacities get awakened into action at all. Natural self-love or "unsocial sociability" invariably brings us into conflict with others. But because we seek to "live comfortably and pleasantly," we learn to take advantage of the civilizing influences of reason. Nature therefore "deserves to be thanked," Kant writes, for without unsocial sociability "all our excellent natural capacities would forever remain undeveloped."[18] So even though Kant insists that morality cannot be grounded on anything empirical and that natural inclinations very often tempt us away from doing our duty, he clearly awards our empirical natures an indispensable role in the realization of morality.

Of course, when we add together the fact that attention to empirical conditions must be involved in the proper formulation of our maxims, and that social institutions are necessary for the development of moral character, and that we have natural inclination to thank for the fact that pure practical reason is awakened into action at all, we do not arrive at the conclusion that the distinction between nature and reason in Kant is anything less than absolute. The efforts of commentators to emphasize the role of the empirical in his practical philosophy, to vindicate him of the charge of empty formalism, presuppose this distinction rather than challenge it. I am not suggesting that they set out to do otherwise. My point is simply that we should not understand these efforts as possible responses to Hegel's critique. There is no evidence supporting the view that, in charging Kant's moral philosophy with empty formalism, Hegel overlooks the role Kant awards empirical content. Hegel recognizes that, for Kant, particular duties are not analytically deducible from the categorical imperative; he knows that, for Kant, the categorical imperative must be applied to our maxims and our maxims must be formulated to reflect the contingencies of context. Hegel is furthermore aware that, in Kant's view, we cannot realize the ends of morality simply by reflecting on what pure practical reason requires. He knows that Kant acknowledges that without the help of social institutions as well as our natural inclinations morality would not be possible for us at all.

Given that Hegel does not ignore the role Kant awards empirical content in any of these ways, why does he claim that the categorical imperative, as formal, must also be empty? As I suggested above, the answer to this question has to do with the link between Hegel's empty formalism critique and his objection to the thesis of absolute opposition. A full treatment of this topic would require a separate paper, but the general idea is this: In Hegel's view, if we treat the categorical imperative as a formal principle (i.e., as the command that we not commit self-contradiction), it will be empty in the sense of insufficiently determinate: it will fail to specify narrowly or clearly enough the range of morally permissible actions. Where is the self-contradiction, after all, in theft or in the absence of property? We can derive a contradiction of the kind Kant is after, Hegel argues, only if we presuppose a *particular conception* of human freedom and of the conditions compatible with it. Kant claims, of course, that it is the formal character of the moral law that is responsible for the fact that it has universal validity – validity, that is to say, independent of any particular conception of human nature, of ends worthy of realization, or of the conditions compatible with those ends. But on Hegel's understanding, if a law is indeed formal in this way, it also will be empty or insufficiently determinate. If what we are after are non-empty laws of reason, laws that can provide for determinate application, then we need to give up the our commitment to the assumption that reason is "pure" or "absolutely opposed" to content.

V

As I said, a full treatment of Hegel's critique of the categorical imperative would require a separate paper; all that I've wanted to suggest here is that his empty formalism charge does not rest on any failure to acknowledge the role Kant awards empirical content. Rather, Hegel's critique of the categorical imperative is motivated by the far less superficial conviction that Kant's very distinction between form and content cannot be maintained.

In order to say more about this, about the motivation for Hegel's objection to the dualism or heterogeneity of form and content, I turn now to the *Philosophy of Right*. The *Philosophy of Right* is one among Hegel's many works in which his argument against the thesis of absolute opposition is carried out. On the interpretation I want to defend, his representation in the *Philosophy of Right* of the ideal State and of practical rationality, his argument for the "identity" of the "rational" and the "actual," all depend on and therefore cannot be understood apart from his rejection of that thesis.

This is the place to insert two clarificatory remarks that bear on the interpretation of the *Philosophy of Right* I am about to offer. First, I don't want to be understood as committed to the thesis that we nowhere in Kant's works find evidence of his own reservations about the absolute opposition of form and content – reservations that may even be taken to anticipate Hegel's objections. Perhaps we do.[19] But even supposing that we do, we nonetheless cannot say of Kant what I believe we can say of Hegel: that his idealism takes as its *point of departure* the rejection of the thesis of original heterogeneity.

Second, the argument of the *Philosophy of Right* is directed against a variety of approaches to political theory, not merely against Kant's approach. Given that in the above discussion I introduced Hegel's critique of heterogeneity as key to understanding his critique of Kant, why am I now suggesting that Hegel's critique of heterogeneity determines the argument of the *Philosophy of Right* as a whole?

The answer to this question derives from the fact that heterogeneity, for Hegel, implies a particular understanding of reason and nature but not a particular understanding of their respective epistemic roles. We assume heterogeneity if we conceive of nature as a bare or unformed content, incapable of supporting necessity or law. This doesn't mean that we need also be committed to the view that necessity or law must derive from elsewhere – from pure reason, for instance. We likewise assume heterogeneity if we understand reason to be pure or to contain nothing empirical. We needn't in addition hold that mere perception unaccompanied by a priori concepts is not for us a possible source of knowledge. We needn't in other words be transcendental idealists to be committed to the thesis of absolute opposition or heterogeneity, according to Hegel. Hegel never in any case suggests that Kant was alone in adhering to the thesis; nor does he claim that the thesis originated with Kant. His view instead seems to be that Kant inherited and took for granted the thesis of heterogeneity, and never subjected it to critique.

VI

So far I've suggested that Hegel holds the thesis of heterogeneity or absolute opposition responsible for what he thinks are inadequate conceptions of reason and nature. As just noted, the thesis is not in his view tied to any particular account of the roles of reason and nature in grounding knowledge. It is also in his view not tied to any particular account of the roles of reason and nature in grounding right. The thesis makes its way into a variety of theories of right, according to Hegel; and it accounts for what he ultimately finds unacceptable about each of them. Since he tells us that the subject matter of the science of right is the idea of human freedom and its actualization,[20] we can so far anticipate this much: That for Hegel any theory of right that depends upon the thesis of heterogeneity will be unable to provide for a fully satisfactory account of human freedom.

Let's first consider what Hegel takes to be unacceptable about the conception of *nature* implied by the thesis of heterogeneity, beginning with a brief look at his treatment of some non-Kantian approaches to right. In the Preface of the *Philosophy of Right,* he declares himself opposed to positivist approaches to law. For the positivist, rational requirements are supposed to have their basis in the will of a people as reflected in actually existing behaviors and practices. Hegel warns us against interpreting his claim that "what is rational is actual" as an expression of his allegiance to this approach to right. Rather, his view is that, "in laws of right, the thing is not valid because it exists."[21]

Not surprisingly, the problem with positivism for Hegel is its conception of nature or of the realm of the actual. The positivist assumes that nature is absolutely opposed to reason since, for the positivist, we can know nature as a bare or unformed content – as something "multifariously concrete" and without unity. Positivism, that is, suffers from what Hegel in the *Encyclopaedia Logic* characterizes as an uncritical empiricism.[22]

Up to a point, Hegel's attack on uncritical empiricism follows Hume's critique of Locke. Even if we grant that objects of nature are given in sensation as bare or unformed particulars, our empirical judgments about nature cannot strictly speaking be *about* bare particulars. They cannot be about bare particulars because it is not possible to demonstrate an immediate causal link from sensation to judgment. Hume claimed that our judgments about matters of fact depend upon the intermediary of imagination, which invariably extends the data of sense. For Hegel, our judgments about matters of fact depend upon the intermediary of thought, and thought necessarily takes what is concrete and via the employment of concepts turns it into something abstract. The empiricist such as Locke supposes that, by relying on perception alone, we can justify for example our idea of matter. What he fails to notice, Hegel writes, is that matter, "is an abstraction, something which as such cannot be perceived." The uncritical empiricist in other words uses "metaphysical categories" of matter, force, and so forth, "without knowing," Hegel says, that he is engaged in metaphysics.

So Hegel follows Hume in arguing against uncritical empiricism that we cannot know the bare or unformed content of sense experience. But whereas for Hume the unknowability of bare content implies skepticism about matters of fact, for Hegel it implies that we need a new account of the proper object of empirical knowledge. Hume concludes skepticism about matters of fact only because he shares with the uncritical empiricist the assumption that what our empirical knowledge *should* inform us about are the unformed particulars presumably given in sensation. This is just the assumption Hegel wants us to reject. What we ought to learn from Hume's critique of Locke, in his view, is that the proper object of empirical knowledge, rather than a bare or unformed content, is an already conceptualized content. We know nature, that is to say, only as a unity of form and content. And since we know nature only as such a unity, the conception of nature as "in itself" or "originally" a bare content that must derive whatever form it has from elsewhere is a mere abstraction. This of course means for Hegel that the thesis of absolute opposition is a mere abstraction as well.

Bearing in mind this revised conception of the proper object of empirical knowledge, we can see why Hegel is unsympathetic not merely to positivist derivations of law, but to state of nature approaches as well – at least in so far as they, too, rely on an uncritical empiricism. In so far as they purport to derive their support from the raw data of sense experience, they are worthy of suspicion, in his view. It is no mere coincidence, after all, that the Hobbesian aiming to justify an absolute form of sovereign power discovers that the state of nature without law is absolutely intolerable: a "war of all against all." Nor is it coincidence that the Lockean seeking to justify a more limited state power observes in human nature a greater capacity for self-regulation. As Hegel puts it in his 1802/03 essay on "Natural Law," the empiricist tacks onto the bare multiplicity a conceptual unity – all in the name of securing his desired conception of law.[23] In so doing, the empiricist engages in metaphysics.

Hegel of course doesn't deny that we sometimes just have sensations (in the absence of any accompanying cognition). We surely do; and insofar as we do, we are like other animals. But we are unlike other animals in that we in addition think about what we sense. Indeed, on Hegel's conception, thinking is so much a part of our experience *qua* rational or reflective natures that it borders on misleading in his view to characterize our experience as involving the purely passive reception of sensations at all. In describing our experience as rational natures, we need to account for the fact that, as rational, we don't merely have but in part also determine our experience. As rational, the contributions of our thinking and of our sensing are inseparable, in his view. This is because in the absence of concepts, sensations for us as reflective, thinking beings are blind.[24]

Appeals to nature in the derivation of right or law are therefore invariably naive and question-begging, according to Hegel. Insofar as they rely on an uncritical empiricism, they misidentify the object of our knowledge as a bare content without form. They enlist the help of a faulty faculty psychology in supposing that, for rational animals seeking to reflect upon or know nature, the activities of thinking and of sensing are separable.

Uncritical empiricism helps itself to an equally implausible faculty psychology, Hegel argues, when it sets out to provide an account of human willing. What it then assumes is the separability of desires or instinct and practical reason. Not surprisingly, Hegel insists that it is misleading to characterize the behavior of rational natures as ever simply determined by desire. As thinking or reflective beings, we no more merely have desires than we merely have sensations. Unlike nonrational animals, we represent to ourselves the objects of our desire. Minimally, we rank them; or, we identify with and attend to some but not others. In this way, we in part determine the objects of our desire. And in arguing that we in part determine the objects of our desire, Hegel is not merely claiming that it is possible for us, as rational, to subordinate the supposedly independent ends of desire to the equally independent ends of reason. This cannot be what he has in mind because in his view, of course, ends of desire and ends of reason for rational natures are not wholly independent. In his view, the faculties of thinking and desiring or willing are as inseparable in us, *qua* rational natures, as the faculties of thinking and perceiving.[25]

VII

These remarks indicate what Hegel believes is unacceptable about the metaphysics of uncritical empiricism and its implied conception of nature. Earlier, however, I noted that in the *Philosophy of Right* Hegel assesses theories of right on the basis of how well they are able to provide for the realization of human freedom. So why does he judge uncritical empiricism to be deficient from this point of view as well?

We can see from Hegel's answer to this question how much he is indebted to Enlightenment rationalism. His view is something like this: It is because uncritical empiricism fails to appreciate sufficiently the extent to which we are thinking or rational natures that it is unable to provide for the fully developed form of freedom of which we are capable. This is obviously true, Hegel believes, for the reductive empiricist for whom reason has no freedom and is a mere slave of the passions. But it is also true, on his account, for the dualist who admits that nature *qua* instinct and desire isn't everything and that we have in addition a rational faculty that can bring instinct and desire in line. Since both positions rely on a conception of nature as "in itself" or "originally" without form or law – as "in itself" without rationality, Hegel would say – both fail to appreciate the way in which our animal natures can be rationally self-determining and therefore the source of our freedom. If uncritical empiricism is able to admit that freedom is possible for us at all, it must locate the source of that freedom outside the realm of nature empirically considered: as deriving from God's will, or from the will of the human subject *qua* intelligible or transcendental. But the need to derive freedom from an external source, Hegel claims, only reveals a failure to appreciate the extent to which thinking determines our being. It is to treat empirical human nature as essentially animal nature instead of as essentially rational animal nature.

Here, of course, the question of Kant versus Hegel raises its weighty head. Both philosophers understand our freedom to derive from our nature as rational beings. Both therefore agree that it is thanks to our rationality that we can be self-legislating or self-determining – that we can give ourselves law, as Kant would put it. But since for Kant thinking or rationality doesn't determine our being through-and-through (or, since for Kant our rational and our animal natures are separable), the most we can hope for, as Kantians, is the successful domestification of our empirical natures, of our brute drives and desires. Because human animal nature on Kant's conception can never itself be the source of laws of freedom, it must be made to submit to the governance of reason. Hegel's complaint, as I understand it, is that in this way Kantian freedom cannot be realized without the aid of coercion.[26]

VIII

This brings us back to where we started. Practical agency and moral imputation according to Kant require as conditions of their possibility the idea of a nonempirical or transcendental form of freedom. Hegel is convinced not only that this model sells human nature short in confining our empirical characters to a state of unfreedom; as should by now be clear, he is convinced in addition that Kant's reliance on a transcendental or intelligible form of subjectivity depends upon an untenable metaphysics. Kant's metaphysics is untenable because, like empiricism's reliance on the conception of nature as a bare content, it presupposes the absolute opposition or heterogeneity of form and content. This presupposition lies at the basis of Kant's conception of the transcendental or intelligible subject. (And as noted above, it is the very *idea* of the transcendental or intelligible subject that Hegel finds unpersuasive; his critique does not depend upon assuming that Kant is committed to its existence or theoretical knowability.)

A central objective of the *Philosophy of Right* is therefore to challenge not just positivist or empiricist approaches to law, but also the assumption that laws of freedom or laws of right derive from a reason supposed to be "pure" or "absolutely opposed" to nature. In the limited space remaining, I'll try to suggest a way to think about the conception of practical reason Hegel urges us to adopt instead.

We might describe the *Philosophy of Right* as a defense of the thesis that reason is historical. It tells a story of the development of various theories of right, each responsive to the needs of its own time, and each presumably more satisfactory than its predecessors. According to this story, social institutions and events play a causal role in making the progress of reason possible, since social institutions and events both aid and awaken the need for reason's development.

But this description of the historical nature of reason doesn't quite capture the specifically Hegelian conception. For one thing, Kant could endorse it as well. Kant surely grants that there has been progress in the development of theories of right; and as we saw above, he also recognizes that the progress of reason has had to depend on the assistance of actual events and institutions.

We can see more clearly where the two philosophers part ways if we consider how they each locate the place of their own philosophizing in this developmental picture. We could perhaps say of Kant that he understands himself to have discovered the given nature of reason. Although surely aware of the role of history in, at least to some extent, setting the agenda for his own philosophizing, Kant does not follow Hegel in deriving from this the conclusion that history or the realm of the actual in part determines the nature of reason itself. Rather, as we saw above, reason for Kant is "in all situations present and the same . . . " (A 556/B 584). The most the realm of the actual can do, on Kant's conception, is assist in the realization of reason's already given nature.

Although he is often represented as doing so, Hegel does not take himself to have discovered the given nature of reason. He cannot understand his own position in this way because, as we have seen, he denies that reason *has* a given nature. By this I mean that he rejects the view that reason is somehow outside time and "absolutely opposed" to what is in time. It is because Hegel does not take himself to have discovered the given nature of reason that he struggles with the problem of how in the *Philosophy of Right* to properly begin his analysis of right. Reason for Hegel is surely not historical in the sense that is a mere slave of the passions or of actual social forces.[27] But reason in his view cannot transcend the realm of the actual either. The philosopher has to begin somewhere in order to philosophize at all, he writes; but the philosopher cannot start from scratch. The philosopher cannot leave his world behind either in his speculations about an original state of nature or in his discovery of laws of a reason supposed to be intelligible or pure. Although philosophy must begin somewhere, its beginning is always "relative," Hegel says, in that it is always the "result" of and so dependent upon some prior philosophical conception.[28] This is why he tells us in his Preface that philosophy (and by implication, the *Philosophy of Right*) comes on the scene too late to instruct the world about how it ought to be. His point is not that because reason is historical rather than transcendent, it can have no legitimate prescriptive force; rather, Hegel means in this passage to draw our attention to the fact that the nature and laws of reason are not given prior to or independent of reason's relation to the actual. Philosophy comes on the scene too late not because laws of reason reduce to nature or history, but because nature and history on Hegel's account are nonetheless in part responsible for what it is possible for us to identify as rational.[29]

Notes

1. See Hegel's 1821 *Grundlinien der Philosophie des Rechts* §135.
2. I am therefore in agreement with Robert Pippin who claims that Hegel's critique of Kant's practical philosophy is "unavoidably metaphysical," or occurs at the level of the "'metaphysics of the person'." See Pippin's "Hegel on the Rationality and Priority of Ethical Life," *Neue Hefte für Philosophie* 35 (1995), esp. pp. 119 and 122. For a different approach, see Allen W. Wood's *Hegel's Ethical Thought* (Cambridge, U.K.: Cambridge University Press, 1990). In the first paragraph of his Preface, Wood writes that the effort to discover in Hegel's metaphysics or "dialectical logic" the "hidden key" to his social thought promises to be not only "difficult" but also "unrewarding." It is not an effort, he says, undertaken by those who are "sensible."
3. Except where otherwise indicated, translations of this as well as all other German texts treated in this paper are mine. Here I rely on the Norman Kemp Smith's translation of "subalternen" as "relative." See his translation, *Critique of Pure Reason* (New York: St. Martin's Press, 1965). In my text I provide in parentheses references to the "A" and "B" Akademie editions of the first *Kritik*.
4. *Grundlegung zur Metaphysik der Sitten* [Ak 389].
5. As Onora O'Neill aptly puts it, what Kant is claiming is that the empirical point of view which can regard human nature only as appearance "lacks closure." See her *Constructions of Reason: Explorations of Kant's Practical Philosophy* (Cambridge, U.K.: Cambridge University Press, 1989), p. 111.
6. Proponents of the "two standpoint" interpretation claim that for Kant appearances are not mental representations of things in themselves (mental representations, that is, of the unknowable reality that causes them). The distinction between appearances and things in themselves refers, that is, not to two different kinds of objects, but to two ways in which empirical objects may be considered. As Henry Allison puts it, Kant intends by "appearances" objects considered, "in relation to the subjective conditions of human cognition," and by "things in themselves," objects as they are "independently of these conditions." This "two standpoint" or "two aspect" reading of the distinction has the obvious advantage over the "two object" or "ontologized" reading, Allison claims, of preserving Kant's "robust empirical realism," according to which appearances, although not objects independent of the subjective conditions of our knowing them, are nonetheless real and mind-independent. See Allison's *Kant's Theory of Freedom* (Cambridge, U.K.: Cambridge University Press), pp. 3 and 18.
7. *Grundlegung* [Ak 458]. Kant is claiming at least this: Our questions about how the intelligible and empirical realms are causally related cannot be answered from within the point of view of theoretical knowledge. According to Christine Korsgaard, it is an implication of Kant's commitment to the two standpoint view that he believes that such questions cannot even be "coherently asked." This is because, on her reading of

322   SALLY SEDGWICK

Kant, "freedom is a concept with a practical employment, used in the choice and justification of action, not in explanation or prediction; while causality is a concept of theory, used to explain and predict actions but not to justify them." From her 1992 essay "Creating the Kingdom of Ends" reprinted as Chapter 7 of her collection, *Creating the Kingdom of Ends* (New York: Cambridge University Press, 1995), p. 204. Korsgaard takes up this distinction between explanation and justification again in *The Sources of Normativity* (New York: Cambridge University Press, 1996), p. 14.

8. For example, the B-Preface of the first *Kritik*. It is not necessary for morality that "freedom be understood," Kant tells us there, "only that it may . . . at least be thought and not be self-contradictory" (B xxix).

9. See again *Grundlegung* [Ak 458].

10. As Kant puts it at A 341/B 399, for example, the "I think" is "purified of the empirical."

11. This language is already present in Hegel's earliest ("Jenaer") writings. See, for example, his discussion of Kant's philosophy in his 1802/03 *Glauben und Wissen,* and the section "Manchelei Formen, die bei dem jetzigen Philosophieren vorkommen," in his 1801 *Differenz des Fichteschen und Schellingschen Systems der Philosophie.*

12. See Hegel's "Jenaer" writings cited directly above.

13. The terms "separable" and "inseparable" may be familiar to us from John McDowell's recent *Mind and World* (Cambridge, Mass., and London: Harvard University Press, 1994). But see §4 A of the *Philosophie des Rechts,* where Hegel characterizes thinking and willing as "untrennbar: sie sind eines und dasselbe, und in jeder Tätigkeit, sowohl des Denkens als Wollens, finden sich beide Momente." (The notion of freedom as our "second nature," also prominent in *Mind and World,* appears in this section of the *Philosophie des Rechts* as well: "das Rechtssystem [ist] das Reich der verwirklichten Freiheit, die Welt des Geistes aus ihm selbst hervorgebracht, als eine zweite Natur . . . ") I discuss the influence of Hegel on McDowell in "McDowell's Hegelianism," *European Journal of Philosophy* 5 (1997): 21–38.

14. See Herman's "The Practice of Moral Judgment," *Journal of Philosophy* 82 (1985): 414–36, reprinted as Chapter 4 of her collection of essays *The Practice of Moral Judgment* (Cambridge, Mass., and London: Harvard University Press, 1993).

15. I cannot for example properly assess the moral worth of my intention to give money to CARE unless my maxim accurately reflects the facts about how much I am actually able to give. To apply the categorical imperative test, I need in this way to attend to empirical content.

16. See Propositions 2 and 6 for these passages.

17. *Grundlegung* [Ak 399].

18. See Proposition 4.

19. A prominent spokesperson for this position is Burkhard Tuschling. In, for example, his essay "The System of Transcendental Idealism: Questions Raised and Left Open in the 'Kritik der Urteilskraft'," he writes that "Kantian Transcendental Idealism involves elements of the Hegelian or speculative understanding," and draws his evidence chiefly from Kant's Introduction to and second part of the *Kritik der Urteilskraft* as well as from Kant's *Opus postumum.* In *System and Teleology in Kant's Critique of Teleological Judgment, Spindel Conference 1991, Southern Journal of Philosophy XXX, Supplement,* ed. Hoke Robinson: 109–27.

20. *Philosophie des Rechts* §1.

21. This passage appears in Hegel's *Zusatz* to the Preface. See also *Philosophie des Rechts* §3.
22. *Enzyklopädie der philosophischen Wissenschaften im Grundrisse (1830), Erster Teil: Die Wissenschaft der Logik,* §38.
23. "Über die wissenschaftlichen Behandlungsarten des Naturrechts, seine Stelle in der praktischen Philosophie und sein Verhältnis zu den positiven Rechtswissenschaften," Section I.
24. As Hegel writes in the *Enzyklopädie Logik,* "Man is always thinking, even when he only intuits; when he considers something, he considers it as a universal; he focusses on the singular . . . in so doing, withdraws his attention from something else, and takes it as something abstract and universal . . . " §24 A 1.
25. I am drawing heavily on §4 of the *Philosophie des Rechts* for this discussion. In Hegel's words, "The animal acts by instinct . . . , but it has no will, because it does not represent to itself what it desires."

    For helpful discussions of the relation of desire to agency in Hegel, see, in addition to the article by Pippin mentioned above, Terry Pinkard's contribution to that same issue of *Neue Hefte für Philosophie,* "Historicism, Social Practice, and Sustainability: Themes in Hegelian Ethical Theory," as well as his book *Hegel's Phenomenology: The Sociality of Reason* (Cambridge, U.K.: Cambridge University Press, 1994), pp. 274ff.
26. As Hegel argues in the *Philosophie des Rechts,* it is this outcome that motivates the advance from the stage of "Moralität" to that of "Sittlichkeit."
27. For Hegel's rejection of the thesis that reason is a mere slave to the passions, see *Philosophie des Rechts* §17; for his rejection of the thesis that reason is a mere instrument of social forces, see §§146, 148.
28. See §2 and the Preface to the *Philosophie des Rechts* for Hegel's remarks on the difficulty of making a new beginning in philosophy. This is a problem which Hegel addresses again and again. See, for example, the Introduction of his 1807 *Phänomenologie des Geistes* and the Prefaces of 1812 and 1831 to his *Wissenschaft der Logik.*
29. This paper appears in the *Bulletin of the Hegel Society of Great Britain* 37 (1998). I owe thanks to the Hegel Society of Great Britain for permission to publish it here as well as for the invitation to prepare it for the Society's annual meeting in September of 1997. I also wish to thank both Rolf-Peter Horstmann and the Alexander von Humboldt-Stiftung for the generous support that made its completion possible.

Bibliography

Primary Sources

Fichte, Johann Gottlieb. *Gesamtausgabe der Bayerischen Akademie der Wissenschaften.* Ed. Reinhard Lauth et al. Stuttgart: Frommann-Holzboog, 1962–.

Fichte, Johann Gottlieb. *Sämmtliche Werke.* Ed. I. H. Fichte. Berlin: Walter de Gruyter, 1965.

Fichte, Johann Gottlieb. *The Science of Knowledge.* Trans. Peter Heath and John Lachs. Cambridge, U.K.: Cambridge University Press, 1982.

Fichte, Johann Gottlieb. *Wissenschaftslehre nova methodo: Kollegnachschrift K. Chr. Fr. Krause.* Ed. Erich Fuchs. Hamburg: Felix Meiner Verlag, 1982.

Fichte, Johann Gottlieb. *Early Philosophical Writings.* Trans. Daniel Breazeale. Ithaca, N.Y.: Cornell University Press, 1988.

Fichte, Johann Gottlieb. *Foundations of Transcendental Philosophy (Wissenschaftslehre) nova methodo (1796/99).* Trans. Daniel Breazeale. Ithaca, N.Y.: Cornell University Press, 1992.

Fichte, Johann Gottlieb. *Introductions to the Wissenschaftslehre and Other Writings.* Trans. Daniel Breazeale. Indianapolis: Hackett, 1994.

Hegel, G. W. F. *Gesammelte Werke.* Ed. Hartmut Buchner and Otto Pöggler. Hamburg: Felix Meiner Verlag, 1968–.

Hegel, G. W. F. *Werke in zwanzig Bänden, Theorie Werkausgabe.* Frankfurt am Main: Suhrkamp Verlag, 1970.

Hegel, G. W. F. *The Difference between Fichte's and Schelling's System of Philosophy.* Trans. Walter Cerf and H. S. Harris. Albany: State University of New York Press, 1977.

Hegel, G. W. F. *Faith and Knowledge.* Trans. Walter Cerf and H. S. Harris. Albany: State University of New York Press, 1977.

Hoffmeister, Johannes, ed. *Briefe von und an Hegel. Band I: 1785–1812.* Hamburg: Felix Meiner Verlag, 1969.

Jacobi, Friedrich Heinrich. *The Main Philosophical Writings and the Novel Allwill.* Trans. George di Giovanni. Montreal: McGill-Queen's University Press, 1994.

Kant, Immanuel. *Gesammelte Schriften.* Ed. Royal Prussian (later German) Academy of Sciences. Berlin: Walter de Gruyter and predecessors, 1900–.

Kant, Immanuel. *Critique of Pure Reason.* Trans. Norman Kemp Smith. New York: St. Martin's Press, 1929.

Kant, Immanuel. *Philosophy of Material Nature.* Trans. J. Ellington. Indianapolis: Hackett, 1985.

Kant, Immanuel. *Opus postumum.* Trans. Eckart Förster and Michael Rosen. Cambridge, U.K.: Cambridge University Press, 1993.

Reinhold, Karl Leonhard. *Über das Fundament des philosophisches Wissens (1791).* Darmstadt: Wissenschaftliche Buchgesellschaft, 1963.

Reinhold, Karl Leonhard. *Beyträge zur Berichtigung bisheriger Missverständnisse der Philosophie, vol. I (1790).* Darmstadt: Wissenschaftliche Buchgesellschaft, 1963.

Reinhold, Karl Leonhard. *Versuch einer neuen Theorie des menschlichen Vorstellungsvermögens (1789).* Darmstadt: Wissenschaftliche Buchgesellschaft, 1963.

Schelling, Friedrich Wilhelm Joseph von. *Sämtliche Werke.* Ed. K. F. A. Schelling. Stuttgart: J. G. Cotta'scher Verlag, 1856–1861.

Schelling, Friedrich Wilhelm Joseph von. *Historisch-kritische Ausgabe.* Ed. Michael Baumgartner et. al. Stuttgart: Frommann-Holzboog, 1976–.

Schelling, Friedrich Wilhelm Joseph von. *The Unconditional in Human Knowledge: Four Early Essays (1794–1796).* Trans. Fritz Marti. Lewisburg, Pa.: Bucknell University Press, 1980.

Schelling, Friedrich Wilhelm Joseph von. *Schriften.* Frankfurt am Main: Suhrkamp Verlag, 1985.

Schelling, Friedrich Wilhelm Joseph von. "Ideas on a Philosophy of Nature as an Introduction to the Study of this Science." In *Philosophy of German Idealism,* ed. Ernst Behler. New York: Continuum Publishing Company, 1987, pp. 168–9.

Schelling, Friedrich Wilhelm Joseph von. *Timaeus (1794).* Ed. Hartmut Buchner. Stuttgart: Frommann-Holzboog, 1994.

Schelling, Friedrich Wilhelm Joseph von. "Treatise Explicatory of the Idealism in the Science of Knowledge." In *Idealism and the Endgame of Theory: Three Essays by F. W. J. Schelling,* trans. and ed. Thomas Pfau. Albany: State University of New York Press, 1994.

Schulze, G. E. *Aenesidemus, oder über die Fundamente der von Herrn Prof. Reinhold in Jena gelieferten Elementar-Philosophie.* Brussels: Culture et Civilization, 1969.

Schulze, G. E. "Aenesidemus, Or Concerning the Foundation of the Philosophy of the Elements Issued by Professor Reinhold in Jena together with a Defense of Skepticism Against the Pretensions of the Critique of Pure Reason." In *Between Kant and Hegel: Texts in the Development of Post-Kantian Idealism,* trans. George di Giovanni. Albany: State University of New York Press, 1985.

Secondary Sources

Allison, Henry E. *Kant's Transcendental Idealism: An Interpretation and Defense.* New Haven: Yale University Press, 1983.

Allison, Henry E. *Kant's Theory of Freedom.* Cambridge, U.K.: Cambridge University Press, 1990.

Allison, Henry E. "Kant's Antinomy of Teleological Judgment." *Southern Journal of Philosophy* XXX, Supplement, *The Spindel Conference 1991* (1992): 25–42.

Allison, Henry E. *Idealism and Freedom: Essays on Kant's Theoretical and Practical Philosophy.* Cambridge, U.K.: Cambridge University Press, 1996.

Allison, Henry E. "Beauty as Mediator between Nature and Freedom." In *Philosophie in synthetischer Absicht,* ed. Marcelo Stamm. Stuttgart: Klett-Cotta, 1998, pp. 539–564.

Ameriks, Karl. "Reinhold and the Short Argument to Idealism." In *Proceedings: Sixth International Kant Congress 1985,* ed. G. Funke and T. Seebohm. Washington, D.C.: The Center for Advanced Research in Phenomenology and the University Press of America, 1989.

Ameriks, Karl. "Kant, Fichte, and Short Arguments to Idealism." *Archiv für Geschichte der Philosophie* 72 (1990): 63–85.

Ameriks, Karl. "Hegel and Idealism." *Monist* 74 (1991): 386–402.

Ameriks, Karl. "Recent Work on Hegel: The Rehabilitation of an Epistemologist?" *Philosophy and Phenomenological Research* 52 (1992): 177–202.

Ameriks, Karl. "The Ineliminable Subject: From Kant to Frank." In *The Modern Subject: Conceptions of the Self in Classical German Philosophy,* ed. K. Ameriks and D. Sturma. Albany: State University of New York Press, 1995, pp. 217–230.

Ameriks, Karl. "Kant and the Self: A Retrospective." In *Figuring the Self,* ed. D. Klemm and G. Zöller. Albany: State University of New York Press, 1997, pp. 55–72.

Ameriks, Karl. "Fichte's Appeal Today: The Hidden Primacy of the Practical." In *The Emergence of German Idealism,* ed. M. Baur and D. Dahlstrom. Washington, D.C.: Catholic University of America Press, 1999, pp. 116–30.

Beiser, Frederick C. *The Fate of Reason: German Philosophy from Kant to Fichte.* Cambridge, Mass.: Harvard University Press, 1987.

Beiser, Frederick C., ed. *The Cambridge Companion to Hegel.* Cambridge, U.K.: Cambridge University Press, 1993.

Berthold, Lothar, ed. *Zur Architektonik der Vernunft.* Berlin: Akadamie Verlag, 1990.

Bowie, Andrew. *Schelling and Modern European Philosophy.* London and New York: Routledge, 1993.

Breazeale, Daniel. "Why Fichte Now?" *Journal of Philosophy* 87 (1991): 424–531.

Breazeale, Daniel. "Philosophy and the Divided Self: On the Existential and Scientific Tasks of the Jena *Wissenschaftslehre.*" *Fichte-Studien* 6 (1994): 117–47.

Breazeale, Daniel. "Certainty, Universal Validity, and Conviction: The Methodological Primacy of Practical Reason within the Jena *Wissenschaftslehre.*" In *New Perspectives on Fichte,* ed. Daniel Breazeale and Tom Rockmore. Atlantic Highlands, N.J.: Humanities Press, 1996, pp. 35–59.

Breazeale, Daniel, and Tom Rockmore, eds. *Fichte: Historical Contexts/Contemporary Controversies.* Atlantic Highlands, N.J.: Humanities Press, 1994.

Breazeale, Daniel, and Tom Rockmore. *New Perspectives on Fichte.* Atlantic Highlands, N.J.: Humanities Press, 1996.

Collins, A. B., ed. *Hegel on the Modern World.* Albany: State University of New York Press, 1995.

Düsing, Edith. *Intersubjektivität und Selbstbewusstsein.* Cologne: Dinter Verlag, 1986.

Düsing, Klaus. "Spekulation und Reflexion. Zur Zusammenarbeit Schellings und Hegels in Jena." *Hegel-Studien* 5 (1969): 95–128.

Düsing, Klaus. *Das Problem der Subjektivität in Hegels Logik.* Bonn: Bouvier, 1976.

Düsing, Klaus. "Hegels Begriff der Subjektivität in der Logik und in der Philosophie des subjektiven Geistes." In *Hegels Philosophische Psychologie,* ed. Dieter Henrich. Bonn: Bouvier, 1979, pp. 201–14.

Düsing, Klaus. "Constitution and Structure of Self-Identity: Kant's Theory of Apperception and Hegel's Criticism." *Midwest Studies* 8 (1983): 409–31.

Düsing, Klaus. "Ästhetische Einbildungskraft und intuitiver Verstand. Kants Lehre und Hegels spekulativ-idealistische Umdeutung." *Hegel-Studien* 21 (1986): 87–128.

Düsing, Klaus. "Die Entstehung des spekulativen Idealismus. Schellings und Hegels Wandlungen zwischen 1800 und 1801." In *Transzendentalphilosophie und Spekulation: Der Streit um die Gestalt einer Ersten Philosophie (1799–1807),* ed. W. Jaeschke. Hamburg: Felix Meiner Verlag, 1993, pp. 144–63.

Edwards, Jeffrey. "Der Ätherbeweis des *Opus postumum* und Kants dritte Analogie der Erfahrung." In *Übergang. Untersuchungen zum Spätwerk Immanuel Kants,* ed. Siegfried Blasche. Frankfurt am Main: Vittorio Klostermann, 1991, pp. 77–104.

Edwards, Jeffrey. "Disjunktiv-und kollektiv-allgemeiner Besitz: Überlegungen zu Kants Theorie der ursprünglichen Erwerbung." In *Recht, Staat und Völkerrecht bei Immanuel Kant,* ed. Dieter Hunning and Burkhard Tuschling. Berlin: Duncker und Humblot, 1998, pp. 113–34.

Edwards, Jeffrey. "Egoism and Formalism in the Development of Kant's Moral Theory." *Kant-Studien* (forthcoming 2000).

Edwards, Jeffrey. *Substance, Force, and the Possibility of Knowledge in Kant's Philosophy of Material Nature.* Los Angeles: University of California Press, forthcoming 2000.

Fleischmann, Eugene. "Hegels Umgestaltung der kantischen Logik." *Hegel-Studien* Beiheft 3 (1965): 181–208.

Förster, Eckart. "Is There 'A Gap' in Kant's Critical System?" *Journal of the History of Philosophy* 25 (1987): 536–55.

Förster, Eckart. "Kant's Notion of Philosophy." *The Monist* 72 (1989): 285–304.

Förster, Eckart, ed. *Kant's Transcendental Deductions: The Three "Critiques" and the "Opus postumum".* Stanford: Stanford University Press, 1989.

Forster, Michael. *Hegel and Skepticism.* Cambridge, Mass.: Harvard University Press, 1989.

Forster, Michael. *Hegel's Idea of a Phenomenology of Spirit.* Chicago: University of Chicago Press, 1998.

Frank, Manfred. *Eine Einführung in Schellings Philosophie.* Frankfurt am Main: Suhrkamp Verlag, 1985.

Frank, Manfred. *Selbstbewusstsein und Selbsterkenntnis.* Stuttgart: Reclam, 1991.

Frank, Manfred, and Gerhard Kurz, eds. *Materialien zu Schellings philosophischen Anfängen.* Frankfurt am Main: Suhrkamp Verlag, 1975.

Friedman, Michael. *Kant and the Exact Sciences.* Cambridge, Mass.: Harvard University Press, 1992.

Fulda, Hans-Friedrich. *Das Problem einer Einleitung in Hegels Philosophie des Rechts.* Frankfurt am Main: Vittorio Klostermann, 1965.

Fulda, Hans-Friedrich, and Dieter Henrich, eds. *Materialien zu Hegels "Phänomenologie des Geistes".* Frankfurt am Main: Suhrkamp Verlag, 1973.

Fulda, Hans-Friedrich, and Rolf-Peter Horstmann, eds. *Hegel und die Kritik der Urteilskraft.* Stuttgart: Klett-Cotta, 1990.

Fulda, Hans-Friedrich, and Michael Theunissen, eds. *Kritische Darstellung der Metaphysik: Eine Diskussion über Hegels "Logik".* Frankfurt am Main: Suhrkamp Verlag, 1980.

Gamm, Gerhard. *Der Deutsche Idealismus: Eine Einführung in die Philosophie von Fichte, Hegel und Schelling.* Stuttgart: Reclam Verlag, 1997.

Giovanni, George di, and H. S. Harris. *Between Kant and Hegel: Texts in the Development of Post-Kantian Idealism.* Albany: State University of New York Press, 1985.

Girndt, H. *Die Differenz des Fichteschen und Hegelschen Systems in der Hegelschen Differenzschrift.* Bonn: Bouvier, 1965.

Görland, Ingtraud. *Die Kantkritik des jungen Hegel.* Frankfurt am Main: Vittorio Klostermann, 1966.

Guyer, Paul. "Kant's Conception of Empirical Law." *Proceedings of the Aristotelian Society* Supplementary Volume 64 (1990): 221–42.

Guyer, Paul. "Reason and Reflective Judgment: Kant on the Significance of Systematicity." *Nous* 24 (1990): 17–43.

Guyer, Paul. "The Systematic Order of Nature and the Systematic Union of Ends." In *Vernunftbegriffe in der Moderne: Stuttgarter Hegel-Kongreß 1993,* ed. Hans-Friedrich Fulda and Rolf-Peter Horstmann. Stuttgart: Klett-Cotta, 1994, pp. 199–221.

Guyer, Paul. "From Nature to Morality: Kant's New Argument in the 'Critique of Teleological Judgment'." In *System und Architektonik bei Kant,* ed. Jürgen Stoltzenberg. Hamburg: Felix Meiner Verlag, forthcoming.

Guyer, Paul. "Organisms and the Unity of Science." In *Kant and the Sciences,* ed. Eric Warkins. Oxford: Clarendon Press, 2000.

Harris, Henry Silton. *Hegel's Development: Toward the Sunlight, 1770–1801.* Oxford: Clarendon Press, 1972.

Harris, Henry Silton. *Hegel's Development: Night Thoughts (Jena 1801–1806).* Oxford: Clarendon Press, 1983.

Hartmann, Nicolai. *Die Philosophie des deutschen Idealismus.* Berlin: Walter de Gruyter, 1974.

Henrich, Dieter. *Fichtes ursprüngliche Einsicht.* Frankfurt am Main: Vittorio Kloster-mann, 1967.

Henrich, Dieter. *Hegel im Kontext.* Frankfurt am Main: Suhrkamp Verlag, 1971.

Henrich, Dieter. "Fichte's Original Insight." In *Contemporary German Philosophy.* University Park, Pa.: Pennsylvania State University Press, 1982, pp. 15–53.

Henrich, Dieter, ed. *Kant oder Hegel: Über Formen der Begründung in der Philosophie.* Stuttgart: Klett-Cotta, 1983.

Henrich, Dieter, ed. *Hegels Wissenschaft der Logik: Formation und Rekonstruction.* Stuttgart: Klett-Cotta, 1986.

Henrich, Dieter. In *The Unity of Reason: Essays on Kant's Philosophy,.* ed. R. Velkley. Cambridge, Mass.: Harvard University Press, 1994.

Horstmann, Rolf-Peter. "Probleme der Wandlung in Hegels Jenaer Systemkonzeption." *Philosophische Rundschau* 19 (1972): 87–118.

Horstmann, Rolf-Peter. "Jenaer Systemkonzeptionen." In *Hegel,* ed. Otto Pöggeler. Freiburg and Munich: Karl Alber, 1977, pp. 43–58.

Horstmann, Rolf-Peter, ed. *Seminar: Dialektik in der Philosophie Hegels.* Frankfurt am Main: Suhrkamp Verlag, 1978.

Horstmann, Rolf-Peter. "Über das Verhältnis von Metaphysik der Subjektivität und Philosophie der Subjektivität in Hegels Jenaer Schriften." *Hegel-Studien* Beiheft 20 (1980): 181–95.

Horstmann, Rolf-Peter. *Ontologie und Relationen: Hegel, Bradley, Russell und die Kontroverse über interne und externe Beziehungen.* Königstein: Hain, 1984.

Horstmann, Rolf-Peter. *Wahrheit aus dem Begriff: eine Einführung in Hegel.* Frankfurt am Main: Anton Hain, 1990.

Horstmann, Rolf-Peter. *Die Grenzen der Vernunft: eine Untersuchung zu Zielen und Motiven des Deutschen Idealismus.* Frankfurt am Main: Hain, 1991.

Horstmann, Rolf-Peter. "Zur Aktualität des Deutschen Idealismus." *Neue Hefte für Philosophie* 35 (1995): 3–17.

Houlgate, Stephen. *Hegel, Nietzsche and the Criticism of Metaphysics.* Cambridge, U.K.: Cambridge University Press, 1986.

Houlgate, Stephen. *Freedom, Truth and History. An Introduction to Hegel's Philosophy.* London: Routledge, 1991.

Houlgate, Stephen. "Hegel, Kant and the Formal Distinctions of Reflective Understanding." In *Hegel on the Modern World,* ed. A. Collins. Albany: State University of New York Press, 1995, pp. 125–41.

Houlgate, Stephen. "Necessity and Contingency in Hegel's *Science of Logic.*" *The Owl of Minerva* 27 (1995): 33–44.

Houlgate, Stephen. "Hegel, Derrida and Restricted Economy: The Case of Mechanical Memory." *Journal of the History of Philosophy* 34 (1996): 79–93.

Inwood, Michael. *Hegel.* London: Routledge, 1983.

Inwood, Michael, ed. *Hegel.* Oxford: Clarendon Press, 1985.

Jaeschke, W., ed. *Transzendentalphilosophie und Spekulation. Der Steit um die Gestalt einer Ersten Philosophie (1799–1807).* Hamburg: Felix Meiner Verlag, 1993.

Janke, W. *Fichte. Sein und Reflexion: Grundlage der kritischen Vernunft.* Berlin: Walter de Gruyter, 1970.

Klemm, David, and Günter Zöller, eds. *Figuring the Self: Subject, Individual, and Others in Classical German Philosophy.* Albany: State University of New York Press, 1997.

Lamb, Andrew. "Fichte's 'Introductions' as Introductions to Certainty." *Idealistic Studies* 27 (1997): 193–215.

Lauth, Reinhard. "J. G. Fichtes Gesamtidee der Philosophie." *Philosophisches Jahrbuch* 71 (1964): 253–85.

Lauth, Reinhard. *Die Entstehung von Schellings Identitätsphilosophie in der Auseinandersetzung mit Fichtes Wissenschaftslehre.* Freiburg: Alber, 1975.

Lauth, Reinhard. *Die transzendentale Naturlehre Fichtes nach den Prinzipien der Wissenschaftslehre.* Hamburg: Felix Meiner Verlag, 1984.

Longuenesse, Béatrice. *Hegel et la Critique de la Métaphysique.* Paris: Vrin, 1981.

Longuenesse, Béatrice. "Hegel, Lecteur de Kant sur le Jugement." *Philosophie* 36 (1992): 40–70.

Longuenesse, Béatrice. *Kant et le Pouvoir de Juger.* Paris: Presses Universitaires de France, 1993.

Longuenesse, Béatrice. "Kant et les Jugements empiriques: jugements de perception et jugements d'expérience." *Kant-Studien* (1995): 278–307.

Longuenesse, Béatrice. "The Transcendental Ideal, and the Unity of the Critical System." In *Proceedings of the Eighth International Kant-Congress, Memphis 1995,* ed. H. Robinson. Milwaukee: Marquette University Press, 1996, pp. 521–39.

Longuenesse, Béatrice. *Kant and the Capacity to Judge.* Trans. Charles Wolfe. Princeton: Princeton University Press, 1998.

Mathieu, Vittorio. *Kants Opus postumum.* Frankfurt am Main: Vittorio Klostermann, 1989.

McFarland, John. *Kant's Concept of Teleology.* Edinburgh: University of Edinburgh Press, 1970.

Neuhouser, Frederick. *Fichte's Theory of Subjectivity.* New York: Cambridge University Press, 1990.

Neuhouser, Frederick. "Fichte and the Relationship between Right and Morality." In *Fichte: Historical Contexts, Contemporary Controversies,* ed. Daniel Breazeale and Tom Rockmore. Atlantic Highlands, N.J.: Humanities Press, 1994, pp. 158–80.

Parrini, Paolo, ed. *Kant and Contemporary Epistemology.* Dordrecht: Kluwer, 1994.

Petry, Michael. *Hegel's Philosophy of Nature.* London: Allen and Unwin, 1970.

Philonenko, Alexis. *La liberté humain dans la philosophie de Fichte.* 2nd ed. Paris: Vrin, 1966.

Pinder, Tillman. "Kants Begriff der transzendentalen Erkenntnis." *Kant-Studien* 77 (1987): 1–40.

Pinkard, Terry. "Hegel's Idealism and Hegel's Logic." *Zeitschrift für philosophische Forschung* 23 (1979): 210–25.

Pinkard, Terry. *Hegel's Phenomenology: The Sociality of Reason.* Cambridge, U.K.: Cambridge University Press, 1994.

Pinkard, Terry. "Historicism, Social Practice, and Sustainability: Some Themes in Hegelian Ethical Theory." *Neue Hefte für Philosophie* 35 (1995): 56–94.

Pinkard, Terry. "Hegel on History, Self-Determination and the Absolute." In *History and the Idea of Progress,* ed. A. Melzer, J. Weinberger and M. Zinman. Ithaca, N.Y.: Cornell University Press, 1995.

Pinkard, Terry. "History and Philosophy: Hegel's Phenomenology of Spirit." In *Edinburgh Encyclopedia of Continental Philosophy,* ed. Simon Glendinning. Edinburgh: Edinburgh University Press, 1999.

Pinkard, Terry. *Hegel: A Biography.* Cambridge, U.K.: Cambridge University Press, 2000.

Pippin, Robert. *Kant's Theory of Form: An Essay on the 'Critique of Pure Reason'.* New Haven: Yale University Press, 1982.

Pippin, Robert. *Hegel's Idealism: The Satisfactions of Self-Consciousness.* Cambridge, U.K.: Cambridge University Press, 1989.

Pippin, Robert. *Modernism as a Philosophical Problem: On the Dissatisfactions of European High Culture.* Oxford: Basil Blackwell, 1991.

Pippin, Robert. *Idealism as Modernism: Hegelian Variations.* Cambridge, U.K.: Cambridge University Press, 1997.

Pöggeler, Otto. *Hegels Idee einer Phänomenologie des Geistes.* Freiburg and Munich: Karl Alber, 1973.

Robinson, Hoke, ed. *System and Teleology in Kant's Critique of Judgment, Spindel Conference 1991, The Southern Journal of Philosophy, Supplement Volume XXX.* Memphis: Memphis State University Press, 1992.

Rohs, Peter. *Johann Gottlieb Fichte.* Munich: Beck, 1991.

Sedgwick, Sally. "Hegel on Kant's Antinomies and Distinction Between General and Transcendental Logic." *The Monist* 74 (1991): 403–20.

Sedgwick, Sally. "Hegel's Critique of Kant's Empiricism and the Categorical Imperative." *Zeitschrift für Philosophische Forschung* 50 (1996): 563–84.

Sedgwick, Sally. "Hegel's Critique of Kant on Matter and the Forces." In *Proceedings of the Eighth International Kant Congress, Memphis 1995,* ed. Hoke Robinson. Milwaukee: Marquette University Press, 1996, pp. 963–72.

Sedgwick, Sally. "McDowell's Hegelianism." *European Journal of Philosophy* 5 (1997): 21–38.

Sedgwick, Sally. "McDowell, Hegel, and Recent Defenses of Kant." *Journal for the British Society of Phenomenology* (forthcoming).

Siep, Ludwig. *Hegels Fichtekritik und die Wissenschaftslehre von 1804.* Freiburg: Karl Alber, 1970.

Siep, Ludwig. *Praktische Philosophie im Deutschen Idealismus.* Frankfurt am Main: Suhrkamp Verlag, 1992.

Simpson, David, ed. *German Aesthetic and Literary Criticism: Kant, Fichte, Schelling, Schopenhauer, Hegel.* Cambridge, U.K.: Cambridge University Press, 1984.

Solomon, R., and K. Higgins, eds. *The Age of German Idealism.* Vol. VI, *The Routledge History of Philosophy.* London: Routledge, 1993.

Stolzenberg, Jürgen. *Fichtes Begriff der intellektuellen Anschauung: Die Entwicklung in den Wissenschaftslehren von 1793/94 bis 1801/02.* Stuttgart: Klett-Cotta, 1986.

Sturma, Dieter. *Kant über Selbstbewußtsein. Zum Zusammenhang von Erkenntniskritik und Theorie des Selbstbewußtseins.* Hildesheim: Georg Olms Verlag, 1985.

Sturma, Dieter. "Präreflexive Freiheit und menschliche Selbstbestimmung." In *F. W. J. Schelling, Über das Wesen der menschlichen Freiheit,* ed. O. Höffe and A. Pieper. Berlin: Akademie Verlag, 1995, pp. 149–72.

Sturma, Dieter. "Self-Consciousness and the Philosophy of Mind." In *Proceedings of the Eighth International Kant Congress, Memphis 1995,* ed. Hoke Robinson. Milwaukee: Marquette University Press, 1996, pp. 661–74.

Sturma, Dieter. "Schellings Subjektivitätskritik." *Deutsche Zeitschrift für Philosophie* 44 (1996): 429–46.

Sturma, Dieter. *Philosophie der Person. Die Selbstverhältnisse von Subjektivität und Moralität.* Paderborn: Schöningh Verlag, 1997.

Tuschling, Burkhard. *Metaphysische und transzendentale Dynamik in Kants Opus postumum.* Berlin: Walter de Gruyter, 1971.

Tuschling, Burkard. "Die Idee des transzendentalen Idealismus im späten *Opus postumum.*" In *Übergang: Untersuchungen zum Spätwerk Immanuel Kants,* ed. Forum für Philosophie Bad Homburg. Frankfurt am Main: Vittorio Klostermann, 1991, pp. 105–45.

Tuschling, Burkhard, ed. *Hegels Philosophie des subjektiven Geistes.* Stuttgart: Frommann-Holzboog, 1991.

Tuschling, Burkhard. "The System of Transcendental Idealism: Questions Raised and Left Open in the Kritik der Urteilskraft." *The Southern Journal of Philosophy* XXX, Supplement, *The Spindel Conference 1991* (1992): 109–27.

Tuschling, Burkard. "The Concept of Transcendental Idealism in Kant's *Opus postumum.*" In *Kant and Critique: New Essays in Honor of W.H. Werkmeister,* ed. R. M. Dancy. Dordrecht: Kluwer, 1993, pp. 151–67.

Tuschling, Burkard. "System des transzendentalen Idealismus bei Kant? Offene Fragen der – und an die – *Kritik der Urteilskraft.*" *Kant-Studien* 86 (1995): 196–210.

Westphal, Kenneth. *Hegel's Epistemological Realism: A Study of the Aim and Method of Hegel's Phenomenology of Spirit.* Vol. 43, *Philosophical Studies Series in Philosophy.* Dordrecht and Boston: Kluwer, 1989.

Westphal, Kenneth. "Kant, Hegel, and the Transcendental Material Conditions of Possible Experience." *Bulletin of the Hegel Society of Great Britain* 33 (1996): 23–41.

334   *Bibliography*

Westphal, Kenneth. "Hegel and Hume on Perception and Concept-Empiricism." *Journal of the History of Philosophy* 33 (1998): 99–123.

Westphal, Kenneth. *Hegel, Hume und die Identität wahrnehmbarer Dinge. Historisch-kritische Analyse zum Kapitel «Wahrnehmung» in der Phänomenologie von 1807.* Vol. 72, *Philosophische Abhandlungen.* Frankfurt am Main: Vittorio Klostermann, 1998.

Westphal, Kenneth. "On Hegel's Early Critique of Kant's *Metaphysical Foundations of Natural Science.*" In *Hegel and the Philosophy of Nature,* ed. S. Houlgate. Albany: State University of New York Press, 1998, pp. 137–66.

Westphal, Kenneth. "Hegel's Internal Critique of Naïve Realism." *Journal of Philosophical Research* 25 (2000).

Wildt, Andreas. *Autonomie und Anerkennung. Hegels Moralitätskritik im Lichte seiner Fichte-Rezeption.* Stuttgart: Klett-Cotta, 1982.

Williams, Robert R. *Hegel's Ethics of Recognition.* Los Angeles: University of California Press, 1997.

Wolff, Michael. *Der Begriff des Widerspruchs: Eine Studie zur Dialektik Kants und Hegels.* Königstein: Hain, 1981.

Wolff, Michael. *Die Vollständigkeit der kantischen Urteilstafel.* Frankfurt am Main: Vittorio Klostermann, 1995.

Wood, Allen. *Hegel's Ethical Thought.* New York: Cambridge University Press, 1990.

Wood, Allen. "Fichte's Philosophical Revolution." *Philosophical Topics* 19 (1991): 1–28.

Wood, Allen. *Kant's Ethical Thought.* New York: Cambridge University Press, 1999.

Wood, Allen. "Fichte's Philosophy of Right and Ethics." In *The Cambridge Companion to Fichte,* ed. Günter Zöller. New York: Cambridge University Press, forthcoming 2000.

Zöller, Günter. *Theoretische Gegenstandsbeziehung bei Kant.* Berlin: Walter de Gruyter, 1984.

Zöller, Günter. "'Des Element aller Gewissheit': Jacobi, Kant und Fichte über den Glauben." *Fichte-Studien* 14 (1998): 21–41.

Zöller, Günter. *Fichte's Transcendental Philosophy: The Original Duplicity of Intelligence and Will.* Cambridge, U.K.: Cambridge University Press, 1998.

Zöller, Günter. "Die Individualität des Ich in Fichtes zweiter Jenaer Wissenschaftslehre (1796–99)." *Revue internationale de philosophie* 206 (1998): 641–63.

Zöller, Günter. "'Die Seele des Systems': Systembegriff und Begriffssystem in Kants Transzendentalphilosophie." In *System und Architektonik in der Philosophie Kants,* ed. H. F. Fulda and J. Stolzenberg. Hamburg: Felix Meiner Verlag, forthcoming.

Zöller, Günter, ed. *The Cambridge Companion to Fichte.* Cambridge: Cambridge University Press, forthcoming 2000.

Index

Adickes, Erich, 75
Aenesidemus *see* Gottlob Ernst Schulze
affection, sensible, 4, 291
affinity, transcendental, 291–3, 302
agency
  free, 158, 255
  practical, 310, 319
  rational, 21, 23–8, 39
Allison, Henry, 73–5, 108, 112, 192, 213, 293, 298, 302, 321
Ameriks, Karl, 169
Amphiboly of Concepts of Reflection, 262
Analogies of Experience, 80, 82, 270, 294–5
Antinomy, 265–7
  of Teleological Judgment, 87
  Third, 278, 307
apperception
  unity of, 3, 63, 74, 79, 225, 232, 272–4, 293–4, 303, 310
  pure, 4, 13, 162
Aristotle, 164, 206–8, 232
autonomy, 106, 154–6 , 159, 188, 256

Baum, Manfred, 87, 89, 91, 230, 282
Beck, Lewis White, 195, 149
Beiser, Frederick, 16, 125, 195
Berkeley, George, 149, 168, 287, 298
Bourgeois, Bernard, 282
Bowie, Andrew, 302
Brandom, Robert, 304
Breazeale, Daniel, 167, 168, 170, 297, 300
Bubner, Rüdiger, 231

Buchdahl, Gerd, 90

category, 82, 209–10, 232–49, 256, 276
  modal, 260, 279
causa noumenon, 70
causality, reciprocal, 240, 244–7, 252, 259
concept
  absolute, 255
  determinate, 265–6
  discursive, 266–7, 270
  empirical, 82, 84, 261, 265
  infinite, 257, 267
consciousness, empirical, 10, 271
Copernican revolution, 79, 253

deduction
  ether, 60–68, 74
  metaphysical, 149, 232–4, 249, 273
  transcendental, 1, 3–9, 16, 177, 180, 188, 198, 232, 272–3, 294, 296, 302
De Flaviis, Guiseppe, 71
De Fries, Willem, 301
dogmatism, 2–3, 99–100, 136, 156, 159, 184–5, 187
dualism, 1, 8, 10, 13, 159, 189, 191, 195, 197, 216, 230, 253, 310–12
Düsing, Klaus, 89, 279, 281, 285, 296, 298, 300

Edwards, Jeffrey, 15, 51
Evans, Gareth, 102
explanation, mechanical vs. teleological, 35–8, 87–8, 142, 259–60, 274

338INDEX